Inventing Maternity

Inventing Maternity

Politics, Science, and Literature, 1650-1865

Edited by
Susan C. Greenfield
and Carol Barash

THE UNIVERSITY PRESS OF KENTUCKY

Publication of this volume was made possible in part
by a grant from the National Endowment for the Humanities.

Editorial and Sales Offices: The University Press of Kentucky
663 South Limestone Street, Lexington, Kentucky 40508-4008

03 02 01 00 99   5 4 3 2 1

Library of Congress Cataloging-in-Publication Data

Inventing maternity: politics, science, and literature, 1650–1865 /
    edited by Susan C. Greenfield and Carol Barash.
        p.   cm.
    Includes bibliographical references and index.
    ISBN 0–8131–2078–0 (cloth : alk. paper)
    1. Motherhood—History.   2. Motherhood in literature—History.
    3. Motherhood—Political aspects—History.   I. Greenfield, Susan C.
    II. Barash, Carol.
    HQ759.I57   1999
    306.874´3—dc21   98–44190

Contents

Preface

This anthology began in the summer of 1992, when we started soliciting articles for a collection on the politics of maternity. At the time we imagined that the volume would cover the seventeenth to the twentieth centuries in England and America, including articles on contemporary literature, film, psychoanalysis, and feminist theory. When it gradually became clear that a tighter historical focus would offer a greater contribution to the burgeoning field of research on motherhood, we tapered the volume to concentrate more closely (though not exclusively) on the long eighteenth century, the period when the idea of the tender, full-time mother was first institutionalized. As scholars of eighteenth-century literature, we were aware that, although there was an accumulating and extremely valuable body of material about motherhood in this time, there was little that offered the kind of immediate variety of perspectives available in a collection of essays. One of our goals in limiting the historical focus of the volume was to open up the range of interpretive approaches to the period.

In determining the final form of the volume, we chose also to include articles based on texts that pre-date and post-date the long eighteenth century, both to help put eighteenth-century depictions of maternity in broader historical perspective and because the articles were particularly effective at anticipating or logically extending some of the major issues raised in the volume. *Inventing Maternity* thus begins with an article on William Harvey's medical study *de Generatione animalium* (1651) and concludes with a discussion of Harriet Jacobs's slave narrative, *Incidents in the Life of a Slave Girl* (1861). The first half of the volume, which covers the mid-seventeenth to the late eighteenth centuries, considers some of the central debates of the period about the mother's role in fetal development, pregnancy, breastfeeding, and childrearing. The second half of the volume, covering the late eighteenth to the mid-nineteenth centuries, charts a historical shift in attention to reproductive regulation, as maternity is increasingly associated with problems of infanticide, population control, poverty, and colonial, national, and racial instability. The essays throughout make reference to a wide range of textual sources, including medical texts, political tracts, literature, domestic conduct books, and cookbooks. Our hope has been to create a volume with both historical depth and discursive and analytic breadth.

In the years we have worked on this project, we have incurred considerable professional debt. We would like to acknowledge some of the people who have helped us here. We are grateful to the numerous authors who responded to our solicitations for essays and are especially appreciative of the patience and support of those whose works were chosen for the volume. Toni Bowers, who commented on the introduction, and Mary Chapman, who shared her thoughts about the connections between eighteenth-century English and American literature, made extra contributions. Paula Backscheider, Cora Kaplan, Ruth Perry, Felicity Nussbaum, Dorothy Roberts, Ellen Ross, and Wendy Wall read and commented on portions of the manuscript or offered crucial bibliographic information or did both. Robert F. Himmelberg, dean of the Graduate School of Arts and Sciences at Fordham University, secured funds for editorial assistance, ably provided by Patricia Manganello. Finally, there were people who offered emotional as well as intellectual support: Allyson Booth, Eve Keller, Jay Greenfield, Judy Greenfield, Matthew Weissman, and Thelma Weissman were indispensable at every stage. Thank you.

Eve Keller's "Making up for Losses: The Workings of Gender in William Harvey's *de Generatione animalium*" appeared previously: © 1998 OPA (Overseas Publishers Association) Amsterdam B.V. Originally published in *Women's Studies* by Gordon and Breach Publishers. Reprinted by permission. Susan Greenfield's "Aborting the 'Mother Plot': Politics and Generation in *Absalom and Achitopel*," is adapted from an essay that appeared in *ELH* 62: 267-94. "The Pregnant Imagination, Women's Bodies, and Fetal Rights," by Julia Epstein, is reprinted by permission of *The Yale Journal of Law & the Humanities* 7: 139-62; the essay appears here with a new prologue. Toni Bowers's "'A Point of Conscience': Breastfeeding and Maternal Authority in *Pamela*, Part 2" appeared in *Eighteenth-Century Fiction* 7, and in her book *The Politics of Motherhood: British Writing and Culture, 1680-1760*, © Cambridge University Press, 1996; it is reprinted with permission of Cambridge University Press and appears here with a new afterword. Claudia L. Johnson's "Mary Wollstonecraft: Styles of Radical Maternity" is excerpted and adapted from her book *Equivocal Beings: Politics, Gender, and Sentimentality in the 1790's, Wollstonecraft, Radcliffe, Burney, Austen*, ©1995 by the University of Chicago; we thank the University of Chicago Press for permission to republish it.

Susan C. Greenfield ⎯⎯⎯⎯⎯⎯⎯⎯⎯⎯⎯⎯⎯⎯⎯⎯⎯⎯⎯⎯⎯⎯⎯⎯

Introduction

This volume springs from the scholarly consensus that the idealization of the full-time mother was an early modern development. Many have argued that it was not until the eighteenth century that woman's social purpose was defined in terms of the bearing, nurturing, and educating of children. This was when the still powerful image of the tender mother took root. *Inventing Maternity* examines the various ways the early modern mother was represented in Great Britain and America between 1650 and 1865. One of the premises of the volume is that even as motherhood evoked an increasingly standardized set of values, the concept was pliant and adaptable. Ideas about female fertility, the maternal body, and the mother's role in producing children and society were themselves produced in different ways for various reasons. Maternity was, in this sense, continuously invented and re-invented. What remained constant was the enormous popularity of the image of the mother—the consistency with which it was invoked and adjusted for a range of political concerns.

One need only consider a few historical details to appreciate the changing interpretation of maternity in the early modern period.[1] Wet nursing, popular among both the rich and the poor, reached an all-time high in England in the seventeenth and early eighteenth century, but by the 1750s maternal breastfeeding had become fashionable, especially among the middle and upper classes. Whereas earlier medical tracts on maternal breastfeeding had primarily been addressed to midwives and nurses, by the mid-eighteenth century such books were directed to mothers themselves and were read throughout England and America.[2]

Change is also evident in the legal arena. The laws against infanticide, invoked almost exclusively against mothers (and not other possible culprits), remained the same in England and America throughout the seventeenth and eighteenth centuries. But both areas witnessed a decline in the rates of conviction as arguments about a mother's love for her deceased child were increasingly accepted as evidence of maternal innocence. Women who could prove that they had made linen for their infants before birth, were tender toward them after birth, or had cried at their deaths were routinely acquitted.[3]

Perhaps no legal change better encapsulates the accumulating emphasis on the importance of maternal love than that concerning the delegation of child custody rights. Until the end of the eighteenth century, English Common Law, granting the father sole custody of children and the sole right to determine their guardianship in the event of his death, prevailed in both England and America.[4] As Justice Blackstone explained in the late 1760s, "a father may by deed or will, dispose of the custody of his child, born or unborn, to any person," but the mother "is only entitled to reverence and respect." This changed in England in 1839 with the passage of the Infant Custody Act, the first law in English history to grant women the right to retain or visit with their children in cases of separation or divorce, as well as the first to acknowledge a married woman's independent legal status.[5]

In America, there were no major legislative changes until the early twentieth century. But, with the significant exception of slaves, American women were regularly awarded custody of young children by the judicial courts as early as 1809, a policy that became known as the "Tender Years Doctrine."[6] The logic for granting maternal custody in cases of separation or divorce was aptly summarized by one court in 1842: "The law of nature has given to [the mother] an attachment for her infant offspring which no other relative will be likely to possess in an equal degree."[7] Thus, in both England and America, the belief in the mother's singular connection to her children had become entrenched enough to revise centuries of exclusive paternal custody rights.[8]

There are countless ways in which motherhood continues to be seen as a natural and timeless female occupation in our day, and the history of such assumptions has been the subject of scholarly analysis for decades. The next several pages of this introduction are devoted to a necessarily selective review of the vast literature on early modern maternity, with more attention paid to the interpretive patterns established by a few influential texts than to the array and nuances of the many important studies that accompanied and followed them. The review points to two central and often related trends in the scholarly treatment of early modern maternity—first, an interest in the way new maternal ideals affected specific groups of women, and second, an interest in the political advantages and liabilities of motherhood as an institution.

Scholarship on the history of the family has been an important source of information on maternity. Discussions about the rise of the tender mother in England appeared in Lawrence Stone's *The Family, Sex, and Marriage* (1977) and Randolph Trumbach's *The Rise of the Egalitarian Family* (1978). Trumbach focuses on the aristocracy and Stone on the middle and upper classes, but both argue that during the eighteenth century "biological mothers became nurturing mothers" and "the dominant figure in children's lives."[9] Both also emphasize the psychological consequences of this shift, suggesting that devoted motherhood fostered the development of intense personal attachments unavailable in previous generations. Critics of this view have pointed out that there is no reliable evidence that such attachments did not exist in earlier periods.[10]

Trumbach and Stone stress the domestic consequences of the new maternity and the effects of being mothered, rather than the experience of being a mother. Several studies by women that emerged in the next decade turned to the mother's point of view and concentrated on both the social power and the disadvantages of women's new image. Thus, in *Liberty's Daughters* (1980), Mary Beth Norton argues that after the Revolution, American mothers saw themselves as playing a major role in strengthening the new republic.[11] Similarly, in her study of the British aristocracy, *In the Family Way* (1986), Judith Lewis suggests that motherhood "became a moral, intellectual, and emotional pursuit" for aristocratic English women: "It became a woman's greatest source of dignity and emotional satisfaction." On the other hand, the obvious ways maternal norms restricted women's lives are also commonly noted. As Elizabeth Kowaleski-Wallace argues, for instance, with the popularization of full-time maternity, woman lost the "ability to conceive of herself as an individual outside the family."[12]

Another important strain of criticism focuses less on the particular history of women and more on the damaging ways in which motherhood—as an institution—has been politically deployed and regulated by the state. One of the obvious sources of this interest is Michel Foucault's *The History of Sexuality* (1976, in English 1978), which focuses on France but has had an enormous impact on English and American scholarship. Foucault places the late-eighteenth-century mother at the center of a bourgeois family, increasingly subject to and supportive of the governmental supervision of sexuality. Preoccupied with its own sexuality and heredity, the bourgeoisie developed a form of "dynamic racism" that had devastating effects on the proletariat class.[13]

Similarly attentive to the governmental regulation of family life and the inequitable class effects of the new maternity in France, Jacques Donzelot argues in *The Policing of Families* (1977, in English 1979) that while the bourgeois mother was deemed responsible for educating her family and for diffusing welfare and educational norms beyond it, the proletariat mother was taught to police her relatives by overseeing the "social retraction of her husband and child."[14]

Foucault's and to a lesser extent Donzelot's influences are evident in Nancy Armstrong's study of domesticity and class in England, *Desire and Domestic*

Fiction (1987). For Armstrong, the image of the domestic woman popular-
ized in British conduct books and novels at the end of the eighteenth century
was essential in the middle class's triumph over the aristocracy, and it became
an important source of the liabilities of bourgeois power.[15]

In keeping with the growing scholarly investment in colonial history and
postcolonial theory, a number of discussions of the political deployment of
maternity have focused on the relationship between domesticity and national
and imperial power—on what we might call the international effects of the
bourgeois family's "dynamic racism." A 1992 issue of *Eighteenth-Century Life*
featured two pivotal essays on the subject, Felicity Nussbaum's "'Savage'
Mothers" and Ruth Perry's "Colonizing the Breast." Perry's and Nussbaum's
articles are linked in their attention to the role that motherhood played in
eighteenth-century English imperial ambition, as the need to generate children for the nation and empire began to constitute "childbearing women as a
national resource," and as England itself was "frequently likened to the benevolent mother of its colonized children."[16]

What differentiates Perry and Nussbaum is their geographical and social
focus. Perry concentrates on the way the "imperatives of an expanding English empire" negatively affected middle- and upper-class English women.
Arguing that maternity became a means of female sexual repression, she suggests that the popularization of maternal breastfeeding represented "the colonization of the [English] female body for domestic life." Interested in the
effects of colonialism abroad as well as at home, Nussbaum contends that in
colonial narratives, "women of the upper and middle classes are pitted against
lower-class women, and 'civilized' English mothers against 'barbaric' mothers—with their difference offered as proof of racial and class superiority, and
their sameness as an indication of their gendered inferiority."[17] In alternate
ways, Perry's and Nussbaum's works draw the two traditional methodological
approaches together, highlighting both the effect motherhood had on particular women and the problematic political history of the institution.

If the range of these scholarly discussions exemplifies the variety of perspectives from which early modern maternity can be interpreted, one of the
interests that has remained most consistent throughout the decades is in the
scientific construction of the female body. Not only have many literary scholars and historians drawn on scientific texts in their analysis of changing maternal ideals and habits, but a growing number of authors, including Ludmilla
Jordanova, Thomas Laqueur, and Londa Schiebinger, have focused specifically on the role of gender in the history of early modern science.[18] A commonly cited source of information in all fields has been Dr. William Cadogan's
Essay upon Nursing and the Management of Children (1748), in which
breastfeeding is represented as a mother's biological responsibility. Popular in

England, America, and France, Cadogan's work was the most influential of its kind and was adopted by the governors of the London Foundling Hospital as their basis for infant care. Schiebinger evokes Cadogan's text in her intriguing suggestion that the idealization of maternal breastfeeding throughout Europe was both reflected in and shaped by Carolus Linnaeus's decision to introduce the term *mammalia*—referring to the presence of milk-producing mammae—into his zoological taxonomy.[19]

While medical texts had long advocated maternal breastfeeding, the cultural importance of the activity in the eighteenth century suggests that it was during this period that maternity began to be popularly defined as a physical predisposition. Laqueur argues that even among doctors the image of woman's anatomy changed, as early modern science generated a female body that was essentially different from the male sexual body and essentially maternal. Thus, whereas women were once seen as being physically analogous (though inferior) to men, bearing internal versions of male reproductive organs, in the eighteenth century reproductive organs became the "foundation of incommensurable difference: 'women owe their manner of being to the organs of generation, and especially to the uterus,' as one . . . physician put it."[20]

Many feminist critics emphasize the way new scientific assumptions about woman's anatomy privileged male authority over the female body. In calling for universal maternal nursing, for instance, Dr. Cadogan's text "earnestly recommend[s] . . . to every Father to have his Child nursed under his own Eye, to make use of his own Reasons and Sense in superintending and directing the Management of it."[21] Scholars routinely contend that it is characteristic of male control over maternity that the doctor came to usurp the midwife.[22] Mary Shelley's *Frankenstein*, which features a scientist who imagines that he can give birth to a human being without involving female labor at all, can be read as a contemporary critique of male scientific proprietorship.[23]

It is important to stress that at the same time that medical science was naturalizing the maternal body and raising questions about who should control it, many groups of women did not have the socioeconomic wherewithal to raise their own children. Maternal duty was increasingly defined as a biological function, but such function was also marked by its exclusivity. In the same era that maternal nursing became fashionable among middle- and upper-class mothers, for instance, slave women were often forced to leave their nursing babies in order to work in the field. As one slave mother recalled: "When I did go I could hear my poor child crying long before I got to it."[24] If middle- and upper-class women were burdened with the limitations and surveillance that full-time maternity entailed, lower-class women and women of color rarely had the luxury either to enforce or self-consciously to reject maternal values.

As both Toni Bowers and Felicity Nussbaum have pointed out, the records from the London Foundling Hospital suggest something of the pain that impoverished women suffered in a society that taught them to cherish maternal love while making it financially impossible for them to care for their children. The governors of the hospital were struck by the "Expressions of Grief of the Women" who relinquished the first children to the institution in 1741. One mother sought employment in the hospital to remain near her child, and others visited regularly to get news of their children's health. Bowers suggests that the anguish of maternal loss is made "disturbingly visible" in the painting that William Hogarth bequeathed to the hospital, *Moses Brought to Pharaoh's Daughter,* which draws attention to Moses's mother's grief. "Moses stands for the London foundlings . . . because his mother, though attentive and affectionate, is forced to resign him to a surrogate for economic and social reasons." Nussbaum notes that the economic and social constraints affecting the foundlings' mothers were typically the products of imperial expansion. Many of the mothers who petitioned for their children to be admitted to the hospital did so because their male partners had gone to war.[25]

Of course, empire also depended on the fertility of African women and West Indian and American female slaves, whose children were regularly taken from them in support of the colonial economy. Several slave narratives open by stressing the emotional pain of this separation, and the production of the narratives themselves can thus be read as an attempt to compensate for maternal absence. Olaudah Equiano, who was kidnapped from Africa, begins *The Interesting Narrative* of his life (1789) by recounting his attachment to the mother he lost.[26] Similarly, in the opening pages of *The History of Mary Prince, a West Indian Slave* (1831), the Bermudan-born narrator describes the morning her mother escorted her and her two sisters to the auction block: "Whilst she was putting on us the new osnaburgs in which we were to be sold, she said, in a sorrowful voice, (I shall never forget it!) 'See, I am *shrouding* my poor children; what a task for a mother!'"[27] In *Incidents in the Life of a Slave Girl* (1861), the first full-length American slave narrative written by a woman, Harriet Jacobs also evokes death imagery in describing a slave mother's last night with her children: "Often does she wish that she and they might die before the day dawns." It is in keeping with the connections among maternal absence, death, and slavery that Jacobs begins her narrative by informing the reader that when she herself was six years old her mother died, and "for the first time, I learned, by the talk around me, that I was a slave."[28]

In recounting her subsequent efforts to avoid being raped by her master, Jacobs makes visible the sexual abuse at the foundation of slave maternity. She stresses that because a slave woman's children were the master's property, he had a double incentive to rape and impregnate her and then to deny a familial relationship with the valuable offspring: "Slaveholders have been cunning enough to enact that 'the child shall follow the condition of the *mother*,' not of the *father*; thus taking care that licentiousness shall not interfere with avarice."[29] The earliest American law concerning mixed offspring, established in Virginia in 1662, highlights the English origins of this economy: "Whereas some doubts have arisen whether children got by any Englishman upon a negro woman should be slave or free. Be it therefore enacted . . . that all children born in this country shall be held bond or free only according to the condition of the mother."[30] Pleading with her implied northern female audience, Jacobs even points to the inevitability of incest in a system where the master need never acknowledge his kinship with slave children: "Talk to American slaveholders. . . . Tell them it is . . . atrocious to violate their own daughters." It was also common for masters to hand-pick slaves and force them to mate.[31]

As Hortense Spillers argues, in such a system, "the customary lexis of sexuality, including 'reproduction,' 'motherhood,' 'pleasure,' and 'desire,' [was] thrown into unrelieved crisis."[32] In addition to fighting to protect the children they bore, slave women in both America and the British West Indies appear to have made concerted efforts to avoid maternity, employing the gamut of possible strategies: sexual resistance, birth control, abortion, and infanticide.[33] At the same time, though, both Jacobs's and Mary Prince's narratives suggest that the brutality of slavery itself hampered pregnancies. Jacobs reports that her aunt had six dead premature babies, and Prince describes a pregnant slave, Hetty, who was stripped naked and whipped "till she was all over streaming with blood. . . . The consequence was that poor Hetty was brought to bed before her time, and was delivered after severe labour of a dead child," shortly after which she herself died. In general, because of such abuse and poor prenatal care, black infant mortality was dramatically higher than white infant mortality, particularly in America. There, fewer than two out of three black children lived to be ten years old.[34]

This overview of recent scholarship on early modern maternity and the sources on which it depends suggests some of the ways in which the political ramifications of maternity can be interpreted. Each essay in *Inventing Maternity* draws on the methodological approaches that typify the discussion about maternity. In addition to exemplifying the characteristic interest in medical, historical, and literary sources, all of the viewpoints emerge from the premise that motherhood is political. Whether the authors analyze the tensions reflected in particular representations of motherhood or consider the effect that domestic ideals had on certain groups of women or do both, they assume that maternal images and practices register cultural conflicts concerning the organization of society and the replication of its values.

The collection is distinguished, however, by its attention to the variety of political meanings attached to early modern maternity. While any anthology is, by definition, an assemblage of different perspectives on a topic, *Inventing Maternity* is founded on the supposition that maternity was (and still is) a contested terrain. As one of the single most important cultural symbols, the mother constituted an open ground for political projections, responding with remarkable flexibility to various efforts to shape its image and ideological implications. Not only does the range of essays here indicate the numerous ways motherhood might be formulated and deployed, but many of the individual essays attend to the tensions underlining even the most specific maternal issues, such as fertility, fetal development, or breastfeeding.

Because it is organized chronologically, *Inventing Maternity* also offers an opportunity to examine how certain tensions shift over time. The early articles about seventeenth-century literature, for instance, focus on competing models of maternal and paternal authority. As the volume turns to examine the eighteenth and nineteenth centuries, however, the father's role gradually becomes a less central topic, in part because the invention of full-time maternity was accompanied by what Jordanova calls "a significant shift . . . away from associating children 'naturally' with their fathers and toward associating them 'naturally' with their mothers."[35] One sign of the shift is that in the seventeenth century, debates about procreation often concern the role that the mother plays in mediating the bond between offspring and some patriarchal source of value—be it God, king, or father. By the end of the eighteenth century and throughout the nineteenth century, images of maternal procreation are often linked with anxieties about mass reproduction in a secularized world where value is no longer clearly defined.

Even as these essays are sensitive to different renditions of maternity and to the impact of historical change, however, they also bear witness to the longevity of certain cultural concerns. Like current debates about abortion and reproductive technologies, early modern discussions of pregnancy and embryology reflect attempts to conceptualize the boundaries between the mother, fetus or offspring, and some governmental body. The articles in *Inventing Maternity* indicate both the endurance of the desire to formulate these borders and the consistency with which they nevertheless prove permeable.

Moreover, questions about maternal authority remain central throughout the volume as they arguably do today. If the invention of the full-time mother could, in practice, include only the most privileged women, and if it inaugurated what many feminists have seen as a regressive period in women's history, it also created a new and potentially threatening image of female control. What Nancy Armstrong says of the domestic woman is especially true of the new mother: "Under her jurisdiction the most basic qualities of human identity were supposed to develop."[36] Or, as Barbara Gelpi writes, with specific reference to maternity, "the power ascribed to women within their sphere could be made so great that it threatened the masculine dominance it was designed to maintain."[37] Even the opening articles of the anthology, which refer to seventeenth-century texts that predate the establishment of full-time maternity, testify to growing cultural anxieties about how to reconcile new ideas about maternal influence with older forms of patriarchal power.

Although the collection focuses primarily on English material, it includes essays on American and Irish literature—Anne Bradstreet's poetry, Maria Edgeworth's *Ennui*, James Fenimore Cooper's *The Last of the Mohicans*, and Harriet Jacobs's *Incidents in the Life of a Slave Girl*—which point both to the widespread impact of new maternal ideals and (in the essays on Edgeworth, Cooper, and Jacobs) to some of the specific consequences of British colonialism. We can begin to imagine the complex ways in which colonialism affected representations of maternity by considering the circumstances of a writer like the English-born Edgeworth, who spent her adult life on her father's estate in Ireland and wrote novels about mothers in both countries. Similarly, Jacobs includes in her narrative a chapter entitled "A Visit to England." In Susanna Rowson's *Charlotte Temple*, popular in both England and America, the seduced heroine moves from England to America, where she dies after childbirth. Rowson herself moved from England to America as a child and back and forth again as an adult.[38] Like people, literary and cultural influence traveled in various directions. Whereas William Cadogan's *Essay upon Nursing* was widely circulated in America, *Uncle Tom's Cabin* was a best-seller in England. Indeed, after the emancipation of English slaves in 1834, the British antislavery movement eagerly adopted the cause of American abolition.[39]

The essays on Irish and American literature included here draw attention to the mother's power to complicate the maintenance of national or racial differences upon which empire depends. *Ennui* features an Irish wet nurse who, after suckling her son and an English heir simultaneously, switches their identities. In *The Last of the Mohicans* and *Incidents in the Life of a Slave Girl*, the mother is associated with miscegenation, a practice common among English colonists but much more visible in postcolonial America than in England itself. By including articles on a variety of primary source materials, *Inventing Maternity* aims both to document the range of political meanings attached to maternity and to help concretize specific discussions, including those about the relationship between motherhood and imperialism.

Organized chronologically, the articles in *Inventing Maternity* concentrate on the political, scientific, and literary uses to which motherhood was put between 1650 and 1865. The collection opens with three essays concerning the mid- to late-seventeenth-century tension between patriarchal models of creation and maternal ones. If motherhood did not epitomize woman's privileged parental authority until the eighteenth century, these articles suggest that before this time it signaled the possibility of a unique creative agency. While the generation of human beings was traditionally linked to some patriarchal origin, in numerous seventeenth-century sources including medical books, political tracts, religious texts, and poems, the mother exerts a potentially competitive form of productive power.

Eve Keller's article, "Making Up for Losses: The Workings of Gender in Harvey's *de Generatione animalium*" (1651), offers a close reading of William Harvey's scientific account of conception, focusing on the problems raised by Harvey's erroneous determination that there is no male semen in the female uterus after intercourse. Harvey's belief in the absence of semen at conception raised the logical possibility that the mother's body exerted greater control than the father's over fetal development. The apparent lack of material contact between semen and female matter threatened the physiology of paternity and by extension the theories of patriarchy that relied on it, since, "according to classic patriarchal arguments, the king ruled his kingdom as a father his children." In a period of civil war and regicide, Harvey's findings were bound to seem disruptive. Keller suggests that one way Harvey's text compensates for the ideological implications of the discovery is by representing the maternal body as the space against which the fetus, as independent male political actor, defines his subjectivity. In this model, the fetus evokes the gradual shift from an English monarchy to a commonwealth, from a system organized around the king as father to one based on individual male sovereignty. The maternal body becomes the place on which the change from one form of political patriarchy to another can be mapped.

In "'Such Is My Bond': Maternity and Economy in Anne Bradstreet's Writing," Kimberly Latta discusses the mother's role in representing a different set of gradual changes in colonial New England—the change from a spiritual to a secular and market economy. In close readings of a number of Bradstreet's mid-seventeenth-century poems and writings, Latta shows how the author details her "profound emotional attachments to her children." At the same time, though, Bradstreet was schooled in the belief that God was the original and ultimate parent. This belief was commonly articulated in the economic terms of God as creditor, the source to which the value of earthly bonds had to be traced. Latta argues that Bradstreet's poetry reveals a tension between the author's sense of her debt to God and her own maternal desert. Often conflating the roles of mother and artist, the author seems "torn between the idea that something valuable," such as a child, a poem, or a book, "could proceed from her and the more dogmatic view that only God can be a source of value." Suggesting that motherhood can serve both as a model of female experience and as a metaphor for social change, Bradstreet's investment in the worldly meaningfulness of her personal creations reflects the growing acceptance of a distinction between secular and spiritual concerns in a culture where value was increasingly determined by market demand.

My own contribution, "Aborting the 'Mother Plot': Politics and Generation in *Absalom and Achitophel*," examines the political usages of seventeenth-century embryology in a close-reading of a particular poem and thus combines different features of the methodological approaches in the articles that precede it. In John Dryden's royalist allegory, *Absalom and Achitophel* (1682), the biblical King David stands for the notoriously philandering Charles II, Absalom is his illegitimate son, Monmouth, and Achitophel is the earl of Shaftesbury, the Whig leader who sought to have Monmouth succeed Charles II instead of Charles's Catholic brother, James. If, as Keller argues, seventeenth-century patriarchalism depended in part on a belief in the king's power to pass his authority through genetic descent, then King David (Charles II) is faced with a paradoxical problem, since the monarchal succession is threatened by his own bastard child. Unless David is absolved of the responsibility of generating Absalom (Monmouth), he must bear the blame for the political instability his son now represents. Arguing that in his efforts to defend the king Dryden rehearses a variety of embryological theories (including Harvey's), I suggest that the author ultimately emphasizes female control over conception and fetal development so as to shift the onus for Absalom's birth onto the mother. In interesting contrast to Harvey's text, in which a new form of patriarchal individualism emerges from the minimization of female procreative agency, Dryden's poem maximizes that agency so as to support the old kingship. At a time when succession had been thrown into doubt and there could be no medical certainty about the process of fetal development, the competing models of procreative agency and embryology assumed enormous political significance.

With Julia Epstein's essay, "The Pregnant Imagination, Women's Bodies, and Fetal Rights," *Inventing Maternity* turns to one of the most important medical and legal debates about female procreative agency in early modern Europe: the question of whether or not the mother was responsible for "monstrous births"—what we now call "birth defects." In a telling indication of the cultural interest in the subject, both Bradstreet and Dryden evoke monstrous births in their poems, the first to describe the unauthorized publication of one of her manuscripts and the second to characterize political chaos. Epstein's article—first published in 1995 and included here with a new preface—offers a detailed explanation of the early modern theory that monstrous births resulted when a pregnant woman's illicit thoughts or desires left a physical impression on the fetus's body. While Epstein argues that this theory gave women "an active role in the development of their fetuses," such authority also made the mother a culprit. Since, above all, a monstrous child "called into question . . . the legitimacy of its parentage," and thus challenged patriarchal inheritance, social organization, and political power, the stakes of her responsibility were high. Whereas my own article indicates that monstrous births could be blamed on the female parent as a means of exonerating the monarchy, Epstein examines the more enduring legal implications of the idea of "mother-blame," suggesting that we see vestiges of earlier beliefs about the mother's responsibility for fetal deformity in current American court cases against pregnant drug users.

All four opening essays deal with questions or metaphors about the nature of female procreation. Toni Bowers's "'A Point of Conscience': Breastfeeding and Maternal Authority in *Pamela*, Part 2" is the first article in the collection to emphasize maternal practice and to focus specifically on debates about the mother's role in childrearing. While such concerns are already evident in Bradstreet's poetry, they assume heightened significance with the idealization of motherhood in the eighteenth century, a significance especially well documented in Samuel Richardson's *Pamela*, Part 2 (1741). First published in 1995 and included here with a new afterword, Bowers's essay opens with a detailed history of maternal breastfeeding, particularly as it was represented in Augustan conduct book literature. Nancy Armstrong describes how eighteenth-century conduct books generally glorify female domestic authority, but Bowers concentrates specifically on the power granted to maternity. The conclusion she draws—that depictions of maternal breastfeeding signal both the triumph of maternal over paternal rule and a middle-class rebellion against aristocratic values—presents a striking alternative to Ruth Perry's suggestion that one of the consequences of the campaign for maternal breastfeeding was the sexual repression of women. The contrast offers a good example of the various ideological uses to which even the most precise maternal images were put in the early modern era and of the way they remain an open ground for divergent interpretations.

Working from the premise that the representation of motherhood in conduct books "provided a rival source of authority from which wives . . . might potentially resist their husbands' commands," Bowers examines Mr. B.'s aristocratically based objection to Pamela's desire to nurse their child in *Pamela*, Part 2. In terms reminiscent of Bradstreet's linkage of religious and maternal duty, Pamela defends her right to breastfeed on the grounds that it marks her service to God. Pamela ultimately yields to her husband's prohibition against nursing, but Mr. B.'s interests nevertheless appear to be "logically flawed and politically suspect." Though finally suppressed, maternal breastfeeding marks the possibility of challenging the male aristocratic power Mr. B. represents.

In the next essay, by Claudia L. Johnson, "Mary Wollstonecraft: Styles of Radical Maternity," motherhood poses a more fundamental challenge to male control. Focusing on Wollstonecraft's posthumously published novel, *The Wrongs of Woman; or, Maria* (1798), Johnson shows how maternity can disrupt its own seeming dependence on heterosexuality. Johnson begins by noting how Wollstonecraft's treatment of sexual difference in A *Vindication of the Rights of Woman* is radically altered in *The Wrongs of Woman*. In the earlier text, Wollstonecraft minimizes the importance of the physical distinction between the sexes, even when she discusses motherhood, but in her final novel she stresses the bodily basis of maternal experience. Nothing indicates the flexibility of maternity more cogently than this example of the same author adjusting the meaning of female physiology to suit the political purposes of the moment. Yet even as Wollstonecraft is increasingly drawn to what might be called a biologically deterministic description of maternity in *Wrongs*, she rejects a deterministic defense of heterosexual passion, which, Johnson argues, emerges as "corrupt beyond the possibility of recovery" by the novel's end. Ultimately motherhood signals the possibility of revolutionary change in *Wrongs* because it offers women of all classes an opportunity to reject men and bond together around their shared physical and emotional experiences. Whereas *Pamela*, Part 2 questions the father's right to dictate the terms of childrearing, *Wrongs* suggests that there are natural affinities between women that make men dispensable.

It is revealing that the father is often irrelevant in the remaining articles in *Inventing Maternity*, which cover the late eighteenth to mid-nineteenth century, a time when the belief in the mother's central role in producing and raising children was widely accepted. The more pressing questions in the final portion of the volume concern the role maternity plays both in defining class, national, and colonial difference and in regulating population. By the end of the eighteenth century, attachment to a sovereign nation became an important source of individual and communal identity in the western world, a shift influenced as well as complicated by colonialism.[40] British colonialism and the investment in African slave labor were well established but nevertheless vulnerable because of the loss of the American colonies, the constant threat of slave revolts in the West Indies, and political upheavals in Ireland.[41] It was by no means clear how colonial subjects were to be controlled. At home, the new science of population was becoming increasingly important to the rising middle class.[42] National and colonial success seemed to depend on the production of healthy citizens, but the expansion of certain kinds of populations (poor, foreign, racially ambiguous) became a source of growing concern. For complex reasons—including the spread of industrialism and urbanization, increases in immigration, and the cost of wars against France, especially over colonial territories—the numbers of poor people in England were rising, as were the debates about how to manage them.[43]

It was in this context that Thomas Malthus published his influential *An Essay on the Principle of Population* in 1798, in which he argued that population growth is driven by sexual and therefore natural forces and that, unless checked by "misery and vice," the "power of population is indefinitely greater than the power in the earth to produce subsistence for man."[44] Malthus saw the future of England as dire, but he was more hopeful about America, not merely because there were greater resources for population expansion there but because he believed Americans had the economic and political liberty to take advantage of them.[45] In America, Malthus's theories tended to be employed on overtly racist grounds, which appalled him.[46] Before the Civil War, proslavery *and* antislavery activists invoked Malthus in arguing that their own cause would reduce the concentration of blacks.[47] In the last decade of the nineteenth century, Malthus's theories were cited in arguments against immigration.[48]

Most important, the association of population growth with sexuality, as opposed to some divine or patriarchal plan, drew attention to the female body as the site for controlling human increase. Women of the poor and laboring classes were singled out for particularly critical inspection. As Deborah Valenze suggests, in Malthus's formulation all women contribute to "a constant effort towards an increase of population," but lower-class women are seen as exercising the least restraint and being the most fertile. Proof of the "domination of nature," poor mothers produce more children than they can afford and are a central cause of the suffering that ensues.[49]

The novel that Julie Costello examines in "Maria Edgeworth and the Politics of Consumption: Eating, Breastfeeding, and the Irish Wet Nurse in *Ennui*" highlights the problem of mothering and poverty in Ireland, an integral subject in Malthusian debates. But Costello suggests that Edgeworth's interest in colonial tensions prompts some original conclusions about the lower-class mother's impact on population and subsistence. Whereas it was common for the poor to be seen as a drain on the British national economy, colonialism often had a reverse effect. In the aftermath of the Act of Union between England and Ireland, for instance, the poverty-stricken Irish subsisted on potatoes while their grains were exported to England. Such ironies, Costello argues, are epitomized in Edgeworth's *Ennui* by the lower-class Irish wet nurse, Ellinor, who suckles an English heir and then exchanges him for her own son. In the novel, "it is Ellinor, and hence Ireland, who feeds England, regulates the consumption of the Ascendancy class, commands their affections, and shapes their identities" so profoundly that the English heir grows up believing he is an Irish peasant. By virtue of maternal affection and nurturance, Ellinor breaks down the difference between populations. Confusing colonizer and colonized along with any semblance of national, racial, and class order, the mother's love proves as subversive as "political intrigue and rebellion."

As Costello points out, the one danger Ellinor does not pose is that of fecundity. As a wet nurse, she is the producer, not the consumer, of food, and the birth control effects of breastfeeding have apparently helped her limit her family. Such an image of moderated fertility belies widespread fears about mass reproduction in Ireland and elsewhere—fears explored in the essay by Anita Levy, "Reproductive Urges: Literacy, Sexuality, and Eighteenth-Century Englishness." Analyzing Malthus's *Essay* as well as works by Charlotte Lennox, Hannah More, and Jane Austen, Levy shows how the language used to discuss problems of sexual reproduction and population emerged from earlier tropes about the growth of print culture. As discussions of biological reproduction integrated the discourse about sprawling literacy and literary production, they "became a way of talking about danger in a social world composed of people whose heritage and blood were often indeterminate." Levy's article returns readers to the metaphor of maternal procreation, so central in the opening articles of *Inventing Maternity*. Her suggestion that the late-eighteenth- and early-nineteenth-century mother is associated with the problem of unauthorized reproduction is reminiscent of the threat that the mother poses to monarchal descent in Harvey's and Dryden's texts, of the links between literary commercialism and maternal creation in Bradstreet's poetry, and of the connections between maternal desire and monstrous births that Epstein describes.

What has changed is the term. As Jordanova and others have pointed out, the word *reproduction* was not used to describe procreation until the late eighteenth century; the earlier word was *generation*. Related to words like *genealogy* and *genesis, generation* suggests a close connection between the object of creation and an original source of patriarchal value; an organized form of lineage, as with the "generations" of a family; and the novelty and difference of the subject produced. The term *reproduction,* on the other hand, evokes the possibility of a simultaneous and endless replication that undermines value, order, and originality. The opening articles discuss how the mother, by infecting the bond presumed to exist between offspring and a sanctioned origin like God, king, or father, might generate a distortion or disruption. But the image of mass reproduction, based in part, Levy suggests, in the growth of print technology, suggests that there is no difference between an original source and the offspring that can numerically outstrip it. In both the early generative and the later reproductive models, the female body is a potential site of pro-creative chaos, but the latter model lacks the compensatory balance of a patri-archal progenitor. Now procreation appears to rest with the sexualized female body alone. Indeed, the erasure of difference implied by the term *reproduction* might be read as a sign that the shift from an earlier patriarchal model of creation to a more modern maternal model has been completed. Whereas the patriarchal progenitor could generate something new, the reproductive maternal body is the place where difference is collapsed. One result of the indistinction connoted by reproduction, Jordanova suggests, is that the words *women and children* become so familiar that they are taken as "two closely related, even equivalent, taxonomic categories."[50]

In "Infanticide and the Boundaries of Culture from Hume to Arnold," Josephine McDonagh shows that the late-eighteenth- and nineteenth-century British preoccupation with excess reproduction was complemented by an obverse obsession with infanticide—usually represented in terms of the infan-ticidal mother. Like images of maternal breastfeeding, tropes of infanticide could be deployed for competing political arguments, which, in this case, included those about overpopulation. Thus, the Malthusians argued that the "refusal to accept the inevitability that the physical world [would] not be able to sustain the population [was] tantamount to child murder." Yet, their oppo-nents, including William Godwin (political philosopher and Mary Wollstonecraft's husband), argued that Malthus implicitly sanctioned child murder as a means of preserving natural resources.

The legal consequences of infanticide, though rarely enforced in the eigh-teenth century, were stark. Between 1624 and 1803, a harsh law made a woman's concealment of pregnancy or birth in the case where the infant died proof of murder in both England and America, constituting infanticide as the one criminal act for which guilt was presumed before innocence. The provi-sion was repealed in England in 1803, partly because of this inconsistency, but also out of a desire to improve the conviction rate. As previously men-tioned, mothers tended to be acquitted as long as there was any sign of tender-ness, and critics argued that judges and juries were unwilling to apply the law because it was so severe. The punishment for infanticide was death by hang-ing. By far, the people most often accused of infanticide in England and America were unmarried women; in England, they were almost always ser-vants. Married women, who did not need to conceal a pregnancy or birth, were less likely to be suspected when an infant died and could more easily rid themselves of unwanted children by neglecting to suckle them, or "overlay-ing" them (smothering them in bed), or leaving them with a disreputable nurse. For single women, and especially servants, such methods were imprac-tical, as propriety dictated that the child be disposed of before anyone discovered its birth; their preferred methods appear to have been strangulation or suffocation.[51]

McDonagh, however, is less concerned with the actual practice and consequences of infanticide than with its symbolic significance. There is no conclusive evidence that infanticide was on the rise in the late eighteenth and nineteenth century, but "the sheer quantity of references" to it in political, philosophical, legal, and literary texts is overwhelming. Making a sweeping survey of works by a wide range of authors (including Arnold, Burke, Eliot, Godwin, Hume, Malthus, Martineau, Smith, and Wordsworth), McDonagh argues that the repeated allusions to child murder and the infanticidal mother are best understood as symptoms of "unresolved problems within the conceptualization of civilized or modern society." She notes that discussions about infanticide frequently break into two central strains of debate, both of which invoke the infanticidal woman to mark the boundaries of civilization. In one strain of the debate, the infanticidal mother is the savage whose behavior "cannot be countenanced within the bounds of a civilized and modern society." In the other argument, particularly resonant in England in the aftermath of the 1834 Poor Law, the infanticidal mother is the oppressed object of sympathy, who signals "the savagery into which modern society has fallen." Both discourses tend to figure the infanticidal mother as a working-class or racially differentiated woman (Indian, Chinese, West Indian, or Irish), but in one version, her difference makes her barbaric while in the other the modern English society that interprets it is more so.

In "'Happy Shall He Be That Taketh and Dasheth Thy Little Ones against the Stones': Infanticide in Cooper's *The Last of the Mohicans*," Mary Chapman shows that infanticide is just as important a trope in eighteenth- and nineteenth-century American literature, where it also serves to mediate concerns about racial otherness and barbarity. The popularity of discussions of child murder on both sides of the Atlantic suggests not just the power of the image but also something of the fluidity that existed between countries, which, among other things, shared a colonial history. At the same time, though, because America was itself a colonized land, the consequences of this shared history were different than in England. Chapman, for instance, focuses on the tensions between Native Americans and English settlers and descendants, tensions not directly experienced in England itself. In American literature, the recurrent child murderer is a Native American, who kills white children as an act of war.

In fact, there is no historical evidence that northeastern Native Americans made a consistent practice of killing white children (their general policy was to adopt them), which suggests that the allusion serves a "discursive rather than strictly documentary significance." This significance, Chapman argues, centers around anxieties about the possibility of miscegenetic relations between Native and white Americans, a mixing feared because it threatens Anglo purity and portends white extermination in the "New Land." As with the common American adaptations of Malthus, the stress is on the need to maintain a white native population. Chapman pays particular attention to a scene in Cooper's *The Last of the Mohicans,* in which the only white mother in the novel stages a sort of sexual striptease to encourage a Huron warrior to return her infant. That both the mother and baby are subsequently murdered suggests she must be punished for her willingness to consider a miscegenetic exchange. In warfare, infants become the battleground in population control, and the reproductive female body, as the potential site of cultural blending, must be eradicated, even though without that body there can be no population at all. Taken together, the articles by Costello, Levy, McDonagh, and Chapman point to some of the political complexities of the new maternal model of procreation and population. Seen as the locus of human increase and the creator of new citizens, the mother appeared to reproduce national identity and health. But she was also a potential hazard—the source of excess population or infant death and the space where national, racial, and class differences could collapse.

The context of colonial slavery further complicated such tensions, particularly those involving miscegenation. Unlike Cooper's novel, for instance, in which a relationship between a white woman and a Native American signals a threat to the white population, Jacobs's *Incidents in the Life of a Slave Girl* points to the white plantation owner's investment in miscegenetic rape as a means of generating new slaves and thus enhancing population growth.[52] If miscegenation is the tabooed sign of racial blurring when it involves the white woman, it is expected of the black woman, whose children—designated slaves—mark not the collapse but the reinforcement of racial difference.

Inventing Maternity concludes with an interpretation of *Incidents,* Ann Gelder's "Reforming the Body: 'Experience' and the Architecture of Imagination in Harriet Jacobs's *Incidents in the Life of a Slave Girl.*" Many readers have discussed how Jacobs highlights the difference between black and white women by emphasizing the impossibility of a slave woman's upholding the dictates of female chastity. "Reforming the Body" extends this tradition by looking at the specific ways in which Jacobs subverts domestic and pastoral imagery in representing her own sexual experience and maternity. Gelder argues that despite Jacobs's publicly requisite claims to the contrary, she reveals that she *was* raped by her master in her depiction of the domestic space where the violence occurred. Her triumph was that she had managed first to become impregnated by a white neighbor, thus denying her master the chance to produce new slaves through his abuse. To the various ways in which a mas-

ter's rape might be rendered unprofitable (birth control, abortion, infanticide), Jacobs adds consensual sex with another white man, "who has the means
to buy and free their children." By virtue of this complex revision of miscegenetic norms, Jacobs could "protect her children from the pain of being products of rape" and try to arrange for their freedom before they were born.

Gelder's article stresses Jacobs's representational strategies and particularly the way she uses spatial images both to articulate the unspeakable experience of rape and to transcend it through her account of pregnancy. Jacobs
undermines "the domestic ideology of the home as sanctified space" to show
that she was raped. But she also describes her grandmother's attic, where she
hid for seven years, as a place of hope. After suggesting that she became pregnant to avoid bearing her master's child, Jacobs presents the attic as the architectural version of the pregnant body, a domestic space from which she herself
is reborn. In the attic, Jacobs inverts the law that the child follows the mother's
condition by securing her children's emancipation before her own, so that she
"follows" them. This "imaginative [use] of pregnancy . . . create[s] a politicized spatial language for enslaved mothers."

In focusing on the representation of procreation, "Reforming the Body"
returns to the subject with which the volume opened. Harvey, Bradstreet,
Dryden, and the writers Epstein discusses offer varying accounts of female
procreative agency, demonstrating the extent to which descriptions of conception and fetal development could be adjusted to suit particular political,
religious, or legal contexts. What distinguishes the slave mother's circumstances, however, is that her children are marked exclusively by maternal
kinship and thus fated to be slaves. The early texts examined in this volume
variously document the relationship between patriarchy and progeny, and
the later ones point to a growing association between reproduction and maternity. But on the plantation the master's part in fathering slave children is
entirely erased. In a world where it is forbidden to name his role in procreation, black maternity is granted a particularly hazardous agency. Jacobs is
victorious because she transforms the onus of reproduction into an advantage. Choosing an alternative white father for her children and depicting the
pregnant body as the source of freedom, she makes fertility a form of escape.

Although Jacobs is at pains to stress the unique difficulty and ultimate
power of black maternity, part of the political force of her argument depends
on her universalization of maternal sentiment. Hoping to provoke her white
female readers to fight for abolition, she tells them that she acted out of "a
mother's love for my children," feelings they surely share and understand.[53]
Both British and American female abolitionists tended to stress such linkages
between black and white women as part of their justification for emancipation. But in both countries, this sense of cross-racial affiliation began to erode

after abolition, as antislavery agitation evolved into the women's rights movement in the latter half of the nineteenth and the beginning of the twentieth centuries. In England, black women tended to be ignored by those struggling for women's rights, and in the United States, the women's suffrage movement was fractured by disagreements about black suffrage and racial equality.[54] Lower-class women's interests also tended to be overlooked. In early-twentieth-century America, for instance, women's rights agitators influenced the passage of legislation mandating funds for needy mothers, but aid was based on whether the mother proved "worthy." Usually reserved for widows, the category excluded poor, working, unwed, and deserted mothers, who were at the greatest risk of having their children removed by the state.[55]

The early twentieth century also witnessed the inauguration of psycho-analytic theory, which, in its most traditional forms, positions a seductive and objectified mother at the center of its model of human development. The value, hazards, and complexities of psychoanalysis as well as the impact it has had on feminist scholarship are subjects of other books; none of the articles in *Inventing Maternity* directly relies on psychoanalytic theory.[56] It is nevertheless worth stressing here that the traditional psychoanalytic account of maternity can be seen as the logical outgrowth of the idealization of full-time motherhood that began in Europe in the eighteenth century. Psychoanalysis is one important register of the changing significance and practice of female parenting. The story of the preoedipal bond, for instance, which posits an unmediated attachment between a mother and infant, is meaningful only for a society that teaches mothers to devote themselves to their offspring, something that neither the woman who sent her child out to nurse nor the wet nurse or slave expected to put that child before her own at her breast was able to do. Texts such as *Pamela*, Part 2, *The Wrongs of Woman, Ennui*, and *Incidents in the Life of a Slave Girl*, which tentatively imply that a child's happiness and health depend on maternal presence and affection, reflect the gradual development of a cultural consensus about childhood needs that psychoanalysis inherits and elaborates.

The debates concerning works by Nancy Chodorow, Carol Gilligan, Luce Irigaray, Julia Kristeva, Sarah Ruddick, and others reveal the profound conflicts among contemporary feminists about how best to use psychoanalytic theories without becoming trapped in essentialist models of motherhood.[57] Drawing on Foucault, Judith Butler helpfully argues that the psychoanalytic account of maternity is of greatest use to feminist theory when treated as the "product of a historically specific organization of sexuality" and not as an abiding precultural truth. Viewed historically, psychoanalysis serves a descriptive value in cultures like our own, which place a premium on mother-infant attachment, and precisely for this reason its conservative implications also provide useful avenues for social analysis. At the same time, though, as Jean Walton shows, critics have only begun to consider how the "articulations of gendered subjectivity" in psychoanalysis are "dependent upon or imbricated in implicit assumptions" about race. Although a racial subtext informs the model of sexual development in a number of early psychoanalytic case histories, the role mothering plays in these negotiations has yet to be carefully analyzed.[58]

In modern-day America, the actual practice of mothering continues to be profoundly affected by race and class. According to recent statistics, one-quarter of American children are poor, nearly half of all children under age six are poor, more than half of these live with single mothers, and minorities constitute 70 percent of all children living in extreme poverty.[59] The Urban Institute has predicted that the 1996 restrictions in the federal welfare policy will move another 1.1 million children into poverty.[60] Patricia Hill Collins points out that while feminist discussions of maternity often center on problems of maternal and child psychological health, poor mothers are faced with the more basic problem of ensuring their children's physical survival.[61]

Arguments for the restriction of welfare benefits for the poor have implicitly been based on negative images of black and often young single mothers—even though this is not an accurate portrait of the majority of women on welfare.[62] Nevertheless, as Dorothy Roberts puts it, "When Americans debate welfare reform, most have single Black mothers in mind. . . . 'Welfare' has become a code word for 'race.'" It has also become a code word for fertility. Assuming that aid encourages its recipients to have too many children, welfare opponents often justify restrictive policies such as "family caps" as a means of limiting the growth of the poor. According to Roberts, these policies are problematic not only because studies have found that there is "no significant causal relationship between welfare benefits and childbearing," but because they divert attention from the true source of poverty.[63] By suggesting that poverty is produced by procreation and not by an inequitable political, social, and economic order, welfare opponents present racial inequality as a function of "nature rather than power," "perpetuated by Black people themselves"—and especially by black mothers.[64] In the context of this volume, such assumptions point to the endurance of the Malthusian attack on lower-class women's reproductive excess, initiated at the end of the eighteenth century. Deborah Valenze suggests that by linking female fertility, overpopulation, and subsistence, Malthus's theories helped make it possible for poor mothers to be blamed for the cycle of poverty.[65]

Questions about abortion and reproductive technologies, also tied to concerns about race and class, have enormously complicated contemporary debates about maternity. It is worth remembering that it was not until the second half of the nineteenth century that abortion became a crime in America. As

Leslie Reagan documents, in both the colonial and postrevolutionary era, terminating a pregnancy before "quickening" was legal under common law, and abortifacients and the services of practitioners were widely publicized and regularly available. The mid-nineteenth-century campaign against abortion was spearheaded by the newly formed American Medical Association, anxious to restrict the services of nondoctors. The promoters gained popular success by evoking Malthusian apprehensions about population growth, arguing that abortions would diminish the numbers of white, native-born Protestants and enable Catholic immigrants to exceed them. Drawing on the idea of the female body as the site of population control, the medical leader of the antiabortion campaign asked: Shall the South and West "be filled by our children or by those of aliens? This is a question our women must answer; upon their loins depends the future destiny of the nation."[66]

The effect of the criminalization of abortion — mandated in all states between 1860 and 1880 — was hardly what its promoters advocated, as privileged women continued to be able to acquire safe and often legal abortions in the following century. By the mid-twentieth century, however, a "nationwide crackdown ended the relative ease of obtaining [safe and legal] abortions," and women who wanted to terminate their pregnancies were increasingly forced to resort to dangerous alternatives. As a result, tens of thousands of them annually poured into emergency rooms. Between 1951 and 1962, the risk of death from illegal abortion nearly doubled and women of color, always less likely to have access to safer measures, experienced almost four times greater risk of death than white women.[67]

Since the legalization of abortion in 1973, the discourse against it, often based on a notion of "fetal rights," has been used not only to challenge a woman's right to terminate a pregnancy but to justify a variety of other measures, including the forced medical treatment of pregnant women and the prosecution of pregnant drug users (these problems are discussed at some length in Julia Epstein's article).[68] Between 1985 and 1995, two hundred women in thirty states were charged with drug use during pregnancy, the majority of them black.[69] One 1990 study of pregnant women in Florida concluded that although black and white women are equally likely to use drugs or alcohol during pregnancy, black women's use is reported to the authorities nearly ten times more often.[70] In South Carolina, the Interagency Policy begun in 1989 resulted in the arrests of forty-two women; all but one were black. There, mothers were shackled shortly before and after childbirth, and one woman was handcuffed to her bed throughout her delivery.[71]

Cynthia Daniels argues that the fundamental issues involved in cases concerning "fetal health" have profound political implications as pregnancy becomes the grounds for exempting women from the right to bodily integrity, one of the most basic principles of liberal individualism and American citizenship. The contradiction at the heart of the legal debates becomes clear when bodily intrusions not permitted under the law are contrasted with those tolerated in cases concerning pregnant women:

> Robbery suspects cannot be forced to undergo surgery in order to remove critical evidence, such as a bullet, from their bodies. Persons suspected of drug dealing cannot be forced to have their stomachs pumped if they swallow evidence. Suspected rapists cannot be forced to undergo involuntary blood tests for AIDS. Parents cannot be forced to donate organs to their children, even if the child's life is at stake and the parent is the only appropriate donor. . . . Organs cannot éven be taken from a cadaver without the prior consent of the dying. . . . [But] pregnant women have been forced to have blood transfusions against their will; they have been sedated, strapped down, and forced to undergo major surgery; they have been physically detained in hospitals when physicians suspected they weren't following medical orders.

Daniels suggests that reproductive politics presses liberal political theory to its breaking point by highlighting the limitations of the concepts of individualism, privacy, and self-determination, which neither capture the relational grounds of pregnancy nor are of consistent use in defending a pregnant woman's rights to terminate a pregnancy or avoid intrusive procedures.[72]

Dorothy Roberts emphasizes a different problem: While much of the debate about reproductive freedom concerns the pregnant woman's right to have an abortion or avoid medical intrusion, black women also suffer from a broad range of governmental policies that limit their ability to bear children — from the coerced sterilizations of hundreds of thousands of minority women in the 1960s and 1970s, to the mass distribution of Norplant among minorities in the 1990s, to the current popularity of "family caps" for welfare recipients. Construing reproductive liberty as the pregnant woman's freedom to make choices about her body without governmental interference fails to address the way governmental incentives against childbearing narrow minority and poor women's range of reproductive choices.[73]

Advances in reproductive technologies have compounded the political tensions surrounding reproduction. On the one hand, these technologies enable motherhood to be separated from heterosexuality and offer "women a greater chance to decide if, when and under what conditions to mother." But on the other hand, they also increase the likelihood that female reproduction will be the subject of medical and governmental surveillance as well as of efforts to reinforce heterosexuality and paternal control. In the 1980s, for instance, the Warnock Committee in Britain advised parliament that only women in stable heterosexual relationships be allowed to take advantage of reproductive technologies, going so far as to suggest that married women offer written consent from their husbands.[74] In the United States, several state courts have wrestled with the difference between seminal donation and surrogate motherhood, generally concluding that the process of pregnancy and birth entitles the surrogate mother to more parental rights than the sperm donor. But individual situations sometimes work to the father's advantage. Thus, in cases involving lesbian and unmarried mothers, sperm donors have been granted parental rights against maternal wishes because there is no competing father.[75]

Questions about reproductive liberty and reproductive technologies are based in part on whether mothers should be seen as the center of procreative control or as a competing interest group. The articles in this anthology indicate that these questions are at once historically enduring and new. The opening essays show that there have long been efforts to conceptualize and prioritize the differences between mother, fetus or offspring, and some greater governmental power, be it God, king, or father. In light of current arguments that put the fetus's rights and health before the mother's, Harvey's celebration of the fetus's individuality seems remarkably familiar as do the many seventeenth- and eighteenth-century theories that fault the pregnant mother for fetal deformity. Similarly, when Bradstreet and Dryden contemplate the difference between the mother's generational agency and that of God, king, or father, they raise still-pressing questions about whether procreative authority rests with the mother or with a governmental body.

As suggested earlier, by the end of the eighteenth century there is an important change in the governing figure's procreative position. In the seventeenth-century models, the argument often turns on the extent to which a higher power actually generates the offspring—the extent to which it supersedes the mother as the privileged point of creation. In the late eighteenth century and beyond, procreation is largely feminized, and the argument is less about a governing power's role in producing the offspring and more about a generalized social need to regulate a process associated primarily with women. The articles at the end of the volume indicate that whether the mother is blamed for excess birth or for infant death—whether she is the space where national, racial, and class differences are reinforced or collapsed—she, and not some governmental figure, has the power to originate (and thereby also exterminate) bodies and populations. It is perhaps telling that after the maternal model of reproduction replaced the governmental model of generation, the mother's fertility was increasingly subject to governmental supervision.

In our own day governmental intervention appears especially pronounced not simply because the assumption that female reproduction needs to be regulated continues, but also because reproductive technologies have created so many new arenas for interference. At the same time, though, such technologies have arguably shifted attention away from the female body as the source of human creation. Terms like *artificial insemination, test-tube baby,* and *in vitro fertilization,* which emphasize science's contribution to conception, make women's procreative role seem as irrelevant as it was for many seventeenth-century theorists.[76]

If procreation was increasingly linked to the female body in the late eighteenth century and maternal practice naturalized partly as a result, this did not preclude the possibility of separating childbearing from childrearing. At least two articles in *Inventing Maternity* explore this possibility. Johnson suggests that the daughter in *The Wrongs of Woman* might be raised by a female couple, only one member of which is the child's blood relative; and Costello describes how the wet nurse in *Ennui* develops as powerful a tie to her foster child as she does to her biological one. In the earlier *Pamela,* Part 2, when Mr. B. overrules Pamela's desire to breastfeed, the mother's value as sexual object and breeder carries more weight than her role as caretaker.[77] In contrast, *The Wrongs of Woman* and *Ennui* demonstrate that women can nurture and care for young children to whom they do not give birth. These later novels indicate that even as motherhood came to be seen as a reproductive disposition, maternal care could be abstracted, idealized, and divided from reproduction itself. Indeed, the prioritization of maternal practice generated, in part, by a biologically deterministic view of the female body may have actually facilitated the conceptual detachment of motherhood and biology.

As suggested at the outset of this essay, the prioritization of maternal care had implications for fatherhood as well. When women gained child custody rights in mid-nineteenth-century England and America, they did so, in part, because paternal kinship became less compelling an argument for guardianship than maternal bonding. It is a testament to the cultural value placed on maternal care that in the hundred years that followed, American mothers were more likely than fathers to gain guardianship of their children in cases of separation or divorce, an important reversal of the centuries of laws treating women and children as the property of men. But most recently, between 1960 and 1990, the judicial presumption in favor of mothers was abolished in nearly all states, and fathers were given equal or nearly equal legal claim to child custody.[78] On the one hand, the change appears to reflect both the feminist call for a more equitable distribution of parental labor and a healthful rejection of the naturalization of maternity. But on the other hand, the change may signal an infringement on maternal authority: in contested custody cases, courts often treat mothers differently than fathers, holding them to a higher standard of parenting and allowing their careers or sexual behavior to be used as evidence against them.[79]

It is not the goal of this volume to gauge the full historical impact these and other measures will have on the understanding of motherhood, but rather to suggest that maternity has long been the site of political change and debate. Certain shifts—like that from a generative to a reproductive model of procreation—mark significant alterations in the political use of maternity. It is possible that we are in the midst of an equally momentous—and oppressive— transition today. Because maternal images and meanings remain malleable over time, at least some political influence can be exerted at the level of representation, and feminist scholarly efforts can be important here. But *Inventing Maternity* also points to the long-term vulnerability of the maternal body—whether that be before medicine, government, or the law. Changing this is the harder task.

Notes

1. For comparable changes in France see Elisabeth Badinter, *Mother Love: Myth and Reality of Motherhood: Motherhood in Modern History* (New York: Macmillan, 1981); George D. Sussman, *Selling Mother's Milk: The Wet-Nursing Business in France, 1715-1914* (Urbana: University of Illinois, 1982); Mary Jacobus, "Incorruptible Milk: Breastfeeding and the French Revolution," in *Rebel Daughters*, ed. Sara E. Melzer and Leslie W. Rabine (New York: Oxford University Press, 1992).

2. Valerie Fildes, *Wet Nursing: A History from Antiquity to the Present* (Oxford: Basil Blackwell, 1988), 79, 116; Valerie Fildes, *Breasts, Bottles, and Babies: A History of Infant Feeding* (Edinburgh: Edinburgh University Press, 1985), 116; Ruth H. Bloch, "American Feminine Ideals in Transition: The Rise of the Moral Mother, 1785-1815," *Feminist Studies* 4 (1978): 109-11; Catherine M. Scholten, *Childbearing in American Society, 1650-1850* (New York: New York University Press, 1985), 71-73. For general trends in England and France see Marilyn Yalom, *A History of the Breast* (New York: Knopf, 1997), 105-23. On the eroticization of the breast see Barbara Charlesworth Gelpi, *Shelley's Goddess: Maternity, Language, Subjectivity* (New York: Oxford University Press, 1992), 43-60.

3. Peter C. Hoffer and N.E.H. Hull, *Murdering Mothers: Infanticide in England and New England, 1558-1803* (New York: New York University Press, 1981), 69, 83-85. For more on English law see R.W. Malcolmson, "Infanticide in the Eighteenth Century," in *Crime in England, 1550-1800*, ed. J.S. Cockburn (Princeton, N.J.: Princeton University Press, 1977): 187-209.

4. For America's dependence on English custody law see Mary Ann Mason, *From Father's Property to Children's Rights: The History of Child Custody in the United States* (New York: Columbia University Press, 1994), 17-18.

5. Bernard C. Gavit, ed., *Blackstone's Commentaries on the Law* (Washington, D.C.: Washington Law Book, 1941), 203, 196; Judith Schneid Lewis, *In the Family Way: Childbearing in the British Aristocracy, 1760-1860* (New Brunswick, N.J.: Rutgers University Press, 1986), 59.

6. Mason, *From Father's Property*, xiii, 50-62, 118. Slave mothers not only had no claim over their children but "the law granted to whites a devisable, *in futuro* interest in the potential children of their slaves." See Dorothy Roberts, *Killing the Black Body: Race, Reproduction, and the Meaning of Liberty* (New York: Pantheon, 1997), 33. Linda Gordon points out that, well into the twentieth century, the legal preference for mothers also "remained an abstraction for most single mothers," since they could rarely afford to maintain their children and were at constant risk of losing them to the state: Gordon, *Heroes of Their Own Lives: The Politics and History of Family Violence, Boston, 1880-1960* (New York: Penguin, 1988), 95, 99.

7. Quoted in Mason, *From Father's Property*, 60.

8. For an argument about the ineffectiveness of maternal presumption and the ease with which fathers have always tended to win contested custody cases despite it see Phyllis Chesler, *Patriarchy: Notes of an Expert Witness* (Monroe, Maine: Common Courage Press, 1994), 38.

9. Randolph Trumbach, *The Rise of the Egalitarian Family: Aristocratic Kinship and Domestic Relations in Eighteenth-Century England* (New York: Academic Press, 1978), 190; Lawrence Stone, *The Family, Sex and Marriage in England, 1500-1800*, abridged ed. (New York: Harper and Row, 1977), 284. For a contemporaneous discussion of changes in Western society see Edward Shorter, *The Making of the Modern Family* (New York: Basic Books, 1975). For similar arguments about America, see Bloch, "American Feminine Ideals in Transition"; Scholten, *Childbearing in American Society*; John Demos, *Past, Present, and Personal: The Family and the Life Course in American History* (London: Oxford University Press, 1986); and Nancy M. Theriot, *Mothers and Daughters in Nineteenth-Century America: The Biosocial Construction of Femininity* (Lexington: University Press of Kentucky, 1996).

10. Linda Pollock argues that there appears to be no "significant change in the quality of parental care given to or the amount of parental affection felt for infants for the period 1500-1900." Pollock, *Forgotten Children: Parent-Child Relations, 1500-1900* (Cambridge: Cambridge University Press, 1983), 235. Also see Bloch, "American Feminine Ideals in Transition," 105. For other problems with Stone and Trumbach, see Gelpi, *Shelley's Goddess*, 36-39.

11. Mary Beth Norton, *Liberty's Daughters: The Revolutionary Experience of American Women, 1750-1800* (Boston: Little, Brown, 1980), 242-50. For another important discussion of Republican Motherhood, see Linda K. Kerber, *Women of the Republic: Intellect and Ideology in Revolutionary America* (Chapel Hill: University of North Carolina Press, 1980), 228-31, 283-88.

12. Lewis, *In the Family Way*, 225; Elizabeth Kowaleski-Wallace, *Their Fathers' Daughters: Hannah More, Maria Edgeworth, and Patriarchal Complicity* (New York: Oxford University Press, 1991), 103.

13. Michel Foucault, *The History of Sexuality*, vol. 1, *An Introduction* (New York: Vintage Books, 1980), 24-35, 103-14, 123-27.

14. Jacques Donzelot, *The Policing of Families* (New York: Pantheon Books, 1979), 45-46.

15. Nancy Armstrong, *Desire and Domestic Fiction: A Political History of the Novel* (New York: Oxford University Press, 1987). Armstrong, however, never directly

discusses maternity, as Toni Bowers points out in *The Politics of Motherhood: British Writing and Culture, 1680-1760* (Cambridge: Cambridge University Press, 1996), 21.

16. Ruth Perry, "Colonizing the Breast: Sexuality and Maternity in Eighteenth-Century England," *Eighteenth-Century Life* 16 (1992): 186; Felicity A. Nussbaum, "'Savage' Mothers," in her *Torrid Zones: Maternity, Sexuality, and Empire in Eighteenth-Century English Narratives* (Baltimore: Johns Hopkins University Press, 1995), 48. "'Savage' Mothers" is adapted from its earlier publication in *Eighteenth-Century Life* 16 (1992): 163-84. Both Perry and Nussbaum indicate that the kind of connections between imperialism and motherhood that Anna Davin describes in her influential article on twentieth-century England began considerably earlier. See Davin, "Imperialism and Motherhood," *History Workshop* 5 (1978): 9-65. For similar arguments about the nineteenth century see Deirdre David, *Rule Britannia: Women, Empire, and Victorian Writing* (Ithaca, N.Y.: Cornell University Press, 1995), esp. 5-7; and Mary Poovey, *Uneven Developments: The Ideological Work of Gender in Mid-Victorian England* (Chicago: University of Chicago Press, 1988), 164-98.

17. Perry, "Colonizing the Breast," 185, 208; Nussbaum, "'Savage' Mothers," 47-48.

18. Ludmilla Jordanova, *Sexual Visions: Images of Gender in Science and Medicine between the Eighteenth and Twentieth Centuries* (Madison: University of Wisconsin Press, 1989); Thomas Laqueur, *Making Sex: Body and Gender from the Greeks to Freud* (Cambridge: Harvard University Press, 1990); Londa Schiebinger, *Nature's Body: Gender in the Making of Modern Science* (Boston: Beacon Press, 1993).

19. Fildes, *Wet Nursing*, 113-14; Schiebinger, *Nature's Body*, 40-42, 69-70. For a current feminist look at the maternal behavior of mammals see Sarah Blaffer Hrdy, "Natural-born Mothers," *Natural History* 104 (December 1995): 30-43. In her fascinating article, Hrdy suggests that infanticide, abortion, and cannibalism may be just as "natural" for mother mammals as suckling.

20. Laqueur, *Making Sex*, 149.

21. William Cadogan, *Essay upon Nursing and the Management of Children from their Birth to Three Years of Age* (London, 1749), 24. Also see William Buchan, *Advice to Mothers on the Subject of Their Own Health and on the Means of Promoting the Health, Strength, and Beauty of Their Offspring* (Philadelphia, 1804). On Cadogan's call for male supervision of the female body see Perry, "Colonizing the Breast," 199, and Kowaleski-Wallace, *Their Fathers' Daughters*, 102-4.

22. Jean Donnison, *Midwives and Medical Men: A History of Inter-Professional Rivalries and Women's Rights* (New York: Schocken Books, 1977); Jane B. Donegan, *Women and Men Midwives: Medicine, Morality, and Misogyny in Early America* (Westport, Conn.: Greenwood Press, 1978); Eve Keller, "Mrs. Jane Sharp: Midwifery and the Critique of Medical Knowledge in Seventeenth-Century England," *Women's Writing* 2 (1995): 101-11. For an alternative interpretation of the dangers of midwife births, see Deborah D. Rogers, "Eighteenth-Century Literary Depictions of Childbirth in the Historical Context of Mutilation and Mortality: The Case of *Pamela*," *Centennial Review* 37 (1993): 305-24.

23. See, for instance, Anne K. Mellor, "*Frankenstein*: A Feminist Critique of Science," in *One Culture: Essays on Literature and Science*, ed. George Levine (Madi-

son: University of Wisconsin Press, 1988), 287-312; and "Possessing Nature: The Female in *Frankenstein*," in *Romanticism and Feminism*, ed. Anne K. Mellor (Bloomington: Indiana University Press, 1988), 220-32.

24. Quoted in Roberts, *Killing the Black Body*, 36.

25. Ruth K. McClure, *Coram's Children: The London Foundling Hospital in the Eighteenth Century* (New Haven: Yale University Press, 1981), 247; Bowers, *Politics of Motherhood*, 10; Nussbaum, *Torrid Zones*, 27. For an excellent study of impoverished mothers in London a century later see Ellen Ross, *Love and Toil: Motherhood in Outcast London, 1870-1918* (New York: Oxford University Press, 1993).

26. Olaudah Equiano, *Equiano's Travels: His Autobiography, The Interesting Narrative of the Life of Olaudah Equiano or Gustavus Vassa, the African*, ed. Paul Edwards (Oxford: Heinemann, 1969), 1-24.

27. *The History of Mary Prince, a West Indian Slave, Related by Herself*, ed. Moira Ferguson (Ann Arbor: University of Michigan Press, 1996), 51.

28. Harriet A. Jacobs, *Incidents in the Life of a Slave Girl, Written by Herself*, ed. Jean Fagan Yellin (Cambridge: Harvard University Press, 1987), 16, 6.

29. Ibid., 76. Dorothy Roberts argues that it is important to see the master's rape as a "weapon of terror that reinforced whites' domination over their human property," not simply as an economically and sexually motivated act (Roberts, *Killing the Black Body*, 29-30).

30. Quoted in Mason, *From Father's Property*, 43. Significantly, though, a mixed child born of a free white woman in the South did not follow the condition of the mother but was instead placed in "a twilight zone between regular apprenticeships and lifetime slavery" (ibid., 29; see also 28, 41).

31. Jacobs, *Slave Girl*, 73; Roberts, *Killing the Black Body*, 27-28.

32. Hortense J. Spillers, "Mama's Baby, Papa's Maybe: An American Grammar Book," *Diacritics* 17 (1987): 76.

33. On American slave women's efforts to protect their children, see Roberts, *Killing the Black Body*, 43-44, 50-51. On resistance to maternity in the West Indies, see Barbara Bush, *Slave Women in Caribbean Society, 1650-1850* (Bloomington: Indiana University Press, 1990), 120-50; for America, see Roberts, *Killing the Black Body*, 45-49, and Stephanie J. Shaw, "Mothering under Slavery in the Antebellum South," *Mothering: Ideology, Experience, Agency*, ed. Evelyn Nakano Glenn, Grace Chang, and Linda Rennie Forcey (London: Routledge, 1994), 247-49. For a summary of the controversy about whether slave women resisted maternity to reappropriate their bodies, see Rosalind Pollack Petchesky, "The Body as Property: A Feminist Re-vision," *Conceiving the New World Order: The Global Politics of Reproduction*, ed. Faye D. Ginsburg and Rayna Rapp (Berkeley: University of California Press, 1995), 398.

34. Jacobs, *Slave Girl*, 143; Prince, *History*, 57; Roberts, *Killing the Black Body*, 36, 49.

35. Ludmilla Jordanova, "Interrogating the Concept of Reproduction in the Eighteenth Century," *Conceiving the New World Order*, 373.

36. Armstrong, *Desire and Domestic Fiction*, 3.

37. Gelpi, *Shelley's Goddess*, 40.

38. Susanna Rowson, *Charlotte Temple*, ed. Cathy N. Davidson (New York: Oxford University Press, 1986).

39. Scholten, *Childbearing*, 71; Clare Midgley, *Women against Slavery: The British Campaigns, 1780-1870* (London: Routledge, 1992), 121-53. Myra Jehlen and Michael Warner point to the inextricable connection between England and America in the title and "General Introduction" of their anthology, *The English Literatures of America, 1500-1800*, ed. Myra Jehlen and Michael Warner (New York and London: Routledge, 1997), xvii-xxiii.

40. Benedict Anderson has been central on this point. See *Imagined Communities: Reflections on the Origin and Spread of Nationalism* (London: Verso, 1991).

41. A fuller summary of these changes appears in my "'Abroad and at Home': Sexual Ambiguity, Miscegenation, and Colonial Boundaries in *Belinda*," *PMLA* 112 (1997): 215-16.

42. Foucault discusses the eighteenth-century emergence of "'population' as an economic and political problem" (25-26); also see Jordanova, "Interrogating the Concept of Reproduction," 382.

43. Patricia James, *Population Malthus: His Life and Times* (London: Routledge, 1979), 127; William Peterson, *Malthus* (Cambridge: Harvard University Press, 1979), 111-12, 128.

44. Thomas Malthus, *An Essay on the Principle of Population*, ed. Geoffrey Gilbert (Oxford: Oxford University Press, 1993), 13-14. In the 1803 edition of *Essay*, Malthus added moral restraint to the list of population checks.

45. J.R. Poynter, *Society and Pauperism: English Ideas on Poor Relief, 1795-1834* (Toronto: University of Toronto Press, 1969), 145; Peterson, *Malthus*, 145. For an alternative view, stressing Malthus's pessimism about America, see Drew R. McCoy, *The Elusive Republic: Political Economy in Jeffersonian America* (Chapel Hill: University of North Carolina Press, 1980), 190-91. For late-eighteenth-century American anxieties about population growth see McCoy, esp. 114, 129-32, 244, 248, 253.

46. Peterson, *Malthus*, 206.

47. Edmond Cocks, "The Malthusian Theory in Pre–Civil War America: An Original Relation to the Universe," *Population Studies* 20 (1967): 343-63, esp. 346-49, 359.

48. Thus, the most prolific American writer on population worried about how to protect "the quality of American citizenship from degradation through the tumultuous access of vast throngs of ignorant and brutalized peasantry" (Peterson, *Malthus*, 206-7).

49. Deborah Valenze, *The First Industrial Woman* (New York: Oxford University Press, 1995), 135-36.

50. For an excellent discussion of the emergence of the term *reproduction*, see Jordanova, "Interrogating the Concept of Reproduction," 371-74.

51. Malcolmson, "Infanticide in the Eighteenth Century," 192-98, 206; Hoffer and Hull, *Murdering Mothers*.

52. It has been estimated that between 1 and 2 percent of the children on slave plantations had white fathers (Roberts, *Killing the Black Body*, 316 n. 23).

53. Jacobs, *Slave Girl*, 85.

54. On England, see Moira Ferguson, *Subject to Others: British Women Writers and Colonial Slavery, 1670-1834* (London: Routledge, 1992), 5; and Midgley, *Women against Slavery*, esp. 154-77. On the United States, see Gerda Lerner, *The Majority Finds Its Past* (New York: Oxford University Press, 1979), 94-111; for the racism of the women's suffrage movement see Angela Y. Davis, *Women, Race, and Class* (New York: Vintage Books, 1983), chaps. 4, 7, and 9.

55. Linda Gordon, *Heroes*, 82-89; Linda Gordon, *Pitied but Not Entitled: Single Mothers and the History of Welfare, 1890-1935* (New York: Free Press, 1994), 30-31; Roberts, *Killing the Black Body*, 204, 206; Mason, *From Father's Property*, 92-101. For a discussion of the Infant Welfare movement in early-twentieth-century England, see Ross, chap. 7.

56. A number of literary scholars have made excellent use of psychoanalytic interpretations of maternity. See Gelpi, *Shelley's Goddess*; Marianne Hirsch, *The Mother/Daughter Plot: Narrative, Psychoanalysis, Feminism* (Bloomington: Indiana University Press, 1989); Margaret Homans, *Bearing the Word: Language and Female Experience in Nineteenth-Century Women's Writing* (Chicago: University of Chicago Press, 1986).

57. For the controversies see Judith Butler, *Gender Trouble: Feminism and the Subversion of Identity* (London: Routledge, 1990), esp. 79-93; Teresa Brennan, "Introduction," *Between Feminism and Psychoanalysis*, ed. Teresa Brennan (New York: Routledge, 1989), 1-14; Janice Doane and Devon Hodges, *From Klein to Kristeva: Psychoanalytic Feminism and the Search for the "Good Enough" Mother* (Ann Arbor: University of Michigan Press, 1992).

58. Butler, *Gender Trouble*, 92; Jean Walton, "Re-Placing Race in (White) Psychoanalytic Discourse: Founding Narratives of Feminism," *Critical Inquiry* (1995), 779-80. For Freud's adoption of colonial metaphors, see Mary Ann Doane, *Femmes Fatales: Feminism, Film Theory, Psychoanalysis* (New York: Routledge, 1991), 209.

59. "One in Four: America's Youngest Poor" (New York: National Center for Children in Poverty, 1996), 47; abridged ed., 12, 17.

60. Peter Edelman, "The Worst Thing Bill Clinton Has Done," *Atlantic Monthly* (March 1997): 46.

61. Patricia Hill Collins, "Shifting the Center: Race, Class, and Feminist Theorizing about Motherhood," *Representations of Motherhood*, ed. Donna Bassin, Margaret Honey, and Meryle Mahrer Kaplan (New Haven, Conn: Yale University Press, 1994), 59-62. For another good summary of the experience of poor African American mothers see Leith Mullings, "Households Headed by Women: The Politics of Race, Class, and Gender," *Conceiving the New World Order*, 122-39.

62. Margaret L. Usdansky, "Single Motherhood: Stereotypes versus Statistics," *New York Times*, Week in Review, 11 February 1996, 4.

63. Roberts, *Killing the Black Body*, 110-12, 218. Also see Usdansky, "Single Motherhood." For the treatment of race and illegitimacy in mid-twentieth-century America, see Rickie Solinger, "Race and 'Value': Black and White Illegitimate Babies, 1945-1965," *Mothering: Ideology, Experience, and Agency*, 287-310.

64. Roberts, *Killing the Black Body*, 102, 5; also see 7, 9, 16-18, 21, 110-12, 179, 200, 203, 209-19.

65. Valenze, *First Industrial Woman*, 136.

66. Leslie J. Reagan, *When Abortion Was a Crime: Women, Medicine, and Law in the United States, 1867-1973* (Berkeley: University of California Press, 1997), 8-14.

67. Ibid., 190-215. Although abortion was legalized in 1973 with *Roe v. Wade*, it continues to remain less available to poor and minority women because of restrictions on Medicaid funding and bans on abortion counseling at federal clinics (Roberts, *Killing the Black Body*, 229-35).

68. For discussions of how the idea of fetal individuality and rights may be related to advances in medical photography and particularly to Lennart Nilsson's photographs in *A Child Is Born* (1966), see E. Ann Kaplan, *Motherhood and Representation: The Mother in Popular Culture and Melodrama* (London: Routledge, 1992), 203-10, and Alice E. Adams, *Reproducing the Womb: Images of Childbirth in Science, Feminist Theory, and Literature* (Ithaca, N.Y.: Cornell University Press, 1994), 117-20.

69. Roberts, *Killing the Black Body*, 153; Cynthia R. Daniels, *At Women's Expense: State Power and the Politics of Fetal Rights* (Cambridge: Harvard University Press, 1993), 103.

70. Daniels, *At Women's Expense*, 127. On why black women are disproportionately affected, see Roberts, *Killing the Black Body*, 172-80.

71. Roberts, *Killing the Black Body*, 166.

72. Daniels, *At Women's Expense*, 5, 33, 137.

73. Roberts, *Killing the Black Body*, 6, and chaps. 3, 4, and 5; also see Davis, *Women, Race, and Class*, 215-21.

74. Michelle Stanworth, ed., *Reproductive Technologies: Gender, Motherhood and Medicine* (Cambridge: Polity Press, 1987), 4, 24-25.

75. Martha A. Field, *Surrogate Motherhood* (Cambridge, Mass.: Harvard University Press, 1988), 115-17. Custody of the famous Baby M, born of an artificially inseminated surrogate mother, was awarded to the father. In another highly publicized case involving reproductive technologies, a divorced couple fought for guardianship of their frozen embryos; custody was awarded to the father, who sought to prevent their being implanted. See Mason, *From Father's Property*, 139-44.

76. On the problem of the terms for reproductive techniques, see Stanworth, *Reproductive Technologies*, 26.

77. As Perry points out in "Colonizing the Breast" (200-201), Mr. B. acts out of sexual self-interest in opposing Pamela's interest in breastfeeding, for he accepts the popular belief that nursing mothers must abstain from intercourse.

78. Mason, *From Father's Property*, 123.

79. For popular representations of nurturing fathers, see Kaplan, *Motherhood and Representation*, 184-88. For women's legal burden, see Chesler, *Patriarchy*, 52-53, and Field, *Surrogate Motherhood*, 140-41. Chesler argues that changes in custody arrangements represent a backlash against the feminist movement, having occurred at the precise historical moment when women began demanding abortion

rights and equal pay (39). For a discussion of how divorced Canadian fathers want joint parental power but not joint childcare responsibilities and are particularly resentful of child support, see Carl E. Bertoia and Janice Drakich, "The Fathers' Rights Movement: Contradictions in Rhetoric and Practice," *Fatherhood: Contemporary Theory, Research, and Social Policy* (Thousand Oaks, Calif.: Sage, 1995), 230-54.

Making Up for Losses

The Workings of Gender in William Harvey's *de Generatione animalium*

By repeated dissection of hen and deer in the 1630s and 1640s, William Harvey determined—as it turns out, erroneously—that there is no mass, either of mixed semina or of male semen and female menstrual blood, to be found in the uterus after intercourse. Although *de Generatione animalium* [Anatomical exercises on the generation of animals] is famous for much else, it seems fairly clear that Harvey considered this experimental discovery momentous, because it unambiguously demonstrated to him that his predecessors, who all assumed the existence of some postcoital mass, had drawn "erroneous and hasty conclusions" about the origins of generation.[1] The new empiricism was once again successful—as it had been earlier in Harvey's discovery of the circulation of the blood—both in banishing what Harvey called the "phantoms of darkness" from traditional knowledge and in establishing a sure foundation for new theories of animal physiology (151).

Historians of science have evaluated the accuracy of the conclusions that Harvey drew from his observational discovery, particularly the roles he assigned to the male and female in procreation and the status of the egg produced.[2] But precisely because it deals with male and female procreative agency, Harvey's text is also available for study in light of its use of historically specific and socially constructed gender relations. Harvey's discovery of the absence of any postcoital mass in the uterus was indeed revolutionary, but not merely because it contravened the biological teaching of Aristotle or Galen; it also threatened to contravene the certain knowledge of male dominion—in both the family and the state—that those theories supported. Starting from an experimentally produced "fact," Harvey suggested a theory of generation that reveals a more or less explicit encoding of gender roles common to his culture. Although he did alter the scientific understanding of generation, he apparently needed to "preserve the phenomena" of gender relations built into the previous theories. I shall argue that Harvey's new theory is a response to the ideological threats, both sexual and political, posed by the absence of semen in the uterus; that his text constitutes a compensatory drama in which an inviolable male agency and an autonomous masculine identity emerge in the face of threatened loss to male sexual and political power; and that both of these are played out against the necessary diminution of the female, particularly in her capacity as progenitor. But if *de Generatione* thus manifests the normative interplay of a priori assumptions about gender and what Harvey called the "obvious truths" of empirical observation, it will also reveal the normative anxieties associated with the empirical method itself—that, though heralded as the sure way *toward* the "citadel of truth" (153), the new empiricism, for all its violent and valiant efforts, could not breach its walls.

This essay thus partakes of two intertwined traditions in the social study of early modern science. The first, perhaps best theorized by Bruno Latour, examines the specific interconnections between epistemological and sociopolitical issues. In the earlier work of Steven Shapin and Simon Schaffer on the competing scientific methodologies of Hobbes and Boyle, and in Shapin's more recent work on the function of gentlemanly discourse in securing credibility for empirical findings, these scholars have sought to show how "solutions to the problem of knowledge are embedded within practical solutions to the problem of social order"—that, in simpler terms, epistemology and social politics are interdependent.[3] The second tradition, roughly called "feminist," tends to be more literary in orientation, as it examines the gendered rhetoric of early modern science texts. Most influential in this regard has been Evelyn Fox Keller, who in her many works has demonstrated with great specificity the constitutive role of metaphors (and particularly those that arise from or correspond to social relations) in the construction of scientific certainties and theories.[4] Although none of these scholars deals explicitly with Harvey's investigations into embryology, they offer methodological models for what will be my approach here in examining the rhetorical and epistemological construction of Harvey's text.[5]

By now it is nearly a truism that the biological body is always culturally inscribed, if not altogether culturally constructed. But the now commonplace assertions of the mechanized body and the passivity of feminized matter in the seventeenth century need to be refined against the specific texts in which those portrayals emerge. Carolyn Merchant, for example, who has been so influential in reappraising the scientific revolution in light of its engagement with women and the environment, nonetheless relies too easily on generalization in her discussion of Harvey's reproductive biology. Merchant claims that "the passive role [Harvey] assigned to both matter and the female in reproduction is consistent with . . . the trend toward female passivity in the sphere of industrial production and with the reassertion of the passivity and inertness of matter by the new seventeenth-century mechanical philosophy."[6]

Merchant misses here what I consider to be crucial aspects of Harvey's theory, among them the suggestion of the female as the efficient—and not merely the material—cause of generation and the vitality (indeed, the vitalism) of biological matter from the first moments of its creation. While I agree wholly with Merchant's general sense that Harvey's theory was constructed in accordance with prevailing gender ideology, I want to consider with somewhat more specificity both the details of the theory and their rhetorical deployment in order to make manifest the specific inscriptions of gender ideology on Harvey's famous text.

In considering the cultural inscriptions in *de Generatione*, it is important to remember that Harvey arrived at his theory of generation in a highly politicized context. As the personal physician of Charles I, Harvey conducted some of his most definitive experiments on the king's lands and at the king's behest,[7] and, although based on work performed for the most part in the 1630s, *de Generatione* was probably written during the second half of the 1640s, when the king was already held captive by parliamentary forces. Harvey was thus for years connected to an increasingly embattled court whose king was engaged in an ultimately unsuccessful struggle to maintain his patriarchal rights over his subjects. While the prefatory matter of the 1651 text argues Harvey's distance from the turmoil of the time, the contention that scientific study was a much needed refuge from the "anxious cares" of the day suggests Harvey's keen awareness of the politicized context in which he worked.

The clearest evidence of the cultural embeddedness of Harvey's work is that his discovery of the postcoital absence of semen in the uterus neatly replicates the threat to political patriarchy that surrounded him. According to classic patriarchal arguments, the king ruled his kingdom as a father ruled his children; political and paternal rights were understood to be analogous or even synonymous. As King James argued in *The Trew Law of Free Monarchies*, "By the Law of Nature the King becomes a naturall Father to all his Leiges at his Coronation: And as the Father by his fatherly duty is bound to care for the nourishing, education, and vertuous government of his children; even so is the King Bound to care for all his subjects."[8]

Harvey's determination that the semen has no material contact with the egg surely threatens the nature of paternity, since without physical continuity between father and child the role of the father in generating the child becomes ambiguous. But it also threatens the nature of patriarchy as a form of civil government, since classical patriarchy—the theory that political right is paternal right—depended, at least implicitly, on the transmission of that right through paternal procreation. Although patriarchal arguments took many forms in the seventeenth century, a common ground of evidence was found in the biblical account of God giving Adam dominion over his wife and children. As Richard Field argued in 1606, "When there were no more in the World but the first man whom God made out of the earth, the first woman that was made of man, and the children which GOD had given them, who could be fitter to rule and direct, than the man for whose sake the woman was created, and out of whose loynes the children came?"[9]

Ignoring the first Creation story, in which male and female are created simultaneously (Genesis 1:26-27), and erasing entirely the female capacity for birth, Field founds Adam's rule on his status as the sole material source of procreation: Eve derives from his body and the children from his loins. Implicit in Field's argument is the biological assumption that the father exclusively creates the child: from *his* body, from *his* loins. Although clearly an inversion of the obvious—that children come from a woman's loins—Field's position, which was common to patriarchal arguments, was actually supported by both Aristotelian and Galenic physiology, which granted the father the greater share of procreative agency.[10]

The patriarchalists' use of Eve's derivation from Adam's body to support claims of paternal rule offers perhaps an exaggerated example of how both biblical stories and biological theories can get enlisted in political argument. When patriarchal writers spoke of rulers in general and not specifically of Adam's rule, however, the connection between generative and political sovereignty could not be made explicitly, since kings could not be said literally to father their subjects. Nonetheless, the connection between paternity and patriarchy continued to function in their claims, if only figuratively. Sir Robert Filmer, for example, founded the right of governance in God's original granting of paternal power to Adam, and he demonstrated that this power descended only through Adam (and not through Eve) because as "the Scripture teacheth us . . . all men came by succession, and generation from one man."[11] But because Filmer recognized that political right was not always transferred by lineal descent—kings could be usurped, for example, or governments consolidated—he did not actually rest his argument for patriarchy on the physiology of paternity.[12] That the two were nonetheless linked in his theory, however, is evident from his telling response to Hobbes's contention that in the state of nature children owe their original obligation to their mother. This could not be possible, argued Filmer, because we know "that God at the creation gave the sovereignty to the man over the woman, as being the nobler and principal agent in generation."[13] Because Adam—as *man*—is the "principal agent in generation," he achieves solitary rule over both wife and children, and it is on that physiological model that we are to understand the paternal rule of kings.

Patriarchal theory in the seventeenth century had grounds of support other than the biology of paternity, but if an analogy between the two was at least implicitly embedded in claims for fatherly rule, then Harvey's discovery, which threatened the traditional understanding of paternity, also threatened the understanding of patriarchy that derived from the father's procreative superiority.[14] Harvey's responses to the two conceptual dangers posed by his experimental work are, however, somewhat different from each other. While he mitigates the threat to paternity by playing out a fantasy of exaggerated male dominion, he counters the threat to patriarchy by transmuting it to a dominion based in a broadly masculine, as opposed to a specifically paternal, right.[15] This emerges in Harvey's depiction of the embryo as an autonomous, free-born male, unbounded by any constraints to either father or mother. In stressing the embryo's masculine autonomy—an autonomy which, as we shall see, characterizes Harvey's endeavors as an empirical researcher as well—Harvey's theory bears certain similarities to the famous myth of origins envisioned by his good friend Thomas Hobbes, who published his own work of anatomy and masculine birth, *Leviathan*, in 1651, the same year that Harvey published *de Generatione*. For both theorists, masculine right reemerges as traditional patriarchy gives way, and the masculine, freeborn individual becomes the basis of the state.

de Generatione is set up as a series of exercises, some detailing Harvey's findings from various dissections and observations, and some presenting the speculative conclusions he drew from them. Although Harvey never sets forth a formal or systematic theory of embryogenesis—in fact, *de Generatione* is deemed valuable less for its positive formulations than for its negative rejection of prior theories—he does provide the *shards* of a theory, speculations and observations that, though they never quite cohere, represent his thinking about what he called "the heart of [nature's] mystery" (153). Working from his determination that there is no semen to be found in the uterus after intercourse, Harvey reasoned that fertilization must occur without the semen having material contact with the egg. For Harvey the "egg" was not what we refer to as the ovum but, rather, the complete origin of the embryo, produced solely by the female; if the female was fertilized through intercourse, the egg would develop and grow on its own, either within the female's body (in viviparous animals) or outside it (in oviparous ones).[16] When Harvey asserted that all living things come from eggs, he was not propounding a universal female contribution from an ovary—Harvey, in fact, thought that the ovary in viviparous animals did not participate in the process of generation at all—but was rather suggesting that oviparous, rather than viviparous, animals should be understood as the paradigm case for understanding generation.[17]

Although *de Generatione* follows Aristotle's teaching in much else, Harvey's discovery of the lack of semen in the uterus compelled him to differ from Aristotle, as well as from Galen, with respect to the components of conception. For Aristotle, the semen acted directly on the female menstrual clot and, though contributing nothing material to the future embryo, actually was responsible for forming it and for determining its *telos*; the female, by contrast, supplied merely the matter on which the semen worked to craft the offspring. Aristotle's analogy for this interaction makes the point: the semen works on the menstrual blood as a carpenter does on a tree, carving out its creation from some prior material.[18] In Aristotle's theory, the female's role as material cause allows her to be rightly considered a parent, but it is the male contribution that provides the motion of the offspring and directs its formation, and so it is the male that is considered the primary progenitor.

The Galenic theory, which vied with Aristotle's for two thousand years, differed from it in attributing procreative seed to the female. But Galen concurred with Aristotle in deeming the female's role to be vastly inferior to the male's. In Galen's anatomy, women were understood to be stunted or deficient versions of males: women possessed the same reproductive organs as men, but because of their lesser perfecting heat, they had to retain those organs inside their bodies to keep them warm. The seed that the female "testicles" produced, therefore, was necessarily inferior in quality and importance to the seed produced by the more perfect organs of men.

As numerous recent scholars have shown, both Aristotle's and Galen's embryological theories align contemporary biological knowledge with prevailing assumptions about gender.[19] Harvey's discovery that these theories misconstrued the makeup of the material body of the fetus threatened to topple their corresponding assumptions about gender, because it undermined their biological support: if there is no postcoital mass in the uterus, then the semen cannot be considered to contribute directly to the fetus. Further, the female must be seen to produce *on her own* the egg out of which the fetus develops. Harvey certainly considered the possibility of female preeminence in generation: he reasoned that since a hen can produce unfruitful eggs without the cock, and since these eggs clearly have some vital principle that propels them from the ovary through the uterus, "all creative force or vital power [*anima*] is not derived exclusively from the male" (288). Harvey even refers to the female as an efficient, and not merely material, cause of generation, and he says that the female may be considered the primary agent in generation: "It seems probable that the female is actually of more moment in generation than the male" (289). As the male role in procreation fades into indeterminacy, the female's role emerges, at least potentially, as predominant.

It is important to understand that Harvey *needed* to assert female agency to explain how an egg can be produced without the semen's direct contribution. But the potential of that agency's really assuming preeminence over the male was troublesome: certainly, if the female herself were considered to control the giving of life to the egg, the traditional association of male with spirit and female with matter would be reversed. Harvey, of course, never portrays his discovery as potentially threatening in this way; his repeated assertions of it are routinely proud and are offered as clear evidence of the efficacy of diligent observation in the unveiling of truth. But although it is possible to read his occasional statements of female agency in procreation as indications of his willingness to alter the established gender hierarchy, the sense that the prospect constitutes more of a threat or, perhaps, a site of anxiety is registered in the vast edifice of explanation that Harvey constructs to counteract both its biological and social implications.

Forced by his discovery into believing that the semen had to act at a distance in order to have any role in generation, Harvey confessed himself unable to determine definitively how fertilization occurs. But it was a problem that fascinated him, one, he said, "full of obscurity," with much that he "admire[d] and marvel[led] at" (575). Harvey even included in *de Generatione* an appendix devoted exclusively to the problem of conception, so that he "would not appear to subvert other men's opinions only, without bringing forward anything of [his] own" (575). Unable to establish any empirical evidence for the process of fertilization, Harvey attempted to figure its workings through analogies. Although presented without apparent order, many of the analogies cohere as a logical series, one that works to foreclose the possibility of female control in generation and to entrench instead male preeminence by progressively reassociating the female with matter and the male with the pervasive power of spirit.

The first in the series—though not the first to appear in the text—is the suggestion that the semen works like a magnet:

> But since it is certain that the semen of the male does not so much reach
> the cavity of the uterus . . . the woman after contact with the spermatic
> fluid in coitus, seems to receive influence and to become fecundated
> without the cooperation of any sensible corporeal agent, in the same way
> as iron touched by the magnet is endowed with its powers and can attract
> other iron to it. When this virtue is once received the woman exercises a
> plastic power of generation, and produces a being after her own image.
> (575)

Of all the analogies Harvey uses, this one most aligns the male with materiality and the female with procreative agency. The semen here is considered the vehicle of an incorporeal "plastic power," but the process necessitates a material "touch" to transfer that power to the female. Once fecundated, though, the female is said to be able to produce a being after *her* own image; through a derivative power, she is given the capacity to re-create *her* own form. It is fairly clear, however, that Harvey was not satisfied with this understanding of fertilization, since he mentions it only a few times.

The second analogy in the series—Harvey's most frequent analogy and the one that apparently made most sense to him as a physician—is that the semen acts like a disease, propagating by contagion.[20] Conception should be understood to occur, Harvey suggests, in the same manner in which "epidemic, contagious, and pestilential diseases scatter their seeds, and are propagated to a distance through the air, or by some 'fomes' producing diseases like themselves, in bodies of a different nature, and in a hidden fashion silently multiply . . . themselves by a kind of generation" (322).

The contagion idea is useful to Harvey's purposes, partly because it helps to explain the multiple births typical of many animals, and partly because it demonstrates the irresistible, exclusive, and multiplicative vigor of the semen. Scattering his seed, the male is still a material cause here. But, unlike the magnet analogy, it is the male who here re-creates *his* image. In fact, every time Harvey mentions the contagion idea, he suggests that the generative ability belongs exclusively to the male: he says, to cite another instance, that animals are procreated "by a kind of contagion, much in the way medical men observe contagious diseases . . . to creep through the ranks of mortal men, and by mere extrinsic contact to excite diseases *similar to themselves* in other bodies" (358; emphasis mine). In marked counterpoint to the "similarity" propagated by the male, the female is implied to be "of a different nature." No longer even of the same kind as the male, the female is relegated to a wholly passive role: she is merely the place in which the male "multiplies" himself.

Whatever its attractions, however, the analogy to contagion did not really accommodate all the particularities of Harvey's understanding of generation. In Harvey's theory the female is not a wholly passive recipient; by whatever means, she does actively produce the egg. Perhaps recognizing the disjunction, Harvey devotes most of his appendix on conception to explaining a third analogy, in which uterine conception is understood in terms of mental conception. He starts from the observation that the inner surface of the uterus, when ready to conceive, "resembles in smoothness and delicacy the ventricles of the brain." Because

> the substance of the uterus . . . is very like the structure of the brain, why should we not suppose that the function of both is similar, and that there is excited by coitus within the uterus a something identical with, or at least analogous to, an "imagination" (*phantasma*) or a "desire" (*appetitus*) in the brain, whence comes the generation or procreation of the ovum? . . . And just as a "desire" arises from a conception of the brain, and this conception springs from some external object of desire, so also from the

male, as being the more perfect animal, and, as it were, the most natural object of desire, does the natural (organic) conception arise in the uterus, even as the animal conception does in the brain. From this desire, or conception, it results that the female produces an offspring like the father. (577-78)

Though starting from a consideration of uterine conception, this analogy works to magnify the male, asserting his association with the incorporeal. As "the more perfect animal" and "the most natural object of desire," the male procreates nonmaterially, imparting to the female an "idea" or "form" of himself through intercourse. Only in response to that incorporeal influence can the female conceive the egg. Furthermore, although the female is said to generate, the offspring is said to be "like the father," not like the mother, as it was in the analogy to magnetism.

The last in the series of analogies completes Harvey's complex balancing act between a female who *must* be said to produce and a male who nonetheless *can* be said to be the primary creator. In this analogy, Harvey takes to its logical extreme the complementary concepts of the male as both "idea" and "the most natural object of desire": here, the semen functions as the original creator, God.

> What is this transitory thing which is neither to be found remaining, nor touching, nor contained, as far as the sense inform us, and yet works with the highest intelligence and foresight, beyond all art; and which, even after it has vanished, renders eggs prolific . . . and makes the hen herself fruitful before she has yet produced any germs of eggs, and this too so suddenly, as if it were said by the Almighty, "Let there be progeny," and straight it is so? . . . In the generation of things is seen the most excellent, the eternal and almighty God. (322)

In this analogy, the semen resembles God in the first moments of the universe, creating by fiat. By mimicking the divine "Let there be light," Harvey's "Let there be progeny" gives to the semen all life-power of creation: the female produces germs of eggs, but they become fruitful, they are endowed with life, only through the agency of the semen. Harvey even suggests the female's awareness of the semen's divinity, since the hen, he observes, after intercourse, "shakes herself for joy, and, as if already possessed of the richest treasure, as if gifted by supreme Jove the preserver with blessing of fecundity, she [is] . . . raised to the summit of felicity" (300). Here, finally, is the realigned balance of matter and spirit: the female produces material eggs, but the male alone gives them the spark of life, for which the female viscerally gives thanks. Although confessing himself "at a standstill" (581), Harvey considers the function of semen that must work from afar and he sees, finally, God.

Taken together, Harvey's analogies reveal his difficulties with the prospect of denying to the semen the formative function possible with the old notion of persistent material contact between male and female contributions to generation. Harvey's conclusion (which he shared with his teacher, Fabricius) that no material contact was involved in embryogenesis is surely polyvalent: it could mean that the semen controlled the process from a distance, but it could also mean that the semen was merely a mechanical trigger, and that life, form, and substance were all imparted to the egg by the female. Harvey's analogies strive to foreclose the possibility of the latter by progressively giving to the male all control in the generation of life.

Harvey in fact sees male predominance in generation not only in the possible explanations for the mechanics of fertilization but even in the act of intercourse itself. de Generatione is filled with sex stories, from traditional lore about female animals that died for lack of regular intercourse to graphically detailed accounts of heterosexual and even homosexual mating practices. Like fertilization, sexual practice was a topic that fascinated Harvey—he even planned a future volume called The Loves, Lusts, and Sexual Acts of Animals—and, as with his consideration of fertilization, he found in it ample evidence of male dominion. What is particularly interesting in his accounts of male sexual prowess, however, is his consistent and unabashed anthropomorphizing: whereas in his writing about fertilization the connection to human beings is always implicit (based on the idea that oviparous generation is the model for viviparous generation), in his discussions of animal sexual behavior, Harvey routinely speaks of a cock's "wives" or the desire of does to protect their "chastity." The result, at least rhetorically, is to see the sex life of animals as a template for that of humans, so that the practices that appear as normative among animals may be considered to be so among human beings as well.

Although de Generatione includes some evidence of female "lustiness," Harvey attends more closely to male sexual aggression, and he repeatedly describes scenes of animal rape. For example, we hear of "a male pheasant kept in an aviary, [which] was so inflamed with lust, that unless he had the company of several hen-birds, six at the least, he literally maltreated them. . . . I have seen a single hen-pheasant shut up with a cockbird . . . so worn out, and her back so entirely stript of feathers through his reiterated assaults, that at length she died exhausted" (193). The females, for their part, are "compelled to submit" to the males' advances, and they are accounted to incite the males' desire whether or not they are actually "inclined" toward sex: "An apparent disinclination on [the hen's] part contribute[s] not a little to arouse the ardour of the male and stimulate[s] his languishing desire, so that he fills her more quickly and more copiously with prolific spirit" (319). Harvey presumably includes this observation to demonstrate that females may, in certain respects, be considered a "first cause" of generation, but the implication is that the females get sex whether or not they want it. Perhaps Harvey's "apparent disinclination" is a seventeenth-century version of "No means Yes": logically, females *must* want sex, since they were known to die for lack of it. But the most straightforward understanding here is that rape is both natural and normative, performed as evidence of power, and not only of the male over the female but between males themselves. Thus Harvey tells us that the "common cock, victorious in battle, not only satisfies his desires upon the sultanas of the vanquished, but upon the body of his rival himself" (193). In this instance, the purpose of sex is not to procreate (which is how Harvey generally portrays it elsewhere) but rather to demonstrate dominion. That Harvey anthropomorphizes here as elsewhere (the cock's "sultanas") suggests that he thought of these animal sexual patterns as normative for human relations: sex is a power play, and females, whatever their desires, are mostly the objects of rape.

Harvey's treatment of the male role in generation, both in the act of intercourse and in the process of fertilization, seems at pains to establish the pervasiveness of male prowess: the male is constructed as a sexual conqueror, dominating his partners and endlessly regenerating himself in them. But Harvey also needed to treat explicitly the female role in generation, and here he met again with a threat to normative gender relations, since the female had to be responsible for producing the egg without direct contribution from the semen. If *de Generatione* alleviates that threat on the male side through analogies that realign the male with the giving of life and through descriptions of male sexual behavior that unambiguously demonstrate male dominance, it deals with the threat on the female side by working nearly to erase her importance, particularly in relation to the being she produces.

Harvey explicitly curtails the possibility of female predominance by taking back his assertions of her procreative agency. For example, just one page after asserting that "the female is actually of more moment in generation than the male" (289), Harvey corrects himself, as it were, to assert that she is "at least equal" to him (290). But, of course, the female cannot be "equal" to the male, as Harvey makes clear in his discussion of female physiology. Even as he rejects the Galenic position of females as stunted forms of males, Harvey manages to maintain the physiological insufficiency of the female in embryogenesis (especially in viviparous animals). In exercise 34, Harvey argues against the Galenic position that females, like males, emit spermatic liquid at orgasm and that it is from the mingling of these two semina that conception occurs. His evidence is threefold: first, he says, not all prolific female animals, and certainly not all childbearing women, experience such emission; second, the liquid is emitted primarily externally—that is, at the orifice of the vulva and never within the uterus—so it could not be mingled with the male emission, which enters the uterus directly (298-99). It would seem that either of these arguments would suffice to cripple the Galenic position. But Harvey's third argument, the one he apparently feels is the most forceful, derives from his already certain knowledge that female physiology cannot attain to the perfection of the male and so cannot be said to produce what the male body can: "I, for my part, greatly wonder how any one can believe that from parts so imperfect and obscure [i.e., the ovaries] a fluid like the semen, so elaborate, concoct and vivifying, can ever be produced" (299). The Galenic position is finally wrong, Harvey believes, because it is illogical to think that the female can match the male. And elsewhere Harvey praises the arrangement of nature to produce perfection by supplying males to compensate for inherent female "deficiencies": "Among the animals where the sexes are distinct, matters are so arranged, that since the female alone is inadequate to engender an embryo and to nourish and protect the young, a male is associated with her by nature, as the superior and more worthy progenitor, as the consort of her labour, and the means of supplying her deficiencies" (362). The arrangement here is not merely that nature requires both a male and a female to perpetuate a kind but that the male "corrects" the female deficiency.

In depicting the female as physiologically inferior to the male, Harvey's work corresponds to the gender assumptions of his predecessors (though for different reasons). But Harvey also shows himself able to break from the teachings of the past while nonetheless maintaining its gender hierarchy; this is clearest in his treatment of the egg. Here the implicit project of de Generatione to aggrandize the father and reduce the mother coalesces, for Harvey makes the offspring the exclusive image of the father, constructed on the near denial of the mother.

Harvey stands enraptured before the egg. It is, he says, "a period . . . of eternity," standing at the midpoint between those who are, those who were, and those who are about to be (271). Like God, it encapsulates the beginning, the middle, and the end of things: it marks the beginning of life, the mean between male and female, and the end of procreation (271). In determining the origin of the chick in the egg, Harvey is therefore delving into what he considers nature's greatest mystery; he says it is not less "arduous [a] business to investigate the intimate mysteries and obscure beginnings of generation than to seek to discover the frame of the world at large, and the manner of its creation" (225). It is important to note this consistent tone of radical amazement in Harvey's search for ultimate origins, because it indicates the value he places on what he finds, namely, the egg's abiding and near complete independence from its mother. He asserts this independence in all phases of the egg's existence: in its initial appearance in the uterus, in its ability to grow and develop into a fetus, and in its eventual birth. In each of these phases, the egg functions on its own as an autonomous entity.

This independence is first established in viviparous animals in the egg's emergence in the uterus. In all things relating to generation other than the function of the ovaries, Harvey insists on the analogy between oviparous and viviparous animals. But whereas he was able to chart with some specificity both the periodic changes in the hen's ovary and the day-to-day changes in the incubating egg, Harvey could not do the same for the viviparous ovary or embryo: he could not see any change in the viviparous ovary before or after intercourse, and he could not see anything resembling a yolk. In his descriptions of viviparous generation, the "eggs," which Harvey describes as masses resembling pudding appended to the uterus, seem to spring up, as it were, by their own volition six to seven weeks after intercourse (483ff.); from their first appearance, the eggs of viviparous animals seem to have no essential connection to the mother. The mother's role as efficient cause in generation reads as if reduced to nothing; the embryo just suddenly appears, as if on its own.

Once visible, whether as a yolk in hens or as a conception in does, the egg proceeds to develop by its own power. Harvey agrees with Fabricius that the function of the uterus is to produce and grow eggs, but he stresses that growth occurs not by means of the uterus but "by a certain natural principle peculiar to itself" (203). In other words, the embryo is responsible for its own development. To make the point, Harvey emphasizes that even while it is within the fowl and connected with the ovary, the hen's egg is not, he says, "to be spoken of as part of the mother" (275); the vital principle that controls its growth is entirely its own.

This idea of the egg's self-regulation and innate vital principle is one of Harvey's most remarkable breaks with Aristotle and is the central point of his entire understanding of the embryo. For Aristotle, the semen formed a fetus out of menstrual blood, endowing it with a vital principle that would direct its growth. But for Harvey, nothing external to the egg is responsible for its vitality; the "anima" is entirely the egg's own. In explaining the process of epigenesis, the doctrine that growth and development happen simultaneously, Harvey uses the analogy of a potter: the potter "educes a form out of clay by the addition of parts, or increasing its mass, and giving it a figure, at the same time that he provides the material, which he prepares, adapts, and applies to this work" (334); the work takes form and increases in size at the same time. Unlike Aristotle's analogy to a carpenter, Harvey's analogy is inexact, because embryologically there is in his theory no distinction between the potter and his creation (the potter cannot be the semen, which never touches the egg). The egg must therefore be understood to make itself. Harvey thus undoes the

Aristotelian distinction between formal and material causes in the embryo: for Harvey, the embryo both en-forms *and* en-matters itself.

This sense of the egg as a self-made entity is bolstered by the metaphors that Harvey routinely uses to describe its autonomy. Not surprisingly, Harvey understands the egg's self-determination in particularly gendered terms. The egg, he says, "even when contained in the ovary, does not live by the vital principle of the mother, but is, like the youth who comes of age, made independent even from its first appearance" (278). Again, in arguing that the egg is neither "the work of the uterus nor governed by that organ," Harvey thinks in terms of sons freed from the control of their parents: the egg, he says, "is free and unconnected, like a son emancipated from pupillage, rolling round within the cavity of the uterus and perfecting itself" (281); "like children come of age," Harvey says, they are "freed from leading-strings, they are maintained and governed by their own inherent capacities" (282). Even in Harvey's other analogy for the autonomy of the egg, which compares eggs to the seeds of plants, the eggs are said to be "perfected in the bosom of the earth . . . by an internal vegetative principle" (i.e., they are not controlled by the tree) (281); and these seeds, "once separated from the plants which have produced them, are no longer regarded as part of these, but like children come of age and freed from leading-strings, they are maintained and governed by their own inherent capacities" (282).

Since Harvey conceives of the egg's autonomy as a release from some prior bondage—from pupillage or from leading-strings—and since the egg's only previous connection is to the mother that "produces" it, that freedom is gained by separation from her. Here again, the radical autonomy of the egg can best be seen in contrast to Aristotle, for whom the "identity" or essence of the embryo is carried by the male, who constitutes the offspring's formal cause. In establishing the egg's identity, Harvey breaks with the Aristotelian pattern by making the embryo self-determining. Because the embryo is self-motive, its identity is generated in and by itself: the embryo becomes the very paradigm of the self-subjectifying man. Because of the implied threat of female control of fetal growth and development that Harvey's initial discovery makes possible, this emphasis on self-regulation, self-determination, and self-subjectification assumes special importance in Harvey's scheme; in this context, the urgent emphasis on the egg's autonomy reads, at least in part, as a safeguard response to that threat.

Just as the egg becomes for Harvey a full subject from its first appearance, the mother, in turn, becomes a fetal incubator, even while gestating her offspring. This is equally true of viviparous as of oviparous females, since Harvey considered the uterus an internal nest, the place where the egg is "cherished, matured and perfected into a fetus" (172). Even the act of birth is a wholly passive process for the mother, since the fetus, both fowl and human, releases itself from its place of growth. In describing the oviparous birth process, Harvey notes that shell fragments are propelled outside the egg; this demonstrates against Fabricius that the chick essentially hatches itself from its shell. Working again on the idea that oviparous processes are the model cases for viviparous ones, Harvey then makes the analogy to human beings: the human fetus "attacks the portals of the womb, opens them by its own energies and thus struggles into day" (535). Birth is the work of the fetus, not of the mother. Battling its way out of its confinement, the fetus works alone and without aid. To press the point, Harvey tells the story—of which he says he has knowledge himself—of a pregnant woman in his village who died one evening; the next morning, Harvey says, "an infant was found between the thighs of the mother, having evidently forced its way out by its own efforts" (536). The fetus here assumes the proportions of a superhero, fighting its way from death into life.

What emerges, then, from Harvey's treatment of embryology is that the mother's role in generation, while initially active, is only fleetingly so: she generates the egg but is unconnected to it. Yet this fleeting agency is crucial to the definition of what becomes the two *male* roles in procreation: in producing the egg but then being separate from it, the mother at once allows the father's role to be conceived of as godlike and allows the egg to be seen as wholly independent and self-determining and thereby decidedly masculine. Acting for only a restricted period between the injection of divine semen and the arising of the self-reliant embryo, the mother becomes that against which males define themselves and in relation to which males grow: for the father she is a place in which to reproduce himself and for the embryo a place to find comfort and nutrition. In other words, and perhaps not surprisingly, the mother in Harvey's theory serves biologically the roles that she was beginning to serve socially in the emerging bourgeois household. When Harvey therefore looks to the "heart of the mystery" of generation, he sees what surrounds him: "self-sufficing and independent" males and the females whose function it is to promote them (408).

Harvey's depiction of the embryo's radical autonomy and masculine identity-formation in the socialized terms of a son who comes of age takes on special significance in the context of the times in which he wrote, during which debates about subjection to a paternal authority were carried out on the battlefield. In the early 1640s, Harvey's friend Thomas Hobbes challenged the natural origin of paternal political right, in part by turning to biology. In Hobbes's state of nature, dominion follows from the physical fact that females give birth: since, he says, it cannot be known who the father of a child is except by the testimony of the mother, and since the mother has it in her power either to nourish the child or to expose it to the elements, the child "is therefore obliged to obey her, rather than any other; and by consequence the Dominion over it is hers."[21] Though this perhaps sounds promising as the basis of a protofeminist politics, recent feminist critics have shown that Hobbes's interest in mother-right inheres less in establishing the dominion of females (or even an enduring equality between men and women) in the state of nature than in countering patriarchal arguments: originary mother-right is a way to deny the natural rights of the father and thus of any civil ruler.[22] But mother-right is a fleeting fixture of Hobbes's thought: useful as a critique of the argument that paternal right is natural, mother-right quickly gives way in Hobbes's theory to a collection of radically autonomous individuals. Although Hobbes is never explicit about how such individuals become free—at one point in *De Cive* he simply asks his readers to consider individuals as if they were sprung up like mushrooms[23]—the state clearly arises from a social contract among free men, not any subject to parents.

It is a logical corollary of Hobbes's theory that if the individuals who contract into the state are wholly autonomous, self-driven, and self-regulating, they must achieve their identity and their independence in their separation from their original obligation to the mother. In tracing such a pattern of psychological development in Hobbes's individual, Christine Di Stefano sees the contours of the modern masculine identity, an identity forged in negative relation to the mother: "The strict differentiation of self from others, identity conceived in exclusionary terms, and perceived threats to an ego thus conceived . . . all recapitulate issues encountered and constructed in the process of securing a masculine identity vis-à-vis the female maternal presence."[24]

While I do not wish to argue explicit influence or even agreement on matters specifically political, I do want to note a confluence between the construction of Hobbesian man and that of Harvey's embryo. Just as mother-right is necessary but fleeting in Hobbes's theory, and just as the Hobbesian individual achieves freedom when mother-right is superseded, so Harvey's embryo achieves its independence in its separation from the mother who is said initially to produce it; and like Hobbes's individual in the state of nature, Harvey's egg is self-determining and wholly autonomous.

Of course, for Hobbes the postulated past of radical freedom is necessary to justify the legitimate rights of a de facto state—the myth of prior freedom justifies subjection to Leviathan's sword—whereas for Harvey the autonomy of the individual seems genuine and enduring. But for both, writing in the mid-seventeenth century in the midst of the greatest social upheaval their country had ever known, the originary human being—for Hobbes in the state of nature, for Harvey in the mother's womb—is autonomous, self-ruled, and distinctly masculine.

The similarity between these two theorists inheres not just in their construction of an insular identity, however; it obtains on a more directly political and public level as well. In studying the contemporary debates between the classical patriarchalists, who identified political with paternal right, and the emerging social contract theorists, who considered political right to be derived from the consent of freeborn individuals, Carole Pateman has argued that patriarchy itself did not so much die out in the seventeenth century as get transformed. Recognizing that patriarchy proclaims man's dominion as both father *and* husband, Pateman suggests that the contract theorists rejected paternal right but "simultaneously transformed conjugal, masculine patriarchal right."[25] Pateman argues, for example, that Hobbes is a "patriarchalist who rejects paternal right": whereas mother-right provides a counter to paternal right, it does not provide a counter to masculine right, since even in the state of nature, Hobbes speaks of families in which the husband unambiguously rules.[26] Pateman shows the crucial transitional role of originary mother-right, which denies paternal right as natural, yet nonetheless coexists with masculine or conjugal right. Hobbes's civil state is therefore postpaternal but not postpatriarchal.

In the context of Pateman's analysis of Hobbes, Harvey's innovative treatment of the embryo as an autonomous individual reads as a physiological version of the same process that Hobbes recorded in his political theory: the transition enacted during the seventeenth century from a patriarchy based on paternity to one founded on a masculine right made manifest in the mastery—and self-mastery—of the (male) individual. If the traditional physiologies held the father to be the prime creator and thereby supported the understanding of the father as the origin of political power, Harvey's discovery, in jeopardizing the father's role in generation, jeopardized its political implications as well. But rather than reassert the old patriarchy—as he did paternity—Harvey substitutes for it the independence of the egg, the new, self-made man, and thereby replicates the political process of his time: from monarchy to commonwealth, from paternal control to independent male sovereignty.

I have been arguing that, given the dangers to sexual and political ideologies posed by his initial discovery, Harvey variously re-creates masculine supremacy in the outlines of his embryological theory and in the rhetoric of his text. It is perhaps an inevitable component of this effort that Harvey encodes the same pattern of self-determining masculinity in his depiction of his own efforts as a scientist: the Harvey that emerges in *de Generatione* is autonomous, heroic, and even at times godlike. Although Harvey follows both Aristotle and Fabricius in many points, and in fact strives wherever possible to align his observations with their opinions, he routinely takes pride in demonstrating his independence from them, in showing them wrong. In fact, Harvey opens *de Generatione* with just such a declaration of independence:

> It will not, I trust, be unwelcome to you, candid reader, if I yield to the wishes, I might even say the entreaties, of many, and in these Exercises on Animal Generation, lay before the student and lover of truth what I have observed on this subject from anatomical dissections, which turns out to be very different from anything that is delivered by authors, whether philosophers or physicians. (151)

There follows a brief statement of the Aristotelian and Galenic positions on embryogenesis, and then Harvey continues:

> But that these are erroneous and hasty conclusions is easily made to appear: like phantoms of darkness they suddenly vanish before the lights of anatomical inquiry. (151)

Harvey here presents himself as the torchbearer, breaking free from the shackles of traditional knowledge, driving away the old bogeys of his predecessors. Just as the egg is characterized as a son free from maternal bonds, so too is Harvey a son free from the bonds of his teachers.

Further on in his introduction, Harvey takes on the role of hero-adventurer, a role commonly assumed by early modern scientists, in which the experimenter explores and seeks to control some uncharted and typically feminized territory.[27] Arguing for the arduous method of direct observation over the more popular but indolent habit of reading books, Harvey says that discoveries have been made only by those who, "following the traces of nature with their own eyes, pursued her through devious but most assured ways till they reached her in the citadel of truth. And truly in such pursuits it is sweet not merely to toil, but even to grow weary, when the pains of discovering are amply compensated by the pleasures of discovery" (153).

The rhetorical suggestion that science is an erotic pursuit takes on special significance in the context of Harvey's particular subject matter, not only because the territory he will be claiming is the female body itself (and not merely a more abstracted feminized nature), but also because his role in achieving dominion over it is characterized by the same aggression and violence that he will elsewhere obsessively describe as normative in male sexuality. Describing the external genitalia of the common fowl, Harvey explains that the three orifices of the pudenda "lie concealed under the velabrum as under a kind of prepuce. . . . So that without the use of the knife, or a somewhat forcible retraction of the velabrum in the fowl, neither the orifice by which the faeces pass from the intestines, nor that by which the urine issues from the ureters, nor yet that by which the egg escapes from the uterus, can be perceived"

(181). This is Harvey's only mention in *de Generatione* of the "forcible" method of dissection, and it is telling that it comes in the context of a unique description of a sexual encounter in which the fowl reveals herself in the same position as the dissected fowl is revealed before Harvey (i.e., with pudenda exposed to sight):

> During intercourse, the hen on the approach of the cock uncovers the vulva, and prepares for his reception. . . . I have myself observed a female ostrick, when her attendant gently scratched her back . . . to lie down on the ground, lift up the velabrum, and exhibit and protrude the vulva, seeing which the male . . . mounted, one foot being kept firm on the ground, the other set upon the back of the prostrate female; the immense penis (you might imagine it a neat's tongue!) vibrated backwards and forwards, and the process of intercourse was accompanied with much ado. (181)

With the use of a knife and a "somewhat forcible" exposure of parts, Harvey displays before himself the pudenda of the fowl in the same way that she readies herself before the cock for sex. In this description—and this is rare in *de Generatione*—the male's approach is seen specifically to be gentle, and the female herself presents her parts for his approach. There is then an odd kind of parallel between Harvey and his scientific subject on the one hand and the cock and his sexual mate on the other: it is as if the female's voluntary self-exposure compensates for the "necessary violence" of Harvey's heroic methods, the "immense penis" an instrument of apparent pleasure, displacing the less pleasurable exposure to a knife.[28] That violence, however, also declares Harvey's dominion, not only over the subject itself—the body of the female fowl—but over his subject matter more generally, for the forcible use of the knife is, as Harvey explains in his introduction, the "devious [and] most assured way" of achieving truth.

Finally, Harvey finds in his work a moment of godlike power. In the course of his researches, Harvey has noticed that the *punctum saliens*, the little beating bit of blood that is the first sign of a chick embryo, stops its motion when removed from incubating warmth, but returns again to life when some manner of heat is reapplied: "After the punctum has gradually languished, and . . . has even ceased from all kind of motion . . . still, on applying my warm finger . . . lo! the little heart is revivified, erects itself anew, and, returning from Hades as it were, is restored to its former pulsations. . . . So that it seemed as if it lay in our power to deliver the poor heart over to death, or to recall it to life at our will and pleasure" (239-40). Such power to bring a "little heart" back from Hades—literally to control life and death—is surely superhuman and is a most distinctive mark of Harvey's self-inscription as the idealized, and even godlike, masculine subject.

Yet for all Harvey's heroic posturing, he cannot, as he freely admits, penetrate to the "heart of the mystery" of generation. In this, too, he mimics the semen, unable to enter the inner sanctum of the womb, where the secrets of life abide. This final similarity, grounded as it is in apparent inadequacy, suggests something about the nature of the idealized images of masculinity that pervade Harvey's text. The godlike semen, the conquering cock, the autonomous egg, the heroic empiric—they are all constructed in response to perceived or threatened failures, of paternity and patriarchy, as well as of the empirical method of science. The images of masculine triumph therefore ultimately appear hollow, generated, like the embryo itself, on a perceived absence. Seen in this way, the workings of gender in Harvey's *de Generatione* can never make up for losses; they can only expose them to view.

Notes

1. William Harvey, *Anatomical Exercises on the Generation of Animals*, in *The Works of William Harvey*, trans. Robert Willis (London: Sydenham Society, 1847), 151. Page numbers appear parenthetically in the text.

2. For discussions of Harvey's embryology, see A.W. Meyer, *An Analysis of the "De generatione" of William Harvey* (Stanford: Stanford University Press, 1936), which is the only study devoted exclusively to Harvey's text and quotes extensively from nineteenth- and twentieth-century scholars; Walter Pagel, *William Harvey's Biological Ideas* (New York: Hafner, 1967) and *New Light on William Harvey* (Basel: Karger, 1978), which both treat Harvey's vitalism and his ongoing indebtedness to Aristotle; and Elizabeth Gasking, *Investigations into Generation, 1651-1828* (London: Hutchinson, 1967), 16-37.

3. Steven Shapin and Simon Schaffer, *Leviathan and the Air-Pump: Hobbes, Boyle, and the Experimental Life* (Princeton: Princeton University Press, 1985), 15. See also Steven Shapin, *A Social History of Truth: Civility and Science in Seventeenth-Century England* (Chicago: University of Chicago Press, 1994) and Bruno Latour, *We Have Never Been Modern*, trans. Catherine Porter (Cambridge: Harvard University Press, 1993), which cites *Leviathan and the Air-Pump* as a model of a "comparative anthropology" of science (15), but also offers an important critique of Shapin and Schaffer's willingness to defamiliarize the assumptions of only one of their protagonists.

There is now, of course, a vast and growing literature on the construction of empirical knowledge in seventeenth-century England, particularly in relation to its modes of cultural embeddedness. In addition to those cited above, see Wolfgang Van Den Daele, "The Social Construction of Science: Institutionalisation and Definition of Positive Science in the Latter Half of the Seventeenth Century," in *The Social Production of Scientific Knowledge*, ed. Everett Mendelsohn, Peter Weingart, and Richard Whitley (Dordrecht: D. Reidel, 1977), 27-55; Michael Hunter, *Establishing the New Science: The Experience of the Early Royal Society* (Woodbridge, Suffolk:

Boydell Press, 1989); and Michael Hunter, *Science and Society in Restoration England* (Cambridge: Cambridge University Press, 1981).

4. See Evelyn Fox Keller, *Reflections on Gender and Science* (New Haven: Yale University Press, 1985), esp. chaps. 2 and 3; and *Secrets of Life, Secrets of Death: Essays on Language, Gender, and Science* (New York: Routledge, 1992), esp. pts. I and II. See also Barbara Duden, *The Woman Beneath the Skin: A Doctor's Patients in Eighteenth-Century Germany,* trans. Thomas Dunlap (Cambridge: Harvard University Press, 1991), which, in reconstructing the body perception of eighteenth-century women from a doctor's reports of their complaints and concerns, reclaims a phenomenological reality constituted by descriptive language.

5. Although there has been some work on the social construction of Harvey's earlier and more famous *De motu cordis,* there is, to my knowledge, no comparable study of *de Generatione animalium* other than the few pages offered in Carolyn Merchant's *Death of Nature: Women, Ecology, and the Scientific Revolution* (New York: Harper and Row, 1980). For *De motu cordis,* see Christopher Hill, "William Harvey and the Idea of Monarchy," in *The Intellectual Revolution of the Seventeenth Century,* ed. Charles Webster (London: Routledge and Kegan Paul, 1974), 160-81, and John Rogers, *The Matter of Revolution: Science, Poetry, and Politics in the Age of Milton* (Ithaca, N.Y.: Cornell University Press, 1996).

6. Merchant, *Death of Nature,* 156.

7. Harvey took advantage of the king's passion for hunting; his well-stocked supply of animals provided Harvey with material for dissection. As Harvey explained: The king's "chase was principally the buck and doe, and no prince in the world had greater herds of deer . . . for this purpose. The game during the three summer months was the buck, then fat and in season; and in the autumn and winter, for the same length of time, the doe. This gave me opportunity of dissecting numbers of these animals almost every day during the whole of the season" (466). See also 477ff., where Harvey describes in some detail his experiment, performed for the king and his game-keepers, designed to demonstrate the absence of semen in does that presumably had had intercourse recently.

8. Quoted in Gordon J. Schochet, *Patriarchalism in Political Thought: The Authoritarian Family and Political Speculation and Attitudes Especially in Seventeenth-Century England* (New York: Basic Books, 1975), 87.

9. Richard Field, *Of the Church,* quoted in Schochet, *Patriarchalism,* 95.

10. Royalist John Maxwell similarly demonstrated the origin of sovereignty in Adam's rule over Eve by recalling her origin in him. "Is it not considerable that God did not make Evah out of the earth, as he did Adam, but made her *of the man;* and declareth too, made her *for him?* It is far more probable then, [that] God in his wisedome did not thinke it fit . . . to make *two independents,* and liked best of all governments of mankind, *The Soveraignty of one,* and that with that extent, that both wife and posterity should submit and subject themselves to him": Maxwell, *Sacro-Santa Regnum Majestas; or, The Sacred and Royal Prerogative of Christian Kings* (Oxford, 1644), 16.

11. Filmer, "Observations Concerning the Original of Government," in *Sir Robert Filmer: Patriarcha and Other Writings,* ed. Johann P. Sommerville (Cambridge: Cambridge University Press, 1991), 187-88.

12. See Filmer, "Patriarcha," ibid., 10-11.

13. Filmer, "Observations," 192.

14. In her feminist analysis of the origins of modern political theory, Carole Pateman claims, perhaps somewhat hyperbolically, that "the patriarchal story is about the procreative power of a father who is complete in himself. His procreative power both gives and nurtures physical life and creates and maintains political right." See Pateman, *The Disorder of Women: Democracy, Feminism, and Political Theory* (Stanford: Stanford University Press, 1988), 38.

15. I am using here Pateman's distinction between paternal and masculine right: in her analysis of the transformations of patriarchy in the classical political theories of the seventeenth century, Pateman notes, "Patriarchalism has two dimensions: the paternal (father/son) and the masculine (husband/wife)": ibid., 37. In this essay, I construe masculine right in the more general terms of man's right over woman, as opposed to a specifically conjugal right.

16. Harvey's fullest explanation of the egg, or "primordium," as he sometimes called it, is as follows: "All living creatures . . . derive their origin from a certain primary something or primordium which contains within itself both the 'matter' and the 'efficient cause'; and so is, in fact, the matter out of which, and that by which, whatsoever is produced is made. Such a primary something in animals . . . is a moisture enclosed in some membrane or shell; a similar body, in fact, having life within itself either actually or potentially; and this, if it is generated within an animal and remains there, until it produces an . . . animal, is commonly called a 'conception'; but if it is exposed to the air by birth, or assumes its beginning under other circumstances . . . it is then denominated an 'egg' or 'worm.' I think, however, that in either case the word 'primordium' should be used to express that from whence the animale is formed" (554-55). A viviparous "conception" is thus to be understood as analogous to an oviparous "egg": i.e., a primary something that has vitality, either actually (if fertilized) or potentially (if not).

17. For more detailed accounts of Harvey's understanding of the egg, see Gasking, *Investigations into Generation*, 27-29, and Joseph Needham, *A History of Embryology* (New York: Abelard-Schuman, 1959), 133-53.

18. Aristotle, *Generation of Animals*, trans. A. Platt, in *The Complete Works of Aristotle*, ed. J. Barnes (Princeton: Princeton University Press, 1984), 729.b.15ff.

19. For gender-inflected readings of biological theories, both ancient and modern, as well as for more detailed accounts of Aristotelian and Galenic embryology, see Nancy Tuana, *The Less Noble Sex: Scientific, Religious, and Philosophical Conceptions of Woman's Nature* (Bloomington: Indiana University Press, 1993); Thomas Laqueur, *Making Sex: Body and Gender from the Greeks to Freud* (Cambridge: Harvard University Press, 1990); Maryanne Cline Horowitz, "The 'Science' of Embryology before the Discovery of the Ovum," in *Connecting Spheres: Women in the Western World*, ed. Marilyn Boxer and Jean Quataert (New York: Oxford University Press, 1987), 86-94; and Londa Schiebinger, *The Mind Has No Sex? Women in the Origins of Modern Science* (Cambridge: Harvard University Press, 1989).

20. The analogy between fertilization, which gives life, and contagion, which breeds death, may at first seem incongruous, but the superimposition of the two

capacities is in fact widespread, particularly when the ability to give birth is appropriated by men (as, for example, in *Frankenstein* or in the production of the A-bomb, Oppenheimer's "baby boy"). See Brian Easlea, *Fathering the Unthinkable: Masculinity, Scientists, and the Nuclear Arms Race* (London: Pluto Press, 1983) and Keller, *Secrets of Life*.

21. Thomas Hobbes, *Leviathan*, ed. C.B. Macpherson (Harmondsworth, Middlesex: Penguin Books, 1968), 254. Although *Leviathan* was published in 1651, similar comments appear in the earlier versions of Hobbes's political theory, as, for example, in *The Citizen*, first published in 1642: "In the state of nature, every woman that bears children, becomes both a *mother* and a *lord*": Thomas Hobbes, *Man and Citizen*, ed. Bernard Gert (Gloucester, Mass.: Peter Smith, 1978), 213.

22. See Christine Di Stefano, *Configurations of Masculinity: A Feminist Perspective on Modern Political Theory* (Ithaca, N.Y.: Cornell University Press, 1991), 85.

23. Hobbes, *The Citizen*, 205; see Di Stefano, *Configurations*, 83ff., for a detailed analysis of Hobbes's mushroom image.

24. Di Stefano, *Configurations*, 82-83.

25. Pateman, *Disorder of Women*, 37.

26. Carole Pateman, "'God Hath Ordained to Man a Helper': Hobbes, Patriarchy, and Conjugal Right," in *Feminist Interpretations and Political Theory*, ed. Mary Lyndon Shanley and Carole Pateman (University Park: Pennsylvania State University Press, 1991), 54-56.

27. See Evelyn Fox Keller, "Baconian Science: A Hermaphroditic Birth," *Philosophical Forum* 11 (1980): 299-308.

28. For an analysis of anatomical illustrations in Renaissance texts in which the dissected subjects appear willingly and even erotically to display themselves before the anatomist's gaze, see Jonathan Sawday, "The Fate of Marsyas: Dissecting the Renaissance Body," in *Renaissance Bodies: The Human Figure in English Culture c. 1540-1660*, ed. Lucy Gent and Nigel Llewellyn (London: Reaktion, 1990), 111-36, and, more generally, Jonathan Sawday, *The Body Emblazoned: Dissection and the Human Body in Renaissance Culture* (London: Routledge, 1995).

"Such Is My Bond"

Maternity and Economy in Anne Bradstreet's Writing

> *Such is my bond, none can discharge but I,*
> *Yet paying is not paid until I die.*
>> "To Her Father with Some Verses"
> *Take thy way where thou art not known.*
>> "The Author to Her Book"

Blending economic, domestic, and theological imagery, Anne Bradstreet (1612-72) painstakingly investigated the nature of her "bonds"—her debts, duties, and loving connections to her mother, father, husband, children, and God. Since Protestant poets commonly represented spiritual realities through everyday worldly figures, Bradstreet's elaborate conceits of binding investments and obligations conventionally expressed the widespread belief in an overwhelming human debt to God.[1] As Robert Daly has observed, Anne Bradstreet "was concerned with figuration, not as a verbal trick the limitations of which gave her opportunity to display her ingenuity, but as a basic principle operative in her perceived universe. She lived in a world in which several orders of reality now often separate—the worldly or earthly or natural or sensible, the biblical, and the eschatological—were the harmonious creation of a single God and were held together by him in a web of intrinsic correspondence."[2] While this is certainly true, it has also been argued that living in a world in which everyday experience was repeatedly invested with spiritual meaning often produced a heightened sense of the distinction between what is and is not religious or spiritual. A separation between the spiritual and the physical became conceivable in the very moment in which it was denied. It is this distinction, many scholars have claimed, that lies at the heart of secularization. I observe the rudiments of this distinction in Anne Bradstreet's terminology of debts, interest, and payments.[3]

By extending the figure of the bond between human beings and God, the original parent and creditor, to herself as both a child and a mother, Anne Bradstreet implicitly searched for the limits of that figure's applicability.

Describing the *religious* force of the bonds between mothers and children, Bradstreet also inevitably underscored the *worldly* force of the obligations that tie family members together. Although, it must be admitted, this does not necessarily mean she understood these two forces as separate, Bradstreet's late work in particular demonstrates her own anguished awareness of and attraction to the material realm as valuable in ways not comprehended by the spirit. She therefore begins to articulate an almost "modern" understanding of a secular realm in which bonds between mothers and children, or authors and their works, might compel and have value in their own right. John Sommerville defines secularization as the gradual transition away from a primarily *religious* culture, in which the world is seen as subsumed by the spiritual and which is characterized by a collective sense of "unmediated access to the realm of supernatural powers, from almost any type of activity or line of thought," to a primarily *secular* culture, in which the sacred and the worldly are seen as *separate* but analogous realms and in which "it would take real thought to make the connections between any activity and one's religious ends."[4] I argue here that the trope of debt or "bondage," which allowed Bradstreet to situate herself within her culture's religious and social hierarchy, also seems to have afforded her a significant means by which to visualize her own creative power. It allowed her to imagine herself as a mother-creator of worldly values that mattered in their own right.

Bradstreet's vexed representation of herself as a maternal creator hinged on her understanding of herself as a maternal obligator or creditor, and it relates to a much broader cultural nervousness over the nature of artificial or autonomous generation. This anxiety is particularly evident in the debates over usury and the growing acceptance that human beings could create, as if out of themselves, wealth that had hitherto not been part of divine creation. Vilifying such "unnatural" production, sixteenth-century antiusury writers frequently depicted usury as a covetous mother uncontrollably breeding monsters or illegitimate offspring (interest) not fathered by God.[5] By Anne Bradstreet's time, people were beginning to accept the usurious production of wealth as benign, and Puritan moralists such as John Winthrop and John Cotton strove to rationalize and sanctify the generation of moderate interest by the elect.[6] But the hybrid tropes of maternal, monetary generation survived, among other places, in seventeenth-century Puritan tracts on the proliferation of knowledge. The millennialist John Goodwin, for example, imagined an "increase" of scientific and spiritual knowledge, which he envisioned as an organic bringing forth of new treasures that heralded the Second Coming.[7] Seventeenth-century writers did not uniformly celebrate the independent or autonomous generation of knowledge and wealth, however, and religious and economic thinkers alike worried about the production of new things that did not seem to issue naturally from God's creation. They contin-ued to regard the bringing forth of something, whether child or thought or profit, that God had neither authored nor authorized as an act similar to, only much worse than, the sin of giving birth to an illegitimate child. To do so was to mother monstrosity and to demonstrate the utter depravity of one's soul.

The poet who represented herself as an artist-mother, the generator of new life and new ideas, must be sure, then, that the material yield of her labor proceeded from a divine source and had value only insofar as it came from the spirit. Yet, by articulating in such loving particularity the worldly mean-ingfulness and value of her own children and poetic creations, Anne Bradstreet seems to have taken steps toward the distinction between the secular and the spiritual, a distinction in which the autonomously generated earthly values (such as "original" poetry or monetary interest) could positively be under-stood as values analogous to, but separate from, spiritual values. She takes those steps by taking her motherhood seriously.

Christian Bondage

A brief summary of the way that Protestant writers envisioned their debt to God is crucial for an understanding of Anne Bradstreet's representation of obligations and bonds between family members. Protestant theologians be-lieved that Adam and Eve's original covenant with God (the Covenant of Works) was a kind of debt contract, which they had to pay immediately after the Fall. Christ sacrificed himself as a surety on that original "bond" between human beings and God, allowing the Father to issue a new contract (the Cov-enant of Grace) between himself and his children.[8] Accordingly, many Prot-estant ministers spoke of the "Spirit of Bondage" as an agency that reminded them of their debt to God for life. "Bondage" meant duty, debt, confinement, imprisonment, servitude, and covenant as well as union or connection in seventeenth-century usage. In much Protestant writing, the "Spirit of Bond-age"—which the New England Puritan Thomas Hooker (1586-1647) called a "spirit of humiliation and contrition"—reminds human beings of their eter-nal debt to God. It restrains, confines, and reforms spiritual waywardness by painfully reshaping the soul to make it worthy of reuniting with its divine origin.[9] Protestant theology held that the loving, parental bond between God and his children would be realized fully only when the children paid off their original debt, but that God, the ultimate creditor, alone enabled payment. Many Protestants therefore imagined the spiritual bond between the divine parent and his children as both a financial and an emotional connection. Redemption was a simultaneous canceling of the financial bond and joyful reunion or rebonding with the spiritual progenitor. Furthermore, because they conceived of bondage as a kind of radical isolation from divinity, many writers imagined release from bondage not as independence but as its opposite: confinement in God. They longed to lose themselves in the Spirit, origin of all value and life in the universe.[10]

As Phyllis Mack has observed, for seventeenth-century Protestants in England and New England, "the paradigm for the experience of spiritual striving and ultimate union with God was the relationship between the mother and her infant child. The labor of childbirth was the archetypal metaphor for the agony of spiritual transformation."[11] One was literally reborn through Christ, but in redemption one also returned to the cosmic womb of Christ. And it was there, paradoxically, that one inherited the riches with which to repay completely the contractual loan incurred at birth. Another important Protestant paradigm for the experience of spiritual striving was the relationship between creditor and debtor, and believers looked to the parable of the talents in Matthew 25:14-30 for the command to return what God had given them with "vantage" or interest.[12] As we shall see, Anne Bradstreet seems to have envisioned earthly bondage, or the contractual obligation to acknowledge continually her spiritual debt to God, as dissolving in a more profound bonding with the heavenly parent. Many Protestant ministers referred to the doctrine of adoption in Romans 8:15 and Galatians 4:21-31 as a consoling lesson that human bondage on earth was a relationship between a parent and a child designated not as a slave but as an heir. While Romans 8 depicts God's relationship to his creatures as paternal ("For ye have not received the Spirit of bondage to feare againe: but ye have received the Spirit of adopcion, whereby we crye Abba, Father"), Galatians 4 also figures that relationship as maternal ("Jerusalem, which is above, is fre[e]: which is the mother of us all. . . . Therefore, brethren, we are after the maner of Isaac, children of the promise").[13] Since Scripture provided patterns for the contractual relationship between humanity and God as both a father and a mother, it was possible for Bradstreet to conceive of her spiritual bondage in terms of her own *paternal* and *maternal* relationships of obligation.

Paternal Bonds

In "To Her Most Honoured Father," the dedication of her quaternion poems, Bradstreet represents her father as her creditor, the source from whom she has derived her poetic skills and personal worth. "I bring my four times four, now meanly clad / To do their homage unto yours, full glad" (lines 14-15).[14] Thomas Dudley, who wrote poetry in addition to serving as deputy governor, provided his daughter Anne with her first and perhaps most significant literary pattern. Cotton Mather recorded, "He had an excellent pen, as was accounted by all; nor was he a mean poet."[15] Bradstreet portrays her own poems as "bounden" or characterized by obligation and connection to him, because they do not cancel but perpetuate her poetic debt and bond. Hence, the worth of her poems "shines" in her father's own poetry ("To Her Most Honored Father," lines 19, 8). The impoverishment of her verses, "meanly clad" and "ragged" "goods," can only barely reflect the immense "worth" of his "rich lines" (lines 14, 43, 39, 8). Her own "true (though poor)" poems are meant to "do their homage" to his rather than to declare her own value (lines 39, 15). Although the poet represents herself as her father's subordinate, there is no indication that she imagines that her "lowly pen" and "humble hand" are inferior because she is female. Bradstreet depicts her poems, which treat the four humors, ages of man, seasons, and monarchies, as "bounden handmaids," yet she also refers to her *father's* poems as "four sisters" (lines 13, 18, 19, 5). "Although it was common practice among English women poets," Eileen Margerum has observed that Bradstreet "never uses her sex as an excuse for writing poor poetry."[16] The subservient position that the poet adopts for herself and her "handmaids" in both "To Her Father" and "To Her Most Honoured Father" proceeds rather from conventional formulae for Christian humility, not only between poets and their patrons but also between children and their parents in Puritan culture.[17]

In "To Her Father with Some Verses," Bradstreet depicts a more complicated relationship with her father by describing it in terms that refer to financial, genealogical, and religious notions of bondage or debt. Like "To Her Most Honoured Father," this poem can be read on two levels of meaning, one secular, the other spiritual. On the secular level this poem defines the vast difference between the genealogical and economic "worth" of the father and daughter. That difference in turn figures the difference in value between creator and creature. On both levels of meaning, economic tropes predominate:

> *To Her Father with Some Verses*
> Most truly honored, and as truly dear,
> If worth in me or ought I do appear,
> Who can of right better demand the same
> Than may your worthy self from whom it came?
> The principal might yield a greater sum,
> Yet handled ill, amounts but to this crumb;
> My stock's so small I know not how to pay,
> My bond remains in force unto this day;
> Yet for part payment take this simple mite,
> Where nothing's to be had, kings loose their right.
> Such is my debt I may not say forgive,
> But as I can, I'll pay it while I live;

> Such is my bond, none can discharge but I,
> Yet paying is not paid until I die. (lines 1-15)

Bradstreet layers terms of poetic and genealogical production on top of terms of capitalist expansion through interest to describe her relationship with her father.[18] These terms were becoming increasingly specialized in seventeenth-century usage, as Bradstreet's poem demonstrates. Here she suggests that a portion of Thomas Dudley has been lent to her as a "principal," which has yielded a smaller "sum" of interest than might have been expected from so "worthy" or large an original investment (lines 6, 5). Her stock, which should be extremely valuable because it is a share of his capital, has been "handled" poorly, or mismanaged; it is "so small" that only a "simple mite" can represent it (lines 7, 8, 10). "Principal" connoted not only origin or source of money, but also rudimentary element, embryo, or seed. Figuring herself as "stock" (which had the sense of the source of a family line of descent before it meant capital or fund) that has not prospered, the poet apologizes for having only the poem itself, a small "crum," or "mite," to return to her father (lines 7-10). The *Oxford English Dictionary* shows that in this period *mite* meant not only a tiny copper coin but also a small child. What the poet has generated is represented as the pitiful financial and familial "yield" of the Dudleys. When Bradstreet implies that expectations of surplus personal value (biological as well as poetic) are meaningless where "nothing's to be had," she laments her barrenness, her inability to reproduce her father—by being unable to produce enough poetic goods and personal value—to succeed her father or to pay off her debt (line 11).[19] Bradstreet can repay her debt only with the yield of the talent that she has received entirely from her father, who is both her procreator and creditor. Her spiritual debt remains the tacit structure through which she explicitly acknowledges her earthly poetic debt. But that her language permits us to distinguish between the two kinds of inheritances, spiritual and earthly, suggests that it was becoming possible to conceive of them as separate but analogous.

"To Her Father" explores the vast difference between the "worth" of the father and the daughter through a multitude of meanings for the word *bond*. For example, Bradstreet divides *oughtworth*, which generally meant "of any value" but was often used to indicate negative worth, into its two components to suggest that she is worth nothing (line 2). The word *ought* also expressed the past tense of the verb "to owe." If Bradstreet is worth "ought," she is negatively worthy in the sense of amounting to only what she must but cannot yet pay. The poet explains this lack by asserting that anything valuable in her is only borrowed from her father, who is "dear" in the sense of "lovable" as well as "expensive" (line 1). Paradoxically, she cannot settle the debt that her loving bond to him entails, and yet she is the only one who can "discharge" it (line 14). Bradstreet also seems to be observing what her contemporary, Henry Wilkinson, termed the "Sacred Debt of Love." "As in the Obligation, such is the Debt," Wilkinson asserted. "Civill obligations cease when the pecuniary debt is paid, but the bond of love among Christians is perpetuall."[20]

Anne Bradstreet's debt of love to her father mirrors her spiritual bond to God, who finally stands as the origin of the value she has borrowed from Thomas Dudley. Only God has the power to cancel her debt, but this fact does not release her from the obligation to honor or to acknowledge it throughout her life. As written documents that declare her debt, Bradstreet's poems themselves do not pay but serve as "bonds" or paper promissory notes. Each poem circulates like a note of credit and only signifies the value of the original who has issued it. That Bradstreet realizes or expresses her perpetual debt to God in terms of her obligation to her father, which she represents in the specialized terms of capital generation, demonstrates that she conceived of her spiritual "worth" and earthly "worth" as values not separate but rather mixed up with one another. Nevertheless, she articulates her *familial* debt in the same terms with which the tacit Christian debt was often recognized. Furthermore, her explicit portrayal of both kinds of nonpecuniary obligation (her debt to her father, her debt to God) in such vividly economic language indicates that separations between divine and genealogical inheritance and between heavenly and earthly values were conceivable.

Anne Bradstreet's economic vocabulary should not surprise us, not only because it conforms to Protestant literary conventions, but also because the poet had extensive familial ties to the merchant community.[21] Her father had served as the earl of Lincoln's steward, or manager of the earl's estate, and helped to found the Massachusetts Bay trading company. Her husband, Simon Bradstreet (1603-97), was a merchant as well as a nonconformist minister. Her sister, Sarah, married the son of Robert Keayne, one of the colony's most prosperous merchants. And Anne Bradstreet's son Samuel made a financially prudent alliance with Mercy, daughter of the prominent merchant William Tyng. Bernard Bailyn has argued that by the 1660s, these very New England merchants had, through intermarriage and close contact with European markets, changed their society from one centered not on the Puritan principles of "social stability, order, and the discipline of the senses" but on the more secular principles of "mobility, growth, and the enjoyment of life."[22]

Bradstreet's language unquestionably does reflect the cultural change in which her family was engaged. But can we read the economic, poetic, and biological metaphors of these poems as registering meanings that can be separated from their obvious religious contexts? The answer to this question is no and yes. Clearly, that she employed the language of the material world to represent the spiritual in no way demonstrates that Anne Bradstreet separated these realms from one another as separate categories of being. It demonstrates quite the opposite point: that she understood them as completely interrelated. Yet Bradstreet acknowledged genuine worldly debts to her father: she felt personally indebted to him for nurturing her poetic gifts, and communally or politically indebted to him for nurturing the colony as an underwriter, deputy governor, and governor.[23] She also knew him to be an economic creditor in the colony. Because Thomas Dudley "engrossed quantities of corn and lent it to his poorer neighbors on credit, to receive ten bushels for seven and a half after harvest," Governor John Winthrop regarded his rigorous and rigid deputy as a usurer, according to Edmund Morgan.[24] Nevertheless, the prevailing tone of Bradstreet's poems about her father is devout, and it would be a mistake to argue that she set worldly debts outside of the religious doctrine to which she adhered.[25] On the other hand, because she aligns various and seemingly nonrelated things—personal obligations, economic debts, and spiritual bondage; poetic productions, biological offspring, and spiritual restitution—we might also say that she sets these things side by side in such a way that they form secular and spiritual categories that later generations would understand as separate but analogous.

Marital Bonds

As in her poems to her father, Bradstreet structured her verses to her husband, Simon Bradstreet, along the lines of Christian bondage. For example, in "To My Dear and Loving Husband," she indirectly compares her husband's love for her, worth more than "mines of gold" and "all the riches" of "the East," to the inestimable value and incomprehensibility of divine love (lines 6-7). Asserting that the love of this merchant and colonial leader is a love she cannot "repay" (line 10), the poet situates herself in the same position of utter lack of value in relation to him that she takes in "To Her Father with Some Verses." Indeed, receiving her husband into her arms after one of his journeys to England frequently inspired Bradstreet to contemplate her overwhelming spiritual debt. In a poem concerning her loneliness during one of Simon's long voyages, she prays for "a better heart" with which to "pay the vowes which I do owe / For ever unto Thee. . . . If thou assist me, Lord I shall / Return Thee what I owe." ("In My Solitary Hours . . . ," lines 48-52). In "May 13, 1657" she thanks God for sending Simon home from a dangerous journey and then wonders how to make up for this bounty: "O studious am what I shall do / To show my duty with delight; / All I can give is but Thine own / And at the most a simple mite" (lines 22-25).[26] In these lines Bradstreet humbly demonstrates her gratitude for God's gifts, which include Simon and his love for her, while simultaneously affirming that reimbursement itself is an activity that her maker has given her the strength and skill to perform. According to this logic, she could only "repay" Simon's richly valued love for her if God makes it possible.[27] Her "mites," the poetic currency of bond notes, only record her debt to him. But this reasoning does not explain the overriding sense, here and in all of Bradstreet's matrimonial poetry, that she freely loves Simon and that she wants her poems to have enough value in themselves to count as earthly payments of worldly love.[28]

As in her poems to her father, the terms that Bradstreet used to celebrate her marital bond suggest that the earthly power of this bond could be, but was not necessarily, subordinated to its spiritual analogy. Hence the rhetorical depth of the marital relation draws upon both the figure of the Christian as the beloved of God and the unmistakable worldliness of marital bliss in lines such as the following:

> Return my dear, my joy, my only love,
> Unto thy hind, thy mullet, and thy dove,
> Who neither joys in pasture, house, nor streams,
> The substance gone, O me, these are but dreams.
> Together at one tree, oh let us browse,
> And like two turtles roost within one house,
> And like the mullets in one river glide,
> Let's still remain but one, till death divide. ("Another," lines 25-32)

In these lines Bradstreet uses the imagery from the Song of Songs (2: 8-12; 8:14) to draw upon the trope of Christian marriage as mirroring the unity of Christ and the church and to explore the opposition between substance and absence, soul and matter. She longs not only for a unification on earth that prefigures the final bliss of oneness with God, but also for a metaphysical miracle—the in-spiriting of matter with true substance, the fusion of soul and body—that the incarnated God (Christ) represents and that Canticles (the Song of Songs) was thought to celebrate. But what stands out is the poet's expressed desire to become like the turtle doves, the mullets, and the deer, to realize the earthly bond of love that ties her to Simon, the bond that death will sever.[29] Her desire to repay her husband's love for her on earth clearly parallels her desire to be reunited with her bridegroom in heaven, but it also registers as an emotion that can be separated from that spiritual inclination insofar as she is longing specifically for Simon's return. It is an emotion which for a moment, at least, seems to supplant her desire for Christ's return. Bradstreet's work generally affirms a religious understanding of the material world as but the shadow of the only true, spiritual reality. Yet her ability to represent the world and its bonds as forceful and, possibly, meaningful in their own right gives her conceits their complex force. This phenomenon is most striking when she meditates on the bond between mothers and their children.

Maternal Bonds

While there is little direct financial imagery in her writings about mother-hood, the poet's representations of the bonds between mothers and children recall the spiritual creditor/debtor relationships in her other work. In "An Epitaph on my Dear and Ever-Honoured Mother, Mrs. Dorothy Dudley, Who Deceased December 27, 1643, and of Her Age, 61," Bradstreet's de-scription of her mother as a spiritually "worthy," "wisely awful," and "true Instructor of her family" recalls her depiction of her father as a "worthy" pro-genitor and teacher.[30] Dorothy Dudley was "worthy" not only because she was descended from a wealthy family but also because she gave generously to the poor.[31] Bradstreet implies that she gave away her handiwork and kindness as well as her money. The poet's representation of her mother as a figure of charity corresponds to traditional representations of this Christian virtue. Charity was frequently represented as a maternal aspect of holiness, perhaps not only because mother's milk was associated with blood, and therefore with the blood that Christ shed to save humankind, but because mothers' gifts were thought to come from self-sacrifice and to sustain life. "In subcurrents of [medieval] religious thought," Londa Schiebinger notes, "mother's milk was thought to impart knowledge. Philosophia-Sapientia, the personification of wisdom, suckled philosophers at her breasts moist with the milk of knowledge and moral virtue."[32] This notion was residual in the seventeenth century and took on special significance in Bradstreet's poetry about herself as a generous mother. But in her poems about her parents, Bradstreet portrays both her mother and father as sources of value and instruction to whom she is obli-gated for any "worth" in herself.

The works in which Bradstreet recounts her own motherhood derive ge-nerically from a literary form that I call the "maternal epistle." Maternal epistles are prose or verse letters to children, from actual or impersonated mothers, which function as contracts that perpetually, emotionally, morally, and spiri-tually bind the two parties together.[33] A common trope in this genre is an overt or indirect association of the author with Paul as a laboring mother in Galatians 4:19: "My little children, of whom I travail in birth again until Christ be formed in you." Bradstreet echoes this verse in her autobiographi-cal "To My Dear Children": "I have brought you into the world, and with great pains, weakness, cares, and fears brought you to this, I now travail in birth again of you till Christ be formed in you" (*Works*, 241). She has de-signed this letter for them so that "when I am no more with you, yet I may be daily in your remembrance . . . that you may gain some spiritual advantage by my experience" (*Works*, 240). The letter outlines what she has done for her children and requires them to learn from her and to remember her daily.

As I have suggested, male and female seventeenth-century colonists frequently imagined their creator in maternal terms, especially when they wanted to convey the special care and love that they felt their spiritual parent had for them. Anne Bradstreet compared God to a "prudent mother" who tailors separate garments of honor, wealth, and health for each child,[34] and Thomas Hooker assured his parishioners that God "hath rocked your Cradles, nursed you at your Mother's Breasts, trained you up in your tender years, taken care of you, and then prayed for you. . . . Oh the Riches of Mercy!"[35] As Hooker illustrates, the merciful, motherly benevolence of God was frequently imagined as the giving of gifts ("riches"), which entailed certain obligations in the receiver. In her spiritual autobiography, Bradstreet passes her spiritual debt to God on, implying that because God gave her children to her as gifts, they are especially obliged to be good Christians: obedient and grateful children of God.[36]

When she depicts herself as a caretaker and religious instructor whose children are obliged to her for their lives on earth as well as their hope for salvation, Bradstreet associates herself with the motherly authority of God. For example, she represents herself as a protector whose "wings kept off all harm" in the maternal epistle "In Reference to Her Children, 23 June, 1659" (line 60). She wants her children to know what her maternity has cost her, as well as the extent to which they are indebted to her for those costs:

> Great was my pain when I you bred,
> Great was my care when I you fed,
> Long did I keep you soft and warm,
> And with my wings kept off all harm,
> My cares are more and fears than ever,
> My throbs such now as 'fore were never. (lines 57-62)[37]

Bradstreet wants to continue to shield her children from the world after they have left her "nest" by instilling moral precepts in them that will allow them to remain good Christians. She instructs them to remember her:

> In chirping language, oft them tell,
> You had a dam that loved you well,
> That did what could be done for young,
> And nursed you up till you were strong,
> And 'fore she once would let you fly,
> She showed you joy and misery;
> Taught what was good, and what was ill,

> What would save life, and what would kill.
> Thus gone, amongst you I may live,
> And dead, yet speak, and counsel give:
> Farewell, my birds, farewell adieu,
> I happy am, if well with you. (lines 85-96)

By repeating this catalog Bradstreet lays out the terms of her children's relationship or "bond" of obligation to her. Her status as a maternal obligator or creditor consists in her having been the nurturer, literally the nursing mother, of their bodies and souls.[38] To repay her, Bradstreet's children must not only be grateful for what she has extended to them but must perpetuate her authority over them by narrating histories of her to their own children. Like her, they exist in a state of perpetual debt and, to use one of Bradstreet's own formulations, must give an "account" describing their "stewardship" of the gifts they have received from her.[39] Bradstreet's children must honor their obligation to her in narratives that resemble her own written offerings to her parents.

By demanding that her own biological reproduction in grandchildren be supplemented with textual reproductions of herself in narrative, Bradstreet again associates children with writing (See "To Her Father with Some Verses"). As with the paternal bond, a child's obligation to his or her mother entails a duty to "yield" upon the "principle." The child's narrative about the mother will both "pay" (by producing the narrative) and perpetuate the debt (by acknowledging it in the narrative) incurred at birth. That debt constitutes the bond or the physical and spiritual link between mother and child. "In Reference to Her Children" further resembles Bradstreet's poems about her father in that it describes contractual obligations between people in the world while it reiterates the bond between God and his children. The poems about Thomas Dudley also differ from the maternal epistles, however. In the former, Bradstreet becomes the child who wants to return to her origin; in the latter, she identifies with the origin and wants to draw her children to herself. If, then, the main emotional thrust of Bradstreet's poems about her bond to her heavenly and earthly fathers articulates her wish to be redeemed through them and with them in heaven, her maternal epistles also express her longing for her children to be redeemed through and reunited with herself.

Although Protestant women were encouraged to think of themselves as serving God when they cared for their children, Bradstreet's longing to preserve her bond with her own seems to compete with her desire to focus solely on spiritual things.[40] This is most evident in her brief poems on the deaths of her grandchildren, where she asserts that children are but loaned by God to their earthly families. "Farewell fair flower that for a space was lent," she calls after her grandchild, Elizabeth Bradstreet. ("In Memory of . . . Elizabeth Bradstreet," line 3). Venting her grief for another granddaughter, who was named after her, she complains, "Experience might 'fore this have made me wise, / To value things according to their price; / Was ever stable joy yet found below? / . . . I knew she was but as a withering flower, / That's here today, perhaps gone in an hour; / . . . More fool then I to look on that was lent / As if mine own, when thus impermanent" ("In Memory of . . . Anne Bradstreet," lines 10-12, 14-15, 18-19). She confesses her deep affection for little Anne even as she chastises herself for having forgotten that no "stable joy" (or fixed value) can be found on earth. The grandmother's mind moves in two directions here, toward the agony of her loss and toward the consolation of her beliefs: "Farewell dear child, thou ne'er shall come to me, / But yet a while, and I shall go to thee" (lines 20-23). Even as she states the religious doctrine that locates all real value in the spirit, she expresses her earthly regret that her granddaughter will never again approach her, never again touch her in this world. The loss of this child, who had brought her "delight" and "bliss," and who now has been re-called by God, has plunged her into sorrow (lines 2, 13). Bradstreet may also mourn her mortality as she realizes that the child will not live to "come to me" or succeed her as another Anne Bradstreet living on earth (line 20).

Although the elegy remains conventional, "In Memory of . . . Anne Bradstreet" suggests that the poet had profound emotional attachments to her children and grandchildren and to her life on earth.[41] Yet how can we reconcile this sense with statements such as "Base world, I trample on thy face. . . . No gain I find in ought below," and "O let me count each hour a day / 'Til I dissolved be" ("My Soul, Rejoice Thou in Thy God," lines 21-22, 27-28). In her mystical "Meditations When My Soul Hath Been Refreshed with the Consolations Which the World Knows Not," Bradstreet seeks solace for her worldly losses through the loss of herself in God, praying: "Let me be no more afraid of death, but even desire to be dissolved and be with Thee which is best of all" (*Works*, 250). But that she feels the need to pray for this favor indicates that she felt she did not long with sufficient fervor for transcendence. She reconciles her wish to hold onto her children and her wish to be released from all her earthly bonds by imagining that her family members will be re-united on the day of redemption, when all debts will be canceled through joining the oneness and absolute value of God. As she wrote to her son Simon, "The Lord bless you with grace and crown you with glory hereafter, that I may meet you with rejoicing at that great day of appearing, which is the continuall prayer of, *your affectionate mother*" (*Works*, 271). In this letter, religious sentiment reinforces earthly love, and maternal bonding eases and promotes desire for the afterlife.

The alleged function of Bradstreet's maternal epistles is to forge a spiritual bond between her children and God: "I have not studied in this you read to show my skill, but to declare the truth, not to set forth myself, but the glory of God" (*Works*, 240). Yet the very accommodating of the spirit to the worldly examples of great "pain" and "care," of keeping the children "soft and warm" ("In Reference to Her Children," lines 57-59), draws attention to the material signifiers and to the earthly experiences themselves. In this case, Bradstreet's desire to be "well" with her children registers on the same level as, and sometimes even seems to compete with, her desire to be "dissolved" in God (*Works*, 250). Finally, the poet seems torn between the idea that something valuable, such as a grandchild or a poem, could proceed from her and the more dogmatic view that only God can be a source of value. This conflict characterizes maternal epistles in general. Because the maternal author focuses with such concentration on the earthly bonds with her children — the bonds established in childbirth, breastfeeding, and daily care — in order to achieve her spiritual ends, these earthly connections seem to take on greater force than the author might admit. In other words, the effect of the attempt to forge a spiritual bond between her children and God is the revelation, and perhaps the realization, of the immense importance of the earthly bond between the mother and her offspring.

The secular thus seems to burst out of the spiritual. As I have already suggested, the mother's hope for reunion with her children has nearly as much weight in the maternal epistle as the mother's desire to lose herself in God. Both of these emotions can be and are expressed in the terminology of spiritual (but also earthly) bondage. In addition to highlighting the earthly importance of a child's life to a parent or grandparent, Bradstreet's focus on the longing for redemption reinforces the worldliness of the economic metaphor that structures the relationship between parent and child. Furthermore, by associating the reproduction of children with the reproduction of narrative, Bradstreet implies that the maternal epistle can "breed," or generate interest upon itself, in the same way that money increases when wisely invested. As in her poems to Thomas Dudley, the terms of debt, obligation, and restitution that characterize the parental bond echo the world from which they are drawn with such intensity that "secular" values seem to separate out from spiritual values.

Maternity and Publication

The interrelation of spiritual, economic, and genealogical meaning in words used to express Christian bondage suggests that notions about redemption, money, and reproduction were only just beginning to come apart from one another during this period of early merchant capitalism. Bradstreet's use of these terms seems to indicate the beginnings of conceptual divisions between these categories, divisions which were not yet present, for example, in John

Donne. The early seventeenth-century poet and Anglican minister connected redemption, money, and reproduction when he preached that Christ came to pay Adam's original debt

> in such money as was lent: in the nature and flesh of man; for man had sinned and man must pay. And then it was lent in such money as was coyned even with the Image of God; man was made according to his Image: that Image being defaced, in a new Mint, in the wombe of the Blessed Virgin, there was new money coyned; The Image of the invisible God . . . was imprinted into the humane nature. And then that there might bee *omnis plenitudo*, all fullness, as God, for the paiment of this debt, sent downe the Bullion, and the stamp, that is, God to be conceived in man, and as he provided the Mint, the womb of the Blessed Virgin, so hath he provided an Exchequer, where this mony is issued; that is his Church.[42]

Donne imagines Christ as appearing on earth in the same "money as was lent." But unlike worthless human currency, the coin that issues from the mint of Mary's womb has miraculous, infinite, and intrinsic value that alone can redeem all of God's human children. Christ's value, mixed with the base metal of human specie, ensures and enables the final return of humanity into its original principle, the heavenly womb of God the Father.[43]

Donne's association of the reproduction of children with money lending was conventional and helps to explain this imagery in Bradstreet's work as well as her uneasiness about her own necessarily fallen generation and spiritual debt. While medieval and Renaissance scholastics accepted what they sometimes called "spiritual usury," which involved the reproduction of children as lawful interest on the loan of life that God had made, they rejected fiscal usury, or moneylending, because it seemed to bring forth illegitimate and indeed blasphemous value from a thing which was perceived to have no intrinsic spiritual value.[44] The antiusury writers looked back to Aristotle, who instructed that money was a barren thing and should not "breed." Money should be used only as a medium of exchange. By the seventeenth century, however, English men and women both at home and in America increasingly accepted modest interest on loans and disapproved only of those who charged exorbitant rates for the sole purpose of enriching themselves. Writing about this topic, John Winthrop distinguished between lending as an act of mercy and lending "by way of commerce," arguing that the former was subject to the biblical injunction to be charitable, whereas "the rule of justice" should govern the latter.[45] He thereby made a categorical separation between the spiritual and the secular in matters of market exchange itself.

Anne Bradstreet must have been aware of the debate over interest, since Thomas Dudley worked closely with Winthrop, and her sister's father-in-law, Robert Keayne, was twice censured for taking too much profit. She may also have known that Winthrop considered her father's grain lending usurious.[46]

An early English proponent of interest, James Spottiswood, also contributes to our understanding of Bradstreet's eschatological concerns about poetry as "mites" generated from an inherited or invested talent. Spottiswood rejected the idea that "money begetteth not money" on the grounds that "there is a lawfull increase & gaine made of artificiall things as well as natural as Houses and Shippes."[47] The yield of money through trade was "artificiall" for Spottiswood, because it was value produced through human management. As such, its "increase" was no less real or legitimate than the profit gained from the increase of natural things, such as livestock or land. From a strictly religious viewpoint, Spottiswood's theory that artificial things (things not found in nature, such as money) can increase appropriates for human imagination the power of generation that properly belongs to God alone. To make things that human beings have made yield of themselves seems from this standpoint covetous or self-glorifying, for it is to assert that human-made values can be as real or as legitimate as values which proceed from God alone. From Anne Bradstreet's perspective, poems could participate in spiritual but not worldly usury. As textual productions, or "artificiall things" generated, they should serve only as mediums of exchange, or currency that acknowledges one's obligation to the spirit, and not as things that increase one's own worldly value.

Yet Anne Bradstreet approaches Spottiswood's potentially blasphemous and therefore dangerous view when she manipulates the idea that one legitimately yields interest on the loan of life through the production of children *as well as of writing*. She does this when she refers to her poem as a "mite," which meant both a coin and a child, in "To Her Father with Some Verses," and in one of her devotional poems, "May 11, 1661." She also treads into potentially heretical territory in her maternal epistles, where she associates the production of children with the production of narrative and seems to imagine her letters to her children giving rise to or "breeding" similar texts. If Bradstreet goes out of her way to emphasize her worthlessness in her poems to her father and her desire to glorify not herself but God in her letters to her children, it may be because she is aware of the danger she courts by imagining her writing as interest. The danger is that she will become a poetic usurer by believing that she has the power to create and to give artificial things the power to generate themselves rather than understanding this power as God's alone. The danger is also that she will set herself up as a creditor in her own right, a source of value and life, to which loans, "notes," and children will return and be redeemed. Finally, the danger is that she will imagine herself as an author in the sense of a person who can generate texts that signify in and of themselves, rather than in the sense of a person whose texts only imperfectly signify higher truths.[48]

The poet contemplates the dangers of generating herself in writing in "The Author to Her Book." It is worth quoting in full:

> Thou ill-formed offspring of my feeble brain,
> Who after birth didst by my side remain,
> Till snatched from thence by friends, less wise than true,
> Who thee abroad, exposed to public view,
> Made thee in rags, halting to th' press to trudge,
> Where errors were not lessened (all may judge).
> At thy return my blushing was not small,
> My rambling brat (in print) should mother call,
> I cast thee by as one unfit for light,
> Thy visage was so irksome in my sight;
> Yet being mine own, at length affection would
> Thy blemishes amend, if so I could:
> I washed thy face, but more defects I saw,
> And rubbing off a spot still made a flaw.
> I stretched thy joints to make thee even feet,
> Yet still thou run'st more hobbling than is meet;
> In better dress to trim thee was my mind,
> But nought save homespun cloth i' th' house I find.
> In this array 'mongst vulgars may'st thou roam.
> In critics hands beware thou dost not come,
> And take thy way where yet thou art not known;
> If for thy father asked, say thou hadst none;
> And for thy mother, she alas is poor,
> Which caused her thus to send thee out of door.

In this poem Bradstreet recounts the history of her manuscript's unauthorized publication in 1650, her initial rejection of the book, and her subsequent editing of the second edition, which appeared posthumously in 1678. She also extends John Woodbridge's metaphor of her book as an "infant" whose "birth" he helped to force.[49] While it circulated in manuscript form among her friends, Bradstreet imagined it to be by her side, still within the purview of her management and interpretive control, as if still connected to her maternal body. This manuscript was kidnapped and introduced into the world before its mother could dress it properly for public—or divine—view. Regarding this "ill-formed offspring of my feeble brain," the poet also seems to view her book "as one unfit for light," as a monstrous birth. Children born misshapen were thought to express their mother's spiritual deformity. Likewise, as Mack points out, "evil opinions or malicious acts . . . were portrayed as monstrous births, and their authors as monster mothers."[50]

Insofar as Bradstreet's earlier "mites" functioned to praise God for lending her the skills with which to repay the immense loan he had made to her, they served as elaborate demonstrations of a bondage that signaled her readiness for glorification—that final union with the paternal/maternal corpus. John Woodbridge disrupted this poetic economy when he surreptitiously removed Bradstreet's manuscript to public view. I am speculating that Bradstreet regarded the copies of *The Tenth Muse Lately Sprung Up in America* (1650) that found their way back to Massachusetts and into public circulation as a kind of illegitimate interest that increased (because it was published and issued in multiple copies) by itself, beyond her control. The book was also illegitimate because it was born without a father; it proceeded from her, but not through the bonds that tie all of her other interestlike offspring to her Father in heaven.[51] Confronting the prospect of her privately written and privately circulated poems roaming "'mongst vulgars," Bradstreet betrays anxiety about how her art will be understood and received in the world: "In critics hands beware thou dost not come." The book, she instructs, must be careful how it presents itself, lest people who do not understand the soteriological function of her writing fail to see or endeavor to undermine its spiritual creditworthiness. Will the poems in this book still register as symbols of her intent to pay her religious debts if they circulate in the material economy and are exchanged for money rather than for the approval and inspiration of those who have helped to guide her to God? Or does the birth of this misshapen child register her own spiritual bankruptcy?

The idea of repayment corresponds to the Protestant soteriological vision of reunion with the parent in the sense that the true value of the child as bond note is realized only when it is paid, when it finds its way back to the original lender, who makes it "good." To make a loan is to disburse a portion of one's money and allow it to circulate independently, like a child or a book, in the world. In Protestant theology, the loan, child, or book needs to return to its parent, to be reunited with its source, in order to have any real value or meaning. As Bradstreet's contemporary, John Robinson, observed, "Writing is the speech of the absent. . . . Great care is to be taken, and circumspection used in writing of Books; not onely (though specialy for conscience of God); but also because the Author therin exposeth himself to the censure of all men."[52] Just as Bradstreet sought to maintain her bond with her children in order to ensure their acceptability as lawful interest to her heavenly father, she wanted to preserve control over her writing so that it would serve as a sacred offering and legitimate increase on her loan of life and talent from him.

In "The Author to Her Book" Anne Bradstreet makes explicit a problem that is only implicit in her maternal epistles: the problem of maintaining control over one's (re)production. In the maternal epistles she associates writing with children and with the perpetuation of herself by regulating her own sons and daughters, who have gone out into the world but who will give accurate "accounts" of her "travail" to their own offspring. She associates writing with children by conceiving of her book as a child that has entered the world, where it will report about her to (and be reckoned by) strangers. The maternal epistle maintains a spiritual bond, a contract and a link, between mother and child. But Bradstreet's "ill-formed offspring" has broken that connection and wanders without guidance. The poet recognizes with some pain that she cannot shepherd her book in the world (as she can shepherd her children through her maternal epistles) and that the accounts it will give of her "stewardship" will be unreliable. "In better dress to trim thee was my mind," she complains, as if she has been unable to tailor garments for this child that accord with divine dispensations.[53]

Finally, the break that the book makes with its mother launches it into a space that is divorced from the spiritual realm at the center of her maternal epistles. Thus Bradstreet's reluctant acknowledgment of maternity and assumption of responsibility for sending her illegitimate child "out of door" because she is "poor" troubles the spiritual water in which we expect to find all of her work. Has she acknowledged this "rambling" (wandering, sinful) "brat" as her own for worldly or economic, as opposed to spiritual, reasons? Does she want to make money with it? Or does she imagine that its proliferation in print yields upon her own poetic value in the world? She admits that "affection" for her earthly, public child has motivated her to "amend" its "blemishes" and make it more fit to be seen. But if no amount of rubbing can wash this child, is this so because, like the hands of Lady Macbeth, its sins cannot be cleansed? Has this creature of an earthly and not a divine womb been permitted to wander in the world because it will never find its way to heaven? And if so, then what kind of existence or meaning does its mother imagine it having, if not a purely worldly one? "Take thy way where yet thou art not known," Bradstreet counsels her book, seeming to encourage it to circulate and become valuable independently in a public, commercial world not enclosed by the spirit. As in all of Anne Bradstreet's work, earthly images figure divine realities. "The Author to Her Book" registers Bradstreet's nervousness that she and her book may have no legitimate spiritual value. That possibility, though denied, remains present in the poem. The potential for worldly value separates from its spiritual complement even as it is asserted as a thing that the spirit overwhelms. Thus the image of her book as an errant child in the world, which will not be redeemed and dissolved in the spirit, becomes embraceable on its own terms. Not quite "profane," it nonetheless exhibits nonreligious value. Rather than taking us to a higher realm, this figure of the book as child exhibits a possibly secular worthiness through its circulation in the material world, a "worth" that Bradstreet only hints at in her poems to her father and that she begins to articulate in her maternal epistles.

Although recent critics have interpreted Bradstreet's nervousness in this poem as the trepidation of a woman worried about offending patriarchal authority by speaking in public, I see it also as gender-neutral anxiety about autonomous generation, a fear of offending the creator by imitating him through the generation of worldly value that both male and female writers shared.[54] George Herbert's (1593-1633) presentation of his "writings" as a "special Deed" in "Obedience," Andrew Marvell's (1621-78) meditation on the insignificance of the "wreaths of Fame and Interest" in "The Coronet," or Edward Taylor's (ca. 1642-1729) endless scrutiny of his value in such lines as "Am I thy Gold? Or Purse, Lord, for thy Wealth" in *Preparatory Meditations* I:6, all worry about the dangers of overweening poetic creation in a language of marketplace terms and values. That said, I have also tried to show how, by embracing the role of mother, Anne Bradstreet assumed a spiritual and creative authority and that the problem of generating value was particularly vexed because of the affective bonds she formed with her real and textual children. These bonds conferred a worthiness that seemed to slip past the boundaries of religious culture and that made her children valuable purely because they sprang from her.

Like many early modern writers, Bradstreet attempted to accommodate the worldly to the spiritual. The world of finance, agriculture, and genealogy is both merged and set into conflict with the spirit in the father-poems. The poems on marriage and biological motherhood sketch out further conflicts between worldly and heavenly values but reconcile these oppositions by imagining all realms and all distinctions as things transcended in the spirit. "The Author to Her Book" seems to disrupt this larger spiritual economy in which Bradstreet located all of her work. The book becomes a child adrift in the world where it has a material value but owes no obligation to its mother, its only parent. Completely dissociated from the contractual bonds that originate in God the Father and that are enforced by the mother, such a production can never be redeemed and therefore will not maintain a spiritual connection to its origin. "The Author to Her Book" also differs from Bradstreet's other poems about parenthood because in it the poet neither longs for her own dissolution in the spirit nor seeks to draw her child up after her; she merely acknowledges the book as her progeny and sends it on its way. The bond Bradstreet establishes with her book, then, remains an earthly connection. She finally does not cast it aside as blasphemy, but sets it apart as a thing that exists in a universe parallel, if inferior, to the spiritual realm that encompasses all her other offspring. It is as if the very effort to articulate the spiritual in graphically material terms, to read religious meaning into all worldly experiences, resulted for her in a nascent distinction between spiritual and worldly experience. "The Author to Her Book" records the culmination of a secularizing trend within the poet's essentially spiritual thought, for it demonstrates how the domestic, the economic, and the theological—which Anne Bradstreet understood as interrelated locations of the bond between parents and children—were beginning to come apart for her as separate but analogous realms.

Bradstreet's writing about obligation and restitution between parents and their offspring demonstrates the complex connections between familial, commercial, and sacred aspects of experience in a culture in which it became possible to conceive of value outside of the spiritual canopy that theoretically encompassed all existence. That she rejected nonspiritual values does not mean that she also repudiated the positive power to create things of earthly significance, which she associated with being a poet and a mother. The metaphor of Christian bondage afforded Bradstreet a position of great authority and creativity, not only as a mother-producer and nurturer but also as the fortunate recipient of priceless gifts from God. Finally, and perhaps most important to her, the ineluctability of her bonds promised reunion in heaven for all time with those she loved most: "Where we with joy each other's face shall see / And parted more by death shall never be" ("To the Memory of My . . . Father," lines 74-75).

Notes

I am indebted to Carol Barash, Anne Coiro, Sarah Ellenzweig, Susan Greenfield, Deborah Kaplan, Phyllis Mack, April Masten, Michael O'Malley, and Steve Pincus for their generosity and critical commentary.

All quotations from Bradstreet's writings are from *The Works of Anne Bradstreet*, ed. Jeanine Hensley (Cambridge: Harvard University Press, 1967). Citations will be listed parenthetically in the text. Poems will be followed by line numbers, other works by page numbers.

1. For a discussion of the Protestant trope of spiritual debt, see Perry Miller, *Errand into the Wilderness* (Cambridge: Belknap Press of Harvard University Press, 1956), 60-61, and C.A. Patrides, *Milton and the Christian Tradition* (Oxford: Clarendon Press, 1966), 133-36. For the conventionality of Bradstreet's location of spiritual meaning in everyday things, see William Haller, *The Rise of Puritanism; or, The Way to the New Jerusalem as Set Forth in Pulpit and Press from Thomas Cartwright to John Lilburne and John Milton, 1570-1643* (New York: Columbia University Press, 1938), 128-33,

140-49; and Michael McKeon's discussion of the Protestant doctrine of accommodation (according to which spiritual truth is only knowable imperfectly through material vehicles) in *The Origins of the English Novel, 1600-1740* (Baltimore: Johns Hopkins University Press, 1987), 73-76.

2. Robert Daly, *God's Altar: The World and Flesh in Puritan Poetry* (Berkeley: University of California Press, 1978), 92.

3. This argument has been made by a number of scholars, including William Haller, *Rise of Puritanism*, 169-72; and C. John Sommerville, *The Secularization of Early Modern England: From Religious Culture to Religious Faith* (New York: Oxford University Press, 1992), 4-8. Michael McKeon observes, "What is crucial to the process of secularization . . . is certainly not an outright assault upon religion; nor, for that matter, either its alliance with or its opposition to the forces of the secular. The crucial element is the categorical self-consciousness itself, the preoccupation with the fundamental problem of boundaries. Religion exercises its authority by a tacit dominion: to inquire closely into its relationship with other realms is automatically to question its claim to superintend and to suffuse them all": "Politics of Discourses and the Rise of the Aesthetic in Seventeenth-Century England," in *Politics of Discourse: The Literature and History of Seventeenth-Century England*, ed. Steven Zwicker (Berkeley: University of California Press, 1987), 35.

4. Sommerville, *Secularization*, 9.

5. See, for example, Thomas Wilson, *A Discourse upon Usury* [1572], ed. R.H. Tawney (New York: Augustus Kelley, 1963), 222, 366. Anne Kibbie analyzes many such images in the antiusury literature of the sixteenth centuries in "The Birth of Capital in Defoe's *Moll Flanders* and *Roxana*," *PMLA* 110 (1995): 1023-34, but she does not acknowledge that, for nearly a century preceding Defoe's works, an entirely different literature far more supportive of usury and capital generation grew up. The sixteenth-century antiusury texts therefore had a less direct influence on his thinking than she implies.

6. See John Winthrop, "Modell of Christian Charity," *Winthrop Papers* (Boston, 1929-47), 2:286, cit. Bernard Bailyn, *The New England Merchants in the Seventeenth Century* (Cambridge: Harvard University Press, 1955), 21-22; and *The Journal of John Winthrop, 1630-1649*, ed. Richard S. Dunn, James Savage, and Laetitia Yeandle (Cambridge: Harvard University Press, 1996), 306-8. For a historical discussion of Calvin's earlier attempt to reconcile interest to the spirit, see Wilson, *A Discourse upon Usury*, 115-21.

7. In *Imputatio Fidei; or, A treatise of Justification wherein the imputation of faith for righteousness is explained* (London, 1642) Goodwin writes, "Well may it be conceived, not only that some, but many truths, yea and those of maine concernment and importance, may be yet unborne, and not come forth out of their Mothers womb (I mean the secrets of the Scriptures) to see the light of the Sun. . . . No man is competently furnished and *instructed to the Kingdome of Heaven, . . . But he that is like unto a man an householder, whiche bringeth forth out of his treasure, things new & old.* i. who is not aswel able, to make som new discoverie, & to bring forth somwhat of himselfe in the things of God in one kinde or other," sig. b4r-v. Cf. John Milton, *The Reason of Church Government* (1642), in *John Milton: Complete Poems and Major*

Prose, ed. Merritt Hughes (Indianapolis: Bobbs-Merrill, 1957), 643. Also cf. Milton, *The Doctrine and Discipline of Divorce* [1643, 1644] and *Areopagitica* [1645], in *Complete Prose Works of John Milton*, ed. Don Wolfe (New Haven: Yale University Press, 1959), 2:224-25, 505, 562.

8. Cf. Genesis 17:7. For a short description of covenant theology, see Miller, *Errand into the Wilderness*, 60-61.

9. Thomas Hooker, *The Soules Preparation For Christ; or, A Treatise of Contrition, Wherein is Discovered How God breakes the heart and wounds the Soule, in the Conversion of a Sinner to Himselfe* (London, 1632). Thomas Hooker was a contemporary of Bradstreet's and a minister who led a settlement in Connecticut. In *A Briefe Exposition of the Lords Prayer* (London, 1645), he wrote, "True, Lord, the talents and debt whereby we are ingaged unto thee are many and great," (63). Cf. *The Covenant of God's Free Grace* (London, 1645), where John Cotton tells his congregation that they will become "free" by paying not money but obedience to God (11-13, 19-21). In *A Treatise on the Covenant of Grace*, 3d ed. (London, 1671), Cotton describes Christ as the "Surety" of the Covenant established between God and Abraham, and he states, "God indeed may give with a purpose to receive back again; but he looketh to receive no more than what he first giveth us, and giveth us strength and Will and Deed to give him back again" (5, 11). In the latter work Cotton referred to the "Spirit of Bondage" as the force that imposes God's will on the soul, drawing it "from sin, and from the world in some measure," and the force which teaches human beings that they can not "lay hold of Jesus Christ" "from any power of our natural gifts and talents" (114, 117). For poetic explorations of this theme, see, for example, George Herbert (1593-1633), "Redemption," and "Obedience"; John Milton (1608-74), "Comus"; Henry Vaughn (1621-95), "Regeneration"; Thomas Traherne (1637-74), "The Recovery"; and Edward Taylor (1642-1729), Meditation 1.41.

10. See, for example, Odet de la Noue, Lord of Teligni, *The Profit of Imprisonment. A Paradox, that Adversitie is more necessarie than Propertie: and that, of all afflictions, close Prison is most plesant, and most profitable*. This is bound with *[Salluste] Du Bartas, His Devine Weeks and Works*, trans. Joshua Sylvester (London, 1605). It is possible that Bradstreet, who adored Du Bartas, either owned or had seen this edition. See Elizabeth Wade White, *Anne Bradstreet: "The Tenth Muse"* (New York: Oxford University Press, 1971), 56-57.

11. Phyllis Mack, *Visionary Women: Ecstatic Prophecy in Seventeenth-Century England* (Berkeley: University of California Press, 1992), 39-40.

12. The King James or Authorized Version of the Bible translated this word (*vantage*) in Matthew 25:27 as *usury*.

13. All references to Scripture are from the Geneva Bible, which was the version Anne Bradstreet used. See White, *Anne Bradstreet*, 60-61. I have used *The Geneva Bible, Facsimile of the 1560 Edition* (Madison: University of Wisconsin Press, 1969).

14. These and the opening lines suggest that Dudley wrote a quaternion poem, now lost to us, "on the four parts of the world."

15. Cit. White, *Anne Bradstreet*, 179.

16. Eileen Margerum, "Anne Bradstreet's Public Poetry and the Tradition of Humility," *Early American Literature* 17 (1982): 152-60, 157. For some influential

arguments in favor of a feminist or prefeminist sensibility in Bradstreet, see also Adrienne Rich's introduction to *Works of Anne Bradstreet,* ed. Jeanine Hensley; and Ann Stanford, "Anne Bradstreet: Dogmatist and Rebel," in *Puritan New England: Essays on Religion, Society, and Culture,* ed. Alden T. Vaughn and Frances J. Bremer (New York: St. Martin's Press, 1977). Timothy Sweet implicitly challenges aspects of these interpretations in "Gender, Genre, and Subjectivity in Bradstreet's Early Elegies," *Early American Literature* 23 (1988): 152-74, asserting that the "constitution of a feminine subject is unproblematic" in Bradstreet's "domestic poetry" where "no strain is put on the dominant discursive conventions. Thus the domestic poetry does not expose the gender-based power relations of the discourse that determines it; rather, it merely reproduces the existing ideology (the gender system), without questioning the 'order of things' created and supported by discourse" (170). Sweet speculates that Bradstreet "surrendered or retreated into less hostile terrain" in her later works. Ivy Schweitzer makes a similar claim in *The Work of Self-Representation: Lyric Poetry in Colonial New England* (Chapel Hill: University of North Carolina Press, 1991), 127-80. I am uncomfortable with the division of Bradstreet's poetry into "public" and "domestic" categories, since these terms oversimplify the nature of her often complex work. Many of the "public" poems express "private" or "domestic" sentiments, and the "domestic" poems arguably concern issues of central concern to the "public" community in which she lived. Furthermore, such a separation presupposes a distinction between private and public "spheres" that may be emergent, but is not realized in her work. As Paula Kopacz points out in "'To Finish What's Begun': Anne Bradstreet's Last Words," *Early American Literature* 23 (1988): 175-85, all of Bradstreet's poems are a form of prayer. I also prefer to think of Bradstreet as moving more valiantly into a spiritual realm in which she willingly gave up her "subjectivity" and where the gender hierarchy breaks down. My reading is therefore more in line with those of Paula Kopacz, "'To Finish,'" and Beth Doriani, "'Then Have I . . . Said with David': Anne Bradstreet's Andover Manuscript Poems and the Influence of the Psalm Tradition," *Early American Literature* 24 (1989): 52-69. Unlike Sweet or Schweitzer, these critics focus on Bradstreet's spiritual strategies rather than on her effort to assert a modern subjectivity.

17. Generally, men and women were held equally subordinate to God, from whom any power in them was wholly derived. Spiritual equality between the sexes did not cancel the superiority of men over women in matters of earthly government or, as William Gouge said, in "domesticall duties." See his *Of Domesticall Duties* (London, 1634). Bradstreet treats Thomas Dudley as her superior not only because he was her father but also because he was her patron. See Margerum for more on Bradstreet's adoption of patron-client literary conventions. There are many fine studies of gender ideology and the social hierarchy in Puritan culture. I have relied on the following texts: Allison Coudert, "The Myth of the Improved Status of Protestant Women: The Case of the Witchcraze," in *The Politics of Gender in Early Modern Europe,* ed. Jean R. Brink, Allison P. Coudert, and Maryanne Horowitz (Kirksville: University of Missouri Press, 1989); John Demos, *A Little Commonwealth: Family Life in a Plymouth Colony* (New York: Oxford University Press, 1970); A.J. Fletcher, "The Protestant Idea of Marriage in Early Modern England," in *Religion, Culture,*

and Society in Early Modern Britain, ed. A.J. Fletcher and Peter R. Roberts (Cambridge: Cambridge University Press, 1994); William and Malleville Haller, "The Puritan Art of Love," *Huntington Library Quarterly* 5 (1941-42): 235-72; Lyle Koehler, *A Search for Power: The "Weaker Sex" in Seventeenth-Century England* (Urbana: University of Illinois Press, 1980); Sarah Heller Mendelson, *The Mental World of Stuart Women: Three Studies* (Brighton, England: Harvester Press, 1987), esp. 62-115; Edmund S. Morgan, *The Puritan Family: Essays on Religion and Domestic Relations in Seventeenth-Century New England* (Boston: Trustees of the Public Library, 1956); Schweitzer, *Work of Self-Representation;* Keith Thomas, "Women in the Civil War Sects," *Past and Present* 13 (1958): 42-62; and Diane Willen, "Women and Religion in Early Modern England," in *Women in Reformation and Counter-Reformation Europe: Public and Private Worlds,* ed. Sherrin Marshall (Bloomington: Indiana University Press, 1989). Finally, Jeffrey Hammond observes, "Although a number of critics interpret [Bradstreet's] difficulties with the faith as rebellion against the androcentric theological and political structures of her time, such difficulties comprised a normal and even mandated dimension of inner experience for all saints, male and female": *Sinful Self, Saintly Self: The Puritan Experience of Poetry* (Athens: University of Georgia Press, 1993), 139.

18. For a discussion of new models of and terms for capital generation through interest, debt, and credit transactions in sixteenth- and seventeenth-century Europe, see Wilson, *A Discourse upon Usury,* 16-169.

19. Her language reiterates the terms of the Parable of the Talents, which the commentary in the Geneva Bible interpreted as teaching that "we ought to continue in the knowledge of God, and do good with those graces that God hath given us," Marginalia for Matthew 25:14 in *The Geneva Bible* (1560).

20. Henry Wilkinson, *The Debt Book, or, A Treatise Upon Romans 13, ver. 8, Wherein is handled: The Civill Debt of Money or Goods, and under it the mixt Debt, as occasion is offered. Also, The Sacred Debt of Love* (London, 1625), 114.

21. Indeed, Bradstreet's concern with written acknowledgments of inheritance may stem not only from Puritan sermons and Scripture but also from her high status among the wealthiest members of the Massachusetts Bay Company. Those without property rarely made wills, but, as I argue below, Bradstreet's will understood her writings to her children as legacies. On women leaving wills, see Susan Amussen, *An Ordered Society: Gender and Class in Early Modern England* (Oxford: Basil Blackwell, 1988), 92-94.

22. See Bailyn, *New England Merchants,* 19, 26, 53, 125, 135-39, and 163. The quotation is from page 139.

23. See "To the Memory of My Dear and Ever Honored Father," in which Bradstreet exhorts her fellow colonists to acknowledge their collective financial and political debt to this man who "spent his state" in order to found the commonwealth: "But now or never I must pay my Sum; / While others tell his worth, I'll not be dumb; / One of thy Founders, him *New England* know, / Who staid thy feeble sides when thou wast low, / Who spent his state, his strength, & years with care / That after-comers in them might have share. / True patriot of this little commonweal" (lines 26-32).

24. "Winthrop regarded this practice as oppressive usury": Edmund S. Morgan, *The Puritan Dilemma: The Story of John Winthrop* (Boston: Little, Brown, 1958), 87. On Dudley's rigidity, see 103-6.

25. Even in her most overt declaration of a "public" and seemingly secular debt, "To the Memory of My Dear and Ever Honored Father Thomas Dudley Esq.," the sacred wholly encompasses the political. By the end of the poem, Thomas Dudley the governor has literally become her father in heaven; see lines 66-75.

26. See also "In Thankfull Remembrance for my Dear Husband's Safe Arrivall, Sept. 3, 1662," where she writes, "I owe so much, so little can / Return unto thy Name" (lines 8-9).

27. John Cotton wrote, "But God himself is said to be our gifts and graces, and therefore they are nothing but his spirit in us," in *The Covenant of God's Free Grace*, 33.

28. This apparent contradiction could be explained through Protestant dogma, as promulgated in Puritan conduct books on marriage. Conjugal love was the result of both God's and human beings' free wills, since those who experienced what the clerics regarded as true matrimonial harmony were thought to have internalized God's will as their own. See William and Malleville Haller, "The Puritan Art of Love," esp. 264-65.

29. Ann Stanford's argument in "Anne Bradstreet: Dogmatist and Rebel" that Bradstreet struggled between dogma and personal feeling regarding her attitude toward her husband (by focusing on their earthly love more than on the ecstasy of the afterlife, and by asking him to remember her after she dies) confirms my point that the poet found it possible to conceive of both the spiritual and the secular worlds as meaningful in and of themselves.

30. See "To Her Father with Some Verses," line 6, and "To the Memory," lines 10-14.

31. Her father was Edmonde Yorke, a substantial yeoman. Cotton Mather described her as "a gentlewoman whose Extract and Estate were considerable": *Magnalia Christi Americana*, quoted by White, *Anne Bradstreet*, 36.

32. Londa Schiebinger, "Why Mammals Are Called Mammals," *American Historical Review* 98 (1993): 394. Of all the virtues, Charity is the only mother. In *The Fairie Queene*, Charissa appears in the House of Holinesse as a woman "of wondrous beauty, and of bountie rare," whose "necke and breasts were euer open bare / That ay thereof her babes might sucke their fill." See I. x.29-31. See also Mack, *Visionary Women*, 36, 40-41.

33. The tradition begins, perhaps, with the first known European woman writer, Dhouda (ca. 803–after 843), who wrote a manual of conduct for her elder son, *Liber manualis*, in *Women Writers of the Middle Ages: A Critical Study of Texts from Perpetua (†203) to Marguerite Porete (†1310)*, ed. Peter Dronke (Cambridge: Cambridge University Press, 1985). But many writings by women in the seventeenth century could be considered "maternal epistles." Among them are Elizabeth Grymeston's *Miscelanea. Meditations. Memoratives* (1604); Dorothy Leigh's *A Mother's Blessing* (1617); Elizabeth Jocelin's *The Mother's Legacie* (1624); Eleanor Douglas's *From the Lady Eleanor, Her Blessing to Her Beloved Daughter* (1644); and Elizabeth Richardson's *A Ladies*

Legacie to her Daughters (1645). Constantia Munda's dedication to *The Worming of a Mad Dogge* (1617) acknowledges the tradition of what Gerda Lerner calls "the theme of female bonding and honoring of motherhood" in explicitly financial terms but is not itself a maternal epistle: Lerner, *The Creation of Feminist Consciousness from the Middle Ages to 1870* (New York: Oxford University Press, 1993), 129. The maternal epistle tradition involves bonding between mothers, their daughters, *and their sons*. Bradstreet's maternal epistles include "In Reference to Her Children, 23 June, 1659," "To My Dear Children," "September 30, 1657," "For My Dear Son Simon Bradstreet," and *Meditations Divine and Morall.*

34. "A prudent mother will not cloth her little child with a long and cumbersome garment; she easily foresees what events it is like to produce, at the best but falls and bruises or perhaps somewhat worse. Much more will the allwise God proportion His dispensations according to the stature and strength of the person He bestows them on": *Meditations Divine and Morall*, no. 39. Cf. Thomas Hooker, *A Brief Exposition of the Lords Prayer*, 49: "A childe happily would have a coat four or five yards too long, and to tyre him, or fire to burne him, but a father will not have it too long, to tyre him, or fire to burne him. So our Father, we would over-flow our measures, out-run our proportions too beyond our need."

35. Hooker, *Lords Prayer*, 32.

36. "It pleased God to keep me a long time without a child, which was a great grief to me and cost me many prayers and tears before I obtained one, and after him gave me many more of whom I now take the care, that as I have brought you into the world. . . . I now travail in birth again of you till Christ be formed in you": "To My Dear Children," 241.

37. Cf. Bradstreet's poem, "Childhood": "My mother did waste as I did thrive / Who yet with all alacrity, / Spending, was willing to be spent by me" (lines 73-75).

38. As a mother, she is like God who gives birth to children but also like the church who nourishes them. We may compare her representation of herself as a nurturer to John Cotton's mystical interpretation of the Song of Songs 7:2 ("Thy navell is like a round goblet") in *A Brief Exposition with Practical Observations upon the whole Book of Canticles* (London, 1655): "The Navell serving for the nourishment of the Infant in the wombe, before it be born, doth fitly resemble Baptisme, which serveth for the nourishment of the Infants of the Church, even before they be born, and brought forth by Spirituall Nativity. If children were born, the breasts were for them (verse 3), but now Navell . . . Infants of Church-members are the seeds of the faithful, and conteined in the wombe of the church. . . . Therefore they had need to be nourished," 191-92. The idea of the church as a mother was common. Cf. for example George Herbert, "The British Church."

39. "Few men are so humble as not to be proud of their abilities, and nothing will abase them more than this: what hast thou, but what thou has received? Come, give an account of thy stewardship": *Meditations Divine and Morall*, no. 17.

40. Linda Crawford, "The Construction and Experience of Maternity in Seventeenth-Century England," in *Women as Mothers in Pre-industrial England*, ed. Valerie Fildes (London: Routledge, 1990), 15, observes that a mother's spiritual obligations could sometimes interfere with her maternal responsibilities in this period.

41. Bradstreet's meditation on her grandchild's death has much in common with Ben Jonson's epigrams "On My First Daughter" and "On My First Son." For some controversial accounts of the attachments of early modern parents to their children, see Demos, *A Little Commonwealth*, 70-74; and Lawrence Stone, *The Family, Sex, and Marriage in England, 1500-1800* (New York: Harper and Row, 1977), 99-102. These views have been rebutted by many scholars. Two good summaries of this debate are Ruth Perry, "Colonizing the Breast: Sexuality and Maternity in Eighteenth-Century England," *Eighteenth-Century Life* 16 (1992): 209n; and Olwen Hufton, *The Prospect before Her: A History of Women in Western Europe, 1500-1800* (New York: Knopf, 1995), 23-24, 209-14. In addition, the first thing Bradstreet requires of her children in "In Reference to Her Children" is to tell that they "had a dam that loved you well" (line 86).

42. John Donne, *Sermons*, cit. E. Pearlman, "Shakespeare, Freud, and the Two Usuries," *English Literary Renaissance* 2 (1972): 234.

43. Similarly, John Milton imagined the mind as a mint, in which "the Deity has imprinted . . . so many unquestionable tokens of himself": *The Christian Doctrine*, in *John Milton: Complete Poems and Major Prose*, 904. Michael O'Malley points out that the word *specie* in the seventeenth century had the sense of both currency and species. "Specie and Species: Race and the Money Question in Nineteenth-Century America," *American Historical Review* 99 (1994): 372.

44. Gabriel Powel defined "Spirituall or celestial usury" as "that gaine and glory wherewith God rewardeth the graces and good workes of his owne children": *Theologicall and Scholasticall Positions concerning Usurie* (London, 1602), 2, cit. Pearlman, "Shakespeare, Freud, and the Two Usuries," 232.

45. Bailyn, *New England Merchants*, 21-22.

46. This last matter prompted John Cotton, whom the Dudley family knew well on both continents, to formulate and publish laws on commercial transactions and interest rates. See Winthrop, *Journal* (1996), 307; and John Cotton, *"An Abstract of the Lawes of New England* (London, 1641), 8, 9.

47. John Spottiswood, *The Execution of Neschech* (Edinburgh, 1616), 33.

48. Robert Daly explains that Puritan poetics "avoided the worship, not the making, of images." Yet, because "Puritans believed that meaning resided in the symbolic world itself, . . . their poetics has far more in common with the Latin concept of the poet as *vates* ('seer'); one who sees and says the truth, than with the Greek concept of the poet as *poeta* ('maker'), one who creates verbal artifacts. . . . [T]heir avowed task was simply to say, to utter, the truths they saw": Daly, "Puritan Poetics: The World, the Flesh, and God," *Early American Literature* 12 (1977): 157-58.

49. In his 1650 dedicatory poem "To My Dear Sister, the Author of These Poems," John Woodbridge writes,

> If you shall think it will be to your shame
> To be in print, then I must bear the blame;
> If't be a fault, 'tis mine, 'tis shame that might
> Deny so fair an infant of its right
> To look abroad; I know your modest mind,

How you will blush, complain, 'tis too unkind:
To force a woman's birth, provoke her pain,
Expose her labours to the world's disdain. (lines 55-61)

Woodbridge secularizes the childbirth metaphor of Galatians by imagining the "travail" that Paul speaks of not as a spiritual effort but as a poetic effort. For the history of the original publication of *The Tenth Muse Lately Sprung Up in America* (1650), see *Works.*, ed. Hensley, xxvii-xxxiv; and *The Complete Works of Anne Bradstreet*, ed. Joseph R. McElrath Jr. and Allan P. Robb (Boston: Twayne, 1981), xx. At the time of this essay's composition, this latter fine edition was sadly out of print.

50. Mack, *Visionary Women*, 41. See also Crawford, "Construction and Experience of Maternity," 7-8; and Jean Marie Lutes, "Negotiating Theology and Gynecology: Anne Bradstreet's Representations of the Female Body," *Signs* 22 (1997): 328-30.

51. Considering the metaphor within the context of contemporary beliefs about mother's and father's roles in generation, Lutes ("Negotiating Theology and Gynecology," 333) has observed that the book as child is a mental offspring arising "not from the material in her womb reacting to a masculine force but, rather, from the material in her mind reacting to her own need for self-expression."

52. John Robinson, *New Essays or Observations Divine and Morall* (London, 1628), 135-37.

53. See *Meditations Divine and Morall*, no. 39; and Crawford, "Construction and Experience of Maternity," 15.

54. See Lutes, "Negotiating Theology and Gynecology," 336-37; Schweitzer, *Work of Self-Representation*, 170-73.

Aborting the "Mother Plot"

Politics and Generation in
Absalom and Achitophel

John Dryden's *Absalom and Achitophel* (1682) is a royalist allegory about the English Exclusion Crisis. It draws an analogy between Absalom's rebellion against King David in 2 Samuel and contemporary conflicts concerning Charles II and the Earl of Shaftesbury, the Whig leader who sought to exclude Charles's Catholic brother, James II, from succession by encouraging Charles's illegitimate Protestant son, the Duke of Monmouth, to claim the throne instead. In the poem, King David represents the notoriously philandering Charles II, Absalom is his rebellious son, Monmouth, and Achitophel is the Earl of Shaftesbury.

Although many critics have pointed to the poem's obvious emphasis on fatherhood and kingship, it has hardly seemed a likely source of information about early modern maternity.[1] But motherhood is actually a pivotal and politically charged problem in *Absalom and Achitophel*. The poem begins and ends with references to mothers: The opening describes how, despite his queen's infertility, the promiscuous King David has still managed to create "several Mothers" (13), and the poem concludes with David's stunning image of a "Viper-like" destruction of the "Mother Plot" against him (1013). Indeed, the shift between these framing images of maternity is a central mechanism in the poem's royalist resolution. Although the text initially suggests that David bears the procreative responsibility for the birth of his rebel son, it ends by transferring the blame for the insurrection onto the Mother Plot, as if only the female power of generation threatens familial and political order and must be suppressed. The shift works because the poem's emphasis on David's promiscuity is gradually replaced by references to a feminine sexual desire and productivity so dangerous that the king appears politically reliable by contrast.[2]

In the process, political questions about the future of monarchal succession are brought into conflict with scientific questions about the nature of conception and the difference between paternal and maternal procreative control. Writing during a period of debate about the source and extent of monarchal authority, as part of a pragmatic effort to defend a king whose own son had challenged him, Dryden is faced with a particularly complex set of issues. Not only was the traditional belief that the king passed his power through genetic descent generally on the wane, but Charles specifically needed to be dissociated from his rebellious child. In an apparent attempt to address these problems, Dryden appropriates and discards various procreation narratives in the poem, finally moving toward a model of maternal generation in order to resolve them.

Before considering the poem closely it is useful to review the cultural—and specifically political and medical—context for its familial and sexual details. Much has been written about the way the king was viewed as the ultimate patriarch of a family of subjects. But to appreciate Dryden's attack on maternity, it is also important to recognize that the most popular patriarchal political theory of the period—best articulated in Sir Robert Filmer's *Patriarcha* (1680)—was fundamentally structured around the erasure of the mother.[3] In trying to prove that "the first kings were fathers of families" and that "kings now are the fathers of their people," for instance, Filmer points out that "the law which enjoins obedience to kings is delivered in the terms of 'honour thy father' . . . as if all power were originally in the father."[4]

As John Locke later suggests in his *Two Treatises of Government* (1690), Filmer is clearly manipulative here, "for God [actually] says, *Honour thy Father and Mother*; but our Author . . . leaves out *thy Mother* quite, as little serviceable to his purpose."[5] Locke here is not especially interested in biblical accuracy or in the question of women's rights but rather in the dynamics of political rhetoric. Arguing against unconditional and exclusive monarchal authority, he understands that the paternal argument can work only if the role of the mother is denied, because to acknowledge her would suggest that the father-king does not have an inherent right to unilateral control. It thus logically follows that to introduce the idea of mother is to disrupt the patriarchal justification of kingship: "It will but very ill serve the turn of those Men who contend so much for the Absolute Power and Authority of the *Fatherhood* . . . that the *Mother* should have any share in it. And it would have but ill supported the *Monarchy* they contend for, when by the very name it appeared that the Fundamental Authority from whence they would derive their Government of a single Person only, was not plac'd in one, but two Persons joyntly."[6] Critics have pointed out that this is hardly a feminist argument, since Locke "uses the mother's 'equal Title' as a *reductio ad absurdum* to refute the derivation of political from parental authority."[7] That is, he uses her to prove the inherent separateness of parenthood and state. Nevertheless, it is worth noting how, by concentrating on the threat that maternity poses to any conservative

understanding of monarchy, Locke ironically demonstrates the mother's political utility.[8]

The *Two Treatises,* composed during the 1680s but published anonymously
nearly a decade after *Absalom and Achitophel,* did not directly influence the
poem. As Steven Zwicker suggests, however, Locke's and Dryden's texts may
be read in relation to each other (as well as to Filmer's *Patriarcha*) "as contemporary rhetorical and political events, as competing interpretations of the
origins of government, the nature of royal authority, and the political meaning of paternity and patriarchy."[9] Locke is particularly useful in the context of
the present discussion about maternity because he articulates an implicit tension in patriarchal theory that was already long evident, clarifying one position about motherhood in an ongoing debate about the relationship between
political and familial power. In both *De Cive* (1642) and *Leviathan* (1651),
for instance, Hobbes had already implied that fatherhood could not be the
ultimate grounds upon which sovereignty is based because "the originall
Dominion over *children* belongs to the *Mother*. . . . The birth followes the
belly."[10] If in many political systems the father acquired control over the mother
and young, that was simply the consequence of civil laws that privileged him,
resulting from the fact that "for the most part Common-wealths have been
erected by the Fathers, not by the Mothers of families."[11] Thus, paternal power
was a sign of conquest but not of unquestionable governmental entitlement.
Fully understanding that any successful argument about the mother's natural
authority could dismantle his defense of monarchy, Filmer challenged Hobbes
in his *Observations Concerning the Originall of Government* (1652) by countering: "But we know that God at the creation gave the sovereignty to the man
over the woman, as being the nobler and principal agent in generation."[12]

Significantly, Filmer here promotes not just the idea of paternal power
but a specific theory of conception, maintaining that the father plays the more
active role in generation and refusing "any acknowledgment of the capacity
and creativity that is unique to women."[13] Hobbes was not alone in
deconstructing such arguments by suggesting that the mother was the more
important creator. In *Of Government and Obedience as They Stand Directed
and Determined by Scripture and Reason* (1654), John Hall reminds his readers that the mother "hath part of her own substance imployed in nourishment
of the young whilst it is within her."[14] And Locke is even more explicit:

> For no body can deny but that the Woman hath an equal share, if not the
> greater, as nourishing the Child a long time in her own Body out of her
> own Substance. There it is fashion'd, and from her it receives the
> Materials and Principles of its Constitution; And it is so hard to imagine
> the rational Soul should presently Inhabit the yet unformed Embrio, as
> soon as the Father has done his part in the Act of Generation, that if it

must be supposed to derive any thing from the Parents, it must certainly owe most to the Mother.[15]

There is something at stake here in addition to the problem of governmental succession. Whether or not the authors were deliberately referring to specific medical theories (and Locke, who was trained in medicine, may well have been), the contrast between their accounts of generation is also characteristic of contemporary scientific debates. Filmer's emphasis on paternal agency evokes the popular Aristotelian notion that the female contributes the matter or passive principle in conception and the male bestows the efficient or active one that creates the movement necessary for the embryo to develop.[16] Like a sculptor, "the male model[s] or mould[s] this [female] material into a form like itself."[17] Aristotle himself explains: "The female always provides the material, the male that which fashions it. . . . While the body is from the female, it is the soul that is from the male."[18]

In his pathbreaking *de Generatione animalium* (1651 [discussed in more detail in Eve Keller's article in this volume]), William Harvey challenged Aristotle's emphasis on female subordination and argued that both mother and father provided the efficient cause of generation.[19] It is unclear exactly how much influence he believed the female primordium had, but Harvey did argue that the material carried by the mother contained its own "power to develop," which was then ignited by the semen.[20] Harvey also suggested that the womb functioned as a kind of brain that "conceived" the fetus like an idea, but this was not necessarily evidence of maternal power, since Harvey considered the uterus an independent organism and also believed that the fetus's life did not depend on the mother's.[21] Those scientists who, unlike Harvey, favored preformation theory (believing that the offspring existed fully formed at conception) were much more willing to credit a single parent with the power to shape the child, insisting that "only one sex could donate the true embryo."[22] By the end of the seventeenth century there were two competing groups in this category of thinkers: the ovists, who argued that the whole embryo existed preformed in the ovary, and the animalculists, who claimed the same for the sperm.[23]

Locke's account of generation blends and revises a number of these medical theories. He never questions the Aristotelian idea that the woman supplies the matter for the embryo, but Locke does insist that it is primarily the work of pregnancy—and not the act of the sperm—that fashions the female material into a child. Contesting the notion that the father gives the soul as well as the notion that the embryo exists fully formed in either the sperm or the egg, Locke emphasizes the process of development, reasoning that because the embryo grows in the mother, she most influences the child's outcome.[24]

Despite their very different scientific assumptions, both Filmer and Locke, like Hobbes and Hall, assume that discourses about the body and state overlap, and they recognize that any representation of conception is thus a political act. This sense of integration was obviously influenced by their own system of government, figured in the body of a ruler who passed his power through genetic descent. At the same time, though, recent historical events—primarily the execution of Charles I—had proved that the royal succession could be broken.[25] The classic seventeenth-century patriarchalism that linked monarchal and paternal procreative power would not endure. As Carole Pateman explains, "Filmer's father . . . stands *at the end* of a very long history of traditional patriarchal argument in which the creation of political society has been seen as a masculine act of birth."[26] In challenging the logic of a political theory based on paternal procreation, Locke's arguments articulate and anticipate permanent changes in the understanding of the origin of government.

Absalom and Achitophel is situated at the crossroads of this change. As he seeks to develop a pragmatic and contemporary defense of monarchal authority, Dryden moves from a story of paternal conception, reminiscent of Filmer's, to an account of maternal creativity that anticipates Locke's. When Dryden finally abandons the model of patriarchal generation at the end of the poem, he, like Locke, marks the cultural turn against the traditional emphasis on masculine birth as well as his own wariness of the role of paternity in political argument.[27] But unlike Locke's work, Dryden's narrative is designed to support the king and, more specifically, to resolve the generative problems posed by Monmouth's bid for the throne. Because Charles was challenged by his own illegitimate child, the paternal control of conception is necessarily associated not with the king's authority but with his vulnerability. In the poem, Charles's counterpart, David, is ultimately acquitted of his generative role when maternal creative power, far from signaling a Lockean need to reconsider the origin of government, emerges as the primary and most dangerous source of any challenge to the status quo. For Dryden it is the very variety and ideological flexibility of accounts of generation that make them useful, and he shapes and reshapes conception to suit his changing narrative needs.[28]

Absalom and Achitophel opens by suggesting that David has, at least in part, conceived his own problems.[29] Most obviously, because he is so "Promiscuous" (6) and has sired bastard children "through the Land" (10), David has encouraged his own destruction, producing a population that has little sympathy for a system of privileges based on legitimacy and hereditary succession. As Howard Weinbrot suggests, "David makes his own rebellion by propagating his own lawlessness in his lawless son and lawless nation."[30] Absalom is especially dangerous because David has overindulged and failed to discipline him, encouraging the favored son to expect rights and opportunities he does not legally deserve.

But the problems of generation in the beginning of the poem are also specifically related to the way David makes mothers at the same time that he does children. We learn first that Michal, the royal wife, is barren because her "Soyl [is] ungratefull to the Tiller's care," and next that

> Not so the rest; for several Mothers bore
> To Godlike *David*, several Sons before.
> But since like slaves his bed they did ascend,
> No True Succession could their seed attend. (13-16)

Precisely because it is confusing, this passage is important, as it generates a variety of ways to interpret David's culpable behavior and the problem of female desire. In many respects, Dryden at first seems remarkably sensitive to the mothers, reflecting what James Winn has described as his "more than occasional insight into the hard lot of . . . women."[31] But as Winn notes of other works, this insight is also balanced by Dryden's tendency to lapse into misogynistic conventions.[32] Ultimately, the competing readings available at the beginning of *Absalom and Achitophel* are narrowed, so that by the end only the negative implications about female sexuality persist.

Let me unpack the various angles of interpretation initially available by beginning with the "several Mothers." A quick reading suggests simply that their problematic status is the source of the trouble with "True Succession"; based on earlier lines, it seems that because the women were not brides but slaves or concubines, their children cannot be kings. But this explanation is not entirely precise. The passage specifically emphasizes the sexual moment when the several Mothers ascended David's bed "like slaves" (15). We are not told that the women *were* slaves, and a careful reading of the opening reveals that some may have actually been among David's many wives (9). Zwicker points out that "the line suggests not just a technical category but sexual slavery or slavishness."[33] Indeed, the stress is on the means by which the mothers came to bed: if they entered like slaves, perhaps they were forced to lie with the king. From this perspective, the problem of succession has as much to do with the way the mothers were impregnated as it does with their status, the implication being that it is because the women were passive objects of David's desire and possibly victims of rape that their children are not fit for royalty.[34]

Lest this emphasis on the absence of female desire seem anachronistic, we need only recall that until the middle of the eighteenth century, it was widely believed that female pleasure and orgasm were necessary for conception.[35] Thus, a seventeenth-century audience would likely have made a connection between the mothers' sexual experiences and their success in generation. Dryden himself need not have been concerned with the question of women's sexual rights to have been interested in the reproductive implications of female pleasure. At this point in the interpretation, however, it is hard to understand how the women's sexual unwillingness would have affected the "seed" of "True Succession" (16), as their enjoyment alone could not guarantee a royal issue.

The relevance of sexual abuse is easier to document, since the poem returns to the problem of rape a few lines later with a reference to the biblical Absalom's murder of Amnon (39). In 2 Samuel, Absalom kills Amnon (his half brother) for raping their sister, Tamar. The narrator in Dryden's poem condemns Absalom's behavior, but nevertheless uses the attack on the brother to foreshadow Absalom's attack on his father. This, plus the fact that Amnon was also the king's son, invites us to consider the resemblance between Amnon and David—even to wonder whether Absalom, who has killed his brother for having offended his sister, may have reason to object to his father's treatment of his mother.[36]

In the context of this layered allusion to David's problem with female desire, the earlier description of how Michal's "Soyl" is "ungratefull" to David's "care" reads not simply as an account of the queen's infertility but also as a satiric comment on her own sexual experience with the king. Michal is clearly distinguished from the "several Mothers" and Tamar, for there is no indication that she has been raped. But given David's apparent neglect of female sexual feeling, as well as his notorious philandering, she may have little reason to be grateful in bed. Perhaps, when it comes to lovemaking, the "Tiller's care" is inadequate.[37] For those seventeenth-century readers who believed that conception depended on female orgasm, such sexual insensitivity could explain Michal's infertility. In order to prevent barrenness, "the man was . . . obliged to ensure the woman's satisfaction."[38] Modern readers have assumed that the burden of infertility lies with Michal without considering the possibility that David has failed to perform his sexual duty to please—and thereby impregnate—his wife.

The connection between female pleasure and conception becomes more complicated when read in relation to the "several Mothers." On the one hand, the seemingly illogical suggestion that the several Mothers have not emitted the "seed" of "True Succession" because the king neglected their desires makes some sense if we interpret it as another account of failed conception. One might argue that while the Mothers obviously prove fertile, their inferior children reflect the inferiority of their own sexual experiences. The passage thereby anticipates the description of Achitophel's son, who is born deformed because he was conceived during a particularly unsavory act of intercourse (170-72). The quality of lovemaking marks the quality of the product.

On the other hand, if the connection between female orgasm and generation is taken literally, then regardless of the means by which they came to David's bed, the several Mothers must have enjoyed themselves; otherwise, they could not have proved fertile. Although there were medical theories that challenged the relationship between female orgasm and conception, a woman's pregnancy could be used to disprove an accusation of rape well into the eighteenth century. As Richard Burn put it in his 1756 *Justice of the Peace,* "a woman can not conceive unless she doth consent."[39] According to this logic, the several Mothers wanted what they got, an implication that anticipates Achitophel's oft-noted suggestion that the king, like all women, secretly longs to be raped (471-74; discussed in more detail below). Along these lines, one can argue that the problem with the royal wife is that David has singled her out and treated her with too much "care." If, like the several Mothers, Michal had been abused in the way women secretly desire, perhaps she too would have conceived.[40]

The competing readings available here serve both a political and a narrative purpose. The poet exposes the king and acknowledges the problem of his promiscuity, something necessary to gain credibility with an audience that would have been well aware of Charles's sexual faults.[41] But Dryden also protects David by leaving open the possibility that the main culpability lies elsewhere — that the production of a rebellious population, and specifically of an illicit son, was fueled primarily by maternal, not monarchal, desire. At this point, however, the balance of responsibility is unclear, and the irresolution generates useful suspense.

If anything, the case against David remains stronger. The king's apparent indifference to female desire, for instance, is highlighted by his contrasting indulgence of Absalom: "To all *his* wishes Nothing he deny'd, / And made the Charming *Annabel* his Bride" (33-34; first emphasis added). These lines continue to draw attention to the problematic objectification of women (the gift of Annabel indicates the extent to which Absalom has been spoiled), while also introducing a homoerotic twist. Pointedly contrasting with his neglect of women, the account of the king's excessive interest in pleasing his son (in this case sexually) highlights David's disorientation. He gazes at the boy with "secret Joy" because in Absalom David sees "His Youthfull Image . . . renew'd" (32), and this narcissistic investment emphasizes the king's attraction to a body that is the same as his own.[42]

The stress on David's physical similarity to Absalom is important for another reason as well because it suggests that as a father he has exerted greater control over the act of conception, corroborating the argument that he is responsible for producing the political problem embodied in the son. In general, stressing what Filmer describes as the man's "principal agen[cy] in

generation," the poem begins by offering an Aristotelian account of fertilization, showing how the king ignites or works on female matter to shape his
progeny.[43] If he has failed to heat the queen's soil, David has nevertheless
fruitfully imparted his "vigorous warmth" (8) throughout the land. In keeping
with later animalculist theories, which suggested that the full embryo existed
in the sperm, the beautiful Absalom seems to have sprung complete from his
father's seed. Apparently bearing no relationship to his mother, Absalom is
the product of his father's great desire and activity, perhaps even "inspir'd" by
David's "diviner Lust" and gotten "with a greater Gust" (19-20).

But then in contrast to the way Filmer celebrates and links male generative and governmental control, Dryden here exposes the political problems
of masculine conception. For if David has determined the development of
his son, then the father is ultimately the source of the troubles that ensue.[44] As
with Achitophel, David's control of procreation is a dangerous one. Granted,
when we learn about Achitophel's act of fatherhood, it is clear that he is considerably less successful than David; his son is an "unfeather'd two Leg'd thing"
who was "born a shapeless Lump, like Anarchy" because he was "Got, while
his [father's] Soul did hudled Notions try" (170-72). But, as different as their
sexual acts may have been and as different as their children now appear, both
David and Achitophel seem unilaterally to have begotten a political problem.

It is not until Absalom himself speaks that this account of paternal conception begins to be redefined and the idea of the mother's participation is
clearly introduced. The moment marks the point at which the poem begins
to develop an increasingly more direct attack on maternal culpability. Tempted
by Achitophel's call for him to seek the political privileges he is denied, Absalom
memorably exclaims:

> Yet oh that Fate Propitiously Enclined,
> Had rais'd my Birth, or had debas'd my Mind;
> To my large Soul, not all her Treasure lent,
> And then Betray'd it to a mean Descent.
> I find, I find my mounting Spirits Bold,
> And *David's* Part disdains my Mothers Mold.
> Why am I Scanted by a Niggard Birth?
> My Soul Disclaims the Kindred of her Earth. (363-70)

On the one hand, Absalom's account of his own production repeats the earlier Aristotelian model, stressing how the mother gives the matter and the
father creates action and soul. As before, the mother here is associated with
"Earth" and the physicality of birth; in addition to the "Soul," the father be-
queaths the "Mind" and "Spirits." However, in contrast to the opening of the
poem, this passage also rebalances the generational model by suggesting that

the female parent's contribution is at least as important as the male's to the development of the child: thus, "David's Part" is evenly balanced by "my Mothers Mold," the latter an arresting formulation since it suggests that the mother has the power to shape her offspring and it conflicts with the way David sees the child as an image of himself. Indeed, what torments Absalom is the extent to which he sees his mother in himself—the extent to which he feels that, as one of her "Kindred," he is indelibly marked by a "mean Descent." Absalom longs to rise out of this maternal boundary, but to his frustration he cannot.[45]

The narrator encourages us to agree with Absalom's account of maternal influence. We are told that, when tempted by Achitophel's promise of power, Absalom is "Half loath, and half consenting to the Ill, / (For Royal Blood within him struggled still)" (313-14), meaning that when he agrees to rebel Absalom is influenced by his ignoble blood, the mother's half.[46] Such intimations would, for a seventeenth-century audience, have been strengthened by the scandalous history of Monmouth's mother, Lucy Walter, a woman rumored to have been a whore of "mean Descent." She died (perhaps of venereal disease) shortly after Charles removed their young son from her care. Not all of the rumors were true, but Lucy was well known for her affairs, and she created considerable trouble for the king, which Monmouth would later compound.[47]

In addition to evoking memories of Monmouth's actual mother, the narrator reinforces Absalom's account of maternal influence by associating him with Milton's Eve throughout the seduction scene. As Frank Ellis points out, "Dryden would not forget that it is Eve whom Satan deceives," and he creates here "an androgynous Monmouth" marked by an effeminate beauty to dramatize the connection.[48] So too, as with Satan and Eve, the serpentine Achitophel "sheds his Venome, in . . . words" (229) that ultimately flatter and provoke the initially resisting child to turn against the father and reach for the "Fruit . . . upon the Tree" (250-51). The desire that Achitophel arouses in Absalom is framed as a feminine one, linked to that experienced by Milton's "general Mother." And the danger that Absalom poses, intensified by the rumors that Monmouth's mother was a whore, shifts attention away from the critique of the king's sexual excesses and toward the earlier intimation that the political problem is the consequence of feminine longing.

Like the description of David's eagerness to please his son, the interaction between Absalom and Achitophel can also be read as a homoerotic one, but whereas his father once indulged him, Achitophel is seducing Absalom to satisfy his own needs.[49] Oblivious to the various ways in which he has been feminized, Absalom himself is attracted by Achitophel's false promise of greater masculinity. Achitophel begins by assuring Absalom that if he dares to seize

the temptress Fortune he can enjoy a kind of sexual conquest reminiscent of
his father's:

> Now, now she meets you, with a glorious prize,
> And spreads her Locks before her as she flies.
> Had thus Old *David*, from whose Loyns you spring,
> Not dar'd, when Fortune call'd him, to be King,
> At *Gath* an Exile he might still remain. (260-64)[50]

Reminding the son of his own debt to David's sexual fertility and invoking an
image of exclusive paternal generation that has already proved problematic
(Absalom springs from David's "Loyns"), Achitophel encourages Absalom to
imitate his father and gain the advantage of sexual dominance. Next, he
changes his strategy and puts David in Fortune's position, arguing that the
king himself is the feminine figure whom Absalom must conquer. After twice
describing David as "Naked" (280, 400) and stressing that he lacks "Manly
Force" (382), Achitophel famously urges Absalom to commit "a pleasing Rape
upon the Crown" (474), suggesting that the king "by Force . . . wishes to be
gain'd / Like womens Leachery, to seem Constrain'd" (471-72). The description does the trick: "And this Advice above the rest, / With *Absalom's* Mild
nature suited best" (477-78).

If the "Mild" Absalom is really moved by the idea that he will be doing
what his father wants, it is notably the image of rape that persuades him to
act. Evoking the opening allusion to the king's capacity to rape and Achitophel's
demand that he ravish Fortune like his father before him, the passage suggests
that Absalom is driven to become his father's sexual replacement, perhaps
hoping that he can exert the very force against David that David has so mag-
nificently displayed, or that he can reverse the abusive act that injured his
birth by becoming his father's abuser. In either case, according to Achitophel,
rape is productive, an implication that plays off the opening example of the
prolific "several Mothers" brought like slaves to David's bed. Apparently consumed by the evidence of his father's virility, Absalom needs to imagine the
king as an effeminate figure whom he can dominate in order to re-create
himself.

But Absalom's fantasy of masculine grandeur proves simply ironic, first
because the rape he and Achitophel imagine performing is pointedly homoerotic and, second, because Absalom is actually the one who, like Eve and the
whorish Lucy Walter, is being seduced throughout the scene. When he thinks
he will become most virile, the son is really the reverse. The contrast highlights David's genuine manliness, reminding us that Achitophel's account of
the king's effeminacy is just as much a ploy as his description of Absalom's
machismo, and that although David may have been too eager to please his

son, he is nevertheless the man who has not only demonstrated the potential to rape but done so with women. So too, Achitophel's efforts to paint David as old and impotent are undercut by the narrator's earlier assurance that Achitophel is actually the one who "Refuse[s] his Age the needful hours of Rest" (166). He may have an impact on Absalom, but Achitophel cannot function successfully enough in bed with a woman to generate a well-shaped child. The accumulating evidence of the sexual differences between David and these men begins to reconfigure the implications about the king's behavior. David's aggressive promiscuity with women is no longer necessarily a problem so much as a mark of his masculine authenticity. And it is in keeping with his virility that far from wishing "by Force . . . to be gain'd" (471), David ultimately proves instead that he is "not Good by Force" (950).

But if Achitophel's description of how women secretly long to be raped finally fails to define the king's position, it nevertheless is gradually validated as an accurate account of feminine sexual desire, a turn that revises the opening emphasis on women's passivity and possible victimization. Not only does Absalom demonstrate a feminine readiness to be seduced, but the crowd, which he (now playing the role of a man) in turn seduces, is lecherously interested in his overtures. Aroused by his good looks, the people open themselves to Absalom, enjoying his penetration. As "He glides unfelt into their secret hearts," his "words" are "easy" and "fit," "slow" and "sweet" (693-97). In this context, the accounts of how "govern'd by the *Moon*, the giddy *Jews*" by "natural Instinct" often "change their Lord" (216-19) and are apt to leave themselves "Defensless, to the Sword / Of each unbounded Arbitrary Lord" (761-62) read as further evidence of the people's sexual exposure and whorish eagerness to be raped.

Some of David's enemies are also marked by their capacity to be "Seduc'd" (498) and by their effeminacy. Zimri (standing for Buckingham, who had a notorious affair with the countess of Shrewsbury) may seem as fertile as the king, but the "ten thousand freaks that dy'd in thinking" (552) that he sires signal his failures of conception and resemble Achitophel's monstrous son. Demonstrating what Weinbrot characterizes as an "impotence of which Charles is free," Zimri may be "Stiff in Opinions" but he performs "every thing by starts, and nothing long" (547-48).[51] And like the fickle and whorish Jews, he too is influenced by the feminine "Moon" (549). Corah (who represents Titus Oates) is just as bad. Although he stands "Erect," Corah's "Monumental Brass" only proves his masculine inauthenticity (633), especially because it was well known that Oates had been dismissed from his office as chaplain for the navy after committing sodomy while on ship.[52]

Like Monmouth, Oates was also rumored to be illegitimate and, echoing the description of Absalom's development from and desire to rise above maternal matter, Corah's "base" birth originates in "Earthy Vapours," although he seeks to "shine in Skies" (636-37). The implicit return to the problem of the maternal prepares us for the later account of Barzillai's son (the earl of Ossory), Dryden's "concept of the ideal" male child, whose legitimate birth and noble death enable him to be free of matter in a way that Absalom and Corah cannot.[53] Unlike Absalom, torn between "David's Part" and his "Mothers Mold" (368), Barzillai's child fulfills "All *parts* . . . of Subject and of Son" (836; emphasis added), suggesting that he reflects his father more completely than the divided Absalom. The passage as a whole, however, does not so much endorse a paternal model of generation as establish the advantages of escaping feminine origins. When Ossory dies

> Now, free from Earth, thy disencumbered Soul
> Mounts up, and leaves behind the Clouds and Starry Pole
> From thence thy kindred legions mayst thou bring
> To aid the guardian Angel of thy King. (850-53)

In echoing Absalom's earlier longing to escape his mother's influence—"I find my mounting Spirits Bold . . . / My Soul Disclaims the Kindred of her Earth" (367-70)—the lines define the essential difference between the men. Where Absalom is grounded in the maternal earth, Ossory's soul can mount above it. Ultimately his "kindred" transcends the feminine.

When David reappears in the finale he seems to have reaped some of Ossory's advantages without having to die. Demonstrating the true superiority of a godly ruler, he is closer to heaven than ordinary mortals and suddenly free of earthly faults. Originally "inspir'd by some diviner Lust" (19), David now speaks "from his Royal Throne by Heav'n inspir'd" (936).[54] He thus bears a greater resemblance to his "Maker" than he did when he was self-indulgently scattering his own image throughout the land. Nevertheless, the difference remains between the legitimate Ossory and the illegitimate Absalom and thus between the virtuous Barzillai and the promiscuous David. As if recognizing the problem of his reputation, David pointedly reconfigures his history of sexual indulgence in his speech, completing the poem's attack on maternal desire and danger, and finally proving that he is not responsible for generating the child of disorder (though he may be guilty of the lesser charge of having raised Absalom "up to all the Height his Frame coud bear" [962] and thus of having given him a false sense of potency). Even as he resolves the initial problem of the poem, then, Dryden leaves open the possibility that David, like Achitophel, is simply developing a rhetorical strategy that is necessary for his own political survival.

Part of David's strategy is to emphasize his phallic advantage, magnified now for readers by the contrasting effeminacy of his enemies. Unlike Zimri, for instance, who is "nothing long" (548), David's "Manly [temper] can the longest bear" (948). And he is prepared to exercise his potency on the "Factious crowds" (1018)—to "rise upon 'em with redoubled might: / For Lawfull Pow'r is still Superiour found, / When long driven back, at length it stands the ground" (1023-25). David here defines governmental repression in terms of his lawful right to phallic conquest, and in so doing, he reverses the opening intimation of his lawless capacity for sexual abuse.[55]

But David's defense of his phallic authority cannot, in itself, solve the problem of the conception of Absalom and the Plot. To extricate himself, the king still needs to prove that the burden of desire and generation lies elsewhere. He is at an advantage with the reader because the text has increasingly emphasized the problem of the people's desire. In addition to the crowd's prostitution before Absalom discussed above, the opening describes how the Jews "led their wild desires to Woods and Caves, / And thought that all but Savages were Slaves" (55-56). At the conclusion David is finally convinced that "no Concessions from the Throne woud please" (925). And when the narrator defends hereditary succession, he specifically insists that the reason subjects should never be given the right to choose their own ruler is that "Then Kings are slaves to those whom they Command, / And Tenants to their Peoples pleasure stand" (775-76). In weighting the problem of desire with the populace, the text reconceptualizes the whole issue of slavery. If it begins by questioning David's enslavement of women, the poem subsequently stresses the savagery of a people in need of control and suggests that the king had better play the part of "Master" (938) lest he himself become a slave. Given Charles's central role in sponsoring the Royal African Company, these passages arguably serve a colonialist purpose, functioning to support England's expanding empire and role in the slave trade.[56]

But by shifting the onus of desire away from the king, the passages also prepare the reader for David's ultimate attack on maternal longing and responsibility. First David links the petitioners' pretended interest in his approval of their choice of king to the way "*Esau's* Hands suite ill with *Jacob's* Voice" (982), recalling another biblical mother who, like Eve, plotted to undermine the father. After all, Jacob deceives Isaac in Genesis 27:13 only because Rebekah urges him to do so, assuring him that "Upon me be thy curse."

Next, David insists that, as with Absalom, he has been far too indulgent with his people—and especially with his enemies in Parliament—who are "Unsatiate as the barren Womb or Grave; / God cannot Grant so much as they can Crave" (987-88). Developing a wonderful counterpart to the opening possibilities that Michal is barren either because he has neglected her needs for sexual arousal or because he has not delivered the force she secretly wants, David instead figures his subjects' ravenous longing as the result of their feminine infertility. The problem is not that he has in some way failed to satisfy feminine desire, but rather that such longing is so uncontrollable that nothing he could have done would have produced a solution. Bearing no relationship to the king's own behavior, the empty womb becomes the driving force of the revolt, reminding us that if only the queen had been fertile all might be well.

David's final maternal image completes the reconfiguration of the several Mothers. Adopting an opposite strategy than the one above, the king now blames his problems on feminine fertility as he anticipates his enemies' self-destruction by exclaiming:

> By their own arts 'tis Righteously decreed,
> Those dire Artificers of Death shall bleed.
> Against themselves their Witnesses will Swear,
> Till Viper-like their Mother Plot they tear:
> And suck for Nutriment that bloody gore
> Which was their Principle of Life before. (1010-15)

Originally unrelated to the rebel son, the mother here becomes the plot against the king, her pregnant body the bloody incubator of revolt. Compared with the description of Achitophel's and Zimri's children, the birth of the vipers is the most monstrous of all, in part because here, for the first time, the mother alone provides the "Principle of Life." Having moved from a paternal to a joint parental model of generation, the poem ends, ironically, with the same emphasis on the power of pregnancy that Locke would later endorse: the offspring "is fashion'd [in the mother's womb], and from her it receives the Materials and Principles of its Constitution."[57] But unlike Locke, Dryden figures maternal generation as the ultimate horror. His emphasis evokes not Harvey's or the ovists' accounts of the importance of the egg so much as an ancient and enduring myth about pregnant mothers (discussed in more detail in Julia Epstein's article in this volume). Mounting embryological research had done little to erode the widespread belief that a woman's mental state and desires could affect and distort the child in her womb, even turning it into a monster.[58] It was assumed that frustrated maternal longings could mark and injure the fetus, and as one eighteenth-century gynecological textbook explained, any excessive feeling might impress "a *Depravity* of Nature upon the Infant's *Mind,* and *Deformity* on its *Body.*"[59] Suggesting that the development and birth of the vipers is the result of a Mother Plot, Dryden's image exonerates the father by emphasizing the gestatory danger of a certain kind of intensive maternal thinking.[60]

Moreover, according to ancient lore about vipers and in keeping with theories about monstrous births, the progeny here is specifically the product of the

mother's excessive desire. In addition to recalling Spenser's Error and Milton's
Sin, the description of the viper is based on popular fables, one of which explains that when vipers copulate, the male puts his "head into the mouth of the
female, who is so insatiable in the desire of that copulation, that when the male
hath filled her with his seed-genital . . . she biteth" off his head and kills him. As
a result, the young she conceives, "in revenge of their fathers death, do likewise
destroy their mother, for they eate out her belly, and by an unnatural issue
come forth."[61] If there were any question at the beginning, the answer is now
unmistakable: the female not only wants to copulate but she is voracious, and
the offspring that result are marked by her hunger. The depiction of the viper
completes David's acquittal, dramatizing the uncontrollable danger of maternal sexuality and his own victimization as father.[62] Far from producing the plot,
David has fallen prey to it. The comfort, however, lies in the certain knowledge that he will be avenged when his rebels turn against their mother and, in
destroying her body and consuming their own placenta, effectively abort themselves. Beautifully, even these vipers will participate in the father's defense.

Because it recalls the way Achitophel developed the plot by shedding
words of "Venome" (229), the image of the viper also completes the attack on
his manliness by associating him with a monstrous mother. Now the earlier
description of his "shapeless Lump" (172) of a son has a different ring. H.T.
Swedenberg suggests that the word *Lump* refers "to the soulless body or to the
primordial matter of chaos."[63] Perhaps, then, Achitophel has not simply failed
in his paternal mission to shape his progeny and give it a soul; perhaps the
child remains a form of chaotic maternal material because that is actually all
he has to offer.[64]

Tearing out of their mother's belly, the vipers are the last in a series of
images suggesting that those associated with the plot have grown too large for
the containment of the body. From the opening, the plot itself is a raging
fever, boiling the blood so that it "bubbles o'r" (136-39) and "Foam[s]" (141)
out of physical boundaries. Similarly, Absalom's "warm excesses . . . / Were
constru'd Youth that purg'd by boyling o'r" (37-38). And Achitophel cannot
stay inside himself, for his "fiery Soul . . . working out its way, / Fretted the
Pigmy Body to decay" (156-57). It is in keeping with such details that, at the
end of the poem, David finally recognizes the way the people, bearing the
"Wound" of a "foment[ing] . . . Disease" (924-26), cannot be placated or
restrained. The recurring ideas of blood, disease, and interior pressure, concluding in the final description of the viper birth, construe the revolt itself as
the inevitable rupture of a swelling pregnancy.[65] And the discussions of how
the "Plot [that] is made" (751) is designed to persuade people that they "have
a Right Supreme / To make their Kings" (409-10, see also 795) read in this
context as warnings about the danger of offering the subjects any kind of

gestatory power. If the populace believes that kings are made, not designated—if it assumes the right to create a ruler—then like the mother viper, it too will become the breeder of chaos.

Dryden's dismissal of the theory of patriarchal procreation reflects a larger political trend. Pateman suggests that "the classic patriarchalism of the seventeenth century was the last time that masculine political creativity appeared as a paternal power or that political right was seen as father-right." Dryden's poem might then be read as marking the end of an ideal, the moment when the generative father-king is no longer a viable image. So too, the attack on maternity anticipates the misogynist implications that, according to Pateman, shaped the contractual body born out of the lost father—the "body of the 'individual'" whose form is "very different from women's bodies. His body is tightly enclosed within boundaries, but women's bodies are permeable, their contours change shape and they are subject to cyclical processes. All these differences are summed up in the natural bodily process of birth."[66] Among other things, Dryden's explosive mother viper proves that the female cannot contain political rights.

But the familial images in *Absalom and Achitophel* are also specifically related to the particular details of the Exclusion Crisis and Dryden's determination to support the king. Given the nature of Monmouth's role, Dryden could not have depended on traditional patriarchal theory to defend the monarch even if he had wanted to, because it appeared in part to be Charles's act of fatherhood that threatened his position as king as well as the endurance of royal succession. To emphasize how a ruler, especially one who promiscuously generated a rebellious son, "had, by right of fatherhood, royal authority over [his] children" and subjects would simply have highlighted the irony of the situation.[67]

The poem's attack on maternity instead enables the king to rise by virtue of contrast. Locke's debate with Filmer suggests that, whether or not it was explicitly acknowledged, the fatherly model of kingship was sustained by denying the role of motherhood in the family. "That the Mother too hath her Title," Locke cautions, "destroys the Sovereignty of one Supream Monarch."[68] Dryden clearly capitalizes on this rhetorical tension between motherhood and monarchy, although for political reasons much different from Locke's. Unable to rely on David's paternity as proof of his right to govern, he turns to the other parent and proves her more harmful. Demonstrating that to introduce the mother into the governmental model is to invite disaster and effectively "Physick [the] Disease into a worse" (810), Dryden argues that the mother must be erased if a stable kingship is to be maintained; in so doing he upholds one of the most basic premises of patriarchal theory.[69]

By insisting on the mother's primary role in conception, the poem can end by disposing of the notion that David was sexually responsible for making his own chaos. Maternal productivity, the consequence of a feminine desire that far outstrips David's own, is the ultimate danger. And David's virtue is marked by his removal from all aspects of the process of generation. The king proves stable both because he suggests that his blood did not create the child of blood and because he rises above average mortals, becoming someone who is not (and should never be) bred or made by them, someone whose origins are fundamentally dissociated from the feminine earth.

But perhaps what is in the end most compelling about the politics of generation in *Absalom and Achitophel* is the variety of narratives about sexuality and the family that emerge before this conclusion. Dryden develops a model of maternal generation in order to defend the royalist tradition as best he can under the circumstances, but because he has adopted and discarded other models along the way, the work ultimately reflects the ideological flexibility of a familial political theory that could be shaped to suit various purposes. At a time when the traditional emphasis on patriarchal procreation was on the wane, when the inevitability of royal succession had long been subject to doubt, and when there was no uniform scientific account of the creation of the human body, any political defense that depended on the image of governmental generation was necessarily unstable and open to rhetorical play. If Dryden ends with an account of maternal monstrosity and a nonprocreative monarchy that solves the problem with which his poem began, he also proves in the process the ease with which his own structure could be dismantled—especially because the questions of who comes next and how are still unresolved.

Notes

1. John Dryden, *Absalom and Achitophel*, in *The Works of John Dryden: Poems 1681-1684*, 20 vols., ed. H.T. Swedenberg Jr. (Berkeley: University of California Press, 1972), 2:2-36. Hereafter lines of poem are cited parenthetically in the text. For discussions of fatherhood and kingship see Larry Carver, "*Absalom and Achitophel* and the Father Hero," in *The English Hero, 1660-1800*, ed. Robert Folkenflik (Newark: University of Delaware Press, 1982), 35-45; Jerome Donnelly, "Fathers and Sons: The Normative Basis of Dryden's *Absalom and Achitophel*," *Papers on Language and Literature* 17 (1981): 363-80; Howard D. Weinbrot, "'Nature's Holy Bands' in *Absalom and Achitophel*: Fathers and Sons, Satire and Change," *Modern Philology* 85 (1988): 373-92; Gayle Edward Wilson, "'Weavers Issue,' 'Princes Son,' and 'Godheads Images': Dryden and the *Topos* of Descent in *Absalom and Achitophel*," *Papers on Language and Literature* 28 (1992): 267-82.

2. Michael McKeon argues that the poem defends patriarchal succession not on "ethical or spiritual grounds" but because of its value as a "known rather than an

unknown quantity": McKeon, "Historicizing *Absalom and Achitophel*," in *The New Eighteenth Century*, ed. Felicity Nussbaum and Laura Brown (New York: Methuen, 1987), 32. It is, I would argue, partly the emphasis on the alternative threat of maternal disorder that proves the safety of the king.

    3. Sir Robert Filmer (c. 1588-1653) may have written *Patriarcha* as early as 1631, but it was not published until 1680, twenty-seven years after his death. For a discussion of the problem of dating the manuscript see Sir Robert Filmer, *Patriarcha and Other Writings*, ed. Johann P. Sommerville (Cambridge: Cambridge University Press, 1991), xxxii-iv. Although it was not written during the Exclusion Crisis, when *Patriarcha* was published the relevance of Filmer's arguments "to the Exclusion debate was immediately recognized by participants on both sides": Richard Ashcraft, *Locke's Two Treatises of Government* (London: Allen and Unwin, 1987), 29. For more on the way Filmer's theory shaped debates about Exclusion see Steven N. Zwicker, *Lines of Authority: Politics and English Literary Culture, 1649-1689* (Ithaca, N.Y.: Cornell University Press, 1993), 132, 161.

    4. Filmer, *Patriarcha*, 1, 10, 11-12.

    5. John Locke, *Two Treatises of Government*, ed. Peter Laslett (New York: New American Library, 1965), 1. § 6. Gordon J. Schochet also notes Locke's attention to Filmer's erasure of the mother in *Patriarchalism in Political Thought: The Authoritarian Family and Political Speculation and Attitudes Especially in Seventeenth-Century England* (New York: Basic Books, 1975), 248-49.

    6. Locke, *Two Treatises*, 2. § 53.

    7. Susan Moller Okin, *Women in Western Political Thought* (Princeton: Princeton University Press, 1979), 200.

    8. I am interested here in the way that, despite other sexist implications, the idea of the mother is pivotal in Locke's attack on the patriarchal justification of kingship. Scholars have long noted the problems with Locke's thinking about women. As Schochet points out, even after insisting on the centrality of maternal authority and the need to acknowledge the duality of "Parental Power," Locke soon forgets "his own injunction" and continues to use the phrase "Paternal Power." Locke also rarely questions the husband's position as "the superior mate" (249). In this respect, Carole Pateman explains, he is no different than Filmer: "Both sides agreed . . . that women (wives) . . . were born and remained naturally subject to men (husbands); and . . . that the right of men over women was *not political*": Pateman, *The Disorder of Women: Democracy, Feminism, and Political Theory* (Stanford: Stanford University Press, 1989), 39. Indeed, "Locke's separation of what he calls paternal power from political power" is predicated on the assumption of woman's inherent inequality: Pateman, *The Sexual Contract* (Stanford: Stanford University Press, 1988), 91, 93. Pateman's feminist analysis of the problems with Locke and the contract theorists is indispensable. See esp. *The Sexual Contract*, 21-25, 52-53, 91-97, and *The Disorder of Women*, 33-57.

    9. Zwicker, *Lines of Authority*, 130. In Locke and Dryden, Zwicker writes, "Filmer had found his shrewdest exegetes" (132).

    10. Thomas Hobbes, *De Cive: The English Version*, ed. Howard Warrender (Oxford: Clarendon Press, 1983), 123; also see the rest of chap. 9, and Hobbes, *Levia-*

than, ed. C.B. Macpherson (Harmondsworth, Middlesex: Penguin Books, 1985), 253-54 (pt. 2, chap. 20).

11. Hobbes, *Leviathan*, 253. As Okin notes in *Women in Western Political Thought*, Hobbes is inconsistent (198-99). Hobbes also maintains that men tend to make better rulers because they "are naturally fitter than women, for actions of labour and danger": *Leviathan*, 250. Still, as Pateman suggests, of all the contract theorists, only Hobbes "proclaims that in the natural condition women are men's equals and enjoy the same freedom": *Disorder of Women*, 5, see also 20, and *Sexual Contract*, 41, 44.

12. Filmer, *Patriarcha*, 192.

13. Pateman, *Sexual Contract*, 88.

14. Quoted in Schochet, *Patriarchalism*, 165.

15. Locke, *Two Treatises*, 1. § 55.

16. For useful discussions of Aristotle's theories, see Eve Keller's article in this volume; Elizabeth B. Gasking, *Investigations into Generation, 1651-1828* (Baltimore: Johns Hopkins University Press, 1967), 27-30; Thomas Laqueur, *Making Sex: Body and Gender from the Greeks to Freud* (Cambridge: Harvard University Press, 1990), 30-59; and Carolyn Merchant, *The Death of Nature* (San Francisco: Harper, 1980), 157-62. For an especially good summary of general trends and debates in theories of generation from Aristotle to the eighteenth century see Marie-Hélène Huet, *Monstrous Imagination* (Cambridge: Harvard University Press, 1993), 37-45.

17. Gasking, *Investigations*, 29.

18. Quoted in Laqueur, *Making Sex*, 30.

19. Dryden praises Harvey's work on circulation in "To My Honored Friend, Dr. Charleton," 1:43-44. But, to my knowledge, he makes no explicit reference to Harvey's work on generation.

20. Gasking, *Investigations*, 28.

21. My summary of Harvey is based on Gasking, *Investigations*, 16-36; Laqueur, *Making Sex*, 142-47; Merchant, *The Death of Nature*, 155-63; and Walter Pagel, *William Harvey's Biological Ideas: Selected Aspects and Historical Background* (New York: Basel, 1967), 270-82, 316, 320-21. For discussions of theories other than Harvey's, see Audrey Eccles, *Obstetrics and Gynaecology in Tudor and Stuart England* (Kent, Ohio: Kent State University Press, 1982), 37-42; and Joseph Needham, *A History of Embryology* (New York: Arno Press, 1975), 115-229.

22. Gasking, *Investigations*, 55.

23. Gasking describes how the early preformationists were all ovists (48), but beginning with Leeuwenhoek in 1683 animalculists became increasingly popular (56). It was not, however, until the beginning of the eighteenth century that there was a well-established division between them. For more on preformation theory see Needham, *Embryology*, 163, 168-70, 175, 205-11.

24. Like Harvey, Locke here favors the theory of epigenesis over that of preformation. It was Harvey who coined the term *epigenesis* to discount the idea that there was what he called "immediate pre-existing material" that produced the fetus. Instead, as Gasking explains in *Investigations into Generation*, "Harvey's account of development is of a simultaneous process of growth and differentiation" (30).

25. For a lucid discussion of the events leading to the "crisis in the theory of royal sovereignty" and of the way this crisis shaped *Absalom and Achitophel*, see McKeon, "Historicizing *Absalom and Achitophel*," 29-34.

26. Pateman, *Sexual Contract*, 89; emphasis added.

27. Zwicker's explanation of Dryden's suspicion about patriarchal theory is very helpful. Dryden, he argues, "was happy to bathe the king in the warm glow of patri- archal indeterminacy; he sought the authority of that argument; he toyed with its plausibility. He was also aware, however, of the less happy associations that might be excited from the patriarchal model of governance, and those are buffered at every point": *Lines of Authority*, 134-35.

28. James Anderson Winn suggests that this kind of flexibility is typical of the poet: *"When Beauty Fires the Blood": Love and the Arts in the Age of Dryden* (Ann Arbor: University of Michigan Press, 1992), 36. Winn's book offers a rich analysis of the way Dryden associates the artistic imagination with sexual energy and concep- tion; see esp. 61, 76, and 349 for discussions of the generation of poetry. In *Absalom and Achitophel*, Winn argues, "there are no sharp lines between the politics of the arts, the politics of sexuality, and the politics of the succession" (249).

29. There is considerable disagreement about the extent to which Dryden opens by blaming David—or Charles—for his sexual behavior. In "'Nature's Holy Bands'" Howard Weinbrot offers a good summary of those who believe Dryden is initially critical of the king (373). Although I am obviously arguing along these lines, I believe that the poem is complex enough to generate multiple and conflicting interpreta- tions. Steven Zwicker, for instance, has consistently argued that Dryden defends the king from the outset. In his first study, Zwicker maintains that "throughout the poem Charles reflects the godhead": *Dryden's Political Poetry: The Typology of King and Nation* (Providence, R.I.: Brown University Press, 1972), 89. In his later *Politics and Language in Dryden's Poetry: The Arts of Disguise* (Princeton: Princeton University Press, 1984), Zwicker argues that "the narrator admits the king's sexual indulgence, but answers the criticism by asserting that in David's sexual excess is evidence of God's creative bounty" (93; see also 26 and 39). More recently he has insisted on the defense of the king implicit in the poem's opening lines in *Lines of Authority*, 132, 138. Wilson also argues for David's consistent divinity in "'Weavers Issue,'" 270-74.

30. Weinbrot, "'Nature's Holy Bands,'" 379.

31. Winn, *"When Beauty Fires the Blood*," 26.

32. See ibid., 26, 36, 101, and 378.

33. Zwicker, *Lines of Authority*, 138. Zwicker goes on to argue that the line is designed to make a "crude joke" out of the word *slavery* (138). Similarly, he views the comment about Michal's infertility, which I discuss below, as simply a joke. Part of my aim in this essay is to argue otherwise. With reference to the slavish mothers, for instance, I would stress that at other points in the poem, the word *slave* connotes a form of serious and humiliating subservience: Adriel is not "a Slave of State" (879), and kings should not be "slaves to those whom they Command" (775). Zwicker, on the other hand, argues that most of the references to slavery are designed to debunk the term, especially when it is used in Exclusionist and liberal arguments "as a way of

denominating the loss of natural rights and political liberty." See Zwicker, *Lines of Authority*, 133-40.

34. This is not, of course, to say that Dryden thought Charles II was a rapist but rather that he found it poetically useful to imply that David, the character, may have been one.

35. Thomas Laqueur discusses the assumed importance of female pleasure in his influential *Making Sex*, arguing that it was not until the end of the Enlightenment that "medical science and those who relied on it ceased to regard the female orgasm as relevant to generation" (3).

36. The biblical description of Amnon's act is similar to the description of David in the poem: Amnon "forced her [Tamar], and lay with her" in his bed; see 2 Samuel 13:5, 14. At the same time, it is worth remembering that the biblical Absalom is also no model of sexual propriety, as he acts on Achitophel's suggestion that he humiliate his father by making incestuous use of David's concubines (2 Samuel 16:20-23). See relevant discussions of Absalom's sexual behavior in Donnelly, "Fathers and Sons," 374; and Weinbrot, "'Nature's Holy Bands,'" 381.

37. Again, I do not mean to make historical claims here—in this case about Catherine of Braganza's sexual experience. Nevertheless, it is worth pointing out that Catherine was troubled by Charles's behavior with his mistresses and by his decision to name the illegitimate James as duke of Monmouth. See Antonia Fraser, *Royal Charles: Charles II and the Restoration* (New York: Dell, 1979), 210-14, 258-60; and Ronald Hutton, *Charles the Second: King of England, Scotland, and Ireland* (Oxford: Clarendon Press, 1989), 187-89. For an alternative analysis of how Dryden's overriding concern is not David's sexual excess but the general problem of "ingratitude" see Steven Zwicker and Derek Hirst, "Rhetoric and Disguise: Political Language and Political Argument in *Absalom and Achitophel*," *Journal of British Studies* 21 (1981): 39-55.

38. Eccles, *Obstetrics*, 36; also see 34-35, and Laqueur, *Making Sex*, 102.

39. On challenges to the relationship between conception and orgasm, see Laqueur, *Making Sex*, 99. Harvey "accepted the stories of women who maintained to have conceived without . . . orgasm": Pagel, *Harvey's Biological Ideas*, 319. See also Eccles, *Obstetrics*, 35. Burn's remark is quoted in Laqueur, *Making Sex*, 162.

40. My reading of David's relationship with Michal and the "several Mothers" owes a great deal to Eve Keller, who commented on an earlier version of this essay and influenced my understanding of the problem of female pleasure in the poem.

41. As Anne K. Krook notes, "On being called father of his people, [even] Charles supposedly once responded, 'Well, I believe that I am, of a good number of them!'": Krook, "Satire and the Constitution of Theocracy in *Absalom and Achitophel*," *Studies in Philology* 91 (1994): 345n.

42. For an interesting analysis of the poem's enduring emphasis on David's similarity to Absalom, see Krook, "Satire."

43. Filmer, *Patriarcha*, 192.

44. Both Donnelly ("Fathers and Sons," 366-67) and Krook ("Satire") suggest that the king's similarities with his son implicate him in Absalom's subsequent behavior.

45. For an analysis of how this passage reveals the role of fate in Absalom's birth and for a discussion of the way Absalom, because he does not descend from God, lacks the dual parentage of kings, see Wilson, "'Weavers Issue,'" 270-73.

46. In many editions "Royal Blood" reads as "Loyal Blood," muting the attack on the mother. Nevertheless, Absalom's Loyal Blood is still arguably the mark of his connection to his father.

47. Lucy, in fact, was not lowborn, but this did not stop Monmouth's enemies from using his mother's "mean Descent" as evidence against him. See Fraser, *Royal Charles*, 64-66, 154-55, 261; and Hutton, *Charles the Second*, 25-26, 96-97, 125-26.

48. Frank H. Ellis, "'Legends No Histories' Part the Second: The Ending of *Absalom and Achitophel*," *Modern Philology* 85 (1988): 402. Winn makes similar associations, suggesting that Monmouth's resemblance to Eve "casts doubt on his authenticity as a hero" and that "the plot to settle the succession on [him] . . . is like [her] false dream": *"When Beauty Fires the Blood,"* 248-49.

49. Winn points out that "in some poetic situations, allusions to . . . homosexual affection were a powerful and acceptable way of indicating intense friendship": *"When Beauty Fires the Blood,"* 84. One might argue that David's charged love for his son is a sign of its strength. At the same time, though, an author might belittle "an adversary by accusing him of sodomy" (ibid., 86). When they specifically refer to dangerous political bonds or threats, the homosexual innuendoes in *Absalom and Achitophel* are designed to sting.

50. Donnelly compares David and Absalom in discussing the motif of sexual conquest in this passage ("Fathers and Sons," 374), but he does not analyze the passage in terms of father-son competition as I do below.

51. Weinbrot, "'Nature's Holy Bands,'" 382.

52. Swedenberg summarizes the sexual scandal in *The Works of John Dryden*, 2:265-66. For good discussions of Dryden's literary treatment of Buckingham and Oates see Donnelly, "Fathers and Sons," 370-72; and Weinbrot, "'Nature's Holy Bands,'" 382.

53. Donnelly, "Fathers and Sons," 375.

54. Weinbrot notes this shift in "'Nature's Holy Bands,'" 389.

55. For an analysis of how the poem ends by making a "sweeping recommendation of the sword" and by suggesting that a "bloody conclusion" is the only possible solution, see Zwicker and Hirst, "Rhetoric and Disguise," 50-53. Zwicker also stresses Dryden's final advocacy of violent revenge against the principals of Exclusion in *Politics and Language*, 87, 90, and *Lines of Authority*, 153.

56. For Charles's role in the Royal African Company, see Richard S. Dunn, *Sugar and Slaves: The Rise of the Planter Class in the English West Indies, 1624-1713* (Chapel Hill: University of North Carolina Press, 1972), 231-32.

57. Locke, *Two Treatises*, 1. § 55.

58. In *Monstrous Imagination*, Huet suggests that "the question of the [power of the] mother's imagination seems to have transcended" scientific disputes; the question survived "not because of the scientific discoveries of the seventeenth and eighteenth centuries, but in spite of them" (45) and became increasingly popular during this period (5).

59. John Maubray, quoted in Julia Epstein, *Altered Conditions: Disease, Medicine, and Storytelling* (New York: Routledge, 1995), 130; the passage is also quoted in her article in this volume. For discussions of the relationship between maternal desire and fetal deformity see Huet, *Monstrous Imagination*, 16-24.

60. The move is fully in keeping with the general implication of the monster myth, which according to Paul-Gabriel Boucé labels "the pregnant mother . . . as the great culprit, the evil scapegoat, much more so than the father. . . . She is finally made responsible for any marks or monstrous deformities of her offspring": Boucé, "Imagination, Pregnant Women, and Monsters in Eighteenth-Century England and France," in *Sexual Underworlds of the Enlightenment*, ed. G.S. Rousseau and Roy Porter (Chapel Hill: University of North Carolina Press, 1988), 98.

61. Edward Topsell, *The History of Four-Footed Beasts and Serpents* (1658), quoted by Swedenberg in *The Works of John Dryden*, 2:285. The lore about the lecherousness of female vipers and the destructiveness of their offspring has a long history. John Trevisa's 1398 translation of Bartholomaeus Anglicus's encyclopedia, for instance, contains a very similar description of the female viper. Bartholomaeus himself compiled his material in the thirteenth century and drew his evidence from even earlier sources. See *On the Properties of Things: John Trevisa's Translation of Bartholomaeus Anglicus De Proprietatibus Rerum*, ed. M.C. Seymour, 3 vols. (Oxford: Clarendon Press, 1975-88), 2:1266-67. I would like to thank Mary Erler for pointing out this reference.

62. Both the earlier image of the barren womb and the description of the fertile viper suggest that insatiable desire originates in the female's reproductive organs. Quoting a contemporary doctor, Boucé characterizes such an association as a typical eighteenth-century sexual myth. "The Womb of a Woman is in the Number of the insatiable things mentioned in the Scriptures . . . ; and I cannot tell whether there is anything in the World, its greediness may be compared unto; neither Hell fire nor the Earth being so devouring, as the Privy Parts of a Lascivious Woman": Boucé, "Some Sexual Beliefs and Myths in Eighteenth-Century Britain," in *Sexuality in Eighteenth-Century Britain*, ed. Paul-Gabriel Boucé (Totowa, N.J.: Barnes and Noble Books, 1982), 42.

63. Swedenberg, in *Works of John Dryden*, 2:249.

64. For an analysis of how "The Medall" also satirizes Shaftesbury for his effeminacy see Winn, "*When Beauty Fires the Blood*," 339. The idea of the self-aborting beasts may also allude to Lucy Walter, who had allegedly aborted two illegitimate children, neither fathered by the king: see Fraser, *Royal Charles*, 154-55; and Hutton, *Charles the Second*, 97. Despite the evidence of Lucy's licentiousness, some of Monmouth's supporters argued that he was a legitimate heir because Charles and Lucy had secretly been married all along. Charles vigorously denied the accusations and even asked an old Counsellor "to recall in public how Lucy was 'a whore to other people'" (quoted in Hutton, *Charles the Second*, 390). By evoking an image of a lascivious mother's unnatural issue, Dryden may have intended to defend Charles's efforts to distance himself from both Lucy and Monmouth.

65. For an excellent and more general account of the image of disease in the poem and the king's role as healer see Wilson, "'Weavers Issue,'" 276-78.

66. Pateman, *Sexual Contract*, 88, 96.

67. Filmer, *Patriarcha*, 6.

68. Locke, 1. § 65. In the context of the Exclusion Crisis, it is worth remembering that Locke was, as Richard Ashcraft explains in *Locke's Two Treatises*, 20-34, both Shaftesbury's closest friend (he was a member of Shaftesbury's household for fifteen years) and his trusted political adviser. Locke's friendship with Shaftesbury may well have had a major impact on the development of his political liberalism. If it would not be entirely precise to argue that Locke learned his liberalism from Shaftesbury, "there is sufficient evidence . . . to establish the fact that, coincidentally with his association with Shaftesbury, Locke began to develop his interests in political and economic issues in a manner that identified his fundamental principles and general political perspective with Shaftesbury's publicly stated position. This was certainly the case with respect to Locke's writing of the *Two Treatises of Government* in the 1680s. . . . It is fair to characterize Shaftesbury's role as that of a catalyst" (22). The *Second Treatise* in particular "was written in the language and from the standpoint of [the] minority of radical Whigs" led by Shaftesbury (31). Locke fled England in 1675, perhaps for his hand in the publication of Shaftesbury's *Letter from a Person of Quality to His Friend in the Country,* but Shaftesbury recalled him in 1679 to assist him during the Exclusion Crisis.

69. Dryden's treatment of the mother thus typifies what Zwicker describes as his general approach to the problem of patriarchal theory: "Without burdening himself with the full run of the patriarchal argument, [Dryden] places it within the poem and by implication and innuendo endorses its language and principles": *Lines of Authority,* 149.

The Pregnant Imagination, Women's Bodies, and Fetal Rights

Prologue

The essay that follows was written in 1994 and appeared in the *Yale Journal of Law and the Humanities* 7 (winter 1995): 198-211. Its statistics reflect its date of publication, although no substantial change has occurred since then to make me rethink the arguments detailed here. The project I undertook after completing this one was, I thought at first, wholly unrelated. I began to collaborate with a colleague at the Temple University School of Law, Jane B. Baron, on a study involving the uses legal scholars have made of narrative theory. The law, many assert, turns on the recounting of stories and their interpretation. Proponents of legal storytelling come primarily from the ranks of feminists, poverty lawyers, and critical race theorists. Having proposed that the law rests on a narrative foundation of human stories, these scholars go on to argue that not everyone in the legal arena has an equal chance to tell her story or to have his story adequately heard. Not surprisingly, these silenced voices tend to be the voices of racial and ethnic minorities, women, the poor, gays and lesbians, and immigrants—in other words, "outsiders." Indeed, much of this work goes by the name "outsider scholarship," and one of the key articles in the field is entitled "Storytelling for Oppositionists."[1]

Some of the legal storytelling scholarship also uses personal narrative, most famously Susan Estrich's account of being raped at knifepoint to introduce an article on rape law, and Patricia Williams's story of her treatment by the clerks in a Benetton store to illustrate the gap between the legal definition and the felt experience of racism.[2] The account I offer below also investigates the personal stories of women. I argue that parallels exist between the eighteenth-century ascription of birth malformations to pregnant women's imaginations and the current trend toward criminalizing the behavior of pregnant women on the grounds that it endangers their fetuses. Looking at this argument from the perspective of the legal storytelling debates, it now seems clear that there is another parallel. In the eighteenth century, women were the arbiters and the authoritative voices in relating their experiences of pregnancy and childbirth. They were trusted to tell their own stories, and those stories were given weight and credence. In the late twentieth century, in contrast, pregnant women have been disenfranchised from storytelling. Their stories are mediated through professional legal and medical discourses that disempower the experiencing subject and turn her into an acted-upon object.

*   *   *

Competing historical and cultural understandings of the human body make clear that medicine and the law construe bodily truths from differing knowledge bases. Jurists rely on medical testimony to analyze biological data, and medical professionals are not usually conversant in the legal ramifications of their diagnoses. In early modern Europe, physicians and jurists recognized that their respective professions were governed by different epistemological standards, a view articulated by Félix Vicq d'Azyr (1748-94), anatomist and secretary to the French Royal Society of Medicine. Vicq d'Azyr noted that whereas lawyers were required to make unyielding decisions based on conflicting laws, customs, and decrees, physicians were permitted more latitude for uncertainty.[3] In the late twentieth century, western medicine and law have become inextricably entwined as technologies have produced new ethical problems for medicolegal jurisprudence.

The authority of women to describe their experiences of pregnancy and childbirth before and during the eighteenth century contrasts powerfully with the twentieth century's reliance on medicolegal decisions to define these experiences. In early modern Europe, women controlled information, experience, and beliefs concerning reproduction, and women held authority over it. A woman only became officially and publicly pregnant when she felt her fetus *quicken*, or move inside her, and she alone could ascertain and report the occurrence of quickening. In 1765, William Blackstone's *Commentaries on the Laws of England* concluded that life "begins in the contemplation of law as soon as an infant is able to stir in the mother's womb."[4]

A pregnancy did not exist until there was quickening, as announced by the pregnant woman, and a child did not exist until it was born alive. Pregnancy in the West today, in contrast, usually entails certification by a medical professional and is verifiable through a number of tactile, laboratory, and visual interventions into a woman's body, from palpation to chemical analysis to ultrasonography. Focus on the fetus as an entity that is available to medical and legal professionals for pronouncement and intervention, and that can be discussed separately from the womb that contains it, is very much a modern phenomenon.[5] In a sense, female interiority has been made public, while women's bodily exterior has attained juridical and moral privacy rights.[6]

It is useful to examine these sharp contrasts between eighteenth- and twentieth-century ideas about pregnancy in order to understand the quagmire that has trapped attitudes toward pregnant women. During the eighteenth century in Europe, heated controversy surrounded the issue of whether the mental activity of a pregnant woman could cause her fetus to become misshapen and thus to be born malformed. Analyzing the way this controversy was articulated in Enlightenment Europe helps us to understand the recent trend toward criminalizing the behavior or status of pregnant women in relation to their gestating fetuses. Knowing the history of the thorny decisions we face concerning women and reproduction can help us to appreciate the controversies in which we are currently embroiled.

In 1991, a Florida appellate court upheld Jennifer Clarice Johnson's 1989 conviction under a Florida statute that criminalizes delivery of controlled substances to minors. Her newborn infant had tested positive for cocaine. Johnson was convicted for "gestational substance abuse" and sentenced to drug rehabilitation and fifteen years probation. The court found that Johnson had passed crack cocaine to her fetus through the umbilical cord; its opinion signaled the first successful prosecution of a pregnant woman in the United States for prenatal damage to a fetus. The following year, the Florida Supreme Court unanimously overturned the conviction, declining "the State's invitation to walk down a path that the law, public policy, reason and common sense forbid it to tread."[7] By mid-1992, more than 160 women had been prosecuted in the United States for drug use during pregnancy through a variety of charges (e.g., criminal child abuse, assault with a deadly weapon, drug trafficking), although at this writing no state or federal laws specifically criminalize prenatal maternal behavior. Most of the women who were prosecuted were women of color living in poverty. Many pleaded guilty or accepted plea bargains, but all twenty-three women who have challenged their prosecutions to date have won their cases on grounds that their prosecutions were unconstitutional or without legal basis.[8]

Jennifer Johnson, twenty-three years old, poor, and African-American, became the first woman in the United States to be convicted of delivering drugs to her fetus in utero. Crucial to her prosecution was the fact that Johnson was not convicted of using drugs, only of exposing her fetus to drugs. Had Johnson terminated her pregnancy, the prosecution would never have taken place. The charges brought against Johnson concerned drug exposure rather than harm. The government introduced no evidence to prove that Johnson's drug use adversely affected her children; on the contrary, there was testimony that Johnson's children were healthy and normal. Dorothy E. Roberts has argued that race and class figured prominently in the Johnson prosecution and generally influence the state's choice to punish, rather than to provide services for, pregnant drug addicts, who are primarily poor African–Americans. "These women are not punished simply because they may harm their unborn children," Roberts asserts. "They are punished because the combination of their poverty, race, and drug addiction is seen to make them unworthy of procreating."[9]

Criminal cases such as the one brought against Jennifer Johnson have profound repercussions for ideas about women's bodies, pregnancy, and fetuses. Such prosecutions necessarily vest fetuses with the status of persons whose rights can be asserted against the rights of their mothers, thereby creating an adversarial relationship between pregnant women and their fetuses. The legal notion of fetal personhood is relatively new in our legal discourse and, ironically, results in part from the 1973 Supreme Court decision on abortion in *Roe v. Wade*. In *Roe*, the court held that "the unborn have never been recognized in the law as persons in the whole sense," and that the word *person*, as used in the Fourteenth Amendment, "does not include the unborn."[10] However, the trimester division that defined "viability" in *Roe* paradoxically relied on the determination of a certain moment at which a fetus becomes an entity separate and separable in law from its mother. Fetal viability as a concept inherits much of the power of quickening, but with the crucial difference that it is decided by physicians and jurists rather than by pregnant women.[11]

In early modern Europe, the pregnant woman was responsible for prenatal care, because pregnancy was not the medicalized condition it is today. The period's advice literature tended to be written by and for women (although only a small percentage of women, mostly in the upper classes, could read), and included counsel on nutrition, exercise, and travel as well as recipes for abortifacients, often described as mixtures to bring on menstruation or to remove false pregnancies.[12] The literature advised pregnant women not to travel in carriages or ride horseback and not to consume strong liquor or spicy foods. Some advice, and its underlying rationale, differed from today's advice for pregnant women. Wine, for example, was often recommended during pregnancy, but strong drink while pregnant or lactating was thought to cause childhood rickets. The traditional diet in England during the seventeenth century was highly salted and included a high consumption of alcohol, estimated by Robert Fogel at the stunning amount of between three and nine ounces of absolute alcohol daily.[13] However, nothing existed that bore any resemblance to our current ideas about the etiology of fetal alcohol syndrome.[14]

A long history predates recent challenges to maternal autonomy in decision–making about pregnancy and in blame for its outcome. In *Dietrich v. Northampton* (1884), Justice Oliver Wendell Holmes denied cause for wrongful death in the case of a premature fetus that died after its mother had fallen.

Holmes argued that the fetus is part of the mother and is not owed a separate duty of care. Courts followed Holmes's analysis concerning prenatal injuries until 1946, when a District of Columbia court recognized a fetus as a "distinct individual."[15] Thus, the concept of fetal personhood in United States law is a post–World War II phenomenon.

"At all stages of pregnancy," writes Lynn M. Paltrow, "the fetus is completely dependent on the woman as everything she does could affect it. . . . Recognizing 'fetal abuse' moves us toward criminalizing pregnancy itself because no woman can provide the perfect womb."[16] Paltrow argues that we face a slippery slope: the prohibition against cocaine could similarly promote bias against alcohol and tobacco, strenuous exercise, poor nutrition, driving a car, riding in an airplane, or owning a gun. The imperfect womb, while not the object of legal sanctions until after 1946, has been targeted for centuries as the source and foundation for birth disabilities and malformations. Although the move toward criminalizing the conduct of pregnant women is radically new in U.S. jurisprudence, it harks back to an ancient tradition of searching for explanations for birth mishaps in the minds and bodies of pregnant women, a tradition that reached its peak during the eighteenth century.

Eighteenth-century physiologists, philosophers, and medical commentators engaged in a heated debate about whether or not imaginative activity in the minds of pregnant women could explain birthmarks and birth defects. Seventeenth- and eighteenth-century developments in embryology and neurophysiology were crucial for the unfolding of this quarrel about pregnancy and the power of mind. The adversarial and internally conflicting discourses that constituted this debate grew out of a range of cultural beliefs about the human body and about women and mothering, and they were embedded in eighteenth-century medical writings.

Bodily borders were ambiguously demarcated in the eighteenth century.[17] The physical body was known to have a skin, which represented not only a boundary but also a fluid surface on which interior life revealed itself.[18] Inside and outside, body/self and external world operated in a process of continual exchange. Early in the century, women did not "reproduce" when they bore children; rather, they participated in *generatio*, or fruitfulness. The reproductive apparatus of a woman's body that today is classified and studied under the medical rubrics of obstetrics and gynecology did not exist as a unit of medical knowledge in the early eighteenth century. Fetuses were nourished and developed by women, whose anatomical structures were far better understood than their functions.

During the eighteenth century, Europeans insisted that bodies serve as classificatory systems in relation to one another. Categories of the body delimited both sensory experience and notions of autonomy and aesthetics. The female body could create monstrosity through its capacity for generation.[19] By the mid-nineteenth century, representations of women's bodies were assimilated into an etherealized domestic ideal, but early-eighteenth-century images of women reflected the perceived threat of an unsocialized, willful, and appetite-driven female sexuality.[20] In the eighteenth century, Europeans believed that ideas manifested themselves across the bodies of pregnant women. The eighteenth-century maternal imagination debates were therefore crucial not only for their cultural representation and medical analysis of women's bodies, but also for the ability of women to control their own lives.

In London in 1714, English surgeon Daniel Turner published a medical treatise called *De Morbis Cutaneis: A Treatise of Diseases Incident to the Skin*. Turner's brief treatise was important as the first English dermatology text in the history of medicine, but its fame rests on the vehement debate it provoked. In *De Morbis Cutaneis*, Turner defined what he called "that Faculty of the sensitive Soul called Phansy or Imagination" as a physiological power that resided in the brain. It operated, he argued, by irradiating nervous fluid inward in response to impressions received by the external organs, admittedly a vague definition from a modern perspective. Turner needed to define the imagination in his treatise on skin diseases because he made a controversial claim in his chapter about the causes of birthmarks. That chapter carried a typically long-winded eighteenth-century title: "Of Spots and Marks of a diverse Resemblance, imprest upon the Skin of the *Foetus*, by the Force of the Mother's Fancy; with some Things premis'd, of the strange and almost incredible Power of Imagination, more especially in pregnant Women."[21] Turner could not explain his claim. In fact, he wrote: "How these strange Alterations should be wrought, or the *Foetus* cut, wounded and maimed, as if the same were really done with a Weapon, whilst the Mother is unhurt, and merely by the Force of her Imagination, is, I must confess ingenuously, . . . *Supra Captum*, i.e., above my Understanding" (116-17).

James Augustus Blondel, a Parisian educated at the University of Leiden and a noted member of the London College of Physicians, responded to Turner's assertion with vituperation. Blondel asked, "What can be more scandalous, and provoking, than to suppose, that those whom God Almighty has endow'd, not only with so many charms, but also with an extraordinary Love and Tenderness for their Children, instead of answering the End they are made for, do bread [sic] *Monsters* by the Wantonness of their Imagination?"[22]

The theory of the maternal imagination, or maternal impressions, embraced two ideas. First, a pregnant woman's longings, if ungratified, were understood to *mark* her fetus. Hence, if a woman's overwhelming desire for strawberries could not be satisfied, her infant would be born with a strawberry mark.[23] Cravings (or aversions) of this sort did not always involve food. They could also pertain to religious or sexual activities or to obsessive acts or thoughts. Yet it is telling that the vast majority of examples of the first type of maternal impression involve a pregnant woman's uncontrollable appetite for fruit. The French physician-theologian Nicholas de Malebranche, a central influence on Turner, had written in his 1674 *De la recherche de la verité* that a mother's desire for fruit caused the fetus to imagine and desire the fruit as well, so that "these unfortunate infants thus become like the things they desire too ardently." It is not hard to find here a theological analogy between monstrous offspring and forbidden fruit.[24]

Second, the pregnant woman needed to avoid disturbing experiences at all costs, on the theory that negative experiences would be mirrored in a related physical deformity in her child. For example, if the sight of a street beggar missing the fingers of one hand startled her, her infant would be born lacking the fingers of the corresponding hand. The pseudonymous early-eighteenth-century midwifery handbook, *Aristotle's Compleat and Experienc'd Midwife*, contained this advice: "Let none present any strange and unwholesome Thing to her, nor so much as name it, lest she should desire it, and not be able to get it, and so either cause her to Miscarry, or the Child to have some Deformity on that Account."[25] John Maubray went further in his popular *Female Physician* (1724). Maubray placed responsibility for these misadventures on the pregnant woman herself. "She ought discreetly," Maubray wrote, "to suppress all *Anger, Passion*, and other *Perturbations* of Mind, and avoid entertaining too *serious* or *melancholick Thoughts*; since all *such* tend to impress a *Depravity* of Nature upon the Infant's *Mind*, and *Deformity* on its *Body*." In addition, Maubray suggested that pregnant women must maintain domestic harmony in their households and marriages. According to Maubray, "There never ought so much as a *Cloud* to appear in [her] *Conjugal Society*; since all such unhappy *Accidents* strongly affect the growing *Infant*."[26]

Families took seriously the desires of pregnant women and the need to satisfy them. A striking example of this truth: when his pregnant wife told the German botanist Joachim Camerarius (1534-98) that she felt overwhelmed by the need to smash a dozen eggs in his face, he obliged her by submitting to her desire.[27] The best-known maternal imagination case in England was actually a fraud: in 1726, Mary Tofts of Godalming in Surrey, commonly known as the "rabbet woman," contrived a lucrative hoax by claiming that she had given birth to seventeen rabbits after being frightened in the fields.[28] In 1746, the *Gentleman's Magazine*, a politically moderate English monthly that covered a wide range of medical topics, published a typical report of a malformed birth ascribed to the maternal imagination: "The wife of one Rich. Haynes of Chelsea, aged 35 and mother of 16 fine children, was deliver'd of a monster, with nose and eyes like a lyon, no palate to the mouth, hair on the shoulders, claws like a lion instead of fingers, no breast-bone, something surprising out of the navel as big as an egg, and one foot longer than the other.—She had been to see the lions in the Tower, where she was much terrify'd with the old lion's noise."[29]

According to the theory of maternal impressions, the birth of a defective infant unveiled the secret passions of its mother. In some ways, one could argue that the birth of an addicted baby today also suggests a secret failing of its mother. The very term *crack baby* implies a fissure or breakage in the autonomy of a mother as well as in her ability to reproduce. It is not surprising, then, that the birth of what was invariably termed a "monster" called into question, above all, the legitimacy of its parentage. Malformed births represented a major social problem in early modern Europe. A monstrous birth lacked legitimacy in a fundamental way. Such an infant failed to resemble its (or any) father; hence, in a social order ruled by the laws of primogeniture and patrilineage, a malformed birth stood for a basic social disruption. Before the sixteenth century, a monstrous birth signified the opposite of its father's stamp. It was a portent, a sign of the wrath of God.[30] Conflicts arose between the ecclesiastical interest in the immortal soul of the infant and the secular authority's concern for determining property rights, inheritance, and legitimacy. Both interests pressured midwives, who were responsible for determining whether a live birth had taken place (hence affecting primogeniture) and for baptizing moribund newborns.

The notion of fetal personhood necessary to such cases as *State v. Johnson* in 1989 was unthinkable in the eighteenth century when newborns did not legally exist unless born alive. The familiar conflict between saving the mother's life and preserving the product of her labor was not at issue in early modern Europe. The mother's health and survival unequivocally came first, as it was the pregnant woman who was being delivered, not the fetus. This clear hierarchy of concern underlay the midwifery practice of manual version, using hands to turn the fetus in the womb, and the more typically male surgical practices of craniotomy and embryotomy, as means of removing a dead fetus from a living woman.[31] This view was not limited to early modern Europe. The *Mishnah*, for example, stipulates that an embryo can be dismembered to save the life of a woman, "for her life takes precedence over its life," as long as its head has not yet emerged. Once its head is visible, "it may not be touched, since we do not set aside one life for another."[32]

The subject of maternal impressions did not by any means originate either in the eighteenth century or in Europe. The belief that the maternal mental state influences fetal development is ancient and can be found in Hindu medical treatises that predate western Hippocratic medicine by many centuries.[33] Ayurvedic texts argue that prenatal beings are sentient and environmentally responsive. The *Garbha Upanisad* and the *Susruta-samhita*, for example, claimed that the fetus expresses its desires through the mother's longings and that such longings must be gratified. The *Caraka-samhita* provides a guide for pregnant women that equates certain eating habits (excessive sweets or fish) or behaviors (sleepwalking, sexual promiscuity) with character traits in the unborn child.[34] The Judeo-Christian tradition also offers a notable example of the theory that maternal sense impressions mark offspring: the story of Jacob placing rods before his flock so that they will bear speckled and spotted cattle.[35]

The two ideas that together form the concept of the maternal imagination are quite different. Although both types are involuntary on the part of the pregnant woman, cravings or obsessions are active, whereas witnessing unsettling persons, or events, or representations amounts to a passive, usually visual, experience that is externally imposed. Both types of maternal impression ultimately raise questions about the formulation of theories concerning female desire and its location in the generative female body. The idea of cravings is the one that persists both as folklore and in obstetric textbooks today—the pregnant woman's desire for pickles and ice cream (or, in the 1959 Disney animated classic *Lady and the Tramp*, watermelon and chop suey).[36] But in their early modern formulation, the maternal imagination debates proposed a continuum between the passive reception of sensory experience and the active production of desire. The maternal imagination debaters derived from the Lockean concept of the primacy of sensory experience the closest approximation we get in the seventeenth and eighteenth centuries to a notion of what women want.

In addition to the array of thinkers on generation from Heliodorus and Empedocles to Étienne and Isidore Geoffroy Saint-Hilaire (the father-and-son founders of teratology, the scientific study of monsters), dozens of writers participated in the debate about maternal impressions during the Enlightenment. Responding to the ideas of Daniel Turner, Blondel published *The Strength of Imagination in Pregnant Women Examin'd: and the Opinion that Marks and Deformities in Children arise from thence, Demonstrated to be a Vulgar Error* (1727). Turner responded in 1730 with *The Force of the Mother's Imagination upon her Foetus in Utero*. Henry Bracken's *The Midwife's Companion* (1737) sided with Turner. Bracken referred to the example of the fingerless beggar and suggested the sociopolitical implications of these ideas: "Indeed, such Objects as these [the beggar] should be driven out of every Town, by express Order of the Magistrate: For it is not hardly credible the Number of Children who are born monstrous on such Accounts."[37]

A French argument in support of Blondel appeared in 1745 when Bordeaux physician Isaac Bellet published his *Lettres sur le pouvoir de l'imagination des femmes enceintes*. Bellet argued against maternal impressions, and he also reported that this mistaken prejudice destroyed the repose and health of pregnant women. The smallest events made them anxious or alarmed, and they lived in fear of experiencing or thinking something that would hurt their infants. This situation was so dreadful, according to Bellet, that he asserted that imaginary maladies became real ones and affected the infant in the womb.[38] Later in the century, in *The Pupil of Nature; or, Candid Advice to the Fair Sex* (1797), Martha Mears presented the same circular argument about maternal passions. Mears wrote that there was no nervous communication between mother and fetus, but that "it is of the utmost moment to root out of the mind those fatal apprehensions; or they will often produce the very evils to which they are so tremblingly alive." Disease during pregnancy may result, or difficulty in delivery, and even "a puny, or distorted infant is sometimes brought forth—the victim of its mother's terrors."[39] In 1747, John Henry Mauclerc published a refutation of Blondel's 1727 treatise: *Dr. Blondel confuted; or, The Ladies vindicated*. Mauclerc's subtitle, *The Ladies vindicated*, reveals the underlying problem in these quarrels: the status of pregnant women as rational beings. The debate made clear both that the locus of responsibility for pregnancy remained with women and that female interiority represented a potential excess that must be policed.

The maternal imagination debate gradually died out, its ideas incorporated in some measure into the science of teratology by the early nineteenth century. No definitive conclusion ever resolved the quarrel, and the power of the maternal imagination remains with us in various cultures' folk beliefs. It is clear from the language of the medical treatises that contributed to the maternal impressions debate that the subject encompassed more than just the maternal imagination's influence on fetal development. This debate was about passion and power with respect to the early modern understanding of the body as an envelope, a coating for the soul, a receptacle whose corporeality was allegorical as well as physical.

Embryology did not emerge as a separate medical discipline until the second half of the sixteenth century. The Turner-Blondel contribution to ideas of generation appeared at the height of beliefs in embryological *preformation*, the view that the whole human structure exists in miniature prior to conception. Preformationist views came in a variety of flavors and were not an eighteenth-century invention, although they had been presented with greater reserve in earlier periods.[40] But around the end of the seventeenth century, preformationist arguments began to appear frequently in medical literature. The usual version of preformation was called *animalculism* or *spermaticism*.

It held that a preformed human being inhabited the male seed. There was an interesting controversy concerning why, if animalculism was valid, children often looked like their mothers. One explanation involved the maternal imagination: vain pregnant women looked at themselves in the glass, and their images then imprinted onto the fetuses they carried. There was also a strain of preformationism called *ovism* which saw the female egg as the repository for the homunculus, a view that seemed to be shored up by Reinier de Graaf's discovery of the ovarian follicle in 1672. The most extreme version of preformationist belief was the notion of *emboîtement*, or encasement, which could be accommodated in either spermatocist or ovist formulations. The Swiss anatomist Albrecht von Haller offered an ovist explanation of this all-inclusive view: "It follows that the ovary of an ancestress will contain not only her daughter but also her granddaughter, her greatgranddaughter and her greatgreatgranddaughter, and if it is once proved that an ovary can contain many generations, there is no absurdity in saying that it contains them all."[41] In other words, all potential human beings existed from the moment of divine creation.

Blondel espoused animalculism, whereas Turner proposed a continuity between fetal and maternal blood vessels, and followed an *epigenetic* view — the view that the embryo develops structurally and sequentially in utero through the growth and differentiation of specialized cells.[42] This debate embraced a central paradox in early modern thinking about fetal development: Turner was relatively accurate about maternal-fetal relations in utero but superstitious about the mental stability of pregnant women, whereas Blondel was medically inaccurate in his knowledge of gestational physiology, but rejected the prevailing folk beliefs about female irrationality and uncontrollability during pregnancy. What is most striking is that both Turner's imaginationist view, which attributed monstrous births to maternal impressions, and Blondel's preformationist view, which argued that the maternal role was merely to house the developing fetus, similarly negated the agency of pregnant women. For preformationists, the mother remained entirely passive and useless except as a vessel; for imaginationists, the maternal imagination operated wholly beyond the will of the mother, who could not shape it or impose meaning upon it.[43]

The imaginationists believed women's stories and gave them an active role in the development of their fetuses, but at a price — they held women accountable for any birth not entirely normal. The preformationists (including the ovists) denied women any role in gestation other than as pack animals but absolved them of blame for the ensuing birth. The eighteenth-century maternal imagination debates make clear that the ideological stakes of assigning responsibility for birth outcomes are especially high. In early modern Europe, assigning blame for the horror of defective or malformed births affected inheritance, social organization, and political power. In a social system dependent on male lineage, it was more than just politically and economically convenient to displace this responsibility onto women's bodies and minds.

The conflicting Enlightenment narratives that explain the etiology of, and thus fix the blame for, "imperfect" infants bear striking similarities to current ethical discussions stemming from the legal battles that pit pregnant women against their fetuses. The underlying significance of these narratives involves the legacy of blaming the mother for her children's appearance and behavior. Blaming mothers serves to justify a wide range of strategies for containing women's minds by containing women's bodies.[44]

Regulatory discourses concerning the physiology and reproductive roles of women have a long social history. In the eighteenth century, physicians and philosophers debated the power of a pregnant woman's mind to influence fetal development. In the nineteenth century, medical practitioners in the United States led an antiabortion campaign intended to establish medicine as a scientific profession and to regulate reproduction. In the nineteenth century as in the eighteenth, assumptions about maternal duty dictated attitudes concerning the behavior of pregnant women. In a passage that makes these assumptions clear, nineteenth-century Philadelphia physician Hugh Lenox Hodge attacked pregnant women for disobeying medical advice: "They eat and drink, they walk and ride, they will practice no self restrainment, but will indulge every caprice, every passion, utterly regardless of the unseen and unloved embryo."[45] The specter of unbridled appetites haunts this passage. The nineteenth-century campaign to criminalize abortion sought to replace a pregnant woman's testimony about her pregnancy with an externally imposed medical authority. Legal scholar Reva Siegel has shown that this campaign had the effect of claiming for physicians "a special competence to mediate between a woman and the state," an effect that continues to be important.[46]

The prevailing views in the nineteenth century permitted physicians to step in and "restrain" women who were unwilling or unable to restrain themselves. Eighteenth-century discourses that attributed fetal malformations to maternal mental activity, and nineteenth-century regulations concerning pregnant women, medical authority, and abortion, both served to make women's role in reproduction conform to prevailing ideas about women's social place. As Siegel notes, "Regulations governing the conditions in which women conceive, gestate, and nurture children express social attitudes about sexuality and motherhood and, in turn, shape women's experience of sexuality and motherhood."[47]

Journalist Katha Pollitt analyzes these social attitudes in a provocative *Nation* article entitled "'Fetal Rights': A New Assault on Feminism." She asks,

"How have we come to see women as the major threat to the health of their newborns, and the womb as the most dangerous place a child will ever inhabit?"[48] As I have shown, that is not such a new question. Women in the United States today who use drugs, especially cocaine, during pregnancy may face criminal prosecution for a variety of offenses, from drug trafficking to criminal child abuse to assault with a deadly weapon. Yet Carol E. Tracy noted in 1990 that only 11 percent of the pregnant women who need substance-abuse treatment get it. Tracy wrote, "We live in a society that romanticizes motherhood but provides virtually no structural supports for mothers."[49] The situation is improving: in 1985 almost no drug treatment programs would accept pregnant users, whereas in 1995 about 75 percent did. At the time of the initial trial of Jennifer Johnson in 1990, however, there were approximately 4,500 drug-addicted pregnant women in Florida, 2,000 of whom were on waiting lists for the 135 drug treatment beds available statewide for pregnant women.[50] Many drug treatment centers routinely turn away pregnant addicts, and few have obstetricians on their staffs. Pregnant drug users avoid even basic prenatal care for fear of being reported. Thirty-seven thousand babies are born in the United States each year to drug-addicted women; fetal alcohol syndrome affects one out of every one thousand U.S. births; and 1.5 percent of newborns in New York City are HIV-seropositive.[51] The Supreme Court, in *General Electric Co. v. Gilbert* (1976), struck down EEOC guidelines requiring employers to provide maternity leave under their benefits programs. In his dissent, Justice William Brennan remarked that the United States is one of the few western nations which has no universal legal or social provisions for maternity.[52]

Motherhood cannot be separated from the social conditions that surround it. The United States confronts the tragedies of teenage pregnancy, women and children with AIDS, single-mother households living below the poverty line, inner-city crime, drive-by shootings, and homelessness. The overwhelming response has been to criminalize acts of desperation such as drug use rather than to provide prevention or treatment services, create jobs programs for inner-city youth, improve the public education system, or devise a system for regulating firearms. The assertion that a person represents a "danger to self and others" constitutes the legal justification for curtailing the individual's civil rights. This justification fuels the discussion of mandatory drug treatment for pregnant women, but it has not led the courts, for example, to impose drug treatment on all drug users or to mandate medical treatment for other untreated diseases.[53] The medicolegal system in the United States, defined as it is by adversarial relations and contests, cannot adequately grapple with the problem of establishing a reasonable standard of care for pregnant women.[54] For example, increasing "fetal rights" will inevitably allow children to bring lawsuits against their mothers for prenatal injuries. *Roe v. Wade* does not prevent tort actions for fetuses before they are viable. At the same time, a maternal duty to utilize prenatal technologies has been emerging.

It is deceptively easy to conclude that eighteenth-century embryology was not sufficiently advanced to produce more scientific explanations for "monsters." The more pressing question is whether we can learn anything from these early medical debates that might illuminate the complicated social, ethical, medical, and legal issues we face.[55] For example, in prosecuting women for drug use during pregnancy, is the state again displacing the systemic socioeconomic problems of unemployment, poverty, and despair onto the bodies of women and taking over control of these bodies because women allegedly lack self-control? Jurists try to translate the moral expectation that a pregnant woman will make every attempt to ensure the healthy development of her unborn fetus into an idea of enforceable legal duty. In this attempt, they unavoidably subordinate a woman's rights to privacy and autonomy to a codification of the state's interest in protecting her fetus from harm.[56] In a 1988 Illinois case, a suit was brought by an infant's father on its behalf against the mother and a motorist for prenatal injuries the child sustained in an automobile accident. The court summarized the situation created by the notion that fetuses have a cognizable "legal right to begin life with a sound mind and body" by stating, "It is the firmly held belief of some that a woman should subordinate her right to control her life when she decides to become pregnant or does become pregnant: anything which might possibly harm the developing fetus should be prohibited and all things which might positively affect the developing fetus should be mandated under the penalty of law be it criminal or civil." The court went on to argue that because any and all actions of a pregnant woman can have an impact on her fetus, any act or omission could render her liable, making a fetus's rights superior to those of its mother, concluding "such is not and cannot be the law of this State." The Supreme Court of Illinois found for the mother, holding that "There is no cause of action by or on behalf of a fetus, subsequently born alive, against its mother for the unintentional infliction of prenatal injuries."[57]

A number of feminist legal scholars have criticized the idea of fetal rights and, consequently, the notion of fetal personhood itself that such rights presuppose. Conceiving and bearing children have never been risk-free, and women have always made, and been expected to make, sacrifices during pregnancy. However, a pregnant woman must have a different status with respect to her fetus than do others, including the state. Otherwise, women's ownership of their own bodies is challenged, and pregnant women are punished for social ills such as poverty, unemployment, malnutrition, and unequal access to education and health care. In juridical terms, there is no "bright line" that may confine this responsibility. "Until the child is brought forth from the woman's body," Janet Gallagher writes, "our relationship with it must be mediated by her. The alternative adopts a brutally coercive stance toward pregnant women, viewing them as means to an end which may be denied the bodily integrity and self-determination specific to human dignity."[58]

The crux of this predicament can be located in the language of rights itself. A focus on rights grounds the discussion in privacy law, which becomes meaningless if the contents of a pregnant woman's womb can be severed from her person and granted separate interests. The constitutional right of decisional privacy detailed in *Griswold v. Connecticut* has begun to yield its place to the rights of fetuses, pitting pregnant women not just against the products of their bodies but against their very bodies themselves.[59] In *Eisenstadt v. Baird*, like *Griswold* a case involving contraceptive practice, the court held that "if the right of privacy means anything, it is the right of the individual . . . to be free from unwarranted intrusion."[60] Privacy rights in law are not monolithic: they include the rights to be left alone, to refuse medical treatment, and to have possession of and power over one's own person.[61] Christyne L. Neff persuasively argues that, for this reason, the doctrine of bodily integrity serves the arguments of reproductive freedom better than does privacy law.

Bodily integrity doctrine underpins legal notions of assault and battery, search and seizure, informed consent, and the right to refuse medical treatment. Separating the fetus from a pregnant woman pursues what Neff calls "an analysis that views the pregnant woman as a duality [and] is itself a violation of woman's bodily integrity."[62] Privacy rights in their multiple forms cannot be distinguished so easily from the legal notion of bodily integrity, since the concept of privacy includes ideas about the body as a refuge, a space protected from state intrusion.[63] Indeed, a version of the idea of bodily integrity seems to have existed for early modern European thinkers, a complex irony given the arguments I have been making. At the same time, the embeddedness of pregnancy within a network of social practices and individual interests may have been more clearly delineated in earlier historical periods in Europe than it is in the United States today.

The eighteenth-century maternal imagination debates were intricate from both biological and philosophical perspectives. To contend that the maternal imagination was impotent, physicians subscribed to preformationism and used the physiologically inaccurate argument that the fully independent fetus shared no circulatory or nervous communication with its mother and, thus, could not respond to her mental or sensory experiences. In contrast, writers who affirmed the power of the maternal imagination chastised those who impugned women's honesty concerning their experiences of pregnancy. This eighteenth-century controversy, then, radically questioned the ontological relation between pregnant women and fetuses and did so in unexpected ways. That ontological relation continues to be vexed. In 1668, François Mauriceau described pregnancy as "a rough Sea" and urged the pregnant woman "to be careful to overcome and moderate her Passions, as not to be excessive angry; and above all, that she be not afrighted; nor that any melancholy news be suddenly told her" because she might miscarry or harm her fetus. He wrote of the pregnant woman's "so great loathings, and so many different longings, and strong passions for strange things." Three hundred years later, David L. Kirp proposes that in light of the problem of environmental and workplace hazards, "the more that is learned about these insidious dangers, the more remarkable it becomes that any fetus navigates the perilous voyage from conception to birth healthy and intact."[64] It is the socioeconomic infrastructure which needs sanction and repair, not the bodies of women.

Notes

The author would like to thank Robert Kieft, reference librarian at Haverford College, and the librarians at the historical collections of the College of Physicians of Philadelphia for research assistance. Jane B. Baron, Estelle Cohen, Ruth Colker, Kathryn Kolbert, Linda McClain, Nigel Paneth, Reva Siegel, and M. Elizabeth Sandel were generous with their expertise in history, medicine, and the law.

1. Richard Delgado, "Storytelling for Oppositionists and Others: A Plea for Narrative," *Michigan Law Review* 87 (August 1989): 2411-41. For overviews and discussions of the legal storytelling movement, see two articles by Jane B. Baron, "The Many Promises of Storytelling and the Law," *Rutgers Law Journal* 23 (fall 1991): 79-105, and "Resistance to Stories," *Southern California Law Review* 67 (January 1994): 255-85. The results of our collaboration thus far are Jane B. Baron and Julia Epstein, "Is Law Narrative?" *Buffalo Law Review* 45.1 (winter 1997): 141-87; and Baron and Epstein, "Language and the Law: Literature, Narrative, and Legal Theory," in *The Politics of Law: A Progressive Critique*, 3rd ed., ed. David Kairys (New York: Harper Perennial, 1998).

2. Susan Estrich, "Rape," *Yale Law Journal* 95 (1986): 1087; Patricia J. Williams, *The Alchemy of Race and Rights* (Cambridge: Harvard University Press, 1991). For a discussion, see Anne M. Coughlin, "Regulating the Self: Autobiographical Performances in Outsider Scholarship," *Virginia Law Review* 81 (August 1995): 1229-1340.

3. See Lindsay Wilson, *Women and Medicine in the French Enlightenment: The Debate over Maladies des Femmes* (Baltimore: Johns Hopkins University Press, 1993), 65. Vicq d'Azyr became the first secretary to the Société Royale, which he helped to found in 1776.

4. William Blackstone, *Commentaries on the Laws of England* (London, 1765), 1:129. Thomas Cobham wrote in his manual for confessors (c. 1216) that striking a pregnant woman in such a way that she miscarried was punishable by death if the fetus were "formed," but required only monetary restitution if the fetus were "un-

formed." Cited by G.R. Dunstan in his introduction to *The Human Embryo: Aristotle and the Arabic and European Traditions* (Exeter: University of Exeter Press, 1990), 5. Angus McLaren comments on the demise of quickening as a juridical definition in *Reproductive Rituals: The Perception of Fertility in England from the Sixteenth to the Nineteenth Century* (London: Methuen, 1984), 138. Barbara Duden also remarks on this phenomenon in *Disembodying Women: Perspectives on Pregnancy and the Unborn* (Cambridge: Harvard University Press, 1993), 82.

5. See Lisa Cody, "The Doctor's in Labour; or, a New Whim Wham from Guildford," *Gender and History* 4 (summer 1992): 175-96. Cody argues that "in the eighteenth century, doctors were forced to listen to women to gain knowledge about reproduction" (191). Like Duden, she dates the silencing of the female body to the nineteenth century, when medicine gained a kind of authority that no longer needed to be authenticated by women's voices. Indeed, a 1959 article in a medical journal not only questions the authority of women's accounts of their own experience of pregnancy but actively terms such accounts a factor in misdiagnosing causes of birth defects. "*Maternal memory bias* is a source of error most difficult to control. The mother of a malformed child is likely to try hard to find a 'reason' for the child's defect in the events of the pregnancy. Thus the mother of an abnormal child will be more likely to remember unusual events during the pregnancy than will the mother of a normal child": F.C. Fraser, "Causes of Congenital Malformations in Human Beings," *Journal of Chronic Diseases* 10 (August 1959): 97-110.

6. Duden argues that this change occurred in the nineteenth century, when the woman yielded to the fetus as the focus of pregnancy, in a chapter entitled "The Uterine Police" in *Disembodying Women*, 94-95.

7. *State v. Johnson*, No. E89-890-CFA (Fla. Cir. Ct. July 13, 1989), *aff'd*, 578 So. 2d 419 (Fla. Dist. Ct. App. 1991), *rev'd*, 602 So. 2d 1288 (Fla. 1992). For discussions of this case, see Christina von Cannon Burdette, "Fetal Protection—An Overview of Recent State Legislative Response to Crack Cocaine Abuse by Pregnant Women," *Memphis State University Law Review* 22 (fall 1991): 119-35; Wendy Chavkin, "Jennifer Johnson's Sentence," *Journal of Clinical Ethics* 1 (1991): 140-41; Dorothy E. Roberts, "Punishing Drug Addicts Who Have Babies: Women of Color, Equality, and the Right of Privacy," *Harvard Law Review* 104, no. 7 (1991): 1419-82; and Ruth Colker, *Abortion and Dialogue: Pro-Choice, Pro-Life, and American Law* (Bloomington: Indiana University Press, 1992).

8. Center for Reproductive Law and Policy, "Punishing Women for Their Behavior during Pregnancy: A Public Health Disaster," 2 February 1993. This pamphlet lists the cases to date and is available from the Center, 120 Wall Street, New York, N.Y. 10005. My thanks to Kathryn Kolbert, vice president of the Center, for this information.

9. Roberts, "Punishing Drug Addicts," 1472. Roberts points out that crack cocaine addiction—much more prevalent in African–American communities than elsewhere in the U.S.—has been singled out for these prosecutions, even though there is compelling evidence that prenatal use of other kinds of drugs, such as alcohol or marijuana, causes fetal harm. These other drugs tend to find niches in middle-class white populations. Johnson's crack addiction came to light because she confided her

drug use to her obstetrician at a public hospital. The state organized its prosecution on the theory that Johnson's efforts to get help for her addiction showed that she knew her drug use harmed her fetus. See Roberts, ibid., 1449; and Roberts, *Killing the Black Body: Race, Reproduction, and the Meaning of Liberty* (New York: Pantheon Books, 1997). In *People v. Hardy*, 469 N.W. 2d 50 (Mich. Ct. App. 1991), the court held that use of cocaine by a pregnant woman cannot be subject to criminal prosecution under a statute that prohibits delivery of cocaine.

10. *Roe v. Wade*, 410 U.S. 113, 162 (1973). An interesting contrast to *Roe*, and a historical precursor of abortion debates, can be found in the *Petition of the Unborn Babes to the Censors of the Royal College of Physicians of London*, 2d ed. (London: M. Cooper, 1751). This document represents a response to two physicians of the Royal College, referred to as Drs. Pocus and Maulus, who argued against an inquiry into the deaths of six children delivered by a man midwife. The petition tried to convince the physicians that "these Children . . . were distinct Beings, . . . and were equally entitled to Preservation with their Mothers" (4-5).

11. Mary Poovey argues that the trimester scheme for viability used in *Roe* produces a tripartite division in authority over a pregnancy: pregnant women have choices in the first trimester, physicians make decisions about the second trimester, and courts regulate the third trimester. Poovey points out that both pregnant women and fetuses challenge the notion of the humanist subject, pregnant women because they are not unitary, and fetuses because they are not self-determining: Poovey, "Feminism and Postmodernism—Another View," *boundary* 2 19, no. 2 (1992): 34-52. See Dawn E. Johnsen, "The Creation of Fetal Rights: Conflicts with Women's Constitutional Rights to Liberty, Privacy, and Equal Protection," *Yale Law Journal* 95 (1986): 599-625; and Johnsen, "Maternal Rights and Fetal Wrongs: The Case against the Criminalization of 'Fetal Abuse,'" *Harvard Law Review* 101 (March 1988): 994-1012, for arguments against the idea of fetal rights. Johnsen points out that criminalizing substance use by pregnant women only hinders them from seeking drug treatment and from getting prenatal care because they fear prosecution. For the most cogent argument on the other side, see John A. Robertson, "Procreative Liberty and the Control of Conception, Pregnancy, and Childbirth," *Virginia Law Review* 69 (April 1983): 405-64. Robertson assumes that all pregnancies carried to term include the free choice to be and to remain pregnant.

For discussions of the personhood status of the fetus from medical, legal, theological, and philosophical points of view, see several articles in *Abortion and the Status of the Fetus*, ed. William B. Bondeson, H. Tristram Engelhardt Jr., Stuart F. Spicker, and Daniel H. Winship (Dordrecht, The Netherlands: D. Reidel, 1983): Leonard Glantz, "Is the Fetus a Person? A Lawyer's View," 107-17; Patricia D. White, "The Concept of Person, the Law, and the Use of the Fetus in Biomedicine," 119-57; Gerald D. Perkoff, "Toward a Normative Definition of Personhood," 159-66; H. Tristram Engelhardt Jr., "Viability and the Use of the Fetus," 183-208; and Caroline Whitbeck, "The Moral Implications of Regarding Women as People: New Perspectives on Pregnancy and Personhood," 242-72. Whitbeck's essay is the only one in the collection that focuses on the experiences and situations of pregnant women. She argues that the maternal-fetal relationship has been "inadequately conceptualized."

A broad discussion of the issues implicated by prenatal technologies and knowledge can be found in Ruth Hubbard, *The Politics of Women's Biology* (New Brunswick, N.J.: Rutgers University Press, 1990), 141-98. Physicians, too, define the maternal-fetal relation as adversarial, in one textbook referring to the possibility that "the intrauterine environment is hostile": Leo R. Boler Jr. and Norbert Gleicher, "Maternal versus Fetal Rights," *Principles of Medical Therapy in Pregnancy*, ed. Norbert Gleicher (New York: Plenum Press, 1985), 141. The authors refer to "a precarious medicolegal situation" and conclude that "it remains to be determined whether fetal indications allow infringement on maternal rights." See also W.A. Bowes Jr. and D. Selgestad, "Fetal versus Maternal Rights: Medical and Legal Perspectives," *Obstetrics and Gynecology* 58 (1981): 209-14.

12. See *Medieval Woman's Guide to Health: The First English Gynecological Handbook*, ed. Beryl Rowland (Kent, Ohio: Kent State University Press, 1981); and John F. Benton, "Trotula, Women's Problems, and the Professionalization of Medicine in the Middle Ages," *Bulletin of the History of Medicine* 59 (spring 1985): 30-53. An excellent account of early modern beliefs can be found in Patricia Crawford, "Attitudes to Menstruation in Seventeenth-Century England," *Past and Present* 91 (1981): 47-73.

13. Robert W. Fogel, "Nutrition and the Decline in Mortality since 1700: Some Additional Preliminary Findings," Working Paper 1802 (National Bureau of Economic Research, 1986), 68-69. It is clear from this figure, and from much of the imaginative literature of the seventeenth and eighteenth centuries, as well as from evidence concerning popular entertainments, that drunkenness was relatively routine. By the mid-eighteenth century, concern had mounted about the effects on infants of their mothers' excessive drinking during pregnancy. See Alvin E. Rodin, "Infants and Gin Mania in Eighteenth-Century London," *Journal of the American Medical Association*, 27 March 1981, 1237-39. Also see Michael K. Eshleman, "Diet during Pregnancy in the Sixteenth and Seventeenth Centuries," *Journal of the History of Medicine* 30 (1975): 23-39. I am indebted here to Linda A. Pollock's excellent overview of pregnancy among the landed elite in England in "Embarking on a Rough Passage: The Experience of Pregnancy in Early-Modern Society," in *Women as Mothers in Pre-Industrial England*, ed. Valerie Fildes (London: Routledge and Kegan Paul, 1990), 39-67. Advice concerning diet differs markedly from culture to culture, and it varies significantly by classes, nations, and ethnic groups.

14. Prosecutions of pregnant women in early modern Europe were confined to those who conceived out of wedlock. See Patricia Crawford, "The Construction and Experience of Maternity," in *Women as Mothers in Pre-Industrial England*, esp. 9-10. The rate of prosecutions for prenuptial pregnancy varied. In addition, laws concerning bastards made unwed motherhood extremely difficult. An illegitimate child could not inherit property, and poor women had few means to force their children's fathers to marry them. Adultery and fornication were also prosecutable offenses. Ellen Fitzpatrick discusses one case of attitudes toward, and treatment of, unwed mothers in America in "Childbirth and an Unwed Mother in Seventeenth-Century New England," *Signs* 8 (summer 1983): 744-49. For historical discussions of prosecuting pregnant women in France, see June K. Burton, "Human Rights Issues Affecting

Women in Napoleonic Legal Medicine Textbooks," *History of European Ideas* 8, no. 4 (1987): 427-34; and Adrienne Rogers, "Women and the Law," in *French Women and the Age of Enlightenment*, ed. Samia Spencer (Bloomington: Indiana University Press, 1984): 33-48. It is important to note that throughout the eighteenth century, western Europeans believed that female orgasm was required for conception. If she became pregnant, then, a woman was in no position to claim rape because pleasure was seen as implying consent. Changes in these views, and changes in views of female sexual pleasure more generally, are traced for North America in Carl N. Degler, "What Ought to Be and What Was: Women's Sexuality in the Nineteenth Century," *American Historical Review* 79 (1974): 1467-90.

15. *Dietrich v. Northampton*, 138 Mass. 14, 52 (1884); *Bonbrest v. Katz*, 65 F. Supp. 138, 140 (D.D.C. 1946). See Tracy Dobson and Kimberly K. Eby, "Criminal Liability for Substance Abuse during Pregnancy: The Controversy of Maternal v. Fetal Rights," *Saint Louis University Law Journal* 36 (spring 1992): 655-94. Leonard Glantz writes, "Although the law rarely lends itself to blanket statements, it can be clearly stated that a fetus is not a person under the law. . . . [F]etuses are not required to be protected": "Is the Fetus a Person?" in *Abortion and the Status of the Fetus*, 116.

16. Lynn M. Paltrow, "No: 'Fetal Abuse': Should We Recognize It as a Crime?" *ABA Journal*, August 1989, 39. See also Paltrow, "When Becoming Pregnant is a Crime," *Criminal Justice Ethics* 9 (winter/spring 1990): 41-47. This issue is a symposium on "Criminal Liability for Fetal Endangerment." It is important to mention that controversy continues over the precise effects of maternal cocaine use on a gestating fetus. It is difficult to single out intrauterine cocaine exposure as a factor in fetal development, because often prenatal cocaine exposure is only one of a number of factors—poor nutrition, lead poisoning, cigarettes, other drugs, as well as multiple short-term foster placements, homelessness, abuse, and the like—determining outcomes such as low birth weight or early cognitive deficits. See Linda C. Mayes, Richard H. Granger, Marc H. Bornstein, and Barry Zuckerman, "The Problem of Prenatal Cocaine Exposure: A Rush to Judgment," *Journal of the American Medical Association*, 15 January 1992, 406-8. The authors argue that factors such as methodologic problems in determining the developmental effects of cocaine use during pregnancy, and bias in clinical decisions about reporting low-income and African-American women for drug use, make it difficult to assess the problem and label a large group of children as "irremediably damaged" (408). Such factors also "work toward exempting society from having to face other possible explanations of the children's plight—explanations such as poverty, community violence, inadequate education, and dimin- ishing employment opportunities that require deeper understanding of wider social values" (408). Physicians have remarked on external factors affecting fetal growth such as socioeconomic conditions and tobacco smoking. See Donald B. Cheek, Joan E. Graystone, and Margaret Niall, "Factors Controlling Fetal Growth," *Clinical Obstetrics and Gynecology* 20 (December 1977): 925-42.

17. See Barbara Duden, *The Woman beneath the Skin: A Doctor's Patients in Eighteenth-Century Germany*, trans. Thomas Dunlap (Cambridge: Harvard University Press, 1991); and Ludmilla Jordanova, "Guarding the Body Politic: Volney's Catechism of 1793," in *1789: Reading, Writing, Revolution*, proceedings of the Essex

Conference on the Sociology of Literature, ed. Francis Barker et al. (Essex, 1982), 12-21.

18. For one view of how mechanistic ideas of physiology operated in eighteenth-century literature, see Juliet McMaster, "The Body inside the Skin: The Medical Model of Character in the Eighteenth-Century Novel," *Eighteenth-Century Fiction* 4 (July 1992): 277-300.

19. On Jonathan Swift's deployment of this idea, see Susan Bruce, "The Flying Island and Female Anatomy: Gynaecology and Power in *Gulliver's Travels*," *Genders* 2 (summer 1988): 60-76.

20. See Mary Poovey, *Uneven Developments: The Ideological Work of Gender in Mid-Victorian England* (Chicago: University of Chicago Press, 1988), 9-10.

21. Daniel Turner, *De Morbis Cutaneis* (London: R. Bonwicke et al., 1714), 102-28, 105. Further references will be given parenthetically in the text.

22. James Augustus Blondel, preface to *The Strength of Imagination in Pregnant Women* (London: J. Peele, 1727). Further references will be given parenthetically in the text. Both Barbara Maria Stafford, in *Body Criticism: Imaging the Unseen in Enlightenment Art and Medicine* (Cambridge: MIT Press, 1991), 314-15, and Marie-Hélène Huet, in *Monstrous Imagination* (Cambridge: Harvard University Press, 1993), 64-67, take up this debate. Huet's suggestive and useful book focuses on resemblance and representation, as does Stafford's visual iconography. See also Philip K. Wilson, "Out of Sight, Out of Mind? The Daniel Turner–James Blondel Debate over Maternal Impressions," M.A. thesis, Johns Hopkins University, 1987.

23. Curiously, an obstetrics textbook first published in 1908 discussed cravings in a very different way. They were taken seriously, even noted as a possible sign of preeclampsia. This text granted that cravings were a common feature of many pregnancies, but it also suggested that such cravings are "deleterious" and that pregnant women must exercise self-control in order to overcome their desires. This text later asserted, "Reproduction is the test of a nervous woman, and should she be in any way mentally or physically weak, her brain may give way under the trial": Ernest Hastings Tweedy, *Tweedy's Practical Obstetrics*, 6th ed., ed. Bethel Solomons (London: Oxford University Press, 1929), 218, 496.

24. Nicholas de Malebranche, *The Search after Truth*, trans. Thomas M. Lennon and Paul J. Olscamp (Columbus: Ohio State University Press, 1980), 117. See Huet, *Monstrous Imagination*, 48-49. Stafford also connects epidermal stains with Original Sin in *Body Criticism*, 318.

25. *Aristotle's Compleat and Experienc'd Midwife*, 4th ed. (London: by the booksellers, 1721). This work was an anonymous and popular version of Aristotle's *De generatione et corruptione* and was continuously in print into the 1930s in Great Britain. See Paul-Gabriel Boucé, "Imagination, Pregnant Women, and Monsters in Eighteenth-Century England and France," in *Sexual Underworlds of the Enlightenment*, ed. G.S. Rousseau and Roy Porter (Chapel Hill: University of North Carolina Press, 1988), 86-100.

26. John Maubray, *The Female Physician* (London: James Holland, 1724), 75-77. Maubray was considered a mystic and not taken seriously by medical practitioners. Cited in Dolores Peters, "The Pregnant Pamela: Characterization and Popular

Medical Attitudes in the Eighteenth Century," *Eighteenth-Century Studies* 14 (summer 1981): 437.

27. This example is cited by McLaren in *Reproductive Rituals*, 40. See also Jacques Gélis, in *History of Childbirth: Fertility, Pregnancy, and Birth in Early Modern Europe*, trans. Rosemary Morris (Boston: Northeastern University Press, 1991), 53-58; originally published as *L'Arbre et le fruit* (Paris: Fayard, 1984), which gives an overview of ideas about cravings and imaginings.

28. This event became a major popular scandal in England, particularly for John Howard, the physician who claimed to have delivered the rabbits, and for Nathaniel St. André and Samuel Molyneux, who traveled to Guildford to ascertain the veracity of the reports. St. André was the royal physician, and when the hoax was exposed, he lost his job and ended his life in poverty. For a discussion of the Mary Tofts story, see S.A. Seligman, "Mary Tofts: The Rabbit Breeder," *Medical History* 5 (1961): 349-60; and Glennda Leslie, "Cheat and Imposter: Debate Following the Case of the Rabbit Breeder," *The Eighteenth Century: Theory and Interpretation* 27 (fall 1986): 269-86.

29. *Gentleman's Magazine* 16 (1746): 270. Cited by Roy Porter, "Lay Medical Knowledge in the Eighteenth Century: The Evidence of the *Gentleman's Magazine*," *Medical History* 29 (1985): 148. The best places to seek case examples of birth malformations ascribed to the maternal imagination are in the casebooks of practicing midwives and obstetricians. Two studies that use these sources are Amalie M. Kass, "The Obstetrical Casebook of Walter Channing, 1811-1822," *Bulletin of the History of Medicine* 67 (fall 1993): 494-523; and Barbara Duden, *The Woman beneath the Skin*, although neither Kass nor Duden focuses on the maternal imagination.

30. For useful background, see Keith Thomas, *Religion and the Decline of Magic* (New York: Scribner, 1971).

31. See Lynne Tatlock, "Speculum Feminarum: Gendered Perspectives on Obstetrics and Gynecology in Early Modern Germany," *Signs* 17 (summer 1992): 725-60.

32. Ohaloth 7.6. Cited by L.E. Goodman, "The Fetus as a Natural Miracle: The Maimonidean View," in *The Human Embryo: Aristotle and the Arabic and European Traditions*, ed. G.R. Dunstan (Exeter: University of Exeter Press, 1990), 88.

33. The Ayurvedic views on embryology also include the notion that children's deformities can be the result of parental sin in this or a previous life. For a discussion, see Vaidya Bhagwan Dash, *Embryology and Maternity in Ayurveda* (New Delhi: Delhi Diary, 1975). See also Lakshmi Kapani, trans., "Upanisad of the Embryo" and Kapani, "Note on the Garbha-Upanisad," in *Fragments for a History of the Human Body*, vol. 3, ed. Michael Feher (Cambridge: MIT Press, 1989), 175-96.

34. See L.D. Hankoff and Ultamchandra L. Munver, "Prenatal Experience in Hindu Mythology," *New York State Journal of Medicine* 80 (December 1988): 2006-14.

35. Genesis 30:31-43, Revised Standard Version.

36. See *Rovinsky and Guttmacher's Medical, Surgical, and Gynecologic Complications of Pregnancy*, 3d ed., ed. Sheldon H. Cherry, Richard L. Berkowitz, and Nathan G. Case (Baltimore: Williams and Wilkins, 1985), which alleges that preg-

nant women act out their conflicts through food: "Examples of cravings are ice cream, and the situation where a woman wakes her husband up in the middle of the night in winter asking for strawberries" (623).

37. Henry Bracken, *The Midwife's Companion; or, A Treatise of Midwifery* (London: J. Clarke, 1737), 40-41.

38. Isaac Bellet, *Lettres sur le pouvoir de l'imagination des femmes enceintes* (Paris: Frères Guérin, 1745), 3.

39. Martha Mears, *The Pupil of Nature; or, Candid Advice to the Fair Sex* (London: privately printed, 1797), 27-28.

40. See Jean Rostand, *La Formation de l'être: Histoire des idées sur la génération* (Paris: Librairie Hachette, 1930).

41. Cited in Joseph Needham, *A History of Embryology* (New York: Abelard-Schuman, 1959), 200; and in Andrea Henderson, "Doll-Machines and Butcher-Shop Meat: Models of Childbirth in the Early Stages of Industrial Capitalism," *Genders* 12 (winter 1991): 100-119, 113. Marie-Hélène Huet points out that the encasement theory "should have excluded the possibility that the maternal imagination could modify the shape of a progeny that had already been formed since the beginning of time": *Monstrous Imagination*, 42.

42. See Needham, *A History of Embryology*, 215-16. See also Shirley A. Roe, *Matter, Life, and Generation: Eighteenth-Century Embryology and the Haller-Woolf Debate* (Cambridge: Cambridge University Press, 1981); Josef Warkany, "Congenital Malformations in the Past," *Journal of Chronic Diseases* 10 (1959): 84-96; F.C. Fraser, "Causes of Congenital Malformations in Human Beings," *Journal of Chronic Diseases* 10 (1959): 97-110; and F.C. Frigoletto Jr. and Suzanne B. Rothchild, "Altered Fetal Growth: An Overview," *Clinical Obstetrics and Gynecology* 20, no. 4 (1977): 915-23.

43. See Marie-Hélène Huet, "Monstrous Imagination: Progeny as Art in French Classicism," *Critical Inquiry* 17 (summer 1991): 718-37. Jean-Baptiste Bérard argued that fetal development took place entirely "à l'insu" of the mother's will and therefore could not be affected by the imagination or the living conditions of a pregnant woman. For proof, he recorded these statistics for 1821: 9,178 of 21,158 infants born in Paris were illegitimate, but none of them were monsters, despite the terrible conditions their mothers had endured during their pregnancies: Bérard, *Causes de la monstruosité et autres anomalies de l'organisation humaine* (Paris: Didot le Jeune, 1835), 7.

44. Katha Pollitt writes about the legacy of blaming women for a host of ills in "Subject to Debate," *Nation*, 30 May 1994, a column that discusses welfare, poverty, and motherhood.

45. Cited in Reva Siegel, "Reasoning from the Body: A Historical Perspective on Abortion Regulation and Questions of Equal Protection," *Stanford Law Review* 44, no. 2 (1992): 301.

46. Ibid., 296. This comprehensive analysis of the nineteenth-century campaign against abortion and its importance for the history and current state of reproductive law fills in many of the gaps in my inquiry between eighteenth-century understandings

of pregnancy and the move in the late twentieth century to criminalize the behavior of pregnant women. I am grateful to Reva Siegel for bringing her work to my attention. For a historical look at reproductive circumstances in the nineteenth century, see Janet Farrell Brodie, *Contraception and Abortion in Nineteenth-Century America* (Ithaca, N.Y.: Cornell University Press, 1994).

47. Siegel, "Reasoning from the Body," 72.

48. Katha Pollitt, "'Fetal Rights': A New Assault on Feminism," *Nation*, 26 March 1990, 410.

49. Carol E. Tracy, "Help the Women Drug Users," *Philadelphia Inquirer*, 14 September 1990, sec. A, p. 21. In ironic contrast to the situation Tracy describes, a hospital program at the Medical University of South Carolina in Charleston allegedly used threats of public exposure and of jail to force pregnant women into drug treatment. In February 1994, the Office of Civil Rights of the U.S. Department of Health and Human Services initiated an investigation into whether the South Carolina program is discriminatory, because most of the women tested for drugs or jailed are African-American. See Philip J. Hilts, "Hospital Is Object of Rights Inquiry: Blacks Make Up Majority of Pregnant Women Tested for Drugs and Coerced," *New York Times*, 6 February 1994, sec. A, p. 29. In January 1993, the Philadelphia Commission on Human Relations and the Women's Law Project held a public hearing to investigate drug treatment programs in Philadelphia that were denying their services to pregnant women. Many drug treatment programs consider pregnant women too high risk to treat because the programs do not have obstetricians on staff or because they believe they cannot handle miscarriages or other emergencies. See Fawn Vrazo, "Some Drug Programs Wary of Pregnant Women," *Philadelphia Inquirer*, 11 January 1994, sec. B, pp. 1-2.

50. Brian McCormick, "Drug Trafficking Conviction Overturned in Cocaine-Baby Case," *American Medical News*, 10 August 1992, p. 11.

51. James F. Drane, "Medical Ethics and Maternal-Fetal Conflicts," *Pennsylvania Medicine* 95 (July 1992): 12-16. The Committee on Bioethics of the American Academy of Pediatrics advises physicians to honor a woman's refusal of fetal procedures, unless the fetus will suffer irrevocable harm without them, the treatment is clearly indicated and likely to be effective, and the risk to the pregnant woman is low. If the woman refuses despite these conditions, the Committee recommends consultation with a hospital ethics committee and turning to courts only as a last resort. See American Academy of Pediatrics Committee on Bioethics, "Fetal Therapy: Ethical Considerations," *Pediatrics* 81, no. 6 (1988): 898-99.

52. *General Electric Co. v. Gilbert*, 429 U.S. 125, 160 (1976). Paraphrased in Caroline Whitbeck, "The Moral Implications of Regarding Women as People," in *Abortion and the Status of the Fetus*, 263.

53. Wendy Chavkin, "Mandatory Treatment for Drug Use during Pregnancy," *Journal of the American Medical Association*, 18 September 1991, 1556-61. Chavkin argues that mandating treatment furthers discrimination against poor minority women, and she cites Veronika Kolder, Janet Gallagher, and Michael Parsons, "Court-Ordered Obstetrical Interventions," *New England Journal of Medicine* 316 (1987): 1192-96. In this 1986 study of court-ordered cesarean sections, 81 percent involved minority

women, 24 percent involved women who did not speak English, and all involved clinic patients. The survey represented women from forty-five states and the District of Columbia who had refused therapy deemed necessary for their fetuses. The data spanned statistics for 1981-86, and the sample included white, Asian, and African-American women.

The study revealed that in Florida, the rate of drug use reporting among pregnant women was ten times higher for African-American women than for white women. Instead of reporting and prosecuting pregnant women who use drugs, Chavkin argues, we need to enhance drug treatment programs so that they welcome pregnant women, serve their needs, and are readily available. As long as such programs are scarce and of poor quality, debates about mandating them remain merely symbolic. Chavkin points out that the American Medical Association and the American College of Obstetricians and Gynecologists oppose court-ordered treatment or penalties for the behaviors of pregnant women. See AMA Board of Trustees Report, "Legal Interventions during Pregnancy: Court-Ordered Medical Treatments and Legal Penalties for Potentially Harmful Behavior by Pregnant Women," *Journal of the American Medical Association*, 28 November 1990, 2663-70, and American College of Obstetricians and Gynecologists Statement, "Patient Choice: Maternal-Fetal Conflict," *Women's Health Issues* 1 (fall 1990): 13-15. See also Wendy Chavkin, "Drug Addiction and Pregnancy: Policy Crossroads," *American Journal of Public Health* 80 (1990): 483-87; Lynn Paltrow, *Case Overview of Arguments against Permitting Forced Surgery, Prosecution of Pregnant Women or Civil Sanctions against Them for Conduct during Pregnancy* (New York: ACLU Reproductive Freedom Project, 1989); M. McNulty, "Pregnancy Police: The Health Policy and Legal Implications of Punishing Pregnant Women for Harm to Their Fetuses," *Review of Law and Social Change* 16 (1987/88): 277-319; and W.K. Mariner, L.H. Glantz, and G.J. Arnes, "Pregnancy, Drugs, and the Perils of Prosecution," *Criminal Justice Ethics* 9, no. 1 (1990): 30-41.

54. See Robert H. Blank, "Emerging Notions of Women's Rights and Responsibilities during Gestation," *Journal of Legal Medicine* 7, no. 4 (1986): 441-69; and Margery W. Shaw, "Genetically Defective Children: Emerging Legal Considerations," *American Journal of Law and Medicine* 3, no. 3 (1977): 333-40. See also Iris Marion Young, "Punishment, Treatment, Empowerment: Three Approaches to Policy for Pregnant Addicts," *Feminist Studies* 20 (spring 1994): 33-57, an article that applies psychoanalytic ideas to formulate "a feminist ethic of care."

55. My focus is on only one aspect of the complicated politics of reproductive change in the late twentieth century: the criminalization of the social conduct of pregnant women. Cases in which courts have forced a pregnant woman to have a cesarean section raise some of the same issues of criminalization and adversarial definitions of mother and fetus (as they also did in the eighteenth century). See Mary Sue Henifin, Ruth Hubbard, and Judy Norsigian, "Prenatal Screening," and Janet Gallagher, "Fetus as Patient," both in *Reproductive Laws for the 1990s*, ed. Sherrill Cohen and Nadine Taub (Clifton, N.J.: Humana Press, 1989), 155-83, 185-235. For an overview of the legal and ethical issues surrounding new reproductive technologies, see Robert H. Blank, *Regulating Reproduction* (New York: Columbia University Press, 1990); Sarah Franklin, "Postmodern Procreation: A Cultural Account of

136   *Julia Epstein*

Assisted Reproduction," in *Conceiving the New World Order: The Global Politics of Reproduction*, ed. Faye D. Ginsburg and Rayna Rapp (Berkeley: University of California Press, 1995): 323-45; Michelle Stanworth, "Birth Pangs: Conceptive Technologies and the Threat to Motherhood," in *Conflicts in Feminism*, ed. Marianne Hirsch and Evelyn Fox Keller (New York: Routledge, 1990): 288-304.

56. In this treatment, the pregnant woman is a medium or vehicle rather than an owner of property in herself. See Judith Roof, "The Ideology of Fair Use: Xeroxing and Reproductive Rights," *Hypatia* 7 (spring 1992): 63-73; and Dawn Johnsen, "From Driving to Drugs: Governmental Regulation of Pregnant Women's Lives and *Webster*," *University of Pennsylvania Law Review* 138 (1989): 179-215.

57. *Stallman v. Youngquist*, 531 N.E. 2d 355 (Ill. 1988). Two issues were on appeal: parental immunity doctrine and the tort liability of mothers. The court's conclusion is significant: "Judicial scrutiny into the day-to-day lives of pregnant women would involve an unprecedented intrusion into the privacy and autonomy of the citizens of this State" (361). Cited and discussed in Robin M. Trindel, "Fetal Interests vs. Maternal Rights: Is the State Going Too Far?" *Akron Law Review* 24 (spring 1991): 743-62.

58. Janet Gallagher, "Prenatal Invasions and Interventions: What's Wrong with Fetal Rights," *Harvard Women's Law Journal* 10 (spring 1987): 57-58. The view Gallagher critiques has been extended to include all women of childbearing age as potentially pregnant, a view that underlies employer-enforced "fetal protection" policies that exclude women from certain jobs. The best known of these recent cases was heard by the U.S. Supreme Court. See *United Auto Workers v. Johnson Controls, Inc.*, 111 S. Ct. 1196 (1991). The Supreme Court ruled for the women, but in an earlier hearing by the Seventh Circuit, Judge John L. Coffey remarked, "This is the case about the women who want to hurt their fetuses." This remark is cited by David L. Kirp in "The Pitfalls of 'Fetal Protection,'" *Society* 28 (March/April 1991): 70. For a full discussion of exclusionary employment policies, see Sally J. Kenney, *For Whose Protection? Reproductive Hazards and Exclusionary Policies in the United States and Britain* (Ann Arbor: University of Michigan Press, 1992). Susan Faludi remarks that no one has tried to prevent women from working at video display terminals, or in day care centers where they are at risk for cytomegalovirus, in "Your Womb or Your Job," *Mother Jones* 16 (November/December 1991): 59-66, 71. See also Elaine Draper, "Fetal Exclusion Policies and Gendered Constructions of Suitable Work," *Social Problems* 40, no. 1 (1993): 90-107; and Lucinda M. Finley, "Transcending Equality Theory: A Way Out of the Maternity and the Workplace Debate," *Columbia Law Review* 86 (1986): 1118-82. Also note that little attention has been paid to the effect of workplace toxins on fathers, despite evidence that men exposed to toxic chemicals can pass birth malformations on to their children. See Ricardo A. Yazigi, Randall R. Odem, and Kenneth Polakoski, "Demonstration of Specific Binding of Cocaine to Human Spermatozoa," *Journal of the American Medical Association*, 9 October 1991, 1956-59. In addition, sperm production in the average male has declined dramatically over the last fifty years, and the reasons appear to be environmental rather than genetic. See Michael Zimmerman, "Working with Chemicals Is a Threat to Fathers," *Philadelphia Inquirer*, 2 May 1993, sec. D, p. 5.

59. *Griswold v. Connecticut*, 381 U.S. 479 (1965) invalidated statutes banning contraception. The idea of holding rights to "property in one's own person" and to bodily self-determination in relation to women's bodies as the media for pregnancies is asserted by Rosalind Pollack Petchesky in "Reproductive Freedom: Beyond 'A Woman's Right to Choose,'" *Signs* 5, no. 4 (1980): 661-85. A recent discussion of privacy law in relation to abortion rights can be found in David J. Garrow, *Liberty and Sexuality: The Right to Privacy and the Making of* Roe v. Wade (New York: Macmillan, 1994). See also Iris Marion Young, "Pregnant Embodiment: Subjectivity and Alienation," *Journal of Medicine and Philosophy* 9 (February 1984): 45-62.

60. *Eisenstadt v. Baird*, 405 U.S. 438, 453 (1972).

61. It is important to maintain distinctions between the constitutional right to privacy, decisional privacy, and tort privacy. For example, Justice Harry Blackmun has been criticized for his failure "to distinguish carefully the physical privacy of seclusion from the decisional privacy of liberty or autonomous choice," when he stated in Roe that "a pregnant woman cannot be isolated in her privacy." See Anita L. Allen, "Tribe's Judicious Feminism," *Stanford Law Review* 44, no. 1 (1991): 187. The political elasticity of the word *right* became clear at the September 1994 United Nations conference on population held in Cairo, during which time United States and European officials made efforts to appease Vatican and Islamic concerns over the language discussing abortion. In a masterly effort at noncommittal speech, Timothy E. Wirth, U.S. undersecretary of state for global affairs, remarked, "The question of 'right' has been a controversial issue. Some people had interpreted the use of the word *right* in the document as establishing an understood right as in the U.N. Declaration of Human Rights, and there is a language that is being proposed by the European Union to define what is meant by *right*." See Alan Cowell, "A Try at a Truce over Population," *New York Times*, 15 September 1994, sec. A, p. 1. The concept remains ideologically if not legally slippery.

62. Christyne L. Neff, "Woman, Womb, and Bodily Integrity," *Yale Journal of Law and Feminism* 3 (spring 1991): 351. See also Petchesky, "Reproductive Freedom"; Katherine De Gama, "A Brave New World? Rights Discourse and the Politics of Reproductive Anatomy," *Journal of Law and Society* 20 (spring 1993): 114-30.

63. Linda C. McClain argues that privacy rights are tied to an imagery of sanctuary and refuge in "Inviolability and Privacy: The Castle, the Temple, and the Body," *Yale Journal of Law and the Humanities* 7 (winter 1995): 195. I am grateful to Professor McClain for sharing her work with me.

64. François Mauriceau, *The Diseases of Women with Child and in Child-bed*, trans. Hugh Chamberlen (London: John Darby, 1683), 58, 65; Kirp, "Pitfalls," 76.

"A Point of Conscience"

Breastfeeding and Maternal Authority in *Pamela*, Part 2

> *Could you ever have thought, Miss, that Husbands have a Dispensing*
> *Power over their Wives, which Kings are not allowed over the Law? . . .*
> *Did you ever hear of such a Notion before, Miss? Of such a Prerogative*
> *in a Husband? Would you care to subscribe to it?*
> — *Pamela to Miss Darnford*

Pamela's outraged description of her husband's domestic tyranny signals the onset of the first conflict in her married life and introduces the reader to a crucial episode in the sequel to Richardson's phenomenally popular first novel. Part 1 of *Pamela* (1740) had been occupied with the violent sexual pursuit of a young servant girl by her wealthy and more experienced master; that pursuit ended, disturbingly for some readers, with the sudden repentance of the master, Mr. B., who condescends at last to marry the girl he had hoped to rape. Part 2 (1741) follows Pamela and Mr. B. into their married life.

What this means for the heroine is that the continuation is largely a record of maternal experience: Pamela is pregnant throughout the sequel (seven times in all), adopts an illegitimate daughter of B.'s from a former liaison, and gives considerable attention in her correspondence to the care and education of her children. Pamela's impassioned complaint to Miss Darnford is also occasioned by her motherhood: she and Mr. B. have disagreed over whether Pamela should breastfeed their first child herself, as she believes is her Christian duty, or hire a wet nurse, as Mr. B. insists. The episode carries significant narrative weight in *Pamela* 2. Pamela recounts each argument between herself and Mr. B. in detail, adding her own ruminations and soliciting the advice of various correspondents.

Despite all this palaver, it is hardly surprising to readers familiar with Part 1 when Mr. B.'s tyrannical "prerogative" wins the day, and baby Billy is placed in the hands of a wet nurse. What does seem odd, however, is the dissonance between the inevitable subordination of Pamela's desires to her husband's and the language that the text uses to represent it. Despite the fact that Mr. B. eventually prevails, Pamela's arguments for maternal breastfeeding are represented as powerful and persuasive. All correspondents except Mr. B. agree that maternal breastfeeding is clearly preferable to wet-nursing, all things being equal; and Mr. B.'s arguments, as we shall see, are deliberately cast as unconvincing and poorly motivated. So clearly does the text valorize Pamela's position, in fact, that the dispute over maternal breastfeeding comes to seem only superficially about the matters ostensibly being debated: the relative merits of mother's and nurse's milk, the practical aspects of maternal breastfeeding (the physical and emotional commitment, the investment of time), and so on. Instead, the struggle to determine whether Pamela should breastfeed is a struggle to define the relative authority of husband and wife over maternal behavior and the status of maternal subjectivity within marriage. Fundamentally, what is being contested between Pamela and Mr. B. is the source of authority over a mother's body.

The vigorous arguments of a generation of conduct books and the increasing enclosure of women in domestic space were finally, by the 1740s, convincing many parents that maternal breastfeeding was preferable to hiring the services of a nurse.[1] In Pamela's central voice, *Pamela* 2 powerfully repeats those arguments, presenting an all-but-watertight case for the dramatic benefits of maternal nursing. Mr. B., on the other hand, mouths stereotypical aristocratic attitudes toward motherhood, attitudes that Augustan conduct literature routinely, even ritualistically, disparaged.[2] The novel sets up a paradigmatic encounter between traditional, patriarchal authority—represented by Mr. B.—and the new authority of conduct literature, a reasoned discourse based (supposedly) on objective observation and predicated on the idea that correct behavior may be defined communally. By teaching objectively correct female behaviors, especially maternal breastfeeding, conduct literature provided a rival source of authority from which wives like Pamela might potentially resist their husbands' commands.

In the end, of course, *Pamela* 2 enforces Mr. B.'s position of authority and so works to curtail the growing influence of conduct literature and to reassert the autocratic rights of individual fathers. But because it represents Mr. B.'s commands as logically flawed and politically suspect, the novel undercuts its own efforts to contain the potential subversiveness of Augustan conduct writers' advice to mothers. The effort to teach wives to obey their husbands even when husbands are wrong backfires, to an extent, as the patently incorrect Mr. B. is obeyed against reason and religion, merely because of his position as husband. As Pamela herself is quick to note, the patriarchal family that *Pamela* 2 defends turns out to be very like the autocratic kingship that England had publicly rejected half a century before.

Pamela 2 sets itself up as a corrective to conduct literature not only politically but aesthetically. Though primarily a didactic work, it sets moral lessons into motion, as it were, making entertainment of material that Augustan conduct books typically delivered in more direct, and even less palatable, forms. Ironically, Richardson's effort to revise conduct writing along novelistic lines is rather too successful for its own good. The "novelization" of didacticism is just convincing enough to invite critical judgments of the work as a novel, but it is not sufficient to make it seem a very good one.

For this reason, *Pamela*, Part 2 has achieved virtually unanimous critical contempt[3] as its readers have looked in vain for the linear structure that most critics still believe must define a good novel.[4] Even the most acute tend to throw their hands up in frustration as the sequel moves with apparent aimlessness from one illustrative vignette to another, tracing Pamela's dilemmas as wife and mother, inculcating lessons and drawing morals. The problem, according to Terry Castle, is that *Pamela* 2 "lacks a unifying plot; nothing 'happens' in it. Plot, character, incident—all fail to produce a satisfying, coherent narrative." Accordingly, most readers have found the text to be, as Castle puts it, "more than a disappointment. At times it seems almost to insult us, to affront our expectations. . . . For the most part, Richardson's sequel is more than just plotless. It is an assault . . . on plot itself."[5]

But from the perspective I am adopting, *Pamela* 2 looks much less like a failed novel than like a fascinating conduct book. Its structure reflects the diffuse, even disjointed, world of domestic detail and daily routine; the episodic nature of the antiplot nicely serves Richardson's didactic purposes. Under this rubric, it makes sense that instead of offering an original story, Richardson's oddly amphibious text dramatizes (and, to an extent, revises) familiar moral instructions and norms for female virtue, norms already coded for eighteenth-century readers of conduct literature as classless and universal, but presented here by means of what Castle rightly calls "a thinly disguised paean to bourgeois values."[6] So although *Pamela* 2 may look like a novel, it doesn't work like one. Instead, the text functions as a generic anomaly, what we might call a "conduct novel."[7] Richardson puts the traditions of conduct literature to work, giving form and voice to the perfect woman whom didactic writers were so eager to define. "What a bewitching Girl art thou!" Lady Davers cries to Pamela in Letter 19. "What an Exemplar to Wives now, as well as thou wast before to Maidens!" (3:104). The Pamela of Part 2 is female virtue personified, the paradigmatic and impossible bourgeois woman brought to life from the sketches of conduct writing, and worthy, as Richardson himself famously put it, "of the Imitation of her Sex, from low to high life."

In particular, Pamela demonstrates the attributes of her culture's vision of a perfect wife and mother. The two duties are, of course, intimately connected. When Lady Davers describes for Pamela the behaviors that will be expected of her as Mr. B.'s wife, she emphasizes the requirement that Pamela produce "a Succession of brave Boys, to perpetuate a Family . . . which . . . *expects* it from you" (3:41-42). Without this, Lady Davers freely informs Pamela, all the rest of her famous virtues will mean nothing, and Mr. B. "by descending to the wholesome Cot . . . will want one Apology for his conduct, be as excellent as you may" (3:42). Pamela's motherhood is the *sine qua non* upon which depend all the rest—her social position, her marital happiness, the continued recognition of her virtue, and its concomitant rewards.

Pamela would not have had to look far for advice on how to be a good mother. At least since the publication in 1673 of Richard Allestree's *The Ladies Calling*, conduct literature had been energetic in its efforts to dictate specific standards for maternal behavior, standards that continue today to influence Anglo-American maternal ideals. Allestree's supremely influential work[8] defined "the office and duty of a Mother" in detail, outlining what would, over the course of the next generation, become standard prescriptions for maternal excellence: feelings of peculiar and overwhelming "tenderness" toward one's children, constant personal care and attendance on them "through the several Stages of Infancy, Childhood, and Youth," responsibility for their early education, and especially breastfeeding.[9]

In a formulation with immense ideological implications, Allestree represents motherhood as an exclusively affective matter: when mothers fail, it is simply because either they love their children too much or they love them too little.[10] Mothers who overdo it are summarily dealt with: "The doting affection of the Mother," Allestree informs his readers, "is frequently punish'd with the untimely death of her Children; or if not with that . . . they live . . . to grieve her eies [sic], and to consume her heart . . . and to force their unhappy mothers to that sad exclamation. . . . *Blessed are the wombs which bare not*" (205-6).[11]

It is when he gets to those mothers who love too little that Allestree formulates the most important touchstone for maternal virtue to emerge in the first half of the eighteenth century, maternal breastfeeding. Allestree argues against "the Mothers transferring the Nursing her Child to another" as an instance of maternal pride, a pride nowhere more clearly seen than among wealthy and aristocratic women, who fail to breastfeed their own children because of a vain belief in their own "State and Greatness. . . . No other motive," Allestree declares "but what is founded in their Quality, could so universally prevail with all that are of it" not to follow "the impulses of Nature" (203).

The denigration of aristocratic mothers as unloving pleasure-seekers who refuse to be inconvenienced by breastfeeding becomes ubiquitous in Augustan conduct literature, reflecting a tendency among writers of the nascent bourgeoisie to "see the aristocracy as deficient in maternal feeling."[12] In the circular reasoning of conduct writing, women of means don't breastfeed because they are unloving mothers, and they are unloving mothers because they fail to establish the unique bond between mother and child understood to be the result of breastfeeding. Maternal breastfeeding, according to an influential compilation of conduct dicta published in 1714, is evidence of the "Affection and Tenderness" that have been "implanted" in mothers by "Nature"; the only "restraint" that breastfeeding places on women is restraint from the vices of vanity, theater, and gambling, all popularly associated with upper-class women.[13] Breastfeeding, the ultimate indicator of maternal virtue, is also the class act *par excellence*, distinguishing the selfless, virtuous, and affectionate domestic mother from the idle, selfish aristocrat.[14]

Experts had long been vociferous about the need for maternal nursing, and such tracts as the Countess of Lincoln's *Nursurie* (Oxford, 1628) demonstrate that a few aristocratic mothers breastfed when it was anything but fashionable to do so. Furthermore, even in the seventeenth century, upper-class women who fed their own children were seen by their contemporaries as exemplifying "true, self-sacrificing motherliness."[15] But it was only in the early eighteenth century that maternal practices actually began to change on a wide scale, so that by the second half of the century a dramatic transformation had taken place. Whereas in 1700 most babies of the upper classes and gentry were sent out to wet nurses for at least the first year of life, by 1750 many mothers from the same classes were nursing their children themselves, at home.[16] In the 1740s, when Richardson published *Pamela*, it was becoming increasingly common — indeed, fashionable — for women of comfortable economic circumstances to nurse their own children.

The shift to maternal breastfeeding was part of a complex of changes in the dominant cultural definition of maternal virtue during the Augustan period. Until the early eighteenth century, middle- and upper-strata husbands, who decided how infants would be fed, tended to disapprove of maternal breastfeeding and often vetoed mothers' deeply felt desires. "There is no doubt," Fildes observes, that "women who wished to feed their own children were frequently overruled by their husbands."[17] By the 1750s, however, many fathers had been convinced that, for a variety of material and economic reasons, maternal breastfeeding was preferable to sending a child out to a nurse or even to hiring a nurse at home (as Pamela and Mr. B. eventually do). Accordingly, reluctant mothers were as likely to be pressured *to* breastfeed as formerly they had been forbidden *from* it. By 1750 the desire to breastfeed was considered to be one of the attributes of "natural" motherhood, part of virtuous womanhood itself.[18] So, in commanding their wives to breastfeed, husbands could imagine themselves as capitulating to a desire natural to any virtuous mother.

This paradoxical state of affairs, where fathers at once continued to exert their unilateral prerogative in determining the method of infant feeding but imagined themselves to be capitulating in the process to the desires of their wives (or to desires their wives *ought* to have felt) is evidenced in the strikingly ambivalent language used by the apothecary James Nelson in 1753. "I cannot help advising in the strongest Terms," Nelson says, "that every Father consent, and even promote, that the Child be suckled by it's [*sic*] Mother." Eliding the difference between paternal "consenting" and "promoting," Nelson's statement evades a recognition of different desires among mothers and further bolsters the notion that virtuous mothers are necessarily breastfeeding mothers.[19]

Nelson's equivocation further suggests that he expects a mixed reception from male readers and the aristocracy (he laments on the same page that there is "little Probability . . . that my Advice herein will be follow'd by Persons in high Life"). Such concern was well founded. Although the trend was definitely toward maternal breastfeeding, there was by no means a universal change in the behaviors of eighteenth-century mothers. Those women of the upper classes who wished to breastfeed had found another source of authorization in the unanimous counsel of conduct literature, but the opinions of many husbands had not changed. In such cases, conduct literature may well have functioned as an incendiary intermediary, a challenge to the univocal authority of the father, a voice that spoke of maternal desire from within the sanction of an established and overwhelmingly male-authored genre. In particular households, then, conduct literature could function as a tool of male dominance or as a challenge to it.

From Allestree on, conduct writers who treated motherhood started from the assumption that virtuous mothers naturally love their children more than do equally virtuous fathers.[20] And especially in the seventeenth century, conduct literature granted special authority to women as mothers, separate from and greater than the authority granted to mere wives. To be sure, such works shared with virtually all other forms of contemporary discourse the belief that women were by nature inferior and rightly subordinate to their husbands. But motherhood was understood as an exceptional circumstance that granted a special dispensation, as it were, from the usual sexual hierarchy.

The Marquis of Halifax, for instance, makes the inequity of women's situation painfully clear to his daughter, but then goes on to suggest that women may offset this state of affairs by means of their extraordinary influence as mothers. "You must first lay it down for a Foundation in general," Halifax writes, "that there is *Inequality* in the *Sexes,* and that for the better Oeconomy of the World, the *Men* . . . had the larger share of *Reason* bestow'd upon them; by which means your Sex is the better prepar'd for the *Compliance* that is necessary." In the overtly politicized domestic realm Halifax describes, the wife functions most often as the submissive subject of a husband who enjoys absolute authority. But strikingly, "in the *Nursery*" she can expect to "Reign without Competition."[21]

Halifax imagines the powerful mother as a Machiavellian strategist who uses a rich array of political devices to appease and cajole a formidable list of potential enemies: children, in-laws, servants, social acquaintances, and husband. And as is well known, Halifax imagines maternal rule as necessarily duplicitous, based on the manipulation of affect and opportunity.

> You must begin early to make them [your children] *love* you, that they
> may *obey* you. . . . You must deny them as seldom as you can. . . . [Y]ou
> must flatter away their ill Humour, and take the next Opportunity of
> pleasing them in some other thing, before they either ask or look for it:
> This will strengthen your *Authority*, by making it soft to them; and
> confirm their *Obedience*, by making it their Interest. . . . Let them be
> more in awe of your *Kindness* than of your *Power*. (22-23)

So while Halifax sees the nursery as a unique realm of female authority, that authority can succeed only when it proceeds with duplicity much like that practiced by the famous "trimmer" himself when negotiating the treacherous worlds of seventeenth-century public politics.

Furthermore, even the heavily coded and self-deprecating maternal reign that Halifax imagined was to be short-lived. Although subsequent works of conduct literature continue to encourage mothers to build their authority on love rather than fear,[22] later writers tend to shun Halifax's explicit identification of maternal affect as a political tool and his suggestion that motherhood might constitute a locus of unique, incontestable authority. The 1714 *Ladies Library* follows Halifax in recommending that mothers elicit "honour" and "obedience" from their children by "natural and gentle Methods" (137), but it also takes pains to warn mothers against attempting to exercise "Craft." And as if in direct rebuke to Halifax's matriarchal vision, *The Ladies Library* is careful to insist that women enjoy no peculiar authority even as mothers.

> The *Father* is . . . Superior to the *Mother*, both in Natural Strength, in
> Wisdom, and by God's Appointment . . . the *Children* are especially to
> Obey their *Fathers*. . . . [I]f it happens, that the Inclinations or Desires of
> the *Mother* should differ from those of the *Father* . . . in . . . Things of
> Moment, . . . the Father is the Superior Authority, and must be obey'd. . . .
> [The mother] is not presum'd to have a Will contrary to her Husband's.
> (33-34)

No longer, by 1714, could a woman expect to "Reign without Competition," even in the nursery.

On the whole, then, Augustan conduct literature privileged motherhood *per se* in new ways. It perceived mothers as uniquely suited, indeed obligated, to be their children's first teachers and constant companions. It dictated maternal behavior across class lines (though according to a middle-class rubric), and used breastfeeding not only as a litmus test for maternal virtue but also as an indicator of broader personal and class virtues. The trend to recognize and extol uniquely maternal behaviors continued as the century progressed. But along with it came increasingly overt efforts to subordinate the power of mothers to that of fathers and to give fathers more direct participation in childrearing.

This development is clearly visible in midcentury conduct handbooks. William Cadogan (1748) calls on "every Father to have his Child nursed under his own Eye" and to do away with traditional attitudes that made infant care "one of the Mysteries of the *Bona Dea*, from which Men are to be excluded." James Nelson is careful in 1753 not to privilege mothers as his chosen audience, insisting that he addresses "every Parent." And writing in 1769, William Buchan extols the great "importance" of mothers, who "have it very much in their power to make men healthy, . . . useful in life, or the pests of society," but he is quick to add a revealing caveat: "The mother is not the only person concerned in the management of children. The father has an equal interest in their welfare, and ought to assist in every thing that respects either the improvement of the body or mind."[23] Writers of eighteenth-century conduct manuals and handbooks continued to teach that mothers love their children more than fathers and are specially equipped to care for them. But the suggestion implicit in late-seventeenth-century handbooks that motherhood might therefore constitute a place where wives' authority is actually *greater* than husbands' was being explicitly discredited. By the middle of the century, mothers were increasingly being elevated as moral and religious exemplars, and mothering was increasingly imagined as a set of behaviors and attitudes entirely peculiar to women. At the same time, fathers were instructed to exert patriarchal authority over even the smallest of nurslings and, in the process, over mothers.[24]

The domestic crisis over maternal breastfeeding that erupts in *Pamela* 2 allows for a direct rehearsal of emerging bourgeois norms against the maternal values associated in conduct books with the morally debilitated aristocracy. When Pamela insists that she ought to breastfeed the coming child, she repeats the arguments, the tone, and sometimes even the language of conduct writing. She reasons that a mother need not breastfeed if she is unhealthy but that breastfeeding is an "indispensable duty" when a mother is well (4:34). It is "most natural" to breastfeed, she says, and "unnatural," even "sinful," not to do so (4:34-35). Pamela's language, though strong, is by no means inflated when compared with that of conduct books, which routinely made a religious duty of maternal nursing. *The Ladies Library* informed its readers in 1714 that maternal breastfeeding was "of a more necessary and indispensable Obligation, than any positive Precept of *reveal'd Religion*." Indeed, this text calls maternal failure to breastfeed "one of the great and crying Sins of this Age and Nation. . . . The neglect of this *Duty*, is a sort of exposing of *Children* . . . it . . . is but little better than the laying of a *Child* in the *Streets*, and leaving it to the Care and Compassion of a *Parish*" (222).[25]

Pamela goes on to draw the conclusion obvious to Protestant readers: if breastfeeding is a spiritual duty for which she will be held individually accountable to God, then it supersedes all lesser duties, including her duty to obey Mr. B. "As great as a Wife's Obligation is to obey her Husband," Pamela says, "it ought not to interfere with what one takes to be a superior Duty. . . . Even a Husband's will is not sufficient to excuse one from a natural or divine Obligation" (4:34, 36).

It is this pious conclusion which causes the unpleasantness between Pamela and Mr. B. For while he clearly understands that "the chief thing" that makes Pamela want to breastfeed "is that you think it unnatural in a Mother not to be a Nurse to her own Child" (4:40), he nevertheless summarily forbids her to nurse. Furthermore, he uses the reasoning assigned specifically in conduct literature to the corrupt aristocracy: he wants Pamela to keep her figure, he wants to have her body at his disposal (not the baby's), and he wants her to continue her education (she is studying French and Latin). He considers nursing to be "beneath" her as his wife. He argues that the child would disturb her sleep; he wants to take Pamela abroad and can't if she's breastfeeding. B. even hints that if Pamela insists on breastfeeding he may take recourse in polygamy, a subject about which he has already made his wife "often somewhat uneasy" (4:39).

> Suppose I put you in mind, that while *Rachel* was giving her Little-one all her Attention, as a good Nurse, the worthy Patriarch had several other Wives.—Don't be shock'd, my dearest Love. . . . I will not think of any more Wives, till you convince me, by your Adherence to the Example given you by the Patriarch Wives, that I ought to follow those of the Patriarch Husbands. (4:39)

And B. threatens to stop loving Pamela if she insists on nursing the baby herself:

> I advise you, my dearest Love, not to weaken, or, to speak in a Phrase proper to the present Subject, *wean* me from that Love *to* you, and Admiration *of* you, which hitherto has been rather increasing than otherwise, as your Merit, and Regard for me, have increased. (4:43)[26]

A problem of conscience emerges for Pamela: ought she to obey what she sees as a divine imperative to breastfeed her own children, or the unequivocal edict of her husband, to whom she owes obedience as the "one indispensable of the Marriage Contract" (4:34). "For if I think it a *Sin* to submit to the dispensation he insists upon as in his power to grant, and yet *do* submit to it, what will become of my Peace of Mind?" (4:44). The dilemma is a serious one. Pamela believes that she will be individually responsible for the decision she makes ("How can a Husband have Power to discharge a Divine Duty?" [4:34]), while she recognizes that it is not really her own decision: her required "compliance" (to use Halifax's term) necessarily compromises her agency. So Pamela is irreducibly the accountable actor behind whatever action she chooses, yet autonomous agency is also, paradoxically, denied her. As Terry Eagleton observes in a different context, Pamela's guilt resides precisely in the fact that she is not a free agent.[27] She agonizes over the compromised nature of her overdetermined choice: "Must not one be one's own Judge of Actions, by which we must stand or fall?" (4:34).

Richardson's answer to this crucial question is clearly "no." Pamela's parents outline the text's rationalization for the necessity of Pamela's capitulation:

> We think, besides the Obedience you have vowed to him, and is the Duty of every good Wife, you ought to give up the Point, and acquiesce; for this seemeth to us to be the lesser Evil: and God Almighty, if it should be your Duty, will not be less merciful than Men; who, as his Honour says, by the Laws of the Realm, excuse a Wife, when she is faulty by the Command of the Husband; and we hope, the Fault he is pleased to make you commit, (if a Fault, for he really gives very praise-worthy Motives for his Dispensation) will not lie at his own Door. So e'en resolve my dearest Child, to submit to it, and with Cheerfulness too. (4:46)

Mr. B. is even more explicit, citing the Old Testament to demonstrate "of how little Force even the *Vows* of your Sex are, and how much you are under the Controul of ours" (4:40).

> Even in such a strong Point as a *solemn Vow to the Lord*, the Wife may be absolv'd by the Husband, from the Performance of it. . . . [A]n Husband may take upon himself to dispense with such a supposed Obligation, as that which you seem so loth to give up, even although you had made a Vow, that you would nurse your own Child. (4:41)

The husband's will takes precedence over what his wife understands as "natural" and "divine" in her motherhood, and makes it excusable—indeed, necessary— for her to commit what she defines as "sin." Even if a husband is incapable of making fine judgments about moral and spiritual duty ("My dear Mr. B.," Pamela notes archly, "was never yet thought so intirely fit to fill up the Character of a Casuistical Divine, as that one may absolutely rely upon his Decisions in these serious Points" [4:44]), his opinions nevertheless have virtually divine authority in *Pamela* 2.[28]

Though hardly one to capitulate easily, Pamela finds the combined weight of all these arguments and threats to be too much, even for her. "Recollecting everything, [I] *sacrificed to my Sex*, as Mr. B. calls it," she writes (4:52). After a good cry, finding that "my heart was relieved by my eye" and that she feels "lighter and easier," she proceeds immediately to hire a wet nurse. "We are quite reconciled," Pamela reports to her relieved parents, "although as I said, upon his own terms" (4:54).

And so, we are to believe, the breastfeeding crisis is resolved. Never mind that immense questions about power relations between spouses, individual responsibility and agency, and maternal authority have been raised—a few tears and a toss of the head presumably make everything right. Although Pamela does regret the decision at one other point, when Billy seems to be dying of smallpox ("Had *I* been permitted—But, hush! all my repining *Ifs!*" [4:252]), her faltering proves unjustified: Billy pulls through and all is well. And apart from this brief qualm, the text refuses to acknowledge that the disturbing problems raised in the breastfeeding crisis are not addressed, only deferred, by the decision to hire a wet nurse.

Nevertheless, the cost of B.'s victory over Pamela's claims to maternal authority and autonomy is high. In order explicitly to subordinate Pamela's will to her husband's, Richardson must necessarily give her arguments a voice, permitting dissonance to sound in his otherwise well–tempered text.[29] Though ventriloquized, contradicted, and finally neutralized, Pamela's subversive maternal voice sounds clearly in the breastfeeding episode, and its echoes disrupt the presentation of virtuous maternity as unproblematically submissive to patriarchal authority.

The exchange between Mr. and Mrs. B. immediately upon her acquiescence—both what is said and what is left unsaid—undermines the ostensible resolution of the conflict and complicates the reductive positions that husband and wife have assumed. Mr. B. begins by complaining that Pamela forces him to "a hated, because an ungenerous, Necessity of pleading my Prerogative. And if this was not like my Pamela, excuse me . . . that I could not help being a little unlike myself." Pamela's response to her husband's complaint is in two parts—her spoken response and her silent thoughts, which she shares only later in a letter. Aloud, she argues again for the priority of her individual conscience and for her innocence:

I am sure, said I, I was not in the least aware, that I had offended!—But I
was too little circumspect. I had been used to your Goodness for so long a
Time, that I expected it, it seems. . . . I thought, Sir, you would have
distinguish'd between a Command where my Conscience was concerned,
and a common Point: You know, Sir, I never had any Will but yours in
common Points. . . . I had no Intention to invade your Province, or go out
of my own. Yet I thought I had a Right to a little Free-will, a very little;
especially on some greater Occasions. (4:49-50)

Pamela's mixture of thick irony and obsequious apology, of course, makes little
impression on her husband. "I forgive you heartily," Mr. B. contentedly informs her. "Give me one Kiss, and I will think of your saucy Appeal against
me no more" (4:51).

But silently, Pamela constructs a different response, equating Mr. B.'s
deployment of his "prerogative" in the breastfeeding crisis with his attempts at
crude sexual force before they were married. "Ah! thought I," she writes in
retrospect, "this is not so very unlike your dear Self, were I to give the least
Shadow of an Occasion; for it is of a Piece with your Lessons formerly" (4:49).
At stake in those former "lessons," of course, was the crucial question of whether
Pamela or Mr. B. had the authority to dispose of Pamela's virginity—that is, to
deploy her female body and its desire. In both Part 1 and Part 2, then, the
central conflict is between autonomy and subordination, choice and constraint,
liberty and tyranny. One might argue that Part 2 revises Part 1 on this issue: in
Part 1, Pamela was right to resist, but in Part 2 she is right to capitulate. On the
other hand, we might note that Pamela managed to come through the har-
rowing situations of Part 1 safely only because Mr. B. chose, at crucial moments, not to rape her after all. From this perspective, choice is B.'s peculiar
privilege in Part 1 as in Part 2. The difference is only that in the breastfeeding
crisis, B. makes a different choice, forcing his desire on Pamela against her
will. Crucially, it is the fact of their marriage that allows B. to perform this new
violence on Pamela *without seeming to violate her*, since as his wife she can
have no desires apart from his anyway. When Pamela pleads for "a Right to a
little Free-will, a very little," Mr. B. responds characteristically: "Why so you
have, my Dear; but . . . I must have your whole will" (4:51-52). As in *The
Ladies Library*, the mother (who is only legitimately visible as a wife) "is not
presum'd to have a Will contrary to her Husband's" (2:33-34).

To her credit, Pamela recognizes these strategies for what they are: manifestations of domestic tyranny.

He is pleased to entertain very high Notions . . . of the Prerogative of a
Husband. Upon my Word, he sometimes . . . makes a body think a Wife

should not have the least Will of her own. He sets up a dispensing Power, in short, altho' he knows, that that Doctrine once cost a Prince his Crown. (4:39-40)

But though the "doctrine" of patriarchal absolutism had long been rejected in the context of royal authority, it remains fully in force in the realm of domestic politics: Mr. B.'s inflexible exercise of husbandly "prerogative" will cost him nothing. As Pamela's parents advise, "It will signify nothing, after all [to resist]; for he will have his Way, that's sure enough" (4:47). Or as Pamela complained to Miss Darnford at the start of all the trouble, Mr. B. enjoys "a Dispensing Power . . . which Kings are not allowed over the Law" (3:389).

Pamela 2, then, initially presents a perfect mother according to the rubric established in Augustan conduct literature: tender, careful, always present, educative, and eager to breastfeed. But by refusing to *let* Pamela breastfeed, Richardson's "conduct novel" challenges not only Pamela's authority over her own motherhood but also conduct literature's authority to dictate maternal behavior. In the process, it redefines virtuous motherhood: specific maternal behaviors become less important than the context of female subordination in which they take place.

But delimiting the authority of conduct literature to dictate maternal behavior is only one of the projects of *Pamela* 2. The narrative of Pamela's unsuccessful attempt to breastfeed her own child also colludes with midcentury conduct literature's effort to further the extent of patriarchal sovereignty over the bodies of children and mothers. Like other conduct works from the first half of the eighteenth century, *Pamela* 2 seeks—with significantly qualified success—to eliminate the possibility that mothers might "Reign without Competition" even over the site of motherhood, and to deny particularity, autonomy, and desire to maternal voices. So Richardson's sequel is an assault to more than our literary sensibilities; in its efforts to reassert patriarchal prerogatives over maternal bodies it constitutes an early statement of a sexual politics only too familiar in our own day.

Afterword

I recently had a pleasure not often reserved for authors, when a reader whom I greatly respect responded to the essay reprinted here in language I might have chosen myself: she called it "disquieting."[30] I confess that I too have been disquieted by "'A Point of Conscience.'" Even when I was drafting the essay, its implications gave me pause. And now that the editors of this volume have asked me to do something else that authors seldom have a chance at—to reflect publicly on my own writing—it strikes me that the disquieting of readers may be an important function of this essay.

When I wrote "'A Point of Conscience'" I was working on a book about eighteenth-century motherhood. What interested me about this episode from *Pamela* 2 was that it demonstrated motherhood's threat to Pamela's control over her own person and her own choices. A few years and another book project later, I think about this material somewhat differently. What seems most illuminating about the episode now is its suggestion that Pamela's identity as privileged wife shuts down her ability to resist B.'s arrogance. As Mrs. B., Pamela can still name her husband's tyranny, but she must finally submit to it, even at the expense of her child's welfare and her own values.

In effect, the conflict over breastfeeding in *Pamela* 2 forces Pamela to put into practice the "injunctions" B. was already catechizing her on in Part 1: "I must bear with him, even when I find him in the wrong. . . . I must be as flexible as the reed in the fable. . . . If he be set upon a wrong thing, [I] must not dispute with him, but do it" (467, 469). Further, the episode clears the way for her submission to the particular demand that formed the immediate context and the main point of those early "kind hints": B.'s demand that she never seek to defend another against him, however unjust his behavior.

In Part 1, we recall, the immediate impetus for the list of injunctions was B.'s rage over his new wife's temerity in daring to interpose with him on behalf of his sister, Lady Davers. "Never think of making a compliment to *her*, or to *any* body living, at my expense," B. thundered during that episode (461), and Pamela dutifully recorded the lesson: "I must think his displeasure the heaviest thing that can befal me. . . . And so, that I must not wish to incur it, to save any body else from it." Significantly, it was during the same episode in Part 1 that we learned about B.'s liaison with Sally Godfrey, whom Lady Davers kept mentioning "accidentally" and whose image kept intruding on Pamela's efforts to memorize B.'s injunctions: "I must bear with him, even when I find him in the wrong.—*This may be a little hard, as the case may be circumstanced. I wonder whether Miss Sally Godfrey be living or dead*" (467).

In Part 2 this Sally Godfrey, the mother of B.'s illegitimate daughter, takes the place of Lady Davers as a woman Pamela might defend against B.'s tyranny. But by now Mrs. B. has thoroughly learned her lessons and avoids repeating that mistake. Indeed, Pamela takes the initiative in enforcing Sally's alienation from her child. For these reasons, the breastfeeding quarrel in Part 2 no longer seems to me separable from the subsequent episode where Pamela colludes in annulling Sally Godfrey's motherhood.[31] The two episodes are intimately connected, as Pamela learns not only to submit to B.'s prerogative herself but also to collude in forcing the submission of others.

Pamela, of course, is a document of eighteenth-century British culture, specific to its time and place; and it is a work of fiction, not the record of a lived life. Any legitimate reading must demonstrate meticulous attention to that historical distance and proceed with humility enough to recognize that Richardson was not writing with twentieth-century readers in mind. But at the same time, the breastfeeding episode in *Pamela* 2 remains disquieting for more than antiquarian or narrowly "scholarly" reasons. Part of the episode's power, I believe, lies in the continued pertinence of the questions it raises about Pamela's autonomy and authority as a married mother.

Marriage does not automatically threaten female subjectivity nowadays: unlike eighteenth-century women, we can become wives and still keep our names, our jobs, and our financial independence. But the vast majority of even the most privileged and autonomous wives still experience constraints when it comes to motherhood. If we keep our names, few among us enjoy sharing our children's names; if we pursue careers, we are resigned to inequitably shouldering the labor of parenting, and we often find motherhood and work to be at odds. The familiarity of this litany should not obscure its importance: despite women's many advances since Richardson's time, motherhood within marriage still too often forces capitulation to—and reinforcement of—patriarchal privilege. That our capitulations may not be identical to those forced on Richardson's heroine is less significant than the continuing necessity of capitulation.

While respecting the profound alterity of Richardson's *Pamela* and of the society in which it appeared, then, it seems to me necessary also to acknowledge the novel's power to delineate structural injustices that continue to shape mothers' lives. And in that light, the most disquieting thing about the breastfeeding episode may not be, finally, the way it facilitates Pamela's own oppression, but the way it prepares her to oppress another mother, Sally Godfrey. The breastfeeding episode not only narrates Pamela's forced capitulation, as a married mother, to her husband's control over her body, her values, and her child's well-being. Even more disquieting, by demonstrating Pamela's submission to the "kind hints" of Part 1, it makes inevitable her collusion in defrauding a less privileged mother.

Notes

Epigraph from Samuel Richardson, *Pamela, or Virtue Rewarded.* 4 Vols. (London: S. Richardson, 1742), 3:389-90. Future page references cited parenthetically in the text.

    1. For the enclosure of women in domestic space, see Nancy Armstrong, *Desire and Domestic Fiction: A Political History of the Novel* (New York: Oxford University Press, 1987); Bridget Hill, *Women, Work, and Sexual Politics in Eighteenth-Century England* (New York: Blackwell, 1989).

    2. For our purposes, Augustan conduct books were behavior handbooks addressed to women and published before 1750. Excluded from concern are manuals specifically devoted to housewifery (cookery books, for example) and the "child management" guides that became so numerous after midcentury, except where these serve as

points of comparison. Conduct books written after 1750 tended to devote more direct attention to mothers than earlier works did; for this reason, the late-century manuals are often assumed to have inaugurated the eighteenth century's obsession with maternal behavior. However, these texts entered an established tradition and relied on definitions and positions that had become current earlier in the century.

Any reader of Augustan conduct books will be immediately struck by their unanimity. This is largely because the majority simply reproduce, abridge, or conflate Richard Allestree's *The Ladies Calling* (1673) and George Savile, Marquis of Halifax's *The Lady's New-Year's-Gift: Or, Advice to a Daughter* (1688—often without attribution). To cite Allestree and Halifax, therefore, is to quote ubiquitous maxims that achieved the status of truth during the Augustan period.

3. Terry Castle reviews the surprisingly uniform critical appraisals of *Pamela* 2 in *Masquerade and Civilization: The Carnivalesque in Eighteenth-Century English Culture and Fiction* (Stanford: Stanford University Press, 1986), 131-32; cf. Lois A. Chaber, "From Moral Man to Godly Man: 'Mr. Locke' and Mr. B. in Part 2 of *Pamela,*" *Studies in Eighteenth-Century Culture* 18 (1988): 213-61, 213-14; and Ruth Bernard Yeazell, *Fictions of Modesty: Women and Courtship in the English Novel* (Chicago: University of Chicago Press, 1991), 266.

4. Susan Winnet provides a perceptive discussion of the genderedness of traditional reading expectations and pleasures in "Coming Unstrung: Women, Men, Narrative, and Principles of Pleasure," *PMLA* 105 (May 1990): 505-18.

5. Castle, *Masquerade and Civilization*, 131, 135, 138. A few readers have found Part 2 slightly more palatable than Castle does; the faintness of the praise it elicits, however, remains damning. Margaret Doody observes that there are "longer and more sustained conversations" in Part 2 than in Part 1 and that "Pamela is not here . . . always the central speaker; there is more variety in style of speech, and of tone": Doody, *A Natural Passion: A Study of the Novels of Samuel Richardson* (Oxford: Clarendon Press, 1974), 80. But these positive comments appear in a chapter entitled "*Pamela* Continued; or, The Sequel That Failed." Donald L. Ball's essay makes similar observations about the sequel's technical improvements, but still *Pamela* 2 "seems to incorporate and to continue needlessly all of the worst features of *Pamela I* and to illustrate very few of the good ones": Ball, "*Pamela II*: A Primary Link in Richardson's Development as a Novelist," *Modern Philology* 65 (1968): 334-42, 334.

6. Castle, *Masquerade and Civilization*, 152. Pamela herself, like *Pamela* 2, is a kind of "hodge-podge" (Castle, 171) at once representing all social classes and none. She was born into what we might today call the lower middle class (her parents once ran a small school), although by the time *Pamela 1* opens her family has fallen on hard times and her father is an aging ditch-digger. We first meet her as a household servant who is oddly also a companion, a kind of daughter, and even a double to her mistress. Eventually raised to the status of a "Lady" (3:6), wife to a wealthy and almost aristocratic husband, she remains ever mindful of her inferior origins and obsessed with bourgeois values and duties.

Pamela 2's amorphous representation of class serves to universalize Pamela's experience. At the same time, the country-house domesticity that Pamela embodies works to subsume under a developing bourgeois rubric all social classes, each of which

Pamela in some sense seems to represent. Cf. Armstrong, *Desire and Domestic Fiction*, 69-75, for a discussion of the shifting valences of the country-house ideal in eighteenth-century conduct literature. Pamela's house epitomizes the apparently classless domestic space that Armstrong says conduct books created for popular emulation.

7. That *Pamela* 2 is essentially a "narrative conduct book" was argued as early as 1968 by Ball ("*Pamela II*," 334). But the work's status as a failed novel has nevertheless been in little doubt among critics.

8. *The Ladies Calling* was almost certainly the most frequently reprinted conduct book in the first half of the eighteenth century, reappearing under many titles and in fragmentary forms in other works. Calling it "immensely influential," Yeazell notes that there were at least eleven editions between 1673 and 1720 and that the work was still being reprinted as late as 1787 (*Fictions of Modesty*, 5, 240). It would be difficult to count the number of times that all or part of Allestree's work was reprinted under other titles; Yeazell offers a partial list (242 n. 27).

9. Richard Allestree, *The Ladies Calling*, 5th ed. (Oxford, 1677), 201-13. Further references cited in text.

10. Allestree's explanation of maternal failure as the result either of an excess of love or of its absence would be reformulated with a vengeance more than a century later by Mary Wollstonecraft, for whom maternal failure seems almost an inevitability: "Woman, . . . a slave in every situation to prejudice, seldom exerts enlightened maternal affection; for she either neglects her children, or spoils them by improper indulgence": *A Vindication of the Rights of Woman* (1790), ed. Carol H. Poston (New York: W.W. Norton, 1988), 151.

11. The overly indulgent mother is a familiar figure in eighteenth-century writing in many genres. In *Ladies Tales: Exemplified in the Vertues and Vices of the Quality, with Reflections* (London, 1714), Mary Davys includes praise for a "most excellent Wife and tender Mother" whose "Tenderness to her child was temper'd with Prudence from that faulty Fondness, that is often of so fatal a Consequence to the unhappy Children of imprudent Parents" (8). Richardson's Lovelace blames his indulgent mother for his own villainy: "Why, why did my mother bring me up to bear no control? . . . Ought she not to have known what cruelty there was in her kindness?": *Clarissa; or, The History of a Young Lady*, ed. Angus Ross (New York: Penguin Books, 1985), 1431. William Cadogan's famous infant feeding essay draws a vivid picture of "the puny Insect, the Heir and Hope of a rich Family," who "lies languishing under a Load of Finery, that overpowers his Limbs, abhorring and rejecting the Dainties he is cramm'd with, 'till he dies a Victim to the mistaken Care and Tenderness of his fond Mother": Cadogan, *An Essay upon Nursing, and the Management of Children, from Their Birth to Three Years of Age, by a Physician*, 1748. *Three Treatises on Child Rearing*, ed. Randolph Trumbach (New York: Garland, 1985), 7. James Nelson asserts that even when fathers try to exert their authority over children, often the "blind Fondness" of mothers interferes and causes the children to be spoiled: Nelson, *An Essay on the Government of Children, Under Three General Heads: viz. Health, Manners and Education* (London, 1753), 32-33. In 1779, *Female Government* actually advocates that sons be kept from their "dangerous," overly indulgent mothers. See

G.J. Barker-Benfield, *The Culture of Sensibility: Sex and Society in Eighteenth-Century Britain* (Chicago: University of Chicago Press, 1992), 278.

12. David Kunzle, "William Hogarth: The Ravaged Child in the Corrupt City," in *Changing Images of the Family*, ed. Virginia Tufte and Barbara Myerhoff (New Haven: Yale University Press, 1979), 99-140, on 127.

13. [Richard Steele], *The Ladies Library* (London, 1714), 225-26.

14. By the time of Marriott's *Female Conduct: Being an Essay on the Art of Pleasing. To be practiced by the Fair Sex, Before, and After Marriage. A Poem, in Two Books* (London, 1759), wealthy women were explicitly barred from readership ("Rich Maids! approach not my Academy," [25]. Yet Marriott also argues that maternal nursing "binds alike each Mother, rich, or poor" (263).

15. Valerie Fildes, *Wet Nursing: A History from Antiquity to the Present* (Oxford: Basil Blackwell, 1988), 85.

16. There is little doubt that maternal breastfeeding was an increasingly valued activity in England from the late seventeenth century on, and it was essentially de rigueur among the privileged by 1750. Barbara Charlesworth Gelpi argues that Rousseau's vision of maternal breastfeeding as the agent of social reform and of the breastfeeding mother as the powerful complement to an infantilized husband "reflects an attitude already widespread in the culture": Gelpi, *Shelley's Goddess: Maternity, Language, Subjectivity* (New York: Oxford University Press, 1992), 44. Edward Shorter notes that in the 1760s "the switch to maternal nursing [was] already well underway among the middle classes," even in France, which lagged behind England: Shorter, *The Making of the Modern Family* (New York: Basic Books, 1975), 182. In *Wet Nursing*, Fildes argues that the "movement toward a different concept of infant feeding received impetus in the publications of man-midwives in the 1730s" (111) and that during the second half of the eighteenth century maternal breastfeeding had become a standard feature of "middle- and particularly upper-class society" (116).

17. Fildes, *Wet Nursing*, 84. During the seventeenth century, Fildes argues, "women with any status in society rarely breastfed their own children," usually because "many husbands did not approve of, or allow, their wives to breastfeed" (83). Even in the early eighteenth century, "the method of infant feeding . . . often depended upon the husband's will" (114). Fildes's observations are supported by James Nelson's *Essay on the Government of Children* (1753), in which he laments that "many a tender Mother, has her heart yearning to suckle her child, and is prevented by the misplac'd Authority of a Husband" (43).

One famous case involves the infant Samuel Johnson (b. 1709), whose father, Michael, overruled the wishes of his wife, Sarah Ford Johnson, in the matter of breastfeeding. At Michael's insistence, baby Samuel was sent to the home of a neighbor for ten weeks, where his mother visited him every day. For a discussion of Sarah Johnson's motherhood, see my "Critical Complicities: *Savage* Mothers, Johnson's Mother, and the Containment of Maternal Difference," *The Age of Johnson: A Scholarly Annual* 5 (1992): 115-46.

18. Fildes, *Wet Nursing*, 118. For the cultural and political functions of the idea of "natural" motherhood in the eighteenth century, see esp. Felicity Nussbaum's

"'Savage' Mothers: Narratives of Maternity in the Mid-Eighteenth Century," *Cultural Critique* 20 (winter 1991-92): 123-51.

19. Nelson, *Essay on the Government of Children*, 45. Moreover, the virtuous mother finds even her sexual desire satisfied in the act of breastfeeding. Nelson says that "there is an inexpressible Pleasure in giving Suck, which none but Mothers know . . . the sensation . . . is said to be mighty pleasing": Nelson, *Essay on the Government of Children*, 44-45. Gelpi observes the sexualized language Nelson employs throughout this passage (45).

20. A mother's love, Allestree teaches, naturally "do's usually exceed the love of the Father" because of the greater "strength of feminine passion": *The Ladies Calling*, 205. And according to *An Essay in Defence of the Female Sex*, 3d ed. (London, 1697), perhaps by Judith Drake, women are by nature "furnish'd with Ingenuity and Prudence . . . for the Relief and Comfort of a Family; and . . . over and above enrich'd with a peculiar Tenderness and Care requisite to the Cherishing their poor helpless Off-spring" (18-19). Cf. *The Ladies Library*, 3 vols. (London, 1714), where mothers have "at least the same, but generally a much greater Affection to them [their children] than the Fathers" (33). Further references cited in text. Rousseau echoed these platitudes when he observed that in their "blind tenderness," mothers are "more attached to the children" than fathers. See *Emile*, ed. Allan Bloom (New York: Basic Books, 1979), 37-38.

21. George Savile, Marquis of Halifax, *The Lady's New-Year's-Gift; or, Advice to a Daughter. The Complete Works of George Savile, First Marquess of Halifax*, ed. Walter Raleigh (New York: August M. Kelley Reprints, 1970), 8. Further references cited in text.

22. In Maria Susannah Cooper, *The Exemplary Mother; or, Letters Between Mrs. Villars and her Family. Published by a Lady*, 2 vols. (London, 1769), the mother is noted for her "empire" over the "inclinations" of her children (17), an empire she attributes to her early breastfeeding and to a combination of Halifaxian tactics (diverting children's attention rather than denying them anything, avoiding contradicting them too much, and so on). She is always begging her children to think of her as a "friend" more than as one with "the authority of a parent" (27).

23. Cadogan, *An Essay Upon Nursing*, 25; Nelson, *An Essay on the Government of Children*, 4; William Buchan, *Domestic Medicine; or, A Treatise on the Prevention and Cure of Diseases by Regimen and Simple Medicines*, 2d ed. (London, 1772), 5-6.

24. The paradoxical development I am describing has been observed recently by Felicity Nussbaum, who calls it a "profound historical contradiction." She explains, "Eighteenth-century Englishmen largely defined themselves, sexually and materially, as fully outside the scope of the maternal yet eager to intervene within it" ("'Savage' Mothers," 126).

25. The aristocratic Halifax had used similar language to discuss his version of maternal failure; but for him, the worst possible maternal behavior is not failure to breastfeed but constant attendance on children and public displays of maternal affection. "You may love your *Children* without living in the *Nursery*," Halifax cautions, "and you may have a *competent* and *discreet care* of them, without letting it break out upon the Company, or exposing your self by turning your Discourse that way; which is a kind of *Laying Children* to the *Parish*, and it can hardly be done any

where, that those who hear it will be so forgiving, as not to think they are overcharged with them." See George Savile, Marquis of Halifax, *The Lady's New-Year's-Gift; or, Advice to a Daughter* 22. By this restraint, according to Halifax, upper-class women may "distinguish" themselves from "Women of a lower size" (22). These pronouncements, not surprisingly, are among the few in Halifax not readily to be found in later writers of conduct literature.

26. B.'s reasoning draws on the traditional notion that sexual intercourse and breastfeeding were incompatible. Linda Pollock notes, "The main reason for wet-nursing seems to have been pressure from husbands to resume sexual relations with their wives," which many believed would curdle breast milk. Pollock, "Embarking on a Rough Passage: The Experience of Pregnancy in Early Modern Society," in *Women as Mothers in Pre-Industrial England*, ed. Valerie Fildes (New York: Routledge, Chapman and Hall, 1990), 39-67, on 50. Cf. Ruth Perry, "Colonizing the Breast: Sexuality and Maternity in Eighteenth-Century England," *Journal of the History of Sexuality* 2 (October 1991): 204-34, 227. Perry observes that in *Pamela* 2 breastfeeding is "less urgent than a woman's duty to sexually serve her husband" (226). Occasionally, eighteenth-century writers offer a somewhat different picture, laying the desire for renewed sexual intercourse at the woman's door. According to the pseudonymous "Gaius," the reason mothers do not want to nurse their own children is "the lack of moderation in their lusts; for whilst they will not contain themselves, they disdain to give suck to the little ones, they have brought forth." See Seius Gaius [pseud.], *The Mother's Looking Glass* (London, 1702), 13.

27. Eagleton, *The Rape of Clarissa: Writing, Sexuality, and Class Struggle in Samuel Richardson* (Minneapolis: University of Minnesota Press, 1982), 35.

28. It is amusing to read *Pamela* 2 against Lady Mary Chudleigh's *Ladies Defence*, since Chudleigh's male speakers—hilarious caricatures of male chauvinist attitudes—often sound very much like Mr. B., whom we are meant to take seriously. Chudleigh's parodic Parson, for instance, instructs wives that "A blind Obedience you from Guilt secures, / And if you err, the Fault is his, not yours": *The Ladies Defence; or, The Bride-Woman's Counsellor Answer'd: A Poem. In a Dialogue Between Sir John Brute, Sir William Loveall, Melissa, and a Parson. Written by a Lady* (London, 1701), 11. And Mr. B.'s threats of abuse sound only too like the Parson's justification of unkind husbands:

> If we are cruel, they have made us so;
> What e'er they suffer, to themselves they owe:
> Our Love on their Obedience does depend,
> We will be kind, when they no more offend. (8)

Pamela's predicament also recalls the dilemma of Daniel Defoe's six-year-old boy in the first part of *The Family Instructor*. The boy tells his father, "Sometimes my Mother won't let me go to Church, if it be but a little ill Weather, and if a little Wind does but blow; and if God requires me to go, and my mother won't let me, *what must I do?* Won't God be angry with me for not going to hear his Word preached?" No, the father replies. "If your Mother won't let you go, then Child, it is none of your Fault": *The Family Instructor. In Three Parts. I. Relating to Fathers and Children. II. To Masters and Servants. III. To Husbands and Wives*, 15th ed., 2 vols. (London, 1761), 1:36-

37. The comparison signals the childlike status of wives in the conventional reasoning of Mr. B. and Pamela's parents. By worrying about her own responsibility, Pamela presumes that she, like B., can claim adult subjectivity and spirituality. *Pamela 1* had validated the lower-class heroine's claim to have a "soul of equal importance with the soul of a princess" (197), but the breastfeeding episode in Part 2 explicitly denies Pamela's claim to have a soul equal to her husband's. Samuel Richardson, *Pamela; or, Virtue Rewarded,* ed. Peter Sabor (New York: Penguin Books, 1980). Further references cited in text.

29. Defoe's 1724 *Roxana: The Fortunate Mistress,* ed. Jane Jack (New York: Oxford University Press, 1964), provides a parallel moment when, in response to the Dutch merchant's arguments that she should marry him for the sake of their child, the protagonist makes her famous Amazonian speeches. Like Pamela's insistence on her own responsibility, of course, Roxana's defiant independence is finally neutralized: she comes to lament ever having spoken against marriage and is careful not to miss her next opportunity to accept the merchant. But despite their eventual containment, Roxana's fighting words, like Pamela's, are never fully absent from the capitulations that follow them.

These proto-feminist speeches strike me as only more resonant and disturbing by virtue of being spoken by an impersonating male. For one recent treatment of the problem of eighteenth-century male authors speaking in the voices of women, see Madeleine Kahn, *Narrative Transvestism: Rhetoric and Gender in the Eighteenth-Century English Novel* (Ithaca: Cornell University Press, 1991).

30. Isobel Grundy in *Scriblerian* 29 (autumn 1996): 29.

31. Cf. Charlotte Sussman, "'I Wonder Whether Poor Miss Sally Godfrey Be Living or Dead': The Married Woman and the Rise of the Novel," *Diacritics* 20, no. 1 (1990): 88-102; Toni Bowers, "Seduction, Coercion, and Maternal Erasure: Sally Godfrey Wrightson's 'Kind Concurrence,'" in *The Politics of Motherhood: British Writing and Culture, 1680-1760* (Cambridge: Cambridge University Press, 1996), 184-89.

Mary Wollstonecraft

Styles of Radical Maternity

I would like to frame this discussion of Mary Wollstonecraft and the politics of the maternal body with a tableau that figures an extraordinary personal drama unfolding against the backdrop of an equally extraordinary national drama. Having journeyed to France to observe a revolution in which she had placed so much hope, Mary Wollstonecraft met and fell in love with Gilbert Imlay, scion of the new American republic, and someone Wollstonecraft looked upon as a sort of natural man, uncorrupted by European affectations and decadence. Needless to say, the enlightened pair never considered seeking any higher sanction to their union than personal honor; indeed, Wollstonecraft even bragged a bit about enjoying the pleasures of conjugal fellowship "without having clogged my soul by promising obedience."[1] In May 1794, a little more than a week after giving birth to her daughter Fanny in Le Havre, Wollstonecraft proudly describes the following scene of republican domesticity: "My little Girl," she writes, "begins to suck so *manfully* that her father [Imlay] reckons saucily on her writing the second part of the R———ts of Woman."[2]

According to Imlay's saucy reckoning, the project of women's emancipation will be complete once infant girls nursing at their mothers' breasts are immasculated, transformed into vigorous men. Because Imlay soon would desert the mother and child, his wit here seems exceedingly painful. After all, breastfeeding was supposed to cement the conjugal tie. In *A Vindication of the Rights of Woman* (1792), Wollstonecraft herself not only had tried to dignify breastfeeding as a civic duty conducive to the formation of sympathetic citizens, but she had also labored to establish the sensuousness of the satisfaction it afforded fond husbands looking on: "Cold would be the heart of a husband, were he not rendered unnatural by early debauchery, who did not feel more delight at seeing his child suckled by its mother than the most artful wanton tricks could ever raise."[3]

But however unfortunate, Imlay's witty comment on the gendering of the suckling scene does not really misconstrue the argument about women, mothers, and daughters that Wollstonecraft advanced in *Vindication*. Regardless of how it ends, liberal theory begins, at least, in Thomas Laqueur's words, "with a neuter individual body: sexed but without gender, in principle of no consequence to culture, merely the location of the rational subject that constitutes the person."[4] Yet although Wollstonecraft repeatedly insists that virtue has no sex, she (like most liberal theorists, and like Imlay here) not only tacitly assumes the maleness of that ostensible sex-neutrality but she also measures women's capacity against the standards set by a very particular kind of masculinity. Having posited rationality, independence, and productive bodily vigor as man's true nature—a nature which culture has perverted into trifling sentimentality, dependence, and weakness—Wollstonecraft's *Vindication* clearly affiliated itself with a modified Commonwealth tradition of English republicanism. This tradition championed the virtue produced by the participation of independent, property-owning, and arms-bearing (male) citizens in civic life. Concomitantly, as G.J. Barker-Benfield has argued, it assailed the "degeneration of both civic virtue and manhood" into vicious effeminacy as the inevitable result of monarchy and hereditary privilege.[5] James Burgh, for example—who seems to have served posthumously as a mentor of sorts for Wollstonecraft—had charged that "adultery, gambling, cheating, rooking, bribing, blasphemy, sodomy, and other frolics" were the elegant amusements of the pampered modern ruling class, whereas Paine damned peers as the "counterfeit" of women and as a "seraglio of males" living in and for "lazy enjoyment."[6]

As if it were possible to transmute misogyny into a form of homophobia that could somehow leave women unscathed, Wollstonecraft attempts to turn a political tradition foundationally scornful of femininity to feminist ends, and she does this not by enlarging or inventing a positive counterdiscourse of femininity but by celebrating a vision of republican masculinity into which women too could be invited. Accordingly, she regards it as crucial for the well-being of the state to differentiate men from fops, from enervated courtiers, from unsexed men and "equivocal beings," but she refuses to consider it important to differentiate men from women (249). Indeed, to allow that difference between the sexes has significance would weaken her liberal argument on behalf of women's political and educational rights. Of course, Wollstonecraft was fighting a losing battle with her own ideological comrades. Historians of the French Revolution have amply demonstrated women's exclusion from the rights of self-responsibility and civic activity within the public sphere that Wollstonecraft recommends in *Vindication*.[7] In the French Republic of Virtue, a woman could be a citizen only through maternity. As Joan Landes has put it, "According to the logic of republican motherhood, woman's major political task was to instill her children with patriotic duty. It followed, then, that the home could serve as the nursery for the state. As citizens, women would be educated beyond their limited horizons and wholly self-oriented concerns in order to embrace the larger polity, but ultimately in a passive and not an active manner."[8] The stoicism, autonomy, muscularity, and self-control of the republican male body was not, in other words, allowed to describe that of the republican female as well. From its vituperative attacks upon Marie-Antoinette's crimes against maternity and sexual propriety to its outlawing of women's political clubs, the Republic of Virtue insisted that women's natural bodily difference mandated the separation of spheres, that female virtue was "naturally" domestic and private.[9]

True, the nurse officiating at Wollstonecraft's lying-in was so impressed by the soldierliness with which Wollstonecraft bore her labor pains that she remarked, "Frenchwoman like, that I ought to make children for the Republic, since I treat it so slightly."[10] Insofar as Wollstonecraft in *Vindication* indeed urges her countrywomen to practice the duties of maternity, she would seem to comply with ultimately defeating imperatives of radical ideology, and feminist historians—more impressed than Wollstonecraft was with the public antidomestic mores of the ancien régime and with the space it accorded to (some) women through salon and court culture—have scolded Wollstonecraft for her ostensible commitment to bourgeois conceptions of motherhood.[11]

But maternity, as Wollstonecraft sees it, in fact entails no necessary or insurmountable division of the public and private spheres. Whereas Burgh recommends that celibacy be penalized by law, Wollstonecraft readily acknowledges that public servants of *both* sexes will probably not want to be married and thus distracted by the private duties of parenthood. Indeed, for her the duties of maternity are striking precisely for what they do not signify: they are not binding upon all women, and they do not block women's participation in civic life any more than the equally important duties of fatherhood customarily inhibit men's participation. A feminist-inflected version of commonwealth ideology as it pertained to domestic sexuality was attractive to Wollstonecraft precisely because it de-specified the female body. Having reclaimed men from debasing and, as Wollstonecraft would have it, feminizing customs of hereditary wealth and privilege, a democratic republic would make men and women alike more manly; it would de-essentialize republican masculinity; it would de-eroticize women's incapacity and foster in them the same sturdiness and self-control recommended for men; and it would rescue and redignify heterosexuality itself—which had been excoriated in Wollstonecraft's early novel, *Mary, a Fiction* (1788/89), as distempered and corrupt—by figuring the mutually respecting married couple not as libertine, frivolous, or idle but as public-minded and purposive, as citizens and as parents busy about their work, productively embodied rather than decadently sensual. With a political and sexual vision like this, it is no wonder that Wollstonecraft did not seem to mind Imlay's wit, which resexed the maternal scene.

The Wrongs of Woman; or, Maria (1796-98) not only explodes this hope in the emancipatory potential of republican masculinity but it represents that hope as the madness from which the heroine must be emancipated. The specificity of the female body, far from being the strategic nonissue it was in the political tracts, here is its starting point. We first encounter Maria as a body that can only be female—a body frustrated in the sentiments which in part constitute it (Maria is "tortured by maternal apprehension" for the daughter who has been torn from her); a body thwarted in its physical functions (Maria's breasts are "bursting with the nutriment for which this cherished child might now be pining in vain").[12] Here, the female body—having been insulted, sold, hunted down, and imprisoned solely because of its femaleness—is accepted in all of its creatureliness, and is offered as the basis for solidarity with other women and as the spring of moral sentiment.

In arguing as much, I am dissenting from the common view of this work, which is seen as a sort of novelization of *Vindication*. To be sure, as far as its negative thesis is concerned—i.e., its determination to exhibit "the misery and oppression, peculiar to women, that arise out of the partial laws and customs of society" (73)—this is the case.[13] But as far as its positive thesis is concerned, *The Wrongs of Woman* grimly narrates the undoing of Wollstonecraft's earlier program: just as the plot works retrospectively to criticize middle- and upper-class masculinity, in the person of the monstrous but altogether conventional Venables, it also carries Maria forward to disenchantment with republican masculinity, in the person of the feckless Darnford. To consider the difference between *A Vindication of the Rights of Woman* and *The Wrongs of Woman*, then, is to consider the difference between Wollstonecraft's revolutionary and postrevolutionary careers. Wollstonecraft, like Wordsworth and Coleridge, was despondent about the failure of the French Revolution and the massiveness of the reaction at home. But these failures exacted different costs from radical women. Wordsworth could leave France, as well as Annette Vallon and their child, behind him. Given the hope Wollstonecraft had invested in republican masculinity throughout *Vindication*, however, Imlay's derelictions spelled a more extensive disillusionment that was political as well as personal. In this essay, I will argue that Wollstonecraft's turn toward the female body, as that body is a daughter and/or mother, is a turn away from the political normativity of the male body in conservative *and* radical discourse.

When *The Wrongs of Woman* opens, Maria has been immured in a decaying mansion that is at once a prison and a madhouse, and it is important to keep the dual nature of her confinement in mind. Insofar as her cell is a prison, it literalizes the condition of women across the kingdom. In chapter 1, the narrator asks, "Was not the world a vast prison, and women born slaves?" (79), and subsequent chapters, constructing an elaborate network of metaphors of entombment and forcible constraint, answer a gloomy affirmative. Maria herself later avers, coining a chilling phrase, "Marriage had bastilled me for life. . . . [F]ettered by the partial laws of society, this fair globe was to me an universal blank" (154-55), and women have the same experience all the way down the social ladder. At the first house where Maria seeks refuge from her husband, she discovers a haggard landlady who timorously declares, "When a woman was once married, she must bear every thing" (170), for her own drunken husband "would beat her if she chanced to offend him, though she had a child at the breast" (171). Maria's second landlady, a craftier dame, irks and bores Maria with a story that is much the same, even foreshadowing Maria's own later experience before the court: having had no choice but to suffer the depredations of a husband who, under the protection of the law, pawns her clothes for whores and drink, she observes, "Women always have the worst of it, when law is to decide" (178). Although these instances blast the myth that heterosexual domesticity affords affective nurturance and protection to women, the case of the unmarried Jemima is more desperate still, for having been raped and debauched of character and reputation since childhood, she is excluded from domestic service and can only subsist through prostitution.

These sections of *The Wrongs of Woman* are clearly devoted to fleshing out the intention Wollstonecraft formulated in a letter that Godwin made into the preface of the novel: "to show the wrongs of different classes of women, equally oppressive, though, from the difference of education, necessarily various" (74). As such, they sometimes appear to be perfunctory inset tales with no other rationale than to show yet another class of woman, like Maria, "caught in a trap, and caged for life" (144). Despite this occasional blatancy—it is, after all, unfinished—*The Wrongs of Woman* is a densely literary novel: texts by Dryden, Rowe, Rousseau, Shakespeare, Johnson, Burney, Radcliffe, and Godwin, to name only a few, are constantly being absorbed and transformed, sometimes with results far more artful than Wollstonecraft is usually given credit for. The quotation just cited alludes to the caged bird in Laurence Sterne's *Sentimental Journey*, whose song—"I can't get out, I can't get out"— moves Parson Yorick to conjure a vivid fantasy about a wretch imprisoned in the Bastille. Anticipating Burney as well as Austen, Wollstonecraft both radicalizes and feminizes the image throughout the novel, as Sterne's bird, taught its song by a servant of the ancien régime, becomes all of England's women, who regardless of class sing the same song: "I can't get out—I can't get out."[14] Moreover, the very bodies of these women both epitomize the unnatural blockage they protest—as when Maria's maternal milk is not permitted to flow—and reproduce that gynocidal blockage, becoming reluctant prisons in and of themselves—as when the wretchedness of Jemima's mother becomes the daughter's manacle, the "heavy weight fastened on her innocent neck" (79), or when Maria "mourning for the babe of which she was the tomb" (202), realizes that her own pregnant belly is a deadly jail.

As determined as this novel is to show the corporeal character of women's confinement, it is even more committed to representing how women's minds are fettered, as Gary Kelly has put it, by the "false consciousness of a society dominated by court and gentry notions of property, family and gender."[15] The orthodox conception of ideology that Kelly employs here is appropriate, for the novel is written with the conviction that rational minds can "advance before the improvements of the age" (73) and achieve a lucidity alien to their blinkered contemporaries. The truth which Wollstonecraft's stunning novel recommends to her enlightened readers is that Maria is immured most strenuously by the ideology of sentimental heterosexuality permeating radical as well as conservative discourse, and that she must cast off the chains that bind women to men and that occlude women's relations to each other and to their children if she is to be free.

The novel's case against heterosexual love is conveyed in part through the pervasive intertextual presence of *Hamlet*. Confined in her own Gothic house, Maria has occasion to meditate upon the rottenness of the kingdom as she looks out her window upon a "desolate garden" gone to seed and a "huge pile of buildings" fallen "to decay" and "left in heaps in the disordered court" (77). But when this feminine embodiment of Hamlet thinks about "the ills which flesh is heir to" (81), she has only women's flesh in mind: only a woman could have her child torn from her, and only a woman could be forcibly incarcerated in the madhouse on her husband's word. Recasting Hamlet's "Frailty, thy name is woman," Maria soliloquizes, "Woman, fragile flower! why were you suffered to adorn a world exposed to the inroad of such stormy elements?" (88), and the fragility she refers to is not women's susceptibility to sexual appetite, but their tragic lack of material, legal, and personal resources with which to withstand the brutality of men. The Ophelia she contemplates is a fellow inmate—"a lovely maniac," yet another womanly "warbler" singing in her cage—driven out of her mind by the "rich old man" to whom she was married "against her inclination" (88).

Although Maria indulges some wishes "to sleep and to dream no more" (85), her body hangs on, and her mind, unlike that of her Ophelian counterpart, is doomed to a painful enlightenment that makes her look like the crazy one in the corrupt world. Writing her "narrative" (85) specifically for her daughter's edification, Maria describes her initial love for George Venables as a fanciful projection onto him of the manly qualities she—like all Wollstonecraftean heroines—possesses in far greater abundance. When he contributes a guinea to Maria's charitable projects on behalf of an old woman, Maria believes him the soul of excellence: "I fancied myself in love—in love with the disinterestedness, fortitude, generosity, dignity, and humanity, with which I had invested the hero I dubbed" (130). But as fantastical as Maria's vision of George is, her delusion is hardly self-induced. As Maria writes of an attorney who is cold to the old woman's tears but moved by the ardent blush of Maria's complexion, "in a world where humanity to women is the characteristic of advancing civilization, the beauty of a young girl was so much more interesting than the distress of an old one" (134). If Maria believes that George's charity reflects anything nobler than the wish to impress the girl, that error is the work of sentimental ideology itself. Maria's sarcasm here targets not only the pretentions of Burke's reactionary inflection of chivalry in particular, already lambasted in the *Rights of Men* and *Vindication*, but also the larger tendency of the sentimental tradition in general, of which Burke partakes, to posit heteroerotic love as the basis for (men's) moral behavior. As Parson Yorick explains, "if ever I do a mean action, it must be betwixt one passion and other" for "one princess or another," for "whilst this interregnum lasts, I always perceive my heart locked up . . . and the moment I am rekindled, I am all generosity and good will again."[16]

In her retrospective memoirs Maria assails the ethos of chivalry without much difficulty, exposing how it invited her erroneously "to consider that heart as devoted to virtue, which had only obeyed a virtuous impulse" (135) inspired by her erotic presence. But her love for the nonchivalric Darnford is criticized far more reluctantly and considerably less frontally. In a subtle structural decision on Wollstonecraft's part, Maria's memoirs to her daughter are withheld from the reader until chapters 7-10, when Darnford reads them. Not until we read them can we appreciate why her love is represented under the shadow of the madhouse and recognize how Maria's love for him recapitulates the error she made with Venables. Here, of course, it is not only the credulity of youth that impels her but also the urgency of sexual desire itself. "Voluptuousness" is a pejorative in Wollstonecraft's earlier work, which links culpable sensuality with the feminine precisely when denoting male vice. But having tried in *Vindication* to dignify women by giving them access to the idealized male body, to which they are fated ever to be inferior in degree of strength, in *Wrongs* Wollstonecraft not only frankly accepts Maria's "voluptuousness" without a sneer but even claims that "it inspired the idea of strength of mind, rather than of body" (98), as if the manifestly (female) sexed substantiality of Maria's body could heighten rather than detract from her dignity. In this novel, when the "air swept across her face with a voluptuous freshness that thrilled to her heart" (89) after Maria has been reading *La Nouvelle Héloïse* in her cell, we are supposed to side with the body and the instincts that seek to expand beyond the constraints that fetter them. And whereas *Mary, a Fiction* had evolved into protolesbian narrative, in *Wrongs* the heroine's instincts are decidedly heterosexual. Mary finds a man as hyperfeminine as her beloved Ann; Maria fantasizes masculine virtues. Darnford's forceful insistence—"I *will* have an answer" (91)—contrasts markedly with Henry's modest reserve, just as the virility of Darnford's presence—"His steady step, and the whole air of his person, bursting as it were from a cloud, pleased her" (89)—contrasts with Henry's languor.

The narrator clearly pities Maria's yearning for propinquity—"What chance had Maria of escaping?" (98), the narrator asks, ominously—but clearly implies that romantic love is another form of incarceration. Yet something more than a purely personal need for love accounts for Maria's readiness to turn Darnford, much as she had earlier turned her husband, into a "statue in which she might enshrine" all "the qualities of a hero's mind" (99). A particular political program encourages the repetition of romantic error. Republican ideology itself, I would argue, remystifies Darnford's masculine sexual privilege in ways that make it hard to recognize. Maria reads Darnford's collection of "modern pamphlets" and a fragment apparently of his own composition about "the present state of society and government" (85-86). The republican sympathies they evidently share make Darnford's account of himself—a remarkably obnoxious mixture of self-pity and braggadocio—sound like a tale of intrepid manhood. Maria could at first plead ignorance to her husband's "libertinism" (130), but she is not ignorant of Darnford's. Indeed, he trumpets his finickiness about the fair sex: "And woman, lovely woman!—they charm every where—still there is a degree of prudery, and a want of taste and ease in the manners of the American women" (96). Even more damaging (given Jemima's presence), he positively flaunts his fancy for prostitutes: "The women of the town (again I must beg pardon for my habitual frankness) appeared to me like angels" (97).

Maria cannot hear Darnford's grossness because republican discourse has intervened and recoded it as frankness, much as it has recoded his selfishness as a lack of servility, his gallantry as generosity of spirit, and his arrogance as the unaffected brashness—the hypermasculinity, if you will—of the natural man, who puts the jaded effeteness—the effeminacy—of other males to shame. Clearly a rendering of Wollstonecraft's experience with Imlay, the Darnford/Maria episodes judge male culture to be so corrupt as to make affective reciprocity between the sexes impossible: republican swashbucklers and gentry and would-be gentry males alike assume the instrumentality of women. The difference between masculinities collapses, carrying with it Wollstonecraft's political hopes. The representation of Maria's relationship with Darnford breaks off with a violence that attests to an investment in it so intense as to be virtually unnarratable. Perhaps the most disturbing indication of Maria's pathetically lingering enslavement to heterosexual romance and to the political hopes it underwrites is her unwillingness to leave her prison. Imagining that in Darnford "she had found a being of celestial mould" (189), she declares that "liberty has lost its sweets." But leave she does, and the way out of prison and the way out of her "false consciousness" are the same. It is Jemima who takes Maria out of her bedlam and Jemima who yanks her back from death in the final fragment. As Janet Todd has put it, Maria's history is marked by two movements, "one circular and repetitive, and the other linear and developmental. The circular binds her to male relationships . . . the linear tends towards freedom and maturity."[17] But this way toward freedom and maturity, I would stress, also carries Maria toward solidarity and affective community with other women, a possibility which had hitherto been occluded.

Theorists such as René Girard and Eve Kosofsky Sedgwick illuminate plots structured by triangulated desire involving one woman and two men. But *The Wrongs of Woman* suggests that the heterosexual dyad represses female rather than male homosociality. Maria first chooses Venable's eldest sister as a "friend" (129), but this friend is no sooner mentioned than she is dropped from the novel altogether. Similarly, although helping her sisters is for Maria "a strong motive for marrying" Venables (143), we never hear from or about them again. Not only are women kept irrelevant to each other but they become jailers as well. Maria's first landlady is ready to betray Maria at the drop of her husband's hat: "A few kind words from Johnny would have found the woman in her," Maria bitterly writes, as if being a "woman" and betraying women go hand in hand (173). For Jemima most conspicuously, the brutality experienced at the hands of men is negligible in comparison to the beatings inflicted by her stepmother or by the wife who "scratched, kicked, and buffetted" Jemima upon discovering her husband raping her (112-13).[18]

In light of this "normal" functioning of female-female violence to sustain heterosexuality, I am more struck by what the relationship between Jemima and Maria tries to achieve than by what it fails to achieve. *Vindication* disdains "square-elbowed drudges" and "servants" who pass on "nasty" sexual tricks to their young mistresses, as if such women did not fall under the rubric "woman" and hence had nothing to do with the "rights" that Wollstonecraft is vindicating.[19] But even though *Wrongs* offends working-class women most egregiously when claiming not to—as when Maria observes of Jemima, "The woman was no fool, that is, she was superior to her class" (78)—its attempt to establish a collective sense of identity inclusive of all women is quite unprecedented. Including prostitutes, landladies, and women of the gentry and the middle class, this fellowship is based on a rational recognition of their mutually oppressive complicity in a system of male privilege as well as on their shared susceptibility to "humanizing affections." At the point where we expect a scene of passion between Maria and Darnford, Wollstonecraft almost comically disrupts the heterosexual dyad: Jemima barges in on the panting lovers and begins telling her very long and chilling story. Although many formidable readers have taken issue with Wollstonecraft's representation of Jemima as magically converted by the middle-class couple's sensibility, in fact it is not Jemima's sympathy with the romantic couple's tender love but her connection to Maria that proves decisive.[20] The upshot of Jemima's narrative is a bond with Maria that supersedes any relation to Darnford. When Jemima asks, "Who ever risked any thing for me?—Who ever acknowledged me to be a fellow creature?" (119), Maria takes her hand, and on the strength of this, Jemima becomes the deliverer that Maria had insanely hoped Darnford would be.

The inset tales show a self-reflexive and self-corrective tendency in light of Maria's gesture of affiliation to Jemima, for their alliance will become an alternative, a way out of the love plot, and it not only permits but invites us to critique the female-to-female violence that the tales elsewhere disclose. Darnford, for example, blunders when bragging/confessing, "I was taught to love by a creature I am ashamed to mention; and the other women with whom I afterwards became intimate, were of a class which you can have no knowledge" (94). But Maria, of course, does know this "class" of "creature"— first as the "wantons of the lowest class" whose "vulgar, indecent mirth" roused the "sluggish spirits" (146) of her husband, Venables. But even as this passage savages Darnford (who went wild over "women of the town" [97]) and Venables, it is in turn corrected by Jemima's own story about being such a "creature," a story that grows out of the section of *Vindication* devoted to "ruined" women.[21] Challenging tales about prostitutes not only as Maria tells them but also as Darnford and Venables tell them, Jemima's experience disproves the arguments that heterosexual propriety employs to shore itself up when it exculpates men who visit prostitutes and when it excludes "unsexed" women or prostitutes from presumably "normal" women. As Jemima's story makes abundantly clear, prostitutes are not wantons who enjoy their work; like wives, they are an exploited class, despising the men on whom they are economically dependent. Similarly, when Maria later heaps scorn on "the savage female," the "hag" (122) who takes over when Jemima temporarily leaves, we can now see—because the Maria/Jemima alliance itself has taught us to see—that this woman may simply be another Jemima and that such epithets are the fetters that keep her and Maria alike in chains.

But if the bond between Maria and Jemima makes possible a rational critique of male domination, it is itself based in a kindred warmth that Maria and Jemima link to the maternal. Representing heterosexual passion as corrupt beyond the possibility of recovery, *The Wrongs of Woman* locates the "humanizing affections" in maternal nurturance instead of in heterosexual love and the benevolizing sentiments it had been said to nourish. Saturated with images of nursing, the novel radically feminizes the imagery of natural blossoming that Paine had employed to characterize revolution itself.[22] The revolution of the seasons, which Paine uses to naturalize the other kind of revolution, the giving way of the old regime to the new, in Wollstonecraft's hands represents the redemptive emergence of woman-to-woman affection. As Maria writes in her memoirs to her missing infant daughter, "The spring was melting into summer, and you, my little companion, began to smile— that smile made hope bud out afresh, assuring me the world was not a desert. . . . I dreamed not of the frost—'the killing frost,' to which you were destined to be exposed" (181). According to this model, it is not subjected men, then, but women and infant daughters at their nursing breasts who are the "tender blossoms" which ought to burst from their cells into the fullness of life, and Darnford shows himself capable of moral feeling only insofar as he can imitate, however imperfectly, the maternal, as when "he respectfully pressed [Maria] to his bosom" (187). Conversely, the "killing frost" depicted in *Wrongs* is not the brutality with which privileged men of the ancien régime extinguish the potential of other men, but the cruelty with which male culture represses women's warmth toward each other: the frost that blights Maria's daughter has already wounded Maria herself—Maria's mother, we recall, preferred Maria's brother. Similarly, Jemima's humanity "had rather been benumbed than killed, by the keen frost she had to brave at her entrance into life" (120), and her mother's coldness toward her makes her unwilling in turn to "succour an unfortunate" such as Maria (79).

   The blight Jemima and Maria share as mothers and daughters they repair in their relations to one another and in their joint relationship with Maria's daughter. Insofar as Wollstonecraft consigns women to their biological roles as tender mothers, her achievement in *Wrongs* may seem to be yet another, implicitly conservative articulation of bourgeois domesticity. But the maternity that Wollstonecraft is serving up is radicalized by its departure from conventional domesticity. Maria first dreams about Darnford in part because she wants her daughter to have "a father whom her mother could respect and love" (90). But when she awakens from this delusion of heterosexual domesticity, she turns to Jemima—not to take the father's place but to stand as maternal coequal in a restructured domestic scene. Enjoining her help in locating her daughter, Maria wins Jemima with an extraordinary promise that has received little attention: "I will teach her to consider you as a second mother" (121). Jemima takes this offer seriously. She persuades Maria to leave the madhouse with her by appealing to the affective duty they owe each other. "On you it depends to reconcile me to the human race" (189), she urges, as if the offer of joint maternity were a sort of marriage proposal valid even after "their" daughter is believed dead. And the household they set up does not conceal class difference. Jemima is neither servile nor calculating. Far from acting out of a selfless devotion that places her outside economic necessity, she insists on her wages and secures her independence. But their parental bond ensures their cooperation. In the concluding fragment, when Maria, having been betrayed by men and their institutions of law and marriage, is in the throes of suicidal agony, Jemima reappears with the lost daughter, whom she has tutored to say the word *Mamma* (203). The dual referent of the word proves doubly redemptive: it takes Maria beyond the plot which heterosexual sentimentality inscribes for her, for that girl child is not cherished *because* she is the progeny of a still-beloved male but quite explicitly *despite* her relationship to her detested father; and it carries Jemima, the girl's "second mother," into an arena for purposive, kindred affection with which biological kinship per se has nothing to do.

This, of course, is not a story which *Wrongs* completely tells. The heaviness of Maria's despair is only barely overcome, and the novel itself is incomplete. And far from degenerating into a powerful and *un*ambivalent physical revulsion of the sort which Maria had felt toward Venables, the lapse of Maria's relation to Darnford into betrayal is hardly depicted at all, and so it is impossible to regard her eventual independence of it as fully voluntary. Still, the outlines discernible beneath the rubble of sentimental heterosexuality at the end invite us to conclude that the emancipated, sturdy, parentally purposive, and rationally loving republican couple that Wollstonecraft spent her career imagining is, finally, a female couple, although their republican virtues can flourish only in a retreat from the insurmountable corruption of the masculine public sphere. The last fragment rewrites the mother/father/child tableau that Imlay joked about years before by expelling men and manliness from the maternal scene, thus undomesticating women and their bodies, and bringing female homosociality into representation as a moral, though not as a clearly political, alternative.

Notes

1. Wollstonecraft to Ruth Barlow, 27 April 1794, in *Collected Letters of Mary Wollstonecraft*, ed. Ralph M. Wardle (Ithaca, N.Y.: Cornell University Press, 1979), 253.

2. Wollstonecraft to Ruth Barlow, 20 May 1794, *Collected Letters*, 256. This description is actually on an addendum to this letter, which Wollstonecraft dates 23 May.

3. *A Vindication of the Rights of Woman*, ed. Miriam Kramnick (Harmondsworth, Middlesex: Penguin Books, 1975), 254. All citations will hereafter be made parenthetically. For a discussion of Wollstonecraft's views on maternity as a means of reforming manners, see G.J. Barker-Benfield, *The Culture of Sensibility: Sex and Society in Eighteenth-Century Britain* (Chicago: University of Chicago Press, 1992), 279-86.

4. Thomas Laqueur, *Making Sex: Body and Gender from the Greeks to Freud* (Cambridge: Harvard University Press, 1990), 196.

5. G.J. Barker-Benfield, "Mary Wollstonecraft: Eighteenth-Century Commonwealthwoman," *Journal of the History of Ideas* 50 (1989): 95-115. As Barker-Benfield points out, Wollstonecraft was rather intimately connected to the Commonwealth tradition through the community of rational dissenters at Newington Green, where she moved in 1783. It was there that she met Richard Price and most probably became acquainted with James Burgh's *Political Disquisitions: An Enquiry with Public Errors, Defects, and Abuses* (1774) through his widow, who regarded Wollstonecraft as a daughter. On this link, see also Claire Tomalin, *The Life and Death of Mary Wollstonecraft* (New York: Harcourt Brace Jovanovich, 1974), 30-33; and Eleanor Flexner, *Mary Wollstonecraft* (New York: Coward, McCann, 1972). For other discussions of the Commonwealth tradition, I am also indebted to Caroline Robbins, *The Eighteenth-Century Commonwealthman: Studies in the Transmission, Development, and Circumstance of English Liberal Thought from the Restoration of Charles II until the War with the Thirteen Colonies* (Cambridge: Harvard University Press, 1961); J.G.A. Pocock, "The Varieties of Whiggism from Exclusion to Reform: A History of Ideology and Discourse," in *Virtue, Commerce, and History: Essays in Political Thought and History, Chiefly in the Eighteenth Century* (Cambridge: Cambridge University Press, 1985), 215-310. Most feminist-based studies into the gendered nature of Commonwealth ideology address versions that influenced the young American republic. See Ruth Bloch, "The Gendered Meanings of Virtue in Revolutionary American Studies," *Signs* 13 (1987): 98-121; and Carroll Smith-Rosenberg, "Domesticating 'Virtue,'" in *Literature and the Body*, ed. Elaine Scarry (Baltimore: Johns Hopkins University Press, 1988), 160-84.

6. James Burgh, *Political Disquisitions*, 3:11; Thomas Paine, *Rights of Man*, ed. Henry Collins (Harmondsworth, Middlesex: Penguin Books, 1969), 102, 249. Also see Burgh, "Of Lewdness," 133-50, and "Luxury Hurtful to Manners, and Dangerous to the State," 59-98.

7. See, for example, Lynn Hunt, *Politics, Culture, and Class in the French Revolution* (Berkeley: University of California Press, 1984); Joan Landes, *Women and the Public Sphere in the Age of the French Revolution* (Ithaca, N.Y.: Cornell University Press, 1988); Dorinda Outram, *The Body and the French Revolution: Sex, Class, and Political Culture* (New Haven: Yale University Press, 1989); and Peter Brooks, "The Revolutionary Body," in *Fictions of the French Revolution*, ed. Bernadette Fort (Evanston, Ill.: Northwestern University Press, 1991), 35-53.

8. Landes, *Women and the Public Sphere*, 138.

9. For a discussion of attacks upon Marie-Antoinette, see Jacques Revel, "Marie-Antoinette in Her Fictions: The Staging of Hatred," in *Fictions of the French Revolution*, 111-29.

10. Wollstonecraft to Ruth Barlow, 20 May 1794, *Collected Letters*, 255.

11. See especially Landes, *Women and the Public Sphere*, 129-38. I believe that Landes greatly exaggerates the importance of maternity in Wollstonecraft's political thought. It is useful to remember that the genre of *Vindication* is decidedly mixed, part liberal manifesto and part treatise on education. As a treatise on education it inevitably emphasizes the domestic duties of wives and husbands. Wollstonecraft intended to write a second volume—the one to which Imlay alludes—addressing women and the law, and presumably this would have taken women into the public sphere. This volume was never written. For the most comprehensive discussion of Wollstonecraft's political thought, see Virginia Sapiro, *A Vindication of Political Virtue: The Political Theory of Mary Wollstonecraft* (Chicago: University of Chicago Press, 1992).

12. Mary Wollstonecraft, *Mary and the Wrongs of Woman*, ed. Gary Kelly (Oxford: Oxford University Press, 1980), 75. All further citations will be noted parenthetically.

13. Critics who view *The Wrongs of Woman* as a continuation of *Vindication* include Mary Poovey, *The Proper Lady and the Woman Writer* (Chicago: University of Chicago Press, 1984); Gary Kelly, *English Fiction of the Romantic Period, 1789-1830* (London: Longman, 1989); and Laurie Langbauer, *Women and Romance: The Consolations of Gender in the English Novel* (Ithaca, N.Y.: Cornell University Press, 1990).

14. Laurence Sterne, *A Sentimental Journey through France and Italy*, ed. Gardner D. Stout Jr. (Berkeley: University of California Press, 1967).

15. Kelly, *English Fiction*, 40.

16. Sterne, *Sentimental Journey*, 128-29.

17. Janet Todd, *Women's Friendship in Literature* (New York: Columbia University Press, 1980), 211-12. Although I disagree with Todd's assessment of the Jemima/Maria relationship, her essay strikes me as one of the most comprehensive written to date on *Wrongs*.

18. For the role of female disidentification in nineteenth-century narrative, see Marianne Hirsch, *The Mother/Daughter Plot: Narrative, Psychoanalysis, Feminism* (Bloomington: Indiana University Press, 1989).

19. See Denise Riley, *Am I That Name? Feminism and the Category of "Women" in History* (Minneapolis: University of Minnesota Press, 1988), for a discussion of the emergence of "women" as a collective category during the eighteenth century.

20. Cora Kaplan, "Pandora's Box: Subjectivity, Class, and Sexuality in Socialist Feminist Criticism," in *Making a Difference: Feminist Literary Criticism*, ed. Gayle Greene and Coppelia Kahn (London: Methuen, 1985), 146-76. I am much indebted to Kaplan's work on Wollstonecraft.

21. In *Vindication*, Wollstonecraft argues, "Asylums and Magdalens are not the proper remedies for these abuses. It is justice, not charity, that is wanting in the world." But in advocating left-handed marriages and assuming that women still love their seducers, she accepts the ideology of heterosexual domesticity abandoned in *Wrongs*. See *Vindication*, 164-65.

22. For a discussion of this imagery in Paine, see Ronald Paulson, *Representations of Revolution, 1789-1820* (New Haven: Yale University Press, 1983), 73-76.

Maria Edgeworth and the Politics of Consumption

Eating, Breastfeeding, and the Irish Wet Nurse in *Ennui*

"The difficulty [facing the enlightened landlord in Ireland] is to relieve present misery, without creating more in the future," claims the good agent, Mr. M'Leod, in Maria Edgeworth's *Ennui* (1809).[1] In the face of spiraling Irish hunger during the 1830s and '40s, Edgeworth would feel this difficulty acutely herself in the years before her death in 1849. Hunger was a problem that she associated explicitly with her own divided (or doubled) responsibility (as the daughter of a wealthy Anglo-Irish landlord)[2] to regulate not only the material but the spiritual consumption of those beneath her—to feed the bodies as well as the minds of the lower-class Irish. Although the political economists she admired had stressed since the turn of the nineteenth century that too generous a system of poor relief in Ireland would foster indolence and over-population, Edgeworth persistently questioned the physical implications of the British government's limited responses to repeated subsistence crises, even before the appearance of the potato blight in 1845.[3] In May 1844 she wrote the Reverend Richard Jones, a staunch supporter of laissez–faire policies, "Take away the horror of seeing human beings perish—without offering aid . . . [y]ou raise, you educate a race of political thugs. There are whole bands of the selfish well-prepared for this education and quite ready to seize philo-sophical reasoning as its pretext." Like incorrigible children, she believed, the Irish necessarily had to be managed, but they also needed, first, to be fed. If she fed the body, however, she might corrupt the spirit. "How shall we get the people who have been fed gratis to believe that the government and their landlords are not bound to feed them always?" she wrote to Jones in 1847. "They evidently have formed this idea. . . . The character of Paddy knows well how to take advantage of his misfortunes and of all fear and blunders."[4]

Edgeworth had given this conflict a sustained treatment in *Ennui* (1809), the second of her Irish novels and one that anticipates many of the concerns that would trouble her during the 1830s and 1840s. Set during the years immediately preceding the Act of Union in 1800[5] (and written during the first half of the decade following the Union [1803-05]), the novel explores Edgeworth's concerns about controlling the consumption of her Irish tenants—largely through its analysis of the figure of the lower-class Irish wet nurse, Ellinor O'Donoghoe. Ellinor epitomizes the gross materiality and political subversiveness that Edgeworth associated with the lower-class Irish, but she also embodies an alternative model of domestic authority. In *Ennui* it is Ellinor, and hence Ireland, who feeds England, regulates the consumption of the Ascendancy class, commands their affections, and shapes their identities. While she is thus in many ways representative of the lower-class Irish mother whose consumption patterns and disorderly housekeeping, Edgeworth persistently stressed, needed to be managed in the broader interests of the state, Ellinor also supplants the duties and rights of the upper-class (and necessarily absentee) English mother, for whom she substitutes. Through the central figure of the wet nurse, Edgeworth poses questions about what kind of woman really has the authority to mother, and what the authority to mother in the hands of the lower classes might portend.

Edgeworth's critics have largely ignored this attention to the physical dynamics of interpersonal and intercultural relations in *Ennui* or, like Elizabeth Kowaleski-Wallace, have stressed that Ellinor represents that which Edgeworth herself "struggled not to become."[6] Katie Trumpener argues persuasively, however, that Edgeworth accentuates in this "national tale" the "imperatives of cultural preservation" and that Ellinor's maternal body becomes a site of "transcultural tolerance."[7] I will argue here that both perspectives are valid, although incomplete unless seen in relation to one another. While playing the role of enlightened mother-educator certainly aligned Edgeworth with the Ascendancy class in Ireland, her focus on the physical dynamics of mothering in *Ennui* helps her to confront simultaneously the difficulties in reconciling maternal sensibility with sound economic practice.[8] She critiques in *Ennui* those aspects of utilitarian colonial policy which seemed to discount the physical suffering of others, and she gestures toward a more maternalized model of Anglo-Irish relations. Yet she nevertheless remains anxious about the potential dangers of ungoverned local affections and loyalties, associating these dangers explicitly with the threat of unqualified maternal love.

Maternal affection, in fact, proves as subversive a force in *Ennui* as political intrigue and rebellion.[9] Ellinor's substitution of her own child for the English earl whom she nurses becomes a form of political rebellion, a means of satisfying her own hungers, if at a distance. (Her own child eventually inherits the estate, while Ellinor raises the real heir as a humble blacksmith.) If she represents a destabilizing threat to individual and cultural identities, however, Ellinor also reveals that the danger of the wet nurse lay not merely in her potential mutinousness but in the very deference which she appeared to present—in the love which she might foster in the upper classes, and the inverse obligations which that feeling engendered.[10] In nurturing and feeding her oppressors, the wet nurse cultivated dangerous sympathies in the ruling classes. Although for Edgeworth these bonds of affection provide a possible foundation for cultural hegemony in Ireland, such intimacy also functions in *Ennui* as a potential threat to the political and economic interests of the Ascendancy.[11] As Edgeworth's contemporary Samuel Ferguson (another Protestant Unionist) would emphasize, "Fosterage was one main instrument in that process of Hibernicization through which the early invaders were invariably withdrawn from their English allegiance."[12] Writing in the immediate aftermath of the political and economic Union of Ireland and Great Britain, Edgeworth questions whether such a distinction between "English" and "Hybernian" allegiances is more destructive than productive—but she also highlights the potentially destabilizing effects of the alternative model of cultural hybridity offered by the Irish nurse.

Before turning to *Ennui*, I will examine the way that the upper- and middle-class maternal responsibility to regulate the consumption of the lower classes was constructed in late-eighteenth-century housekeeping guides and cookbooks in England. I will suggest, then, that the problem of Irish hunger complicated this responsibility for enlightened reformers such as the Edgeworths, given their desires to, like the agent M'Leod, "relieve present misery without creating more." Turning to the case of the lower-class Irish wet nurse, I will argue that she problematizes the issue of controlling the consumption of the lower classes. As a food source, the wet nurse provokes the question, "Who is feeding whom?" and thereby foregrounds acutely the material dynamics of power relations in Ireland. In *Ennui*, Edgeworth suggests that, like Ireland, Ellinor is valued only as much as she can be consumed, although as with Ireland, Ellinor will threaten to turn the tables and become a devouring consumer herself.

The politics of domestic consumption and the role of the middle- to upper-class woman in managing the diets of her family as well as those of the lower classes were clearly spelled out in a genre that was relatively new to the eighteenth century and dominated by the work of women writers after mid-century—the cookbook.[13] Although many scholars have examined the way in which conduct literatures of the late eighteenth and early nineteenth centuries participated in the construction of specifically classed and gendered English subjects,[14] cookbooks have been widely disregarded as a field of inquiry, despite the fact that these texts anticipate concerns central to our understanding of nineteenth-century class and gender relations in Great Britain. The domestic homemaker functioned in cookery books of the period as the "unacknowl-edged legislator" of a society increasingly defining itself through the food it consumed and increasingly wary of the choices it thereby confronted. The careful regulation of diet became a means to a higher (national) end after midcentury, as English cooking was usually defined in opposition to the more costly, elaborate, and time-consuming French culinary methods promoted in cookbooks of the first half of the eighteenth century. Cookbooks helped to foster a sense of solid national identity, addressing an increasingly urbanized population that evidenced growing signs of imported disease.

Hannah Glasse's *The Art of Cookery Made Plain and Easy* (1747) was perhaps the most successful cookbook of its day, and it set the tone for works to follow in advocating economy and moderation in consumption patterns, while characteristically condemning extravagance as a French national trait: "I have heard of a Cook that used six pounds of butter to fry twelve Eggs; when any Body knows (that understands cooking) that Half a Pound is full enough — or more than need be used. But then it would not be French!"[15] Regulating this habit of extravagance, according to Glasse and other women writing cook-ery texts in the second half of the eighteenth century, would correspondingly elevate the character of the British nation.[16] Integral to this process was the suggestion that waste might be controlled. (Glasse offered her readers, for example, hints such as how "To Save Potted Birds That Begin to Go Bad.")

The implication that this type of ingenuity was an integral component of good housekeeping increasingly assumed broader social significance in sub-sequent best-selling cookbooks, and by the century's end, the social dynamics of eating became a central issue in works like Maria Rundell's *A New System of Domestic Cookery; Formed on Principles of Economy, and Adapted to the Use of Private Families* (1806). Rundell encouraged domestic homemakers to feed the urban poor with the leftovers from their tables (thus eliminating the need for organized soup kitchens and other forms of governmentally regu-lated relief), and she stressed that this type of domestic economy would help to cure the British nation of its blight of poor. In addition to her "receipts" and her extensive coverage of most aspects of thrifty household management, Rundell included detailed instructions to middle- and upper-class housewives on economic cooking practices for the relief of the lower classes. After a lengthy description of how to make nourishing soup from scraps and bones, for ex-ample, she noted:

> I found, in the time of scarcity, ten or fifteen gallons of soup could be dealt out weekly, at an expense not worth mentioning, though the vegetables were bought.

> If in the villages of London, abounding with opulent families, the
> quantity of ten gallons were made in ten gentleman's houses, there would
> be a hundred gallons of wholesome agreeable food given weekly for the
> supply of forty poor families, at the rate of two gallons and a half each.[17]

Like Glasse, Rundell maintained that the business of feeding a family involved the regulation of its waste—the laboring classes might then receive
that which would otherwise be discarded: "broken potatoes, the green heads
of celery, the necks and feet of fowls," etc. She further stressed that this careful
management of detail radiated or circulated throughout the system of the
nation. Not only would "the pieces of meat that come from the table and are
left on the plates after eating" yield "nutritious soup for the poor two or three
times a week," but servants could be taught to subordinate their own needs to
those of others less fortunate: "It very rarely happens that servants object to
seconding the kindness of their superiors to the poor; but should the cook of
any family think the adoption of this plan too troublesome, a gratuity at the
end of the winter might repay her, if the love of her fellow-creatures failed of
doing it a hundred fold."[18]

Rundell's domestic philosophy emphasized the inherent value of disinterested acts of "kindness," which enriched both giver and receiver. But ultimately her goal was to teach others to help themselves, most especially the
"industrious mother, whose forbearance from the necessary quantity of food,
that others may have their share, frequently reduces the strength upon which
the family depends."[19] Rundell suggested that there were concrete means
through which women contributed to the material as well as the spiritual
well-being of their families and the families of others, but she stressed, too,
that if the body of the mother ran to waste, the welfare of the entire family
would be jeopardized.

Edgeworth drew upon these domestic values in her 1798 pioneering work
on child management, *Practical Education* (cowritten with her father, Richard Lovell Edgeworth), but she put a somewhat different spin on the question
of the mother's duty to regulate the consumption habits of her family. She
cautioned her readers most specifically about the dangers of enjoying food to
excess, noting that in homes where "the pleasure of eating is associated with
unusual cheerfulness, and thus [with] the imagination," parents "conspire to
make [their children] epicures": "All children may be rendered gluttons, but
few, who are properly treated with respect to food, and who have any literary
tastes, can be in danger of continuing to be fond of eating."[20] Promoting the
values of moderation and self-control, Edgeworth also suggests explicitly that
proper literature can become a kind of substitute for food. Needless to say,
she clearly hoped that her own moral and educational tales (which preach

self-discipline and the control of appetites) might provide her readers with just such a form of alternative nourishment.

Yet circumstances in Ireland complicated the more immediate sense of responsibility to the poor that Edgeworth associated with her own position as daughter of an enlightened landlord. Targeting the agricultural practices in Ireland as the "root" of the country's trouble, she aligned herself with political economists who found the potato to be an inferior food that pinned the Irish to the bottom of civilization's ladder, linking the Irish dependence on the potato to indolence and spiritual decline. She would note years later that potato farming did not require "industry or labor sufficient for the moral purpose."[21] It was not only the scarcity of food in Ireland that concerned women like Edgeworth, in other words, but the abundance of the wrong type of food. Elizabeth Smith, of County Wicklow, expressed attitudes that were, by the mid-nineteenth century, widespread: "The cheapness of this low description of food encourages idleness, pauper marriages and dirty habits, and neither mind nor body could be fully developed upon such nourishment."[22]

Ironically, although it would be consistently associated in this way with economic and moral decline, Irish potato farming had developed in response to the increased export of grain to England and its other colonies. Christine Kinealy notes that an estimated two million people within Great Britain were fed, on the eve of the Great Famine, with food imported from Ireland, "and the demand for this food was increasing." Agricultural Ireland was in fact described "as a granary for the remainder of the United Kingdom." Exportation was facilitated under the auspices of protectionist legislation, the infamous Corn Laws, which guaranteed minimal prices for "home-produced corn," of which Ireland was England's "largest single supplier." Ireland served, in other words, as a wet nurse of sorts to the English. While Irish exports filled English stomachs, the potato provided a local substitute food source that was both nutritious and easy to produce. Large quantities of potatoes could be cultivated in poor soil and on small parcels of land. Moreover, the cottier system, whereby Irish laborers leased a small portion of land from a larger tenant farmer in exchange for a certain number of hours of contracted labor, meant that subsistence might be maintained without cash transactions. Irish cottiers farmed potatoes on small plots of land on a rotating basis. The potatoes helped prepare the soil for other cash crops, and were given to the laborers as "left-overs." While they were thus cash-poor, the consumption of up to fourteen pounds of potatoes a day[23] generally kept the lower classes healthy.

Yet overreliance on the potato crop was increasingly associated with rampant subdivision, earlier marriages, and an ever-burgeoning population in Ireland. Thomas Malthus had anticipated the trend to scapegoat the potato in his *Essay on the Principle of Population* (1798), in which he details "the disadvantageous effect of a low relative price of food on the consumption of the poor":

> The great quantity of food which land will bear when planted with potatoes, and the consequent cheapness of the labor supported by them, tends rather to raise than lower the rents of land . . . to keep up the price of the materials of manufactures and all other sorts of raw produce, except potatoes. . . . The exchangeable value of the food which the Irish laborer earns, above what he and his family will consume, will go but a little way in the purchasing of clothing, lodging, and other conveniences; and the consequence is that his condition in these respects is extremely miserable, at the same time that his means of subsistence, such as they are, may be comparatively abundant.[24]

While he may be well fed, Malthus explains, the Irish laborer produces no capital with which to reinvest in the Irish economy. In 1826 Malthus would amend this passage, noting that the "indolence and want of skill which usually accompany such a state of things tend further to render all wrought commodities comparatively dear."[25] Increasingly in this way, the negative influence of diet on character was linked to its deleterious effects on economic stability.

Increasingly too, the "indolence" which was held to "accompany such a state of affairs" in Ireland was associated with an even more threatening disorder—that of the fecundity of Irish mothers. Kinealy notes that besides indolence, "the production of children" was alleged to be the favorite pastime of the Irish people: "Hypotheses about human reproductive behavior . . . in the context of the provision of poor relief, were popular among the intellectual elite, linking high birth rates to indolence and the inactivity associated with poverty on the one hand, and too generous a system of poor relief, on the other." As the fear mounted that the number of Irish mouths was growing more rapidly than the food supply, concerns escalated regarding the "tendency," as Malthus so ominously expressed it, for population "to increase beyond the means of subsistence."[26] Writers like Malthus and Adam Smith suggested that Irish women's natural capacity to bear children contrasted sharply with their abilities to rear them—and that the dependence of Irish children on the state would mean the further loss of English revenues.[27] As excessive (re)producers (not unlike the potatoes which fueled that reproduction), Irish women were held to be necessarily conspicuous consumers.

The Irish wet nurse, however, radically challenged such assumptions. By definition she was a producer (the word *foster* derives from the Old English "fostrian," which means "feed" or "nourish") despite her lower-class status. The wet nurse utilized her body to turn a profit (she turned body into bread, so to speak). While the nature of this transaction—the nurse's ability to substitute for the biological mother—suggests a sympathetic model of intercultural relations, the wet nurse also becomes an uncomfortable reminder of the tenuousness between outside and inside, self and other. So too, while maternal value was grounded during the late eighteenth and early nineteenth centuries in the mother's supposed separateness from the public world of exchange and competition, the wet nurse testified to the fact that a woman "has value only in that she can be exchanged."[28] Rousseau had suggested this point explicitly, if ironically: "The best nurse is the one who offers the highest bribe." Indeed, as Valerie Fildes has stressed, wet-nursing had been a rather lucrative career for working-class women before 1800. Extended breastfeeding was widely acknowledged, moreover, to be an effective (if not always reliable) form of birth control, and the contraceptive advantages of nursing may have been complemented by the Roman Catholic doctrine of women's abstinence from sexual intercourse while breastfeeding.[29] Lower-class Irish wet nurses helped limit their burgeoning families by prolonging the period of lactation, while enabling aristocratic women to increase the size of their own families. The relationship between the aristocratic mother, her child, and the lower-class nurse constituted a kind of self-contained economy of mutual benefits and rewards.

During the 1790s, however, the years in which the action of *Ennui* unfolds, the practice of fostering out children began to decline in Ireland. Terry Eagleton, following Kevin Whelan, connects this trend to the political turbulence of that decade, which culminated in violent rebellion in 1798.[30] Yet we should note that the Irish wet nurse had long been the victim of English prejudice. As early as 1596, Edmund Spenser had suggested that fostered children might be corrupted by the *love* they received from their nurses, whom they might come to prefer over their mothers. Spenser appealed to this anxiety in venting his racial as well as class antipathy for the Irish wet nurse in *A View of the Present State of Ireland*, where he argues that the fostering system in Ireland is a "dangerous infection," and laments that "the child that sucketh the milk of the nurse must of necessity learn his first speech of her. . . . The smack of the first will always abide with him, and not only of the speech, but of the manners and conditions. . . . They moreover draw into themselves, together with their suck, even the nature and disposition of their nurses . . . so that the speech being Irish, the heart must needs be Irish."[31] This concern that the child might pick up the language habits of its nurse reveals Spenser's deeper anxieties about children learning to love "things Irish"—his fears that milk might be thicker than blood.[32] Edgeworth echoes this concern early in *Ennui*, where she interrupts the narrative with a footnote in which she quotes Sir John Davies: "Fostering hath always been a stronger alliance than blood" (36). For Davies, as well as Spenser, the fostering system was one cause of the English failure to subdue Ireland. The embrace of Irish custom, via the embrace of the lower-class wet nurse, had led "the English, which hoped to make a perfect conquest of the Irish," to be "perfectly and absolutely conquered" by the Irish.[33]

Edgeworth clearly draws on such anxieties in *Ennui* via the baby-switch plot. But she also offers a more complex and more decidedly sympathetic response to the Irish wet nurse. Her portrait of Ellinor O'Donoghoe emphasizes the (invariably) lower-class nurse's historical role in sustaining and nurturing the bodies of the English—her ability to be herself a food source that fosters British strength. The rural nurse's milk, in particular, had been frequently hailed in the late eighteenth century as a healthy alternative for upper-class children. Lord Glenthorn is placed with Ellinor as an infant for precisely this reason. His father, an English aristocrat, "had an idea that this would make me hardy" (5). The impulse proves to be sound, as the sickly heir regains his health at the breast of his Irish nurse, who claims later that she had been "sure . . . that he would die wid me" (289).

Although Ellinor is clearly a subversive presence in other ways, whose duplicity is equal to any of Spenser's or Davies's charges, she is not an abusive or neglectful nurse (like those targeted by Rousseau, for example), nor does she possess a nature somehow deviant from her maternity, like Lady Clonbrony or Lady Dashfort in *The Absentee* (1812). Those aspects of Ellinor's behavior that ultimately prove most threatening, rather, are those most explicitly associated with her mothering: her unqualified love, her intimacy with her children (both biological and fostered), her ability to produce enough milk (and affection) for not just one but two. As with the middle-class housekeepers of Glasse's and Rundell's texts, who contribute through their thriftiness to the financial well-being of the family, Ellinor channels surplus (the breastmilk which she produces for her own child as well as another's) into profit—both immediate financial profit and an added contraceptive payoff. Extended breastfeeding has (apparently) limited the size of her own family (only two biological children are mentioned in the text, both sons). Combining the features of the good middle- and upper-class English mother with those qualities valued in the good Irish nurse, Ellinor serves as a possible figure of reconciliation in the context of the impending union between England and Ireland—a union which is materialized through her act of suckling the heir to the Glenthorn estate.

Yet Edgeworth insists too that there are dangers inherent in this union. If it is in fact the Irish mother who is feeding the English, in whose breast does the real power lie? The question of who controls the "means of consumption" thus becomes a central issue in *Ennui*, where the regulation of diet proves in fact to be a slippery business. Ellinor is valued as a food source, but only insofar as she furthers the strength of those who would consume her. Ellinor's own appetites are an uncomfortable variable within this equation, not merely because they represent a potential drain on British resources but because they mirror the unregulated appetites of the English aristocracy in Ireland—those who, according to Edgeworth, ought rather to have been teaching the Irish the value of subordinating desire. As one of the novel's Irish aristocrats, Lady Geraldine, explains, "We, Irish, might live in innocence half a century longer, if you [English] didn't expedite the process of profligacy" (177). Lady Geraldine refers to the influence of the English in Ireland as a "contagion," from which the Irish need to be "quarantine[d]" (177). But how is it, Edgeworth wants to ask, that English national character had become so degenerate when transported to foreign soil? To admit, like Spenser and Davies, the dangerous influence of the Irish fosterage system (the English child's absorption of "Irishness" at the breast of the nurse) is at once to reaffirm the natural inferiority and infectiousness of Irish national character and to concede the alarming fragility of English identity—a concession which undercut the Ascendancy's claim to innate cultural superiority. Are the English, then, merely that which they eat? Does national character determine consumption patterns, or might the reverse prove true?[34]

Rather than providing us with definitive answers to such problematic questions, Edgeworth sidesteps them in *Ennui* by shifting her attention away from the problem of Irish national character (so central to her earlier *Castle Rackrent*) and focusing instead on the more overtly "natural" dangers of maternal love. She scapegoats, in other words, not Ellinor's inherent Irishness but her seemingly natural maternal responsiveness (her loyalties to both the child of her body and her nursling). Ellinor's original crime, the substitution of one child for another, dramatizes these split loyalties. By Ellinor's own account, this substitution represents an attempt to support—not to subvert—the status quo. She claims to have been motivated by sympathy for the Glenthorn family, stressing especially her consideration for their financial interests: "I thought with myself, what a pity it was the young lord should die, and he an only son and heir, and the estate to go out of the family, the Lord knows where; and then I thought, how happy [the Senior Lord Glen- thorn] would be if he had such a fine *babby* [sic] as [mine]" (289, emphasis Edgeworth's).

While we might detect more than a shade of Thady Quirk–like dissimulation here (even the turn of phrase, i.e., "I thought *with* myself," suggests a doubleness of perspective), Ellinor never denies her consciousness of the future benefits that would ultimately accrue to her own child as a result of her actions. She rather stresses her sense of responsibility to all parties concerned: "I thought . . . what a gain it would be to all, if it was never known" (290). Such apparent disinterestedness, of course, masks dangerous local interests, although Ellinor herself seems unconscious of this. Her allegiances have become blurred—not just for the reader but for Ellinor herself. And this, Edgeworth wants to stress, is precisely what is best and worst about the Irish fostering system. While fosterage breaks down cultural barriers, it also threatens to destroy the objectivity of both the English and the Irish, who can no longer, like the reader, distinguish who is who.

Edgeworth is careful to emphasize to this end that Ellinor's seemingly benevolent actions produce their share of casualties, not the least of which is her natural son, who believes himself to be an orphaned English earl. Raised without the benefit of a mother-legislator (Lady Glenthorn has died shortly after giving birth), Lord Glenthorn does not learn the values of moderation and self-control so necessary for happiness and sound leadership. He has rather been "bred up [in England] in luxurious indolence . . . surrounded by friends, who seemed to have no business in this world but to save me the trouble of thinking or acting for myself" (1). This faulty education (whereby idleness rather than industry is rewarded) produces in Glenthorn, "whilst yet a boy," a "mental malady" characterized by melancholy and boredom, which he refers to as "ennui" (2-3). That ennui is a disease foreign to healthy English subjects is reinforced by Edgeworth's detailed attention to the manifestations of Glenthorn's disorder: his French epicurism (19-24) and his taste for revolutionary upheaval (236). While his bad eating habits and inclinations for political intrigue might be viewed as marks of Glenthorn's "natural" Irishness, Edgeworth persistently stresses that her protagonist's character flaws are rather the products of his decadent upbringing among English aristocrats—themselves rendered corrupt through exposure to French culture.[35]

The thorny path down which Glenthorn has been led, however, takes a radical swerve when he is confronted in England, on the birthday that marks his coming of age, by Ellinor herself, whom he believes to be his Irish wet nurse. To highlight this transitional moment, Edgeworth has Ellinor, in a burst of joyous enthusiasm, provoke Glenthorn's "fortunate fall" from his horse—fortunate, that is, because the accident allows him a glimpse of the "true characters" of his wife (whom Glenthorn has "purchased . . . by the numeration table" [17]) and his friends (who he realizes are anxious "to get rid of me" [35]). The accident is fortunate, too, in that it provides Ellinor with an opportunity to nurse Glenthorn back to health, both physically and spiritually. The recovered Glenthorn (whose wife has eloped with his crafty financial manager) decides to return to his estate in Ireland, where he believes he can enjoy what he imagines to be "feudal power" and live "as a king" (39). Upon discovering his actual identity, however, Glenthorn assumes his real name (Christopher O'Donoghoe), relinquishes his estate to his foster brother,

Christy (the actual earl, who has been raised by Ellinor), and begins to live by his own wits. Through industry and perseverance he attains self-made happiness and the bride of his choice (upon whom his former estate has been conveniently settled). When Christy, the restored earl, later relinquishes the estate (which has all but been destroyed by his wife's extravagant consumption patterns), a wiser, more deserving Glenthorn/Christopher reassumes his former position — "the demon of ennui [now] cast out forever" (359).

Ennui thus plays out (on the surface) Edgeworth's program for the development of legitimate Ascendancy authority. If Glenthorn/Christopher is unqualified to rule by virtue of the birthright which he has been led to believe is his own, in learning the values of hard work, just principles, and affectionate duty, he appears to be so qualified upon the completion of the novel, which is written as his memoir. As with English rule in Ireland, his authority will in the end be merited rather than arbitrarily inherited. "Honors of your own earning," notes Lord Y****, who oversees Christopher's education and facilitates his class transition. "How far superior to any hereditary title!" (393). Moving away from an explanatory model of political legitimacy that is rooted in blood ties or in ties to the land helps Edgeworth to validate the claims of the ruling Ascendancy over those of the displaced Irish landowners. Yet the confusion of identities that attends this movement also helps to obscure the fact that an Irish O'Donoghoe eventually assumes control of the Glenthorn estate. Edgeworth pushes this sense of confusion still further. Local lore holds that the lowborn O'Donoghoes were once "kings of Ireland" (304), whereas the Glenthorns, "long and long before they stooped to be *lorded*," were at one time but mere "O'Shaughnasees" (37, emphasis Edgeworth's). Perhaps there is something of poetic (as opposed to utilitarian) justice at work here after all.

Even if obliquely, these references to familial decline and ascent raise specters of a violent past marked by the rapid (and coercive) reordering of the social classes in Ireland. Ellinor's methods of political conversion, by contrast, constitute an alternative to the problematic colonial model that history offered Edgeworth. In reforming Glenthorn through love, Ellinor teaches him in turn *to love* and, moreover, to love Ireland, a country for which he has previously felt only antipathy (5). Love will eventually become the motivating force of his life, driving him to pursue the law laboriously so as to make himself worthy of Cecilia Delamere. Ellinor's resumption of her mothering of Glenthorn is in this sense his enlightenment, a point that Edgeworth accents through the promise Ellinor asks of him: to be allowed to light his fire in the morning and draw open the shutters (81). The name Ellinor is, in fact, from the French Hélène, meaning "light." Glenthorn's coming into the light is rendered, furthermore, as a return to nature. "You want the natural touch, you do," Ellinor tells him, specifically in the context of Glenthorn's initial "virtuous resolution" not to be merciful, when mercy might interfere with "what was due to justice" (281-82). Ellinor's function in the text becomes to "touch" Glenthorn, to personalize his understanding of just rule. Her affection cures not only his "hard heart" (282) but, via his heart, also his ennui. Hers is a revisionary model of politics, similar to what Anne Mellor has identified as a feminine Romantic "ethic of care."[36] At her death, Lord Glenthorn loses "the only human being who had ever shown me warm, disinterested affection" (321).

Yet precisely because all of Ellinor's ideas of virtue "depended upon the principle of fidelity to the objects of her affections, and no scrupulous notions of justice disturbed her understanding, or alarmed her self-complacency" (299), there are troubling implications for this ethic. Ellinor is a threat to the social order specifically because her affections take precedence over justice. While she inspires in Glenthorn a broader concern for the physical well-being of others that dramatically reorients his sense of personal and social responsibility (and that consequently enables him to abandon his former absenteeism), she also reveals that ungoverned sympathies can be problematic. Ellinor, in fact, cultivates in both her natural son and her foster son sympathies that threaten the broader political and financial interests of the Ascendancy. She teaches them to be, in other words, "bad mothers," who cannot control the appetites of others or reform the consumption patterns that threaten both Ireland and England.

The true heir (and former blacksmith), Christy, for example, is a seemingly natural gentleman, who appears to be content enough with the life he has been given and who is motivated by affection and a sense of responsibility to others. Nonetheless, he is thoroughly unprepared to govern the estate when he is confronted with his true responsibilities. "Tribes of vagabond relations" descend on Glenthorn Castle when Christy takes up residence there, and the estate becomes "a scene of riotous living, and of the most wasteful vulgar extravagance" (369). Although Christy himself "has lived all his days upon potatoes and salt, and is content" (283), his contentment can be read as complacency that actually helps facilitate the near destruction of the estate. His degeneration resembles, however, that of the English aristocrat as much as it does that of the Irish laborer rendered dull from a potato diet. Christy's degeneration, like Glenthorn's early self-indulgent behavior, is produced by a faulty education. From Ellinor, whose heart rules her head, Christy has learned the wrong lessons. He cannot recognize the dangers of overindulgence, and so he cannot understand the benefits of long-term vision that will improve the land and all its inhabitants.

Although Ellinor provides Glenthorn similarly with an education of the heart, the sympathies that she inspires in him are as problematic as the liberality she has fostered in Christy. Foremost among the traps to which Glenthorn is susceptible upon his return to Ireland is the tendency to "give" injudiciously to those he should be disciplining. This is a dramatic improvement over the neglect that characterized his absentee status, although his behavior is nonetheless still qualified by the same sense of apathy: "The method of doing good, which seemed to require the least exertion, and which I, therefore, most willingly practiced, was giving away money" (101). Although "well-meaning," Glenthorn's initial charitable attempts to improve the conditions of his tenants are fundamentally unsound because he is indiscriminate: "I did not wait to inquire, much less to examine, into the merits of the claimants; but, without selecting proper objects, I relieved myself from that uneasy feeling of pity, by indiscriminate donations to objects apparently the most miserable" (101). Glenthorn's "pity" (an "uneasy" condition because, like Ellinor's pity for the Glenthorn family, it smacks of his guilt) is targeted by his agent, M'Leod, as an improper impulse in the greater design to "do good." For M'Leod, a student of Adam Smith, the task of feeding the poor is inseparable from the goals of education: "to teach men to see clearly, and follow steadily, their real interests" (111). It is the confusion of interests, he suggests, which leads to economic degeneration and hunger—a confusion spurred by inappropriate emotional responses on the part of the aristocracy. Glenthorn has, for example, given marriage portions to the daughters of his tenants and rewarded those who have children, so as to encourage population. M'Leod notes, in response, that Glenthorn's estate "was so populous, that the complaint in each family was that they had not land for the sons. *It might be doubted* whether, if a farm could support but ten people, it were wise to encourage the birth of twenty. *It might be doubted* whether it were not better for ten to live, and be well fed, than for twenty to be born, and to be half-starved" (105, emphasis Edgeworth's).

Controlled giving, on the other hand, which encouraged the industrious, while teaching the indolent to reform, is represented as an acceptable mode of aristocratic philanthropy. Thus Glenthorn's later desire to reward the daughter of a tenant for her self-restraint in delaying marriage, by providing her with a small farm on which she and her future husband can live comfortably and care for her aging father, inspires a broader pattern of assumed responsibilities, and this benefits the estate as a whole. (The family does not, in this case, subdivide and thus devaluate the father's portion of land, and they achieve self-sufficiency at minimal cost and maximum benefit for all.) Acts of charity when motivated solely by pity, on the other hand, constitute unsound investments and further destructive patterns of consumption. M'Leod argues, "Pity for one class of beings sometimes makes us cruel to others. I am told that there are some Indian Brahmins so very compassionate, that they hire beggars to let fleas feed upon them; I doubt whether it might not be better to let the fleas starve" (102). Shifting to a more remote colonial context, M'Leod at once presents the colonial problem as universal (i.e., all colonial situations are alike, in that the colonizers—as much as the colonized—need to be educated to abandon archaic and unreasonable methods of confronting unpleasant problems), *and* invokes sympathy for the colonized figure who is himself being devoured by the current state of affairs. The Brahmin's "philanthropy" merely disguises his displaced consumption of the beggar, whose body is the only commodity that the beggar has to sell, and who must be eaten so as to satisfy his own hunger temporarily. The same is equally true of the wet nurse. But more broadly, this dynamic underscores the relationship that Edgeworth saw between England and Ireland. M'Leod stresses, above all, that one cannot always distinguish the difference between eating and being eaten.

Ellinor's tragedy is explicitly this inability to distinguish between being consumed and being the consumer. Her willingness, for example, to "sacrifice all she had in the world for anybody she loved" leads her to be "as generous of the property of others, as of her own" (299). Such selfless generosity not only threatens the broader interests of the community but blinds Ellinor to the fact that in attempting to prioritize the needs of others, she has starved herself of the emotional and physical rewards of mothering Glenthorn/Christopher, her "jewel" (285, 288, 292). She recalls the pleasure of holding and nursing him and despairs when he initially denies the preference he owes his "old nurse, that carried ye in her arms, and fed ye with her milk, and watched over ye many's the long night, and loved ye: ay, none ever loved, or could love ye, so well" (280). Depriving both herself and her child of that love has created a chain of events that not only endangers the happiness of each but distorts the nature of the mother-child bond. Ellinor does not know, in fact, how to *be* a mother to her real son when he acknowledges their relationship. Faced with Glenthorn's rebirth as Christopher, Ellinor wills her own end and falls victim to her son's decline in fortune (to his weaning from the taste for fashionable life).

Ellinor's death suggests that while the influence of the mother is vital to the cultivation of bonds of affection, her authority must in some measure be contained. She dies when the classes are reordered for a second time (when Christopher/Glenthorn gives up his right to the estate), but she also precipitates with her death the further restructuring of the social order by freeing her son to move beyond her orbit and releasing him from the promise he has made to nurse her back to health and take her with him when he leaves the estate. Only through physical separation from her body, Edgeworth suggests, can he differentiate himself from her powerful control and move forward. The death of the Mother becomes the originating act that founds society within this text. In the end, this is the "secret" Ellinor must conceal, even to herself.

If, however, Edgeworth necessarily had to bury the mother in *Ennui*, she also insisted that maternalized sympathies must be resurrected in Ireland in something of a new form, which feeds the mind while simultaneously acknowledging the primacy of the body. Restoration in *Ennui* thus comes through Cecilia Delamere, who inherits the Glenthorn estate after it has been all but ruined by Christy's mismanagement. Via the intermarriage of an English Delamere with an Irish O'Donoghoe (like those in the traditional endings of Walter Scott's future novels), Edgeworth gestures toward the possibility of a legitimately hybrid (and explicitly feminized) Anglo-Irish culture. Cecilia, in fact, renames Christopher/Glenthorn (he takes the name Delamere in marriage), and thus offers him a new identity, which prioritizes the influence of the maternal (Delamere, as Elizabeth Kowaleski-Wallace points out, is "de la mere," of the mother).[37] Cecilia inspires in her husband healthy appetites that are neither self-destructive nor disabling for others. Rather she motivates him to "persevere" in his "intellectual labours" so as to attain "the pleasures of domestic life" that can come only through "exertion" (396). In this sense her domestic legislation is grounded in reciprocal affections that produce responsible middle-class behavior and the possibility of real social progress. Moreover, this progress is not accomplished through the consumption of the labor and bodies of others, but through a steady diet of words, through Glenthorn's "*eating [his] terms* at the Temple" (384, emphasis Edgeworth's).

This movement away from the consumption of the Irish body to that of the English word recalls Edgeworth's own educational intentions. For Edgeworth, as with her protagonist, the task of inverting the consumption dynamics in Ireland necessarily began with the reappropriation of cultural authority in the form of the educational text. Yet Edgeworth struggled throughout her career with the contradictions embedded in her novels, which could only gesture toward romantic resolutions to the tensions that she continued to see escalate in Ireland, without effecting real relief for the starving Irish lower classes. Significantly, with the assumption of full managerial duty for the family estate in 1826 (she would run Edgeworthstown until 1839), her public writing declined dramatically. During these years, she increasingly questioned in her private correspondence the physical implications of the laissez-faire doctrine she had hesitantly promoted in novels like *Ennui*. It is as though she played out those concerns with which she had struggled in her fiction, in an Ireland that became "impossible to draw," as "realities [were] too strong, party passions too violent to bear to see."[38]

In the year before her death, however, Edgeworth found something of a tentative resolution to her own imperative to feed both minds and bodies. In 1848, she wrote one last story set in Ireland, *Orlandino*, which took as its subject the value of temperance. Thus fulfilling her duty to regulate the consumption patterns of the Irish, she evidenced her continued commitment to an educational model based on reason and the control of the appetites. Donating her profits to famine relief, however, she was simultaneously able to provide literal nourishment for the poor. Metonymizing the book (or, more precisely, the pen) into figurative breast, she could nurture this once both bodies and souls.

Notes

This essay benefited vastly from the advice and encouragement of Seamus Deane, Susan Greenfield, Greg Kucich, Willa Murphy, and Kevin Whelan.

1. Maria Edgeworth, *Ennui* (New York: Garland, 1978), 102. All further references will be cited parenthetically in the text.

2. Edgeworth would not have used the term *Anglo–Irish*, but rather would have described herself as Irish. In this essay I will use the term *Irish* to designate, however, those whom she considered "Hybernion" by descent.

3. Histories and economic studies of the Famine and pre–Famine years are appearing rapidly. See Austin Bourke, *"The Visitation of God?" The Potato and the Great Irish Famine* (Dublin: Lilliput, 1993); Mary E. Daly, *The Famine in Ireland* (Dundalk: Dublin Historical Association with Dundalgan Press, 1986); R.D. Edwards and T.D. Williams, *The Great Famine: Studies in Irish History* (1957; reprint, Dublin: Lilliput, 1994); Christine Kinealy, *This Great Calamity: The Irish Famine, 1845-52* (Dublin: Gill and Macmillan, 1994); Helen Litton, *The Irish Famine: An Illustrated History* (Dublin: Wolfhound, 1994); Cormac O'Grada, *The Great Irish Famine* (London: Macmillan, 1989) and *Ireland: A New Economic History, 1780-1939* (Oxford: Clarendon, 1994); and Rita M. Rhodes, *Women and the Family in Post-Famine Ireland: Status and Opportunity in a Patriarchal State* (New York: Garland, 1992). See also Cecil Woodham-Smith's recently reissued *The Great Hunger: Ireland, 1845-1849* (New York: Penguin Books USA, 1992).

4. Quoted in Michael Hurst, *Maria Edgeworth and the Public Scene: Intellect, Fine Feeling, and Landlordism in the Age of Reform* (Coral Gables, Fla.: University of Miami Press, 1969), 134, 167. See also letters quoted on 103, 157, 165.

5. The Act of Union abolished the Irish Parliament and annexed Ireland to the "body" of Great Britain.

6. Elizabeth Kowaleski-Wallace, *Their Fathers' Daughters: Hannah More, Maria Edgeworth, and Patriarchal Complicity* (New York: Oxford University Press, 1991), 172. Kowaleski-Wallace argues convincingly that Edgeworth betrayed an attraction to the lifestyle of the Irish peasantry which ran counter to her policy of reform. She stresses, however, that Edgeworth necessarily had to suppress her attraction to the "excessively physical" embrace of Ireland so as to maintain her "defense of Anglo-Irish privilege" (166).

Most postcolonial critics of Edgeworth's work have focused, however, on her understanding of duty in terms of intellectual rather than physical influence. Michael

Hurst claims (in *Maria Edgeworth and the Public Scene*), for example, that Edgeworth had a "social gospel" (104), which was spurred by her "passion for justice under the rule of the best educated" (148), although it contained the elements of which "the potentials of autocracy [were] made and, with certain more modern accretions, Fascism too" (123). See also Barry Sloan, *The Pioneers of Anglo-Irish Fiction, 1800-1850* (Gerrards Cross, Bucks: Colin Smythe, 1986); and Mary Jean Corbett, "Another Tale to Tell: Postcolonial Theory and the Case of *Castle Rackrent*," *Criticism* 36 (summer 1994): 383-400.

Anne Mellor, in a somewhat different vein, notes that Edgeworth's colonial model was familial and that her Irish peasants were rhetorically assigned to the category of children, "who need to be well treated, with justice and benevolence and understanding." (Mellor does not consider specifically, however, the ways in which justice and benevolence might operate at cross purposes within this maternalized frame of influence.) See Mellor, *Romanticism and Gender* (New York: Routledge, 1993), 78.

7. Katie Trumpener, "The Old Wives' Tale: The Fostering System as National and Imperial Education," in *Bardic Nationalism: The Romantic Novel and the British Empire* (Princeton: Princeton University Press, 1997), 216, 214.

8. Seamus Deane makes a similar case with respect to *Castle Rackrent* (1800), arguing that Edgeworth confronts in this earlier novel a version of what Deane identifies as the "Burke problem," that is, "the reconciliation of sensibility with economics": Deane, *Ireland: Strange Country. Modernity and Nationhood in Irish Writing Since 1790* (Oxford: Clarendon, 1997), 38.

9. See Mitzie Myers, "'Like the Pictures in a Magic Lantern': Gender, History, and Edgeworth's Rebellion Narratives," *Nineteenth-Century Contexts* 19, no. 4 (1996): 373-412, for a reading of *Ennui* through the lens of the 1798 Rebellion in Ireland.

10. Ellinor, of course, resembles in this sense another of Edgeworth's most ambiguous characters, Thady Quirk (*Castle Rackrent*).

11. Terry Eagleton makes a similar point: "There is a question with Edgeworth . . . of how near to or distant from a situation you need to be in order to pass judgement on it": Eagleton, *Heathcliff and the Great Hunger: Studies in Irish Culture* (London: Verso, 1995), 172.

12. See Samuel Ferguson's "Review of Hardiman's Irish Minstrelsy, no. III," *Dublin University Magazine*, October 1834, 452. Ferguson stresses the acutely physical nature of the threat posed by the fostering system to English cultural identity: "Certainly no institution could be better calculated for incorporating foreign families with the greater body of the people; so that, when we consider the danger to English interests attending on the admission of a custom thus destructive of the whole scheme of conquest, we can readily find an excuse for laws against communication with the Irish, which, if not justified by the existence of a contagion so catching, would appear unnecessarily and atrociously cruel."

13. See Stephen Mennell, *All Manners of Food: Eating and Taste in England and France from the Middle Ages to the Present* (Oxford: Basil Blackwell, 1985), 202.

14. Nancy Armstrong's *Desire and Domestic Fiction: A Political History of the Novel* (New York: Oxford University Press, 1987) is the obvious example. Toni Bow-

ers observes that Armstrong's study "virtually omits consideration of the eighteenth-century domestic woman as mother, obscuring motherhood's central status in Augustan women's lives": Bowers, *The Politics of Motherhood: British Writing and Culture, 1680-1760* (Cambridge: Cambridge University Press, 1996), 21.

15. Quoted in Eric Quayle, *Old Cook Books: An Illustrated History* (New York: Dutton, 1978), 72.

16. Educational guides written by women betray the same preoccupation. Catharine Macaulay, in her 1790 *Letters on Education: With Observations on Religion and Metaphysical Subjects* (New York: Garland, 1974), drew on evidence from past civilizations to support her claim that overindulgence in "luxuries which belonged only to opulence" signaled the weakening of "a robust habit of body," leading to an affliction of "mental powers," and consequently giving "a taint to the morals" (24, 25). Macaulay linked "those refinements of sense which are only mischievous in their excess" to the increasing "ostentation of the table" (301).

17. Quoted in Quayle, *Old Cook Books*, 125.

18. Ibid.

19. Ibid.

20. Maria Edgeworth and Richard Lovell Edgeworth, *Practical Education* (London: J. Johnson, 1798), 1:200-201.

21. Quoted in Hurst, *Maria Edgeworth and the Public Scene*, 165.

22. Elizabeth Smith, *The Irish Journals of Elizabeth Smith, 1840-1850*, ed. David Thomson and Moyra McGusty (Oxford: Clarendon, 1980), 101.

23. Kinealy, *This Great Calamity*, 4, 5; Daly, *Famine in Ireland*, 8, 13-19; Bourke, *Visitation of God?*, 94.

24. Thomas R. Malthus, *An Essay on the Principle of Population; or, A View of Its Past and Present Effects on Human Happiness* (1798; reprint, Cambridge: Cambridge University Press, 1992), 127-28.

25. Ibid., 127 n. 4.

26. Kinealy, *This Great Calamity*, 5, 2; Malthus, *Principle of Population*, 15.

27. Ludmilla Jordanova discusses representations of maternity in the theories of eighteenth-century political economists in "Sex and Gender," in *Inventing Human Science: Eighteenth-Century Domains*, ed. Christopher Fox, Roy Porter, and Robert Wokler (Berkeley: University of California Press, 1995), 152-83, esp. 172-76.

28. Luce Irigaray, "Women on the Market," in *This Sex Which Is Not One*, translated by Catherine Porter with Caroline Burke (Ithaca, N.Y.: Cornell University Press, 1985), 176. Irigaray holds that mothers "as both natural value and use value . . . cannot circulate in the form of commodities without threatening the very existence of the social order" (185).

29. Jean-Jacques Rousseau, *Emile*, trans. Barbara Foxley (London: Dent, 1993), 27; Valerie A. Fildes, *Breasts, Bottles, and Babies: A History of Infant Feeding* (Edinburgh: Edinburgh University Press, 1986), 162, 107-9, 105. See also Londa Schiebinger, *Nature's Body: Gender and the Making of Science* (Boston: Beacon Press, 1993), 66.

30. The 1790s, Eagleton argues, constituted a turning point in relations between the gentry and their tenantry: "The newly militant Catholic Committee broke with

the obsequiousness of its predecessors, and if some of the tenantry still respected the Big Houses, an increasing number had taken to plundering them": Eagleton, *Heathcliff and the Great Hunger*, 56. The Edgeworths had, in fact, been forced to flee their estate during the 1798 Rebellion. See Myers, "Magic Lantern," on Edgeworth's allusions to the Rebellion in *Ennui*. See also Jim Smyth, *The Men of No Property: Irish Radicals and Popular Politics in the Late Eighteenth Century* (New York: St. Martin's Press, 1992); and Kevin Whelan, *The Tree of Liberty: Radicalism, Catholicism, and the Construction of Irish Identity, 1760-1830* (Cork: Cork University Press, 1996), on the political turbulence of the 1790s.

31. Edmund Spenser, *A View of the Present State of Ireland*, ed. W.L. Renwick (Oxford: Clarendon, 1970), 68.

32. Clare Carroll also notes of this passage that Spenser's "analogy between the child's learning language and sucking milk through the breast suggests the most physical and erotic sense of language, as well as a linguistically conditioned way of perceiving the world." The problem for Spenser is that Irish women (through intermarriage as well as fostering) "are responsible for raising and thus forming the cultural identity of [Anglo-Irish] children": Carroll, "Representations of Women in Some Early Modern English Tracts on the Colonization of Ireland," *Albion* 25 (fall 1993): 384.

33. Sir John Davies, *A Discovery of the True Causes Why Ireland Was Never Entirely Subdued*. Excerpted in *The Field Day Anthology of Irish Writing*, 3 vols., ed. Seamus Deane (Derry: Field Day, 1991), 1:216.

34. *Ennui* confronts more overtly in this sense the provocative question that concludes *Castle Rackrent*: "Did the Warwickshire militia, who were chiefly artisans, teach the Irish to drink beer? or did they learn from the Irish to drink whiskey?" (70). See Deane's *Ireland: Strange Country*, 28-48, for a good analysis of the problem of national character in Edgeworth's fiction.

35. See David Simpson, *Romanticism, Nationalism, and the Revolt Against Theory* (Chicago: University of Chicago Press, 1993), 64-83, on the "Myth of French Excess" during the late eighteenth and early nineteenth centuries.

36. Mellor, *Romanticism and Gender* (3), borrows this phrase from Carol Gilligan's *In a Different Voice* (Cambridge: Harvard University Press, 1982).

37. Kowaleski-Wallace, *Their Fathers' Daughters*, 180.

38. Letter dated 19 February 1834, in Maria Edgeworth, *Chosen Letters*, ed. F.V. Barry (1931; reprint, Boston: Houghton-Mifflin, 1979), 384.

Reproductive Urges

Literacy, Sexuality, and Eighteenth-Century Englishness

As its starting point, this essay takes the period in eighteenth-century England when the power of words changed profoundly and writing took on unprecedented authority in a field of symbolic practices. With cultural meaning no longer legitimated and stabilized through its intimate association with monarchy or church, Raymond Williams, Michel Foucault, and others argue, it could be determined in other arenas and serve other interests.[1] There is evidence to suggest that the ability to read and write vernacular English effectively produced communities, on both sides of the Atlantic, who shared interests and affiliations, whose power and increase in numbers depended on publications that addressed their interests. Early efforts to regulate the English language were based on the implicit assumption that an individual's writing attested to the quality of its human source.[2] The ability to read and write common speech distinguished the individual from his inferiors and identified his interests in common with others outside his immediate geographic area, commercial ties, or kinship network. As vernacular English came to represent a person's capacity for thoughts, feelings, and actions, it apparently identified those who possessed it as true English people, those most suited, even obligated, to govern.[3]

With the gradual proliferation of print, increase in written forms, and improvements in printing techniques and methods of distributing information, the relationship presumed to exist between the elite individual who could read and the quality of his literacy was implicitly threatened. The manner in which writing preserved and strengthened elite ties is suggested in Alvin Kiernan's description of the books filling aristocratic libraries "celebrating the great princes and their courts, their kingdoms and their languages, legitimating and reinforcing the aristocratic ethos and the hierarchical social structures that entered the entire political and artistic enterprise."[4] In contrast, periodical writers, moralists, and intellectuals of the late eighteenth century were particularly alarmed by the propensities of the novel to call into question this kinship between literacy and the quality of individual consciousness. Hannah More warned that "frivolous reading" would "produce its correspondent effect" in the character of young people exposed too early and too often to its charms.[5] Fiction was perceived to be powerful and hence dangerous for a number of reasons. Not only was it easily imitated, with its multiple spin-offs widely disseminated and avidly read, but it had the mimetic capability of representation that could point to something that was not really there. It could simulate personal and social qualities lacking in essential value.

Sometime around the end of the eighteenth century, to put it simply, a problem with literacy and mass cultural reproduction became a problem with sex or biological reproduction. Mid-eighteenth-century authors and intellectuals responded to the popularizing tendencies of print culture with a slew of dictionaries, grammar books, and novels in a concerted attempt to make vernacular English behave, to control a language that took new shape every day in the pages of novels, journals, chapbooks, pamphlets, and the like, and to make it conform to aristocratic ideals of historical and dynastic continuity and divine authority.[6] By 1800, many writers, moralists, and journalists warned of the dangers of linguistic reproduction out of control. They did so in the same vocabulary deployed by political economists, Thomas Malthus foremost among them, to warn of the biological power and arithmetic increase of population, the seemingly inevitable result of unchecked sexual reproduction among the wrong sorts of people.

The discourse on population imparted a new sense of urgency to the problem of early mass culture because it seemed to provide a natural basis for reproduction, a phenomenon previously understood not in sexual terms but in its cultural capacity as a problem unique to print language.[7] What had become a tradition assuming the unlimited capacity of print language to reproduce itself, despite efforts to control its spread, now merged with a preoccupation about the sexual reproduction of bodies and populations. As a new way of thinking about sex and literacy (or the relationship between sexual and cultural reproduction) came into being, it displaced or dissolved the links between reading, writing, and individuality characteristic of an older cultural logic to become a way of talking about the social and political dangers confronting the newly consolidating middle class. It is tempting to argue that the longevity and political efficacy of this late-eighteenth-century logic is nowhere more evident than in contemporary American newspaper accounts, senatorial debates, and "scholarly" books linking the sexual habits of "welfare mothers" to the economic plight of the American middle class.

There is a difference then between the eighteenth and the nineteenth century in terms of the cultural work done by the novel and the problem it must rationalize or solve. As a historical scholar of nineteenth-century fiction,

I want to map out a tentative trajectory from mid-eighteenth-century optimism about the production of mass literacy and the reading subject, as figured in Charlotte Lennox's *The Female Quixote* (1752), to the sudden anxiety about cultural and sexual reproduction out of control, texts unhooked from their sources, bodies without end, which characterizes turn-of-the-century morality tracts, political economies, and novels of the kind represented by Hannah More, Thomas Malthus, and Jane Austen. This essay will trace the discursive swerve taken by the language of cultural reproduction as it is linked to figures of sexual reproduction and the maternal body, especially in discourse about what the novel should be and in the novel itself. For it is there that the problems with language and sex overlap and interact in the most provocative manner.

Patrilineage, Continuity, and the Trouble with Language

The troubles of Lennox's misguided aristocratic heroine in *The Female Quixote* stem from a problem with language. Raised in splendid isolation by her father, the marquis, after his banishment from court, Arabella cultivates a fondness for reading French romances in "very bad Translations." That Arabella's odd behavior results from the French romances she reads is crucial. As Margaret Anne Doody suggests, "The volumes of romances are Arabella's only inheritance from her mother, and the female inheritance is customarily presented by women in their novels as dangerous or double-edged."[8] What Doody's reading elucidates is the manner in which the figure of the mother increasingly becomes the space onto which the problem of unauthorized reproduction, as I will argue, will be mapped as the century progresses.

Arabella's first turn of the page leaves her unable to distinguish fiction from fact, copy from original. "Her Ideas," writes Lennox, "from the Manner of her Life, and Objects around her, had taken a romantic Turn; and supposing Romances were real Pictures of Life, from them she drew all her Notions and Expectations" (7). Comical consequences ensue when Arabella's misreading launches her on a series of adventures making plain, in Lennox's words, "the Bad Effects of a whimsical Study"—in other words, the influence of reading on women. Deluded by bad books, Arabella transforms noblemen into knights, gardeners into disguised lovers, and women of easy virtue into distraught maidens. Thus, she is unable to distinguish the knight from the suitor out to claim her fortune, the disguised lover from the gardener out to steal her carp, and the maiden from the prostitute out to gull her. But this is a minor problem. What is most at issue in such illicit reproduction is the challenge to patriarchal authority implicit in Arabella's refusal to marry the man chosen by her father, her cousin Glanville.[9] By transforming "a Lover of a

Father's recommending" into an "impropriety," Arabella's misreading of romance protocols challenges the demands of alliance governing the aristocratic community. According to this logic, the sexual and the political were united within one elite, enclosed domain so represented earlier by John Milton in *Paradise Lost* as the "Union of Pure with Pure."[10] Her resistance to make so appropriate a match endangers the longevity and stability of aristocratic power. Because aristocratic rule was predicated on the purity of blood and the antiquity of ancestry, the unique character of marriage alliances was a crucial element connoting rank, status, and power in early modern England.[11]

Despite the challenge to patriarchal authority mounted by Arabella's illicit reproduction of French romance, the literacy problem is never represented as a problem of desire. The novel certainly problematizes the troublesome relationship between individual identity and textual replication by playing out the consequences of a female reader's inappropriate transference of copy to original, representation to "reality," thereby highlighting the potential within literacy to call forth unauthorized behaviors and practices. Nonetheless, *The Female Quixote* never seriously calls into question what form social and sexual reproduction will assume; it is always perfectly clear how these aristocrats will reproduce themselves. Literacy played only a slight role in this political drama as Benedict Anderson observes: "The relatively small size of traditional aristocracies, their fixed political bases, and the personalization of political relations implied by sexual intercourse and inheritance, meant that their cohesion as classes were as much concrete as imagined. An illiterate nobility could still act as a nobility."[12] In Lennox's isolated aristocratic milieu, personal relationships are played out within an overarching model of continuity ensuring the uninterrupted and unchanging connection between its members that is never seriously jeopardized by literacy gone awry.

In Glanville's eyes, Arabella's aristocratic beauty, bearing, and grace are only magnified by her unique reading style, whereas in Arabella's somewhat eccentric affections no comparable suitor emerges to rival Glanville—whose appropriateness, desirability, and suitability to marry are never at issue. If anything, Arabella's persistent efforts to reproduce in Glanville the features of a romantic hero pay off by enhancing his attractions. He is transformed from a bad reader, who did not obey her when "she made a Sign for him to retire" because "he was quite unacquainted with these Sorts of dumb Commands" (36), into a good reader, who "understood" when she made "a Sign to leave her alone" (304). Arabella's interpretative difficulties hardly amount to anything more than a series of comical mix-ups, mistaken identities, and near misses threatening little or nothing of consequence in the social world she orbits. Given this, the problem motivating the plot, indeed rescuing it from

Lennox's tedious repetition of a comedy of errors, is precisely what form Arabella's cure will take.

Conservative intentions to the contrary, *The Female Quixote* neither argues against cultural reproduction itself nor figures language as an uncontrollable force. Although Arabella's adventures illustrate the power of fiction to form and authorize her subjectivity, she nevertheless is cured in the end. Marriage to Glanville brings desire squarely into alignment with the demands of the kinship system and guarantees the continuity of aristocratic fortune and blood. Whereas some feminist critics read Arabella's renunciation of Romance as a portent foretelling her precipitous decline into domesticity, and see Arabella herself as a powerless victim of the forces of patriarchy beyond her control, such conclusions, I would argue, are based on ahistorical premises.[13] Because they represent the alliance that ends the novel in terms more appropriate to nineteenth-century domestic fiction, Arabella's dynastic union is rewritten as middle-class matrimony. Only in so doing can feminist readings argue that the demands of gender make subordinate privileges of rank and status clearly belonging to Arabella, the marquis's daughter, even after marriage. There is little evidence to suggest that her vast estate, material wealth, formidable education, regal bearing, and pure blood, all political prerogatives of her aristocratic station, will summarily be replaced upon marriage by the narrow confines of a gendered identity alone. It is possible to argue, however, that the marriage of Arabella and Glanville is represented in terms blending features of the kinship system governing aristocratic unions and those of the companionate system characterized by the enactment of a sexual contract between properly gendered individuals. The contractual exchange so performed by Glanville and Arabella figures the newlyweds as persons possessed of unique internal qualities uniting them "as well in these as in every Virtue and laudable Affection of the Mind" (383). Like Samuel Richardson's Pamela and Mr. B., Lennox's happy couple achieves the best of both old and new orders when hereditary wealth is augmented in conjunction with a notion of integral personal worth.

Matrilineage, Reproduction, and the Trouble with Sex

It is fair to say that mid-eighteenth-century intellectuals were not preoccupied with the possibility of prolix authors writing too many books or fertile people having too many children.[14] While the rich versatility of written English certainly fascinated many, their concerns seemed to converge on the repair and maintenance of traditional continuities—between books and their readers, words and their meaning, aristocrats and their bloodlines. Discourses of cultural reproduction, like aristocratic kinship practices, looked back to notions of origin, authenticity, and the metaphysics of blood as purveyors of meaning and quality from the past to the present. Inasmuch as the authenticity of the cultural or social source could be verified, the futurity of texts and bodies was never in doubt and appeared immune to the incessant quantifying demands of print culture. Certainly the anxiety of illicit reproduction — readers copying books, words escaping original meanings, and bloodlines becoming sullied — was always present.[15] Yet the proper regulation of literacy remained a promising means to affect desired forms of subjectivity well into the century.

Sometime around the end of the eighteenth century, the language problem suddenly took on crisis proportions. With the spread of literacy, increase in book production, and the tendency of the novel to generate multiple spinoffs, the presumed relationship between writing and the individual, copy and original began to deteriorate.[16] If the increasingly frequent diatribes against popular novels are any measure, intellectuals and authors were now more intrigued and horrified by the dangers of reading and writing out of control. By contrast, Dr. Johnson's attitude toward mass literary production had been sanguine, as these words, so recounted by Boswell, make plain: "There is a great difference in favour of that crab-apple tree which bears a large quantity of fruit, *however indifferent*, and that which produces only a few."[17] Even Johnson acknowledged the value of abundance independent of the intrinsic value of the composition. Late-eighteenth-century writers, in contrast, no longer knew, as Johnson believed he did, how to tell the good apple from the bad when the standard was no longer qualitative but quantitative. Put another way, if literacy is a sign of innermost character, what happens when the democratization of reading and writing begins to obscure or to erase this original relationship?

With the links between literacy and consciousness strained, moralists and educators increasingly located the problem of authenticity with the literate individual rather than with the continuity of language itself. Hannah More was particularly alarmed by "that profusion of little, amusing, sentimental books with which the youthful library overflows." Where Johnson found merit in plenty, More warned of its sinister side. "Abundance has its dangers as well as scarcity," she writes in *Strictures on the Modern System of Female Education* (1799). "May not the multiplicity of these alluring little works increase the natural reluctance to those more dry and uninteresting studies, of which . . . the rudiments of every part of learning must consist?" (157). From such seductions comes the frivolous reader unable to regulate her own conduct. "Girls who had been accustomed to devour frivolous books," writes More, "will converse and write with a far greater *appearance of skill* as to style and sentiment at twelve or fourteen years old, than those of a more advanced age who are under the discipline of severer studies . . . and those who early begin talking and writing like women, commonly end with the thinking and acting like children" (160, emphasis added).

What More fears from unregulated literacy is the disruption of the proper relation of reader, writer, and book. The reader of trifles, in her logic, becomes a frivolous writer, one whose conduct is similarly marred by the mere appearance of skill and style lacking in essential substance. In so linking reading, writing, and conduct, More implies that the wrong kind of literacy can produce an individual who is a bad copy, a person of no intrinsic value, but one who does have the skills to simulate such value. Put another way, if writing indicates the quality of its human source, it can also attribute value (or lack thereof) to the origin (writer) rather than the origin lending value to the text.[18] Since the text can no longer be hooked to its origin, moreover, it displaces the original, thereby initiating an endless chain of reproduction with no definitive source.[19] Not only is the cultural artifact devalued in More's logic, but the social value formerly believed to inhere in the literate individual vanishes. For if literacy is no longer an accurate measure of individual consciousness, how is the capacity for thought, feeling, and action to be determined? If the quality of literacy among one group of people had been the basis upon which they gained prestige and power over others, as I suggested earlier, how might mass cultural reproduction endanger their claim?

It is not easy to imagine how fiction could have acquired so much linguistic power in such a short time had its dissemination in England not coincided with the growth of the notion that the wholeness of the individual, as well as the strength of the nation, depended on what came to be understood as a universal drive toward sexual reproduction. Elaborated in the writing of political economy, this concept of the English nation imagined it to be a social body composed of sexualized populations. Because writing about population incorporated and adapted tropes of production and popular consumption common to earlier writings on the proper regulation of cultural reproduction, it achieved unprecedented rhetorical power.

Nothing brings the history of this transformation into more visible relief than the work of Thomas Malthus. In his 1798 *Essay on the Principle of Population*, Malthus radically reconfigures the notion of reproduction, transforming it from the controlled, determinable process imagined earlier in the century to a biological force that overpowers efforts to contain it. Malthus structures his argument around two basic postulates that, in effect, separate the body from history and reanchor it in universal nature: "First, That food is necessary to the existence of man. Secondly, That the passion between the sexes is necessary and will remain nearly in its present state. These two laws, ever since we have had any knowledge of mankind, appear to have been *fixed laws of our nature*."[20]

Three points simultaneously established here need emphasizing. First, notice how sexual desire is configured according to a model of the natural body and its need for food. Malthus equates sex with food, both driven by an uncontrollable hunger; in each case, the magnitude, intensity, and frequency are identical. Second, so naturalized and biologized, sexual passion becomes the principle, the "fixed law" defining and organizing so-called human nature. This tendency is evident, for example, in his survey of the "hunter state," where Malthus argues, "In the rudest state of mankind, in which hunting is the principal occupation and the only mode of acquiring food, the means of subsistence being scattered over a large extent of territory, the comparative population must necessarily be thin. It is said that the passion between the sexes is less ardent among the North American Indians than among any other race of men" (27).

"Passion between the sexes" becomes the basis for his analysis of the economic and social organization of Native Americans, as well as "the shepherd state," "the tribes of barbarians that overran the Roman Empire" (27), Chinese peasants, and English tradesmen. Malthus romps through time and space violating historical and cultural boundaries, yoking together radically different peoples, places, and histories according to their shared reproductive urges. "The passion between the sexes," Malthus declares confidently, "has appeared in every age to be so nearly the same that it may always be considered, in algebraic language, as a given quantity"(52).

Through its unification of culturally and temporally diverse peoples around the principle of sexual reproduction, *Essay* contributed to a new classification system that, according to Foucault, is extraordinarily powerful precisely for its ability to dissolve older political and economic demographies to reconfigure them according to shared "natural" desires. Malthus's *Essay*, in this respect, provides a blueprint for the nineteenth-century literature of urban exploration, including James Kay Shuttleworth's *Moral and Physical Condition of the Working Classes* (1832), Frederick Engels's *Condition of the Working Class in England in 1844* (1845), and Henry Mayhew's *London Labour and the London Poor* (1861). As Judith Walkowitz notes, Mayhew introduced his investigation by linking the street folks of London to the ethnographic study of "wandering tribes in general" by arguing for their common promiscuity, irreligiosity, and laziness.[21] Although sexual proclivities may be common to all, in Malthus's logic and later in Mayhew's, some lack the requisite self-discipline to prevent natural urge from turning into natural disaster. "The labouring poor," Malthus writes, "seem always to live from hand to mouth, their present wants employ their whole attention, and they seldom think of the future" (41). So consumed by appetite, the poor appear as bearers of bad culture, the absence of economic restraint pointing to a more fundamental lack of sexual discipline and self-restraint.

Finally, Malthus's postulates underline the fear of biological reproduction so crucial to his argument and transform it from a sign of cultural and social vitality to a harbinger of sexual chaos. With his insistence that healthy bodies eventually produce an impaired social organism, Malthus departs from predecessors Adam Smith and David Hume, who saw rapid reproduction as simply an index of a healthy society. The *Essay*, moreover, posed a threat to the traditional Christian doctrine, embodied by Tory poet laureate Robert Southey, that man must be fruitful and multiply.[22]

Thus emptied of cultural meaning and linked to nature, the sexually reproducing body becomes the geometric foundation for the tremendous "power of population" that Malthus fears. "Assuming then, my postulata as granted," Malthus continues, "I say that the power of population is indefinitely greater than the power in the earth to produce subsistence for man" (20). So overwhelming are the voracious demands of population that popular consumption will always outstrip the production of food for the multitudes. Even the presence of plenty in the realm of production will not reduce demand, as one might imagine, but instead will lead to more consumption. Malthus argues, to wit, that "population does invariably increase where there are the means of subsistence, the history of every people that have ever existed will abundantly prove"(26). Illicit cultural reproduction is no longer attributable to a failure of linguistic continuity, paternity, or lineage, as Lennox believed. Instead, Malthus locates the problem in biological reproduction, itself out of control. When Malthus uses the number of women of childbearing age to indicate the rate of increase of a given population, he imagines the social body as female. In so measuring illicit reproduction in terms of the issue from the body of the mother, he shifts its source from paternity to maternity, lineage to reproduction. This shift is consonant with a more general historical trend in the latter half of the eighteenth century, so described by Felicity Nussbaum as "a fascination with the maternal." Malthus's focus on maternal reproduction is consistent with what Nussbaum calls a "significant historical change in reproductive politics."[23]

While it is tempting to argue that in the political economy of population lies the source of the problem of sexual reproduction and population, it is more reasonable to assume that Malthus's work was a symptom rather than a cause of a more widespread shift in cultural categories. Earlier writers anticipated and in some sense facilitated the figure of overpopulation with their frustrated and often comical efforts to contain the euphoria of print language released from age-old political, practical, and material constraints. Writing about the so-called population problem contributed another vital component to this process when it effectively shifted the burden of mass reproduction from the cultural domain to the natural world. In so doing, it provided biological ground for the fear of popular consumption raised decades earlier with the acceleration of print culture. With the lineaments of this transformation in mind, I want to turn to figures of population and popular consumption as they resurface in fiction and nonfiction as vital signs of social and cultural danger.

This metonymic overlap is particularly intriguing in late-eighteenth-century writing about the novel and what it should be. Easily copied, widely disseminated, popularly consumed, and sentimentally powerful, the novel proved particularly troublesome to those desiring to control the effects of mass literacy. "Who are those ever multiplying authors," Hannah More demands to know, "that with unparalleled fecundity are overstocking the world with their quick succeeding progeny? They are novel writers; the easiness of whole productions is at once the cause of their own fruitfulness, and of the almost infinitely numerous race of imitators to whom they give birth" (169-70).

More rewrites the figure of the author who becomes a fecund mother spawning an "infinitely numerous race of imitators." Since women were, by the late eighteenth century, identified as producers of novels, More's language acquires added resonance.[24] Like Malthus, who imagines the social body as female, More identifies prodigious literary production with female reproductive capacities. As textual progeny "overstock" the cultural world, the original relationship between author and text is irrevocably weakened by successive generations of novels, thereby diluting the quality of culture itself. This is not a sign of cultural health. Rather, More's rhetoric transforms the productive "body" of the writer, like the sexually reproductive body in Malthus, into a degenerative body figured in terms of its association with maternal reproduction.

What the novel loses by its copies, in Walter Benjamin's terms, is its original aura. "The technique of reproduction," he writes, "detaches the reproduced object from the domain of tradition. By making many reproductions it substitutes a plurality of copies for a unique existence."[25] This loss of aura might best be seen as the displacement of patriarchal continuity, so crucial to earlier writers, by maternal "reproduction" as the means by which western culture is transmitted.[26] By symbolic extension, from a cultural world of purity and originality comes one of frivolity and cheap imitation. The degeneration from one cultural moment to the next, moreover, is understood solely as a product of the reproductive vigor of language itself. The effects of overproduction on the cultural world that More depicts are remarkably similar to the social chaos produced by overpopulation in Malthus's model. Overproduction, in each case, threatens the "natural" balance between production and consumption; a social or cultural world thus "overstocked" is a system out of balance. Reproduction, so imagined in its sexual form by Malthus and in its cultural shape by More, is a force in need of regulation and control. More unwittingly problematizes the status of the novel as mass cultural object by calling into question the relationship between quality and quantity. The novel is a form of popular culture that is easily reproduced and widely read. Literary popularity becomes both boon and blight—marker of success and sign of degeneracy—as Walter Scott would lament some years later in his introduction to *The Abbey*.

With the fear of the mass reproduction of the novel came the anxiety over its popularity. "Women of every age, of every condition, contract and retain a taste for novels. . . . The depravity is universal," wrote the periodical writer known as the Sylph in a 1795 testimonial worth quoting at some length:

> My sight is everywhere offended by these foolish, yet dangerous books. I find them on the toilette of fashion, and in the work-bag of the sempstresses; in the hands of the *lady, who lounges on the sofa*, and of the *lady, who sits at the counter*. From the *mistresses of nobles* they descend to the *mistresses of snuffshops*—from the belles who read them in town, to the chits who spell them in the country. I have actually seen *mothers*, in miserable garrets *crying for the imaginary distress of an heroine, while their children were crying for bread*: and the mistress of a family losing hours over a novel in the parlour, while her maids, in emulation of the example, were similarly employed in the kitchen.[27]

Novels are most dangerous not only because they are most illicitly reproducible, as More maintains, but also because they are most disruptive of social order, as the Sylph argues. Ironically, as the Sylph's rhetoric actively links ladies who lounge on sofas to ladies who wait at counters, mistresses of noblemen to mistresses of snuffshops, it discursively constructs a new social trajectory of disorder. The danger of cultural reproduction thus out of control is that literacy no longer differentiates among social groups—the woman of fashion from the seamstress, the belle from the chit.

The passage comes to rhetorical fruition with the figure of the mother whose self-indulgence in reading novels renders her unable to distinguish between "the imaginary distress of an heroine" and the real distress of her children "crying for bread." Meanwhile, the inattentive mistress, careless of her duties and servants, jeopardizes the welfare of the household. No longer the occasion for comedy, as in *The Female Quixote*, the consequences of compulsive reading are so grave as to pose a threat to the very existence of the family itself. Mass reproduction is now held responsible for this breakdown in social and economic order, poverty, hunger, and the mismanaged household.

It is rhetorically equated with the dangers of mass literacy itself, among them the pleasures of reading novels giving rise to the reader's sentimental overidentification with the heroine.[28]

The rapid growth of the novel-reading public, depicted in the novel's progress from toilette to work-bag, parlour to garret, genders female both the novel and the social network it supposedly establishes by virtue of its promiscuous circulation. In so doing, this scene of reading establishes one link in the historical chain associating mass culture with "woman" that will become a prevalent mode for its representation in nineteenth- and twentieth-century Europe and the United States. Literary historians generally consider the association of the novel with the female in the eighteenth century to be the explanation for its status as a low, even dangerous, cultural form. Yet this connection could also work the other way round, as Armstrong suggests. "If it was on the basis of gender that people condemned fiction, . . . it was also on the basis of gender that fiction received its strongest endorsement."[29] Few studies, if any, have explored the relationship between the novel, the figure of "woman," and the construction of early mass culture traced briefly here in the Sylph's disquisition.[30] While such an inquiry is beyond the scope of the present essay, some preliminary conclusions may be suggested. The Sylph's just-so story of girls and their novels materializes early mass culture as a social pattern cohering only in the novel's wake as it perversely links readers whose social ranks otherwise hold nothing in common. It is a culture composed of individuals who consume the wrong kind of cultural object, one that is overly sentimental, easily reproducible, and too popular with the wrong sort of people. In the seductions of the novel, so powerful as to lead a mother to neglect her children, we can just make out the lure of mass culture, traditionally described, according to Andreas Huyssen, as "the threat of losing oneself in dreams and delusions and of merely consuming rather than producing."[31] As debates about the novel would have it, popular novel reading was no way to reproduce the kind of individual necessary to ensure the uninterrupted integrity and continuity of one's social group, much less secure the stability of the nation. Large-scale literacy, by extension, endangered the class of people whose claim to power rested not on heritage or blood but on their superior consciousness made visible in the quality of literacy itself.

Under the old system, we know that aristocrats reproduced themselves through the maintenance and continuation of a pure metaphysical body, whereas the underclass, according to Malthus, simply did it too much. But how were the diverse groups of people who composed the middle class at the end of the eighteenth century to make sense of their social experience and to reproduce it in continuous form? How were they to preserve continuity when social reproduction was based neither on the metaphysics of blood nor on the common physical urges of the body? As incipient mass culture undermined early class continuity maintained by limited literacy, the discourse of cultural reproduction, energized by semiotic contact with discourses of sexual reproduction and population, became a way of talking about danger in a social world composed of people whose heritage and blood were often indeterminate and whose literacy might prove an unreliable measure of personal integrity.

Jane Austen and the Perils of Reading Novels

Jane Austen went to great lengths to reconcile these two conflicting traditions of social reproduction—genealogy and self-production through literacy. Often, her novels focus on the need to preserve the continuity of an elite community while incorporating new social elements. To figure out a new bourgeois aristocracy on the basis of blood and individual value, Austen employs a variety of narrative strategies. As the daughter of a privileged woman who made an "untoward choice" in marriage, *Mansfield Park* heroine Fanny Price's heritage connects her by her mother's marriage to one of the most distinguished families of the area. There is little else to suggest why Fanny, who comes from relatively squalid circumstances (a Malthusian scenario, as it were), will be the one to continue the Bertram line. Yet in shaping her various "homes" in terms of the appearance of self-restraint or its lack, Austen provides ample justification for Fanny's good fortune. Fanny's possession of "moral restraint," "regulation," and "direction," in Malthus's words, ensures that she will be the bearer of good culture. Austen's social logic resembles Malthus's mathematics of sexual reproduction in that both privilege the same features as indicators of true culture—one that eschews sexual appetite. In contrast to the Crawfords, who are rendered fraudulent because they culturally reproduce what "breeding" is supposed to supply, only Fanny possesses the requisite self-discipline entitling her to make a prestigious alliance with Edmund. In the end, she becomes the daughter whom Sir Thomas wanted and the most suitable candidate should Mansfield Park be in need of a new mistress.

Unlike Fanny Price and Edmund Bertram, Catherine Morland and Henry Tilney of *Northanger Abbey* come from different social circles. Of all Austen's heroines, Catherine is the most unpretentious. As Austen writes, "A family of ten children will be always called a fine family . . . ; but the Morlands had little other right to the word, for they were in general very plain, and Catherine, for many years of her life, as plain as any."[32] Daughter of a clergy who "had never been handsome" and "a woman of useful plain sense, with a good temper and . . . a good constitution," Catherine has very little in the way of heritage or breeding to fit her for an alliance with a member of one of the elite country families dotting Austen's social landscape. What is more remarkable is the initial absence in Catherine of those sensibilities that immediately distinguish Fanny upon her entry into the Bertram household. Indeed, Austen takes every opportunity to emphasize Catherine's unsuitability for heroism of the kind for which Fanny is destined. Not only is she possessed of "a thin awkward figure, a sallow skin . . . dark lank hair," but her mind is decidedly unpromising, empty of intrinsic virtue. "She never could learn or understand any thing before she was taught," Austen writes, "and sometimes not even then, for she was often inattentive, and occasionally stupid" (37). Whereas Lennox's Arabella is amply suited by wealth, beauty, and lineage to take up her role as a heroine, Austen seems to intend Catherine for a much less distinguished career. In so devoting an entire chapter to unmaking her heroine, Austen sets out the terms by which she will remake Catherine into a true heroine according to a new set of narrative standards. Much of the energy of *Northanger Abbey* goes into narrowing the demographic distance between Catherine and Henry to make them alike.

Henry Tilney's virtues are as apparent as Catherine's are absent. "A very gentlemanlike young man," Henry "was rather tall, had a pleasing countenance, a very intelligent and lively eye, and if not quite handsome, was very near it" (47). Not only does he talk "with fluency and spirit" but he is exceedingly knowledgeable on matters of style and taste. To the astonished Mrs. Allen, he demonstrates his "understanding" of muslin, assuring her further that he buys his own cravats and has gained his sister's trust "'in the choice of a gown.'" His estimation of the writing style of women's letters links good taste in appearance to good taste in reading. In both matters he is equally confident, finding female writing "faultless except in three particulars. . . . A general deficiency of subject, a total inattention to stops, and a very frequent ignorance of grammar"(49). He is furthermore a member of a distinguished family of excellent breeding, whose virtues are embodied with grace and civility by sister Eleanor. Henry is supremely well suited to enact the education Catherine requires to reproduce socially and culturally the old squirearchy into which she will enter with as little disruption as possible.

Because there was not one lord, not even a baronet, to be discovered in Catherine's family, no lost inheritance to be claimed, the question remains how Austen makes the difference between Catherine and Henry go away. How does she make her a fit companion for him, the one most entitled to get the man and the goods? To close the gap between her protagonists, Austen employs two strategies. First, she introduces the Thorpes, Isabella and her brother John, whose manifest falseness, lack of manners, and dishonorable conduct become egregious as the novel progresses. Austen's first rendering of Thorpe is particularly important for my purposes: "He was a stout young man of middling height who, with a plain face and ungraceful form, seemed fearful of being too handsome unless he wore the dress of a groom and too much like a gentleman unless he were easy where he ought to be civil, and impudent where he might be allowed to be easy" (66). Austen thus fixes Thorpe on the boundaries of social identity, a liminal figure whose dress and demeanor, so oddly juxtaposed, expose the absence of definitive interior value.

Not only is Thorpe quarrelsome and dishonest but he does not read novels. This is perhaps the most shocking of his failings in a novel in which one's reading habits and tastes determine one's nature and value. Whereas Catherine and Henry share a mutual pleasure in gothic novels that will become the basis for Henry's prescription on the right way to read fiction, Thorpe has "something else to do" (69). Austen takes Isabella's measure in much the same manner. False modesty, coquetry, and husband-hunting notwithstanding, Isabella is, above all, an ill-informed reader with secondhand opinions. Without having read Samuel Richardson's *Sir Charles Grandison*, she pronounces it "an amazing horrid book" because her friend "Miss Andrews could not get through the first volume"(62).

Austen represents the Thorpes as pretenders, counterfeit goods whose class claims are shown to lack essential value. They are illicit copies with no heritage, fortune, or breeding, but only manners that simulate them. Thus they fail to answer correctly the most important questions of social interpretation that Austen raises: Are you what you say you are? And do you come from where you say you come from, or are you making it up? Because the answer is no in the first two cases, the Thorpes provide the false reproduction against which the authentic articles, the true Catherine and the true Henry, come to appear essentially valuable. Since it is John Thorpe who initially misleads the general, feeding him false information about Catherine's prospects, the Tilneys are linked to the Thorpes. General Tilney is turned into a greedy man who wants a moneyed woman for his son, someone who merchandises love, in contrast to the bourgeois Morlands who separate love from money. With the Tilneys' value thereby compromised, the gap between Catherine and Henry is further narrowed.

For those circulating within Austen's society, the most pressing danger then resides in the failure of interpretation. "Launched into all the difficulties and dangers of six weeks' residence in Bath" at the height of the social season, with only the languid guidance of Mrs. Allen, Catherine must learn to distinguish among the crowd, to know the worthy acquaintance from the pretender, the "good" copy from the "bad." This social process is not unlike the heroine's first physical passage through the Pump Room, which Austen describes with characteristic precision. Determined to get a good view of the dancers, she finds "to her utter amazement . . . that to proceed along the room was by no means the way to disengage themselves from the crowd; it seemed rather to increase as they went on, where she had imagined that when once fairly within the door, they should easily find seats. . . . But this was far from the case, and though by unwearied diligence they gained even the top of the room, their situation was just the same; . . . Still they moved on—something better was yet in view; and by continued exertion of strength and ingenuity they found themselves at last in the passage behind the highest bench" (44-45).

Not only must Catherine jockey for space in the overcrowded Pump Room, but she must also be able to distinguish the sight worth seeing ("something better was yet in view") from the multitude before her eyes.[33] Danger, in this world, is located in the ersatz bourgeois aristocrat, like John Thorpe, who is the real threat to the social reproduction of the bourgeois aristocracy that Austen envisions. Thorpe excels in the ability to simulate personal integrity and social worth, while in essence lacking such qualities. In merely reproducing what is represented as essential or natural among Austen's gentry, the ersatz bourgeois jeopardizes a social economy founded on the assumed link between identity and appearance.[34] This is the importance of the author's second strategy making Catherine and Henry alike, for if Henry teaches Catherine nothing else, he equips her with the reading skills to navigate such treacherous social waters. In prescribing the right way to read gothic novels, Henry solves the problem of illicit reproduction by translating from fiction to real life. His lecture to the embarrassed heroine, who has mistaken the manor house for the Gothic castle, the patriarch for the murderer, makes this distinction clearly. "Remember the country and the age in which we live," Austen writes. "Remember that we are English, that we are Christians. Consult your own understanding, your own sense of the probable, your own observation of what is passing around you—Does our education prepare us for such atrocities? Do our laws connive at them? Could they be perpetrated without being known, in a country like this, where social and literary intercourse is on such a footing; where every man is surrounded by a neighborhood of voluntary spies, and where roads and newspapers lay every thing open? Dearest Miss Morland, what ideas have you been admitting?" (199-200).

That the only danger Henry's speech admits is the failure to interpret properly the evidence of one's senses—"what is passing around . . . in a country like this"—is extraordinary considering the historical moment in which Austen writes. Despite this placid picture of a community ringed by "voluntary spies," united in mind and manner by print and transport, the late 1790s finds England at a dangerous crossroads following the upheaval of the French Revolution. While bands of displaced men roamed the English countryside in search of their daily bread, the promise and peril of mass literacy was at no time more evident than in the widespread circulation and tremendous popularity of radical political tracts, broadsheets, declarations, and charters. Yet the only danger preoccupying Austen originates in the compromise of one's sense-making abilities to the allure of the cheap reproduction, be it gothic novel or bourgeois impersonator. It is from these dangers that Henry rescues Catherine. Austen's solution for Catherine thus takes quite a different turn from that of Lennox, whose heroine similarly lacked clarity of vision and the good judgment that goes with it. Although counseled to separate good from bad forms of textual reproduction, Arabella was encouraged, nevertheless, to model herself after books, albeit the right kind of books. Henry tutors Catherine to sever the links binding literacy to subjectivity when he calls upon her to privilege her "own understanding," her "own sense of the probable," and her own "observation"—all presumably distinct from literacy. According to Austen, social problems and sexual relations do not come from "outside." They are a matter of inner drives to be regulated and contained by self-surveillance. Only might such a sensible woman be desirable to a man of education and taste if, together, they would achieve the pleasures of a well-governed household and an orderly family.

Let me conclude by pointing out that during the nineteenth century, the literature of sociology, anthropology, psychology, and sensational fiction came into being in response to accounts of various sexualized populations in need, at risk, threatening, or threatened—the industrial poor cohabiting overcrowded bedrooms; colonial peoples beckoning enticingly from harems and huts; middle-class families drinking tea in well-appointed drawing rooms.[35] What such representations share, among other features, is the idea that there exist populations whose sexuality is entirely out of control, in need of regulation, or properly managed. If these images have long since become the stuff of common sense, Dickensian kitsch, Raj revivalism, *Masterpiece Theater*, or American welfare reform schemes, perhaps it is because we too share the nineteenth-century conviction that problems of the social world are sexual problems. So construed, they appear to originate with women, who, because their desires are improperly regulated, have either too many babies or not enough.

Notes

1. See Benedict Anderson, *Imagined Communities: Reflections on the Origin and Spread of Nationalism* (London: Verso, 1983); Nancy Armstrong, *Desire and Domestic Fiction: A Political History of the Novel* (Oxford: Oxford University Press, 1987); Nancy Armstrong and Leonard Tennenhouse, *The Imaginary Puritan: Literature, Intellectual Labor, and the Origins of Personal Life* (Berkeley: University of California Press, 1992); Roger Chartier, *The Order of Books: Readers, Authors, and Libraries in Europe between the Fourteenth and Eighteenth Centuries*, trans. Lydia G. Cochrane

(Stanford: Stanford University Press, 1994); Michel Foucault, *The Order of Things* (New York: Vintage, 1970), and *The History of Sexuality*, vol. 1, trans. Robert Hurley (New York: Random House, 1978); Alvin Kiernan, *Printing Technology, Letters, and Samuel Johnson* (Princeton: Princeton University Press, 1987); Michael Warner, "The Mass Public and the Mass Subject," in *Habermas and the Public Sphere*, ed. Craig Calhoun (Cambridge: MIT Press, 1992); Raymond Williams, *The Long Revolution* (New York: Columbia University Press, 1961).

2. As one writer warned his audience in the early seventeenth century, "It is shame both to employ a notary to subscribe for thee in any security, and to want that good token of education which perhaps thine inferior hath, for wheresoever any man of honest rank resorteth who cannot write, *chiefly where he is not known*, he is incontinent esteemed either to be base born or to have been basely brought up . . . that is, far from any city where there be schools of learning, discipline, policy and civility": David Brown, *The New Invention Instituted Calligraphia* (St. Andrews, 1622), quoted in David Cressy, "Literacy in Context: Meaning and Measurement in Early Modern England," in *Consumption and the World of Goods*, ed. John Brewer and Roy Porter (New York: Routledge, 1993), 308.

Since only a worthy source could lend value to the written text, the person who could not write, by extension, must be "base born" or "basely brought up"—his lack of literacy indicating a more essential absence of civility or polity.

3. Eighteenth-century fine arts criticism, according to John Barrell, imagined a similar model of political power in which the capacity for aesthetic judgment evidently identified those most suited to rule the realms of both taste and politics. See Barrell, "'The Dangerous Goddess': Masculinity, Prestige, and the Aesthetic in Early-Eighteenth-Century Britain," *Cultural Critique* (spring 1989): 101-31.

4. Kiernan, *Printing Technology*, 28.

5. Hannah More, *Strictures on the Modern System of Female Education* (1799; New York: Garland, 1974), 1:159. Further references cited in the text.

6. For a discussion of the literature of the daily, the trivial, and the common that extended well beyond traditional linguistic boundaries, see J. Paul Hunter, "'News and New Things': Contemporaneity and the Early English Novel," *Critical Inquiry* 14 (1988): 493-515. On the rise of literacy and print culture in early modern England, some of the most consulted sources are Richard Altick, *The English Common Reader: A Social History of the Mass Reading Public 1800-1900* (Chicago: University of Chicago Press, 1957); Lawrence Stone, "Literacy and Education in England, 1640-1900," *Past and Present* 42 (1969): 69-139; and Williams, *Long Revolution*. Also see Roger Chartier, *The Order of Books*; Cressy, "Literacy in Context"; and Elizabeth L. Eisenstein, "Some Conjectures about the Impact of Printing on Western Society and Thought: A Preliminary Report," in *Literacy and Social Development in the West: A Reader*, ed. Harvey J. Graff (Cambridge: Cambridge University Press, 1981). For the larger implications of the work of linguists, lexicographers, and grammarians on the conceptualization of nation and empire, see Martin Bernal, *Black Athena: The Afroasiatic Roots of Classical Civilization*, vol. 1 (New Brunswick, N.J.: Rutgers University Press, 1987); and Olivia Smith, *The Politics of Language, 1791-1819* (Oxford: Clarendon Press, 1984).

7. As Julia Epstein notes, "Early in the [eighteenth] century, women did not 'reproduce' when they bore children; rather, they participated in *generatio*, or fruitfulness. The reproductive apparatus of a woman's body that today is classified and studied under the medical rubrics of obstetrics and gynecology did not exist as a unit of medical knowledge in the early eighteenth century." See "The Pregnant Imagination, Women's Bodies, and Fetal Rights" in this volume.

8. Margaret Anne Doody, introduction to *The Female Quixote; or, The Adventures of Arabella*, by Charlotte Lennox (1752), ed. Margaret Dalziel (Oxford: Oxford University Press, 1989), xxi. All further references to this edition will be cited in the text.

9. The word *patriarchy* here identifies a particular early modern formation of political power locating the head of the household and his family in homologous relation to the king and his subjects. See Gordon Schochet, *Patriarchalism in Political Thought: The Authoritarian Family and Political Speculation and Attitudes Especially in Seventeenth-Century England* (Oxford: Basil Blackwell, 1975).

10. See John Milton, *Paradise Lost and Paradise Regained* (1667; New York: Signet, 1968), 627.

11. See Lenore Davidoff and Catherine Hall, *Family Fortunes: Men and Women of the English Middle Class, 1780-1850* (Chicago: University of Chicago Press, 1987); Michael McKeon, *The Origins of the English Novel, 1600-1740* (Baltimore: Johns Hopkins University Press, 1987); and Anne Laurence, *Women in England, 1500-1760: A Social History* (New York: St. Martin's Press, 1994).

12. Anderson, *Imagined Communities*, 77.

13. For examples of feminist readings under discussion, see Jane Spencer, *The Rise of the Woman Novelist: From Aphra Behn to Jane Austen* (Oxford: Basil Blackwell, 1986); and Patricia Meyer Spacks, "The Subtle Sophistry of Desire: Dr. Johnson and *The Female Quixote*," *Modern Philology* 85, no. 4 (1988): 532-42.

14. Rather than fearing overpopulation, many midcentury writers warned against the consequences of underpopulation. In his *Dissertation on the Numbers of Mankind* (1753), for example, Robert Wallace argued that England needed more people to settle its lands and to develop vast expanses of uncultivated land and other natural resources. See Frances Ferguson, "Malthus, Godwin, Wordsworth, and the Spirit of Solitude," in *Literature and the Body: Essays on Populations and Persons*, ed. Elaine Scarry (Baltimore: Johns Hopkins University Press, 1988):106-24.

15. This preoccupation is also apparent in Jonathan Swift's *Gulliver's Travels*. See Susan Bruce, "The Flying Island and Female Anatomy: Gynaecology and Power in *Gulliver's Travels*," *Genders* 2 (1988): 60-76; and Terry Castle, "Why the Houyhnhnms Don't Write: Swift, Satire, and the Fear of the Text," in *Critical Essays on Jonathan Swift*, ed. Frank Palmeri (New York: G.K. Hall, 1993).

16. From 100 books published in the 1750s, the figure rises to 370 in the years 1792-1802. On the intensification of print culture and literacy rates at the end of the eighteenth century, see Williams, *Long Revolution*, 162ff. Clifford Siskin calculates the statistical rise of the novel as follows: "Growth until the 1780s had been slow and erratic. From an annual rate of only about four to twenty new titles through the first four decades, and remaining—despite Fielding and Richardson's popularity—within

a range roughly twenty to forty for the next three, new novel production peaked briefly near sixty in 1770 before a steep decline to well below forty during the latter half of that decade. Within the next seven years, however, the output jumped—more than doubled—to close to ninety, and continued to increase sharply into the next century." See Siskin's "Epilogue: The Rise of the Novel," in *Cultural Institutions of the Novel,* ed. Deidre Lynch and William Warner (Durham, N.C.: Duke University Press, 1996), 423-40.

17. James Boswell, *Life of Samuel Johnson,* ed. G.B. Hill (New York: Harper, 1950), 1:418-19.

18. This point follows from Jessamyn Jackson, "Why Novels Make Bad Mothers," *Novel* 27, no. 2 (1994): 161-74.

19. That the relationship between notions of originality and reproduction is ultimately historically determined is illustrated in Richard Shiff's postmodern analysis of their status. "The status of the original," he writes, "comes retroactively to whatever has been repeated—the greater the number of copies, the greater the originality of the source (think of how often Michelangelo or Raphael have been reproduced)." The contrast between Shiff's complacency toward cultural reproduction and More's anxiety is highly instructive. See Shiff, "Original Copy," *Common Knowledge* 3, no. 1 (1994): 96. Also see Christopher Jenks, *Cultural Reproduction* (London: Routledge, 1993), for a useful overview of recent theories of cultural reproduction.

20. Thomas Robert Malthus, *An Essay on the Principle of Population as It Affects the Future Improvement of Society, with Remarks on the Speculation of Mr. Godwin, M. Condorcet, and Other Writers* (New York: W.W. Norton, 1976), 19. All further references to this edition will be cited in the text.

21. Judith Walkowitz, *City of Dreadful Delight: Narratives of Sexual Danger in Late-Victorian London* (Chicago: University of Chicago Press, 1992), 19. See also Gareth Stedman Jones, *Outcast London: A Study in the Relationship between Classes in Victorian Society* (Oxford: Clarendon Press, 1971); and Anita Levy, *Other Women: The Writing of Class, Race, and Gender, 1832-1898* (Princeton: Princeton University Press, 1991).

22. See Catherine Gallagher, "The Body versus the Social Body in the Works of Thomas Malthus and Henry Mayhew," *Representations* 14 (1986): 83-106; and Thomas Laqueur, "Sexual Desire and the Market Economy during the Industrial Revolution," in *Discourse of Sexuality from Aristotle to AIDS,* ed. Domna Stanton (Ann Arbor: University of Michigan Press, 1992): 185-215.

23. Felicity Nussbaum, "'Savage' Mothers: Narratives of Maternity in the Mid-Eighteenth Century, *Eighteenth-Century Life* 16, no. 1 (1992): 172.

24. On women as "producers" of novels in the late eighteenth century, see J.M.S. Tompkins, *The Popular Novel in England, 1770-1800* (London: Constable and Co., 1932). More's language of excessive biological reproduction is also significant in light of Jackson's assertion that early-nineteenth-century British culture witnessed a reaction against the literary authority previously granted women authors due to "an increasing investment in maternal authority." See Jackson, "Why Novels Make Bad Mothers," 162.

25. Walter Benjamin, "The Work of Art in the Age of Mechanical Reproduction," in *Illuminations*, ed. Hannah Arendt (New York: Schocken Books, 1969), 221, 243.

26. See Nussbaum, "'Savage' Mothers"; Epstein, "Pregnant Imagination."

27. John Tinnon Taylor, *Early Opposition to the English Novel: The Popular Reaction from 1760 to 1830* (New York: King's Crown Press, 1943), 53.

28. On the role of fiction in facilitating this imaginary sympathetic link between reader and "nobody" in particular, the fictional character, Catherine Gallagher writes, "Because they [fictional characters] are unmarked by a proprietary relationship to anyone in the real world . . . , they become a species of utopian common property, potential objects of universal identification." See Gallagher, *Nobody's Story: The Vanishing Acts of Women Writers in the Marketplace, 1670-1820* (Berkeley: University of California Press, 1994), 171-72.

29. Armstrong, *Desire and Domestic Fiction*, 106.

30. Andreas Huyssen takes up this project in his work on nineteenth-century European culture; see his "Mass Culture as Woman," in *After the Great Divide: Modernism, Mass Culture, Postmodernism* (Bloomington: Indiana University Press, 1986). On the relationship between gender and the history of fiction, see Armstrong, *Desire and Domestic Fiction*; Ballaster, *Seductive Forms: Women's Amatory Fiction from 1684 to 1740* (New York: Oxford University Press, 1992); Gallagher, *Nobody's Story* (1994); Ruth Perry, *Women, Letters, and the Novel* (New York: AMS Press, 1980); and Tompkins, *The Popular Novel in England* (1932).

31. Andreas Huyssen, "Mass Culture as Woman," 55.

32. *Northanger Abbey* (1818; New York: Penguin Books USA, 1972), 37. All further references to this edition will be cited in the text.

33. See Lenore Davidoff, *The Best Circles: Women and Society in Victorian England* (Totowa, N.J.: Rowman and Littlefield, 1973), 20-35, on the social season as the means of ensuring the reproduction of the bourgeois elite. This venue is especially important in *Northanger Abbey* in view of the fact that the arranged aristocratic marriage is rendered something appropriate only to gothic fiction.

34. See McKeon, *Origins of the English Novel*.

35. The narrative strategies shared among Victorian social sciences are discussed in Levy, *Other Women*. On the relationship of gender, sexuality, and public policy, see Judith Walkowitz, *Prostitution and Victorian Society: Women, Class, and the State* (Cambridge: Cambridge University Press, 1980); Jeffrey Weeks, *Sex, Politics, and Society: The Regulation of Sexuality since 1800* (London: Longman, 1981); Frank Mort, *Dangerous Sexualities: Medico-Moral Politics in England since 1830* (New York: Routledge and Kegan Paul, 1988); and Epstein, "Pregnant Imagination." For analyses of the historical interaction among categories of colonialism, race, and gender, see Sander Gilman, "Black Bodies, White Bodies: Toward an Iconography of Female Sexuality in Late-Nineteenth-Century Art, Medicine, and Literature," *Critical Inquiry* 12 (autumn 1985): 204-42; Malek Alloula, *The Colonial Harem* (Minneapolis: University of Minnesota Press, 1986); Gayatri Chakravorty Spivak, "Three Women's Texts and a Critique of Imperialism," in *"Race," Writing, and Difference*, ed. Henry

Louis Gates (Chicago: University of Chicago Press, 1986); Jenny Sharpe, *Allegories of Empire: The Figure of Woman in the Colonial Text* (Minneapolis: University of Minnesota Press, 1993); and Antoinette Burton, *Burdens of History: British Feminists, Indian Women, and Imperial Culture, 1865-1915* (Chapel Hill: University of North Carolina Press, 1994).

Infanticide and the Boundaries of Culture from Hume to Arnold

Although recent critical work has had much to say about the masculine usurpation of maternal culture as *the* characteristic Romantic metaphor for the creative process, comparatively little attention has been spared for the Romantics' less insistent and yet more menacing use of the figure of the woman who kills her child.[1] Blake's Proverb of the Devil in *The Marriage of Heaven and Hell* (1798), "Sooner murder an infant in its cradle than nurse unacted desires," and Wordsworth's ballad, "The Thorn" (1798), in which the poetic intensity is achieved by the never confirmed possibility that Martha Ray *may* have killed her child, both present texts in which child murder is posed as a sublime object, a provocation to imaginative transcendence, a spur to creativity. The metaphorical uses of mothering, or "natural" reproduction, within an aesthetic that privileges nature over industry, are self-evident. The potential of infanticide as a recurrent figure for imaginative work is more difficult to understand. The purpose of this essay is to unpick some of the meanings of infanticide in British culture in the late eighteenth and early nineteenth centuries to ascertain the appeal of this appalling trope.

There is no conclusive evidence that infanticide was on the rise during this period, although demographic changes may well have made such instances more visible.[2] Percy Bysshe Shelley was not alone in noticing, on a visit to the Lake District in 1812, that "the manufacturers . . . [have] deformed the loveliness of Nature with human taint," as "children are frequently found in the river which the unfortunate women employed at the manufactory destroy."[3] Shelley's remark reverberates with contemporary concerns having to do with town and country, industry and nature: it is the barbarity of industry that causes women to throw away children and transform the loveliest and, of course, the most poetic of landscapes—the quintessential locus of British Romanticism—into a "suburb of London." As this suggests, what is striking in this period is not the number of infant corpses but the intense cultural investment in them. When one surveys the literature of the period, one is struck by the sheer quantity of references to infanticide and the variety of purposes they serve: for example, infanticide occurs as a cause for humanitarian concern in parliamentary discussion, as an example in philosophical debate, as a subject of tragedy on the stage, as a check on population in political economy, as an argument against the use of birth control, and as a marker of racial difference or of the moral depravity of the poor.

In this essay I will focus on debates either about infanticide or in which infanticide occurs as a significant term in the law, philosophy, political economy, and literature in eighteenth- and nineteenth-century Britain.[4] In each of these, infanticide tends to occur as a pretext for the discussion of one of the larger questions that preoccupied thinkers of the time, that is, the constitution and characteristics of a civilized society. In the philosophical literature, for instance, as we shall see, infanticide provides an opportunity for the discussion of whether a capacity for sympathy or a capacity for reason is the true mark of a civilized society. As has been well documented, such debates took place in a context in which elite English culture struggled to conceptualize and articulate its sense of its own difference from and superiority to older and foreign societies. It did so through the development of the discourses of the natural and human sciences, but also through its interest in manners, domesticity and the family, and the massive wave of humanitarianism that arose in the second half of the eighteenth century.[5] In this period, the concerns that cluster around the figure of infanticide are set in a climate in which the modern is felt to be an improvement on older forms of culture, in which child murder thrived. By the mid-nineteenth century, however, the infanticidal woman will come to represent the barbaric modern, rather than the barbaric archaic, in a context that privileges tradition over modernity.

Although the materials that I present in this essay are complex and varied, it is possible to trace in them two recurrent and opposing narratives of civilized society. In both, infanticide holds a pivotal position. In one, a version of society derived from the tenets of reason, civilization is staked upon the exclusion of certain groups it defines as barbarous. In this case, the practice of infanticide marks the epitome of savage behavior, which cannot be countenanced within the bounds of a civilized and modern society. The second narrative uses the idea of infanticide to provide a humanitarian critique of rational society. The injustices of this society are shown to drive people to the desperate measures of infanticide: a civilization based on reason does not exclude barbarians but creates them. Infanticide remains as the sole humane act, an act of salvation in a corrupt world. In this critique, another version of civilized society is produced, one based on sympathy and feeling. These two versions can be identified in writings by Adam Smith and David Hume, Lord Ellenborough and Edmund Burke, Thomas Malthus and William Godwin,

Harriet Martineau and Matthew Arnold. My contention in this essay is that the repeated occurrences of infanticide in the literature of the period are best understood as symptoms of unresolved problems within the conceptualization of civilized or modern society.[6] The literature of infanticide tends to be dominated by the figure of the infanticidal woman, whether she be the abandoned fallen woman, the wretched object of pity and concern, like Martha Ray or Hetty Sorrel; the depraved, unnatural working-class woman who, in the words of Tennyson, "kills her babe for a burial fee";[7] or the racially differentiated woman, the Indian, Chinese, or Irish, who kills her child because her culture teaches her no better. Nevertheless, the anxieties and desires that each of these women embodies have little to do with mothers in particular or in general. Rather, the murdering mother gives face to a peculiar spectrum of social and cultural concerns, all of which nevertheless affect the treatment of real infanticidal women. As a rhetorical device, the infanticidal woman operates within a range of distinctly social and material concerns. Like Martha Ray, she appears as an overdetermined term in British culture. She is the sign of poverty or of depravity, of the impossibility of culture and civilization, the sign of the barbarian, the marker of cultural alterity. And as she bears the burden of arguments that are beyond her immediate sphere, the infanticidal woman is always tantalizing, assuming a strangely ephemeral quality—the sign of something in excess of her bodily person.[8]

In the eyes of the law, the infanticidal woman tended to be unmarried. The particularly severe 1624 law "to prevent the murder of bastards" was not amended until 1803, and even then it did not stop targeting unmarried mothers. The 1624 law had been unique in English legislation in that it presumed guilt until innocence was proved. If an unmarried woman were to have a child, and if that child were to die, and if she had concealed the birth and failed to inform anyone of her pregnancy, then she would be considered guilty of murdering the baby, the penalty for which was death by hanging. The sequence of events was not unusual, given the ignominy surrounding the bearing of illegitimate children and the high rate of infant mortality. Lord Ellenborough's 1803 Offenses against the Person Act (43 Geo. III, c.58) made child murder the same as any other murder: innocence was presumed and guilt had to be proved. Concealment of the birth was a secondary charge that could be leveled if the case for murder could not be upheld, and concealment bore a penalty of two years in prison.[9]

Although a humanitarian lobby had argued unsuccessfully for legal reform in the 1770s, when the law did change thirty years later it was motivated by rather different concerns.[10] Lord Ellenborough, who introduced the successful bill in his position as the newly appointed lord chief justice, was driven not by humanitarian concern but by a desire to rationalize the law, to draw into line legislation concerning different acts of harm to other bodies and to make the laws of Ireland match those of England following the Union in 1800. Ellenborough introduced the bill with a view "to generalise the law with regard to certain penal offenses, and to adapt it equally to every part of the United Kingdom."[11] His Maiming and Wounding Bill, which was to become the 1803 Act, encompassed a variety of offenses—"malicious shooting, attempting to discharge loaded fire arms, stabbing, cutting, wounding, poisoning and the malicious using of means to procure the miscarriage of women, and also the malicious setting fire to buildings"—in addition to the repealing of the earlier 1624 law against "murdering infant bastards."[12] The bill was proposed initially in lieu of a so-called Chalking Bill, a law against "wounding and cutting" that was specific to Ireland. If the Maiming and Wounding Bill were accepted, Ellenborough argued, then the Chalking Bill would be unnecessary.[13] However, while the bill was proposed in the spirit of a necessary rationalization of the statute books at a time of political restructuring, it should also be seen as a strategic intervention in the maintenance of colonial control.[14] The inclusion of arson in the bill is a case in point. In his presentation, Ellenborough noted the anomaly that in Ireland it was not an offense to set fire to one's own house, and he argued that it should be, in order to prevent the defrauding of insurance companies. However, it seems highly significant that at the time the bill was proposed, Irish nationalists, led by Robert Emmet, were purchasing buildings in Ireland and burning them, as a confusion tactic, in a campaign to overthrow the British that came to an abortive climax in Dublin in 1803.[15]

At a time when humanitarian reformers of the law were seeking to reduce the number of capital offenses, which had risen to a record high level during the eighteenth century, the act was noteworthy in that it created ten new capital offenses.[16] As far as the humanitarian reformers were concerned, the sole positive aspect of the new act was the repeal of the 1624 infanticide provisions. However, this gesture was incorporated within an attempt to make the law more effective: due to the excessive severity of the penalty, courts had become increasingly reluctant to find women guilty of the crime, and the law had become inoperative.[17] The new law gave opportunities for scrutinizing a case in greater detail and punishing with a broader range of penalties. It thereby participated in the intensified medical and legal supervision of parturition and motherhood that took place in the nineteenth century.[18]

One significant effect of the act was that it drew together domestic and criminal offenses as "offenses against the person." Murderous mothers and the dissident Irish were thus drawn together as co-offenders against the civil body. The legislation clearly divided civil and uncivilized behavior, and infanticidal women were firmly placed, along with the barbarous Irish, on the wrong side of the divide.

An earlier attempt to change the law had been made in the House of Commons in 1772, led by Burke, Fox, Harbord, and Meredith. They were motivated by a sympathetic concern for the fate of women under a law whose severity, they claimed, was matched by no other in the legal system. Significantly, Ellenborough and Burke had been adversaries in an earlier situation, as Ellenborough had served as the leading counsel for Warren Hastings in a trial that had been provoked by Burke.[19] Their strategy was to focus on the inconsistency of the law, which encouraged unmarried women to conceal a pregnancy, since illegitimate pregnancy incurred a public whipping and a fine, while making concealment itself a capital offense: "Nothing could be more unjust or inconsistent with the principles of all law, than first to force a woman through modesty to concealment, and then to hang her for concealment."[20] The argument also invoked the cause of "humanity and justice" for the humane treatment of women, and for the equal treatment of bastards and legitimate children: "While all due praise was allowed to legitimate children, it was not just to give a squeeze in the neck to bastards."[21] The resolution was passed in the Commons, but failed in the Lords, as was a second bill proposed by Lockhart the same year.

In the legal debates infanticide is construed in two very different ways. In Ellenborough's attempt to redraw and bolster the boundaries of the nation, infanticide is the sign of the barbarian. For Burke et al., infanticide provides an occasion for sympathy, for an affective or even sentimental response. Implicit in both are narratives about the nature of civilized society, but one is based on strategies of exclusion developed from a project of rationalization, whereas the other is based on the values of humanitarianism.

The same narratives can also be found in the philosophical literature of the period. Adam Smith outlined the first—in which infanticide serves as a marker of the limits of civilization—in his *Theory of Moral Sentiments* (1759, rev. 1761). Although Smith's moral system is based on a belief in the human capacity for sympathy, he also holds that only certain *civilized* forms of social organization allow the full expression of sympathy. In the section entitled "On the Influence of Custom and Fashion upon the Sentiments of Moral Approbation and Disapprobation," he draws attention to practices that for him lie beyond the boundaries of civilized human behavior, a list in which footbinding and child murder figure prominently. "Can there be greater barbarity," he asks, "than to hurt an infant? Its helplessness, its innocence, its amiableness, call forth the compassion of an enemy, and not to spare that tender age is regarded as the most furious effort of an enraged and cruel conqueror."[22] Yet, he goes on, "we find, at this day, that this practice prevails among all savage nations." Smith's point is that in distant places and ages, people murdered infants, whereas in the civilized here and now, babies enjoy the sympathy that is the mark of civilized humanity. Infanticide marks the absolute antithesis to modern civilization, the negation of cultured life.

Such beliefs seemed to be confirmed by travelers who returned to Britain from journeys to distant lands. In the 1770s, Captain Cook, for instance, told of "the children who are so unfortunate as to be begot" in the promiscuous intimacies that marked Tahitian life. They were "smothered at the moment of their birth."[23] In this case, infanticide is a sign of the licentiousness of a people who had begun to achieve notoriety in the West for their excessive enjoyment of sexual pleasures. In 1789, reports were first made to the Asiatic Society on the practices of female infanticide that had been discovered in some regions of India.[24] A long campaign was thereby set in motion by the British—akin to the campaign to outlaw sati—to suppress these practices and to protect the women of India from the cruelty of their barbarous menfolks.[25] Although different, these cases demonstrate that the existence of infanticide in the ethnographic record became a measure by which English society could apprehend and celebrate its own humanity, sobriety, and restraint.

The other narrative concerning infanticide also begins to assume prominence at this time. In this narrative infanticide—wherever it occurs—is represented as an event capable of raising deep human emotions. This is because children are an eternal object of sympathy, and sympathy is identified as a common human attribute that somehow precedes cultural differentiation. Thus David Hume, contributing to a major midcentury debate on the claim that modern society was far less populated than antiquity, was able paradoxically to claim that "by an odd connection of causes, the barbarous practice [of infanticide] of the ancients might rather render those times more populous,"[26] because the availability of infanticide as a form of family limitation would encourage early marriages, yet the "force of natural affection" was such that "very few" could carry out their intentions. Here, in Hume's estimation, infanticide is preferable to the corrupt modern practice of placing unwanted children in foundling hospitals.[27]

Hume's position on infanticide prefigures one based on self-interest which had fairly widespread currency at the end of the century. William Alexander, for instance, provides a version of it in his two-volume *History of Women* (1779), a comparative history of manners in barbarous and civilized societies, in which the difference between the two is marked by the degree of respect paid to women. As was the case for Hume, infanticide is the most unnatural of acts, for the maternal bond is the "most powerful of all human feelings." However, Alexander draws our attention to "some savage countries" in which the lives of women are so abject that mothers are impelled to kill their own female infants to save them from the horrible future that awaits them.[28] As evidence, he cites the case of a woman standing on the banks of the Oronooko who laments the fact that her mother had not killed her at birth, so intolerable is her life. Here the argument has taken an interesting turn, for under these conditions infanticide is an act of kindness, even of heroism. To cap his case, he cites the Abbé Raynal's account of slave women who murder their female children in a frenzy of "revenge and compassion, that they may not become the property of their cruel masters." To kill a child, to save her from a life of misery, under this construction, is a humanitarian act of salvation. For Alexander, child murder is not in itself an act of savagery but, ironically, a course imposed by savagery as the only means of escaping the life of abuse that, in Alexander's account, is the very definition of savagery. Thus the tables have turned, for infanticide, which begins as a mark of the savage society's inhumanity, in contrast to the humanity of modern society, has now become, through the idea of a noble or salvific infanticide, a sign of the savagery into which modern society has fallen.

These philosophical arguments about the nature of civilized society were repeated in the population debates of the turn of the century. Hume's essay had made an influential contribution to the discussion of the comparative sizes of ancient and modern populations. By the end of the century, after the depopulation thesis had been disproved, the debate shifted to the scarcity of resources and the question of whether the physical world might sustain an ever-increasing population.[29] Those who held that it might not—the most prominent of whom were Malthus and the political economists—believed that society would always be dogged by the limited resources of nature and that progress would always be impeded. Their opponents, among whom figured Godwin, Condorcet, and Marx, agreed with Hume that the world's capacity for sustaining population was unlimited, as was the potential for social and scientific improvement. Entwined in these debates, then, are different beliefs about the power of science and technology and the possibilities for social and scientific progress. Malthus and the political economists believed that science and rational thought could be used only to expose the limits of progress, to demonstrate its inability to change the course of nature.[30] Their opponents, on the other hand, believed that science would give mankind the capacity to control nature and bring about unbounded and positive social change.

What is curious, however, is that in the debates between them, the charge of child murderer flies freely from both sides. For the Malthusians, their opponents' refusal to accept the inevitability that the physical world will not be able to sustain the population is tantamount to child murder. For the Godwinians, however, a belief in this very analytical model makes the Malthusians guilty of the same crime. For the Godwinians, to kill a child to save it from a life of misery—like the slave mother or the unfortunate Oronooko woman—is a comprehensible moral act, but to kill a child to save resources, as is suggested by the Malthusian model, is morally reprehensible.

Malthus articulated his influential argument from scarcity in his 1798 *Essay on the Principle of Population as it affects the Future Improvement of Society, with Remarks on the Speculation of Mr. Godwin, M. Condorcet, and other Writers.* In Malthus's scheme, human life is ordered by a competition between competing desires or passions—the passion for sex and the passion for food. In the 1798 text, the former is the stronger. The drive for sexual reproduction, he claims, is responsible for the formation of civilized society—demographic changes, the division of labor, the enclosure of land, the formation of property. But sex also threatens civilization, for population will increase at a higher rate than the resources that are needed to sustain it: as population increases at a geometric rate, resources increase at an arithmetic rate. Various checks—famine, disease, volcanoes, floods, and wars—are always clawing back population to a sustainable and civilized level.[31]

Malthus denied that mankind and society could be in a state of exponential improvement because limitations on resources will always tend to make societies oscillate between states of civilization and decay. In the much expanded second edition of *Essay on the Principle of Population*, published just five years later in 1803, its rhetorical scheme is clearer: the domestic haven of middle-class English life is juxtaposed to barbarous foreign and ancient states in which infanticide is a frequent trait. Malthus's vision of a civilized society is similar to Adam Smith's in that it, too, is based on the idea of exclusion of certain groups—which, like Smith, he identifies on the basis of behavior such as killing babies. But for Malthus there is a persistent danger that society may slip back into this state of savagery. Foreign societies thus provide an endless specter of the state of decay into which civilization may fall. By exercising moral restraint and the simple device of the late marriage, however, Malthus claims in the second edition, society can stave off a collapse into savagery, which would be the inevitable outcome of the profligacy recommended by his opponents such as Godwin and Condorcet, who believed in free love and the perfectibility of mankind.

The seemingly optimistic Godwin, in contrast, admitted that he was not averse to infanticide. "Neither do I regard a new-born child with any superstitious reverence," he wrote in his response to Malthus in 1801. "I had rather a child should perish at the first hour of existence, than that a man should spend seventy years of life in a state of misery and vice."[32] A similarly pragmatic view was put forward by the socialist medical practitioner Charles Hall.

Writing in 1805, Hall argued for the greater humanity of the Chinese, on the grounds that the killing of children would be an act of kindness when the alternative was a life of impoverishment: "The Chinese, who suffer the exposition of their children, and even appoint men to destroy them, seem to act more humanely than the Europeans, who cause the long, languishing sufferings of children."[33] Like Godwin, Hall invokes the idea of the salvific infanticide as a critique of the social conditions and ideologies of his time.

Ironically, however, in a later work Godwin was one of the many to level the charge of child murder at Malthus. He attacked Malthus on the grounds that his theory appeared to legitimate child murder as a positive check on population growth. "It is obvious all through, that Mr. Malthus trusts to the destruction of infants and young children as the street anchor of our hope to preserve the population of Europe from perishing with hunger."[34] In Godwin's logic, this is because Malthus considered the value of a child's life to be far in excess of any other; that is to say, a child with seventy years to live would incur a far greater expenditure of resources than one with just twenty years to go. For Godwin, it is not the simple fact of child murder that is the problem: to kill an infant to save it from a life of misery is an act of noble kindness; to kill an infant to save resources is a self-serving act of vice.

The debate between Malthus and Godwin provides a useful gloss on Blake's proverb, cited at the beginning of this essay: "Sooner murder an infant in the cradle than nurse unacted desires." Blake's remark could be read as a Godwinian expression of the belief that it is better to die at birth than to live a miserable life of "unacted desires." But the insertion of the word *nurse*, and its implications of sympathy, care, affect, when set against the word *murder*, suggest a critique of Godwin's rationalism. The proverb expresses neither party's view, but it articulates something of the ontological crisis that is provoked when it is presumed that lives have relative values, whether these be assessed in relation to other lives or, indeed, to potential lives.

That the implications of Malthus's work were perceived by his critics to be extremely worrying is clear by the outlandish list of crimes that were laid at his door: in addition to child murder, he was found guilty of encouraging cannibalism and sexual licentiousness. Anna Letitia Barbauld, in a diatribe against the Napoleonic wars entitled "Dialogue in the Shades," sardonically alluded to Malthus as the "great philosopher [who] has lately discovered that the world is in imminent danger of being overpeopled, and that if twenty or forty thousand could not be persuaded every now and then to stand and be shot at, we should be forced to eat one another. . . . This discovery has had a wonderful effect in quieting tender consciences."[35] Hazlitt, for his part, complained not that Malthus assumed the disposability of human life but that his work presumed licentiousness to be a necessary feature of human nature. Malthus's work, Hazlitt asserts, "rests on a malicious supposition that all mankind . . . are like so many animals *in season*," and he warned against the dangerous pornographic potential of the work in the hands of "young women of liberal education."[36] Ironically, in this roll call of perversions, the Reverend Malthus was metamorphosed into a dangerous libertine—one version of the savage life to which his barbarizing influence would reduce us all.

These two versions of infanticide circulated widely in the writings of the period—and, with them, two opposing constructions of motherhood. The infanticidal woman epitomizes the bad mother, the barbaric, uncivilized woman, who rejects the maternal role and all it represents; frequently the bad mother is a single mother.[37] On the other hand, the woman who kills her child is, paradoxically, the heroic mother, the martyr—the one who is willing to make the ultimate sacrifice, that of her child's life. Distinct as these two constructions are, the boundaries between them are frequently blurred.

This is most apparent in the furious debates that took place around the 1834 Poor Law. Of particular significance were the bastardy provisions. The effect of these was to put an end to outrelief and the availability of financial assistance from the child's father, thus casting the sole responsibility for illegitimate children onto their mothers. With some justification, critics of the law saw it as an *incitement* to infanticide.[38] In 1838, for instance, a pseudonymous author named "Marcus" wrote a pamphlet entitled *An Essay on Populousness*. In the spirit of Swift's *Modest Proposal*, Marcus outlines his theory of painless extinction, how to "revoke or continue a child's existence without infringing the laws of humanity, that is, without inflicting pain."[39] With mock scientific precision he travesties the discourse of political economy, particularly Malthus's work, echoing Godwin's critique of Malthus that he advocated the slaughter of infants for reasons of economic expediency.[40] For its critics, the New Poor Law meant the sacrifice of working-class babies for the enrichment of the ruling class. In this, we can recognize a version of the rhetorical strategy that was identified in earlier social criticism: the poor law's effective institution of the practice of infanticide demonstrated the barbarity to which society had been reduced by the social policy of the political economists. As far as women were concerned, however, the effect of this powerful rhetoric was double-edged. Although it undoubtedly brought attention to the material plight of single mothers, it did so in such a provocative way that it made them the objects of a general fear and loathing. The result of this rhetoric was to focus attention on the deviancy of the unmarried mother. In the moral panic that was generated by the New Poor Law, the broader issue—the impoverishment that was a direct result of the new provisions for illegitimate children—

slipped out of the frame. There was little payoff for single mothers in a rhetoric that capitalized on the fact that their position was so extreme that they might be forced to kill their children.

This demonization of single mothers should, of course, be set in the context of the idealization of married mothers, which was brought about through the strengthening of the ideology of domesticity and separate spheres that occurred in the late eighteenth and early nineteenth centuries and reached its pinnacle in the Victorian period.[41] As the family was increasingly designated the ideal social, economic, and moral unit, the mother was held responsible for imparting social and moral values to children and servants. Through nurturing, suckling, and nourishing, the good mother reproduced not only the population but also the values of the nation. Thus the deviancy of the infanticidal woman appeared particularly acute, as she violently and symbolically rejected not only her own baby but the whole institution of motherhood, which was a defining force in bourgeois society.

The concept of social incorporation is central to the domestic ideology. The good mother, as the agent of incorporation, acculturating new generations, inducing them into the body social, holds an organic function in society. The infanticidal woman, who rejects her child, is rejected by society: she is the pariah, the outcast, the barbarian. The barbarian is now quite specifically the undomesticated and the anti–maternal woman, and civilization has been narrowed to encompass only bourgeois families nurtured by good, middle-class mothers. Now motherhood has come to symbolize civilization itself, and infanticide represents its boundaries.

In the period of the New Poor Law, writing about society tends to revolve around the two metaphorical figures of the good mother and the bad mother, the latter epitomized as the infanticidal woman. Infanticide continues to hold the two rhetorical functions identified in the earlier period. For some, it is used to mark the groups that must be expelled from the body social in the construction of the nation as a civilized and moral entity. It is often associated with the Irish during the period in which Irish immigrants were feared as the major disruptive force in the British workforce. For others, infanticide provides the basis of a humanitarian critique of government social policy, as in Godwin's and Hall's earlier work. The significant point, however, is that both uses of infanticide converge in the construction of the domestic ideal of the good mother and the simultaneous demonization of the sexualized, deviant woman.[42]

A good example of the first is provided by Harriet Martineau in her multi–volumed *Illustrations of Political Economy* and *Illustrations of Taxation*, published between 1832 and 1834. In "Ella of Garveloch" and "Weal and Woe in Garveloch," numbers five and six of the *Illustrations*, she combines Malthusian population theory with ideas about the moral and educational roles of mothers, to demonstrate that bad mothering colludes with shortages of resources to perpetrate a selective culling of certain racial and class groups. Thus she expands on the premonitions of Mary Wollstonecraft, who in *A Vindication of the Rights of Woman* (1792) had asked, "How many children are absolutely murdered by the ignorance of women!"[43] to explain the cultural and social roots of this "ignorance" and how it operates in a context of uneven and unreliable resources.

In "Ella of Garveloch," the small Scottish island community of Garveloch increases its wealth through careful husbandry and the development of trade and industry. In "Weal and Woe in Garveloch," the advantageous conditions of this new state of wealth have led to an increase in population such that, when the harvest fails one year, the community can no longer produce the resources to sustain itself. Included in the story is a romance between Ella's brother, the noble and upstanding Ronald, and the Widow Cuthbert, who is already the mother of three children. As a true Malthusian, Ronald exercises moral restraint and, for the sake of the community, decides against marrying the widow. At a point in the story at which the conditions of deficiency reach a crisis, Martineau includes a conversation between Ella, a mother of six, and the Widow Cuthbert, excellent mothers both, sitting with babies on their laps, in which they discuss the connection between population and class. Widow Cuthbert says, "I have heard that neither the very rich nor the very poor leave such large families behind them as the middling classes; and if the reason is known, it seems to me very like murder not to prevent it."[44]

Ella continues the discussion by demonstrating that the reasons for the physical superiority of the middle-class family are well known: both very rich and very poor women are bad mothers. While the rich mother lives in luxury and dissipation, plays cards all night in hot rooms, and drives in carriages rather than taking constitutional exercise, the poor woman dangles her baby "as if she meant to break its back and gives the poor thing nothing but potatoes." Neither, she goes on, are much better than the mothers in China — where "in great cities, new-born babes are nightly laid in the streets to perish, and many more are thrown into the river and carried away before their parents' eyes" — or in India — where "it is a very common thing for female children to be destroyed as soon as they are born."

In these tales, Martineau reiterates the point made by the Malthusians, that infanticide functions as the benchmark of the barbarous society — the state of decay that only the middle classes can fend off. The barbarity that is to be protected against is now located in specially designated racial and class groups — the Chinese, the Indians, the very rich and the very poor, and the potato-eaters (a barely coded reference to the Irish). In Garveloch the barbarous group is indeed an Irish family, whose indolence and vice will be the cause of its own downfall. Much is made of the supposed proclivity of the Irish for excessive reproduction and their subsequent failure to be responsible for their children, their unwillingness to work, to save, to be sober, and so on. It is not claimed directly that the Irish kill their children, but their excessive reproduction and inability to support them, in this context, amounts to the same thing. Martineau's narrative is one in which the good, middle-class, Protestant, Scottish mothers bear strong and healthy children by exercising restraint, thrift, industriousness, and so on, while the Irish family withers into a state of decay and eventual extinction on Garveloch.

Ebenezer Elliott, the "Corn Law Rhymer," provides an example of the second use of infanticide, the salvific infanticide, as a means of social critique. As for Godwin et al., Elliott's infanticide is a sign of the barbaric state to which England has been reduced by current social policy. In one infanticide poem he writes:

> Upon her pregnant womb her hand she laid,
> Then stabb'd her living child! and shriek'd, dismay'd
> "Oh, why had I a mother!" wildly said
> That saddest mother, gazing on the dead —
> Hurrah for the bread tax'd England.[45]

This mother commits the only heroic act possible in the morally and materially derelict world that she inhabits. At the end of the poem, the responsibility for the murder is laid squarely at the feet of the government, "Wholesale Dealers in waste, want, and war!" (line 31). The infanticidal woman in this case is the heroic martyr, and by performing a self-denying act of moral distinction in a fallen world she epitomizes the domestic ideal of the good mother.

A much more complex example of the salvific infanticide is provided by Elizabeth Barrett Browning in her arresting poem "The Runaway Slave at Pilgrim's Point" (1850). Here the black woman murders her white male child — the result of rape by her master — "to save it from [her] curse" (line 146). The sex and the color of the infant in this example are crucial. Unlike in the earlier account provided by the Abbé Raynal, this slave mother does not murder a female child to save her from a fate similar to her own. Rather, she identifies her child with her oppressor ("in that single glance I had / Of my child's face, . . . / I saw a look that made me mad! / The *master's* look" [lines 141-44]), and she transforms the act into one of revenge. The force of the word *save* in line 146, then, is profoundly ambiguous. The idea that she "saves" the child from the "curse" of negritude, the "curse" that is indeed her own, is complicated by the fact of the child's color and gender. But the idea that she "saves" the child from her own wish for violent retribution — her own "curse" — is complicated by the fact that she "saves" him by acting out that very retribution and strangling him. Despite this complexity, however, the poem works by using the infanticide in much the same way that Elliott does: in this case, to demonstrate the degradations of slavery and racism.

For Elliott and Barrett Browning, the act of infanticide suggests a certain kind of nobility in mothers and a capacity to bring about social redemption. For Martineau, child murder means moral deviancy and a concomitant physical degeneracy. However, these opposing formulations share a belief in the centrality of mothers to the definition of civilized society. For all of these writers, civilization finds metonymic representation in the figure of the good mother—the guardian and reproducer of the values of civilized society. For all, the good mother is identifiable by her self-sacrifices, her capacity to nurture, and her possession of moral goodness—the same figure in all cases. The good mother is, of course, an idealized, monumental figure who casts a shadow of underachievement over all real mothers. In such a context, unmarried women who become pregnant, especially at a time when all extramarital sex is the cause of moral and social stigma, have no hope of being anything but deviant bad mothers.

In cultural ideation, however, such ideals stand and amass multiple meanings that bespeak the anxieties and desires of the time. By the middle of the nineteenth century, under the force of the domestic ideology, the figure of the good mother, in its dominant uses, tends to stand for tradition, against the incursions of industrial society. The infanticidal woman is associated with the disorder and change brought about by industrialization. As the good mother stands for tradition, the infanticidal woman is the harbinger of the modern. This is in sharp contrast to the situation at the end of the eighteenth century and in the early nineteenth century described in the opening sections of this essay. Then infanticide was considered an archaic, atavistic practice that signaled the prelude to modern, humane society. In this later period it is still proposed as the antithesis to the humane society, but now it is set in the context of a rhetoric that concentrates anxieties on modernity rather than archaism, the present and future rather than the past.

This shift, I would suggest, coincides with the development of a particularly pervasive (and still dominant) notion of Culture that Raymond Williams and Terry Eagleton have charted through the works of the major writers of the century.[46] In this formation, Culture provides a place for social critique and for the expression of humane qualities of sympathy and compassion. Based on the terms of organicism, Culture usually provides a narrative in which tradition—equated with organic, land-based, usually rural, face-to-face societies—is pitched against industry—that is, mechanized, commercial, urban, alienating societies. By extension, Culture encompasses nature, natural reproduction, and families. On the other side of the fence are grouped machines, science, profits—and, we might add, perverted practices such as child murder.

George Eliot's *Adam Bede* (1859) exemplifies this point. Here Hetty Sorrel, the infanticidal woman, is contrasted with Dinah Morris, the civilized and civilizing woman who is a Methodist preacher. The final scenes of soft-focus domestic bliss with the now married Adam and Dinah (no longer a preacher) and their children suggest that the novel could be read as a Malthusian narrative—an expanded version of Martineau's parable—in which the world will be peopled by the vigorous and morally superior offspring of the civilized classes, whereas the barbarians, in the person of Hetty, will be expelled from the nation and will eventually perish.[47] Joan Manheimer has pointed out that the novel's ending is a nostalgic celebration of past times, and that Hetty, in contrast, "challenges traditional assumptions about the immutability of class distinctions, about the stability of community, and about the sanctity of the family."[48] In this reading, Hetty is the bearer of modernity, representing progress through sexual liberation, a notion that cannot be countenanced in the novel. Thus Hetty presents an early example of a figure that recurs frequently in the second half of the century with both disapprobation and approbation: the sexually liberated woman as a sign of modernity. The New Woman of the 1890s will provide one version of this figure.[49] Moreover, the representation of progress through a woman's sexual behavior continues even now, as a society's capacity for being modernized or otherwise is frequently staked on its attitude toward birth control. A supposedly "backward" society such as Ireland then is "barbarous" precisely in its resistance to contraception and abortion. From another perspective, of course, it is traditional and civilized in fending off the barbarous—and murderous—practices of modern society.[50]

In mid-nineteenth-century cultural theory, however, the most striking child murderer is to be found in Matthew Arnold's essay "The Function of Criticism at the Present Time" (1864). Midway through this powerful and pervasive articulation of high cultural values, there is a reference to a girl named Wragg who strangled her illegitimate child.[51] In the rhetorical construction of high Culture, or Arnoldian civilization, Wragg represents the barbaric work of industry—or anarchy—that will be fended off by the formation of the realm of Culture. And if anarchy is represented by the bad mother, Culture, in its civilizing mission, appropriates the function of the good mother. Like the good mother, Culture provides a site in which a class can reproduce its values, and it does so precisely by regulating modes of literary consumption, in the same way that the good mother performs her acculturating function through the metaphor of feeding.

However, Arnold's presentation of Wragg is more ambivalent than this might suggest. In an essay that deplores the current state of English cultural life and looks to a former generation of poets for regeneration, Wragg's Romantic ancestry is significant: like Martha Ray, Wragg performs the function of the sublime object. For Arnold, Wragg's case controverts the jingoistic sentiments of self-satisfied Tories and Utilitarians that prevail in English intellectual work, both of whom have celebrated the "old Anglo-Saxon race" as "the best breed in the whole world." Wragg, on the contrary, represents the "touch of grossness in our race," its "original short coming in the more delicate spiritual perceptions," not by her crime, curiously, but rather by her name, which Arnold calls a hideous "Anglo-Saxon name," like "Higginbottom, Stiggens and Bugg." Her crime becomes but a device of her characterization, a constituent in a list of props: "the gloom, the smoke, the cold, the strangled illegitimate child" — a metonymic representation of her gross nature that is merely the fulfillment of her charmless name. In fact, the infanticidal Wragg makes an important contribution to Arnold's formulation of the case for disinterested criticism, characterized as the free play of the imagination, by which the mind, detached from material and practical concerns, might contemplate "the best that is known and thought in the world." Not only does she expose the ideologically transparent rhetoric of politicians and social critics, who fail to see the true nature of English society that is represented by her, but her "gross" name and the starkness of the writing of the report that Arnold relishes — "Wragg is in custody. . . . Wragg has strangled her child" — these together produce a superior, unencumbered prose style that, for Arnold, will be the facilitator and organ of higher critical insight.

Wragg has strangled her child. But, ironically, by doing so, she provides the conditions for English intellectuals to raise themselves from the philistinism that, for Arnold, dogs them. As the barbarian, she also offers the occasion for an imaginative leap that will provide the basis of intellectual regeneration. Embedded in the figure of Wragg are the traces of the redemptive or salvific infanticide identified earlier in this essay.

Arnold's ambivalence toward Wragg rests on the convergence of the two uses of infanticide that I have traced. Wragg is the barbarian who must be expelled from the social body that constitutes the nation, but she is also the occasion for a critique of that very process of national identity formation. Furthermore, I would suggest that the arresting intervention of Wragg in the essay marks a profound ambivalence within Arnold's notion of Culture toward the idea of modernity: Arnold's work is as much a discourse of improvement as it is of nostalgia and tradition. Wragg becomes a repository for these unresolvable longings: for the past and the future, for incorporation and disavowal, for improvement and stasis.

Arnold's Wragg gives both name and face to a range of deeply rooted anxieties about modernity and progress, on the one hand, and about tradition and the past, on the other. In the context of this history of infanticide, that the woman who kills her child should bear the burden of these anxieties is neither new nor extraordinary. But it is highly significant that these concerns should remain buried in Wragg's criminal figure in a text that subsequently assumes a determining role in the reproduction and continuity of central definitions of Englishness. It suggests that the idea of infanticide will maintain a shadowy presence in subsequent constructions of nationhood, holding within it, as we have seen, contrasting ideas about the nature of civilized society. The infanticidal woman thus goes forward at the end of the century, a complex and contradictory figure, carrying with her the marks of unresolved tensions within long-standing debates over the boundaries of culture at this formative period in the development of the modern nation.

Notes

1. See in particular Margaret Homans, *Bearing the Word: Language and Female Experience in Nineteenth-Century Women's Writing* (Chicago: University of Chicago Press, 1986).

2. For historical accounts, see Mark Jackson, *New-Born Child Murder: Women, Illegitimacy, and the Courts in Eighteenth-Century England* (Manchester: Manchester University Press, 1996); R.W. Malcolmson, "Infanticide in the Eighteenth Century," in *Crime in England, 1550-1800*, ed. J.S. Cockburn (Princeton, N.J.: Princeton University Press, 1977), 187-237; Lionel Rose, *The Massacre of the Innocents: Infanticide in Britain, 1800-1938* (London: Routledge and Kegan Paul, 1986); Roger Sauer, "Infanticide and Abortion in Nineteenth-Century Britain," *Population Studies* 32, no. 1 (1978): 81-93. For a comparative account, see René Leboutte, "Offence against Family Order: Infanticide in Belgium from the Fifteenth Century through the Early Twentieth Century," *Journal of the History of Sexuality* 2, no. 2 (1991): 158-85. The history of infanticide is tied inextricably to the history of bastardy. On this, see Peter Laslett, Karla Oosterveen, and Richard M. Smith, *Bastardy and Its Comparative History* (London: Edward Arnold, 1980); and Adrian Wilson, "Illegitimacy in Mid-Eighteenth-Century London," *Continuity and Change* 4, no. 1 (1989): 103-64.

3. *The Letters of Percy Bysshe Shelley*, ed. F.L. Jones (Oxford: Clarendon Press, 1964), 1:222-23. See Nathaniel Brown, *Sexuality and Feminism in Shelley* (Cambridge: Harvard University Press, 1979), 198-200.

4. This essay, therefore, is not an attempt to uncover the historical realities of infanticide. Nevertheless, my interest in the widespread rhetorical uses of the idea of infanticide comes in the context of a recognition that such uses framed contemporary perceptions and documentation of cases of infanticide as much as they were inspired and motivated by real instances of the crime. I examine this relationship in my more extensive work-in-progress on infanticide between 1760 and 1880.

5. On the general context, see Paul Langford, *A Polite and Commercial People: England, 1727-1783* (Oxford: Oxford University Press, 1992). On intellectual movements, see Peter Gay, *The Enlightenment: An Interpretation*, esp. vol. 2, *The Science of Freedom* (New York: Alfred A. Knopf, 1978). On the affectionate family, see Philippe Ariès, *Centuries of Childhood: A Social History of Family Life*, trans. Robert Baldick (New York: Alfred A. Knopf, 1962); and Lawrence Stone, *The Family, Sex, and Marriage in England, 1500-1800* (London: Weidenfeld and Nicholson, 1977). On humanitarianism, see Thomas L. Haskell, "Capitalism and the Origins of the Humanitarian Sensibility," in *American Historical Review* 90 (1985): 339-61, 547-66; and Thomas W. Laqueur, "Bodies, Details, and the Humanitarian Narrative," in *The New Cultural History*, ed. Lynn Hunt (Berkeley: University of California Press, 1989), 176-204.

6. I differ here in emphasis from many of the historical accounts of infanticide, which tend to see it as a pathological product of socioeconomic change, particularly of the bastardy clauses of the New Poor Law of 1834. See Ann R. Higginbottom, "'Sin of the Age': Infanticide and Illegitimacy in Victorian London," in *Victorian Scandals: Representations of Gender and Class*, ed. K.O. Garrigan (Athens, Ohio: Ohio University Press, 1992), 257-88; and Rose, *Massacre of the Innocents*, 22-34. See also Margaret L. Arnot, "Infant Death, Child Care, and the State: The Baby-Farming Scandal and the First Infant Life Protection Legislation of 1872," *Continuity and Change* 9, no. 2 (1994): 271-311; and George K. Behlmer, "Deadly Motherhood: Infanticide and Medical Opinion in Mid-Victorian England," *Journal of the History of Medicine* 34 (1979): 403-27. These accounts tend to underplay the cultural investment in infanticide.

7. Alfred, Lord Tennyson, *Maud: A Monodrama* (1855), line 45.

8. In this respect she resembles another recurrent figure in nineteenth-century aesthetic representation, the dead or dying woman. Recent critical interest has focused a great deal on this figure. As Elisabeth Bronfen has shown in *Over Her Dead Body* (Manchester: Manchester University Press, 1992), the dead woman functions as an ambivalent sign of transcendence: as the dead mother, she marks the refusal of materiality, the possibility of entering the (Kantian) sphere of disinterestedness. But as a dead being, she is also the sign of the impossibility of that transcendence, a reminder of mortality, the eventual extinction of all flesh. See also Cynthia Chase, "Primary Narcissism and the Giving of Figure: Kristeva with Hertz and de Man," in *Abjection, Melancholia, and Love: The Work of Julia Kristeva*, ed. John Fletcher and Andrew Benjamin (London: Routledge, 1990), 124-36. Similarly, the infanticidal woman marks the intrusion of gross materiality and provides the occasion for critical transcendence. However, since the most interesting accounts of the dead woman have been rooted in psychoanalysis, emphasis has been laid on the fantasy of her role within the family as the dead mother, as the basis of psychic development and trauma. While the fantasy of the murdering and destructive mother is similarly pervasive in psychoanalytic work, the figure of the infanticidal woman in the nineteenth century demands to be located within a social context that might encompass a psychoanalytic understanding of these desires but that would also extend beyond them. Hence my interest is in her complex role as a defining term within a society's self-representation.

The relationship of this to the familial model of psychoanalysis is beyond the scope of this discussion.

9. In 1828, the concealment charge was extended to cover any mother, not only illegitimate ones. In 1861 concealment of a birth became a separate, substantive crime that applied to any person, not just to the mother. On the social implications of the legal context, see Angus McLaren, *Reproductive Rituals* (London: Methuen, 1984), 129-35. The best discussions of the 1624 law and its 1803 repeal are Peter C. Hoffer and N.E.H. Hall, *Murdering Mothers: Infanticide in England and New England, 1558-1803* (New York: New York University Press, 1981), esp. 65-87; Mark Jackson, "Suspicious Infant Deaths: The Statute of 1624 and Medical Evidence at Coroners' Inquiries," in *Legal Medicine in History*, ed. Michael Clark and Catherine Crawford (Cambridge: Cambridge University Press, 1994), 64-86; and Jackson, *New-Born Child Murder*, 158-77. On the 1828 and 1861 amendments, see Roger Smith, *Trial by Medicine: Insanity and Responsibility in Victorian Trials* (Edinburgh: Edinburgh University Press, 1981), 143-50; and Rose, *Massacre of the Innocents*, 70-78.

10. This is a significant point. Most accounts of the law reforms allude to an accumulating humanitarian concern that gradually wins through. See, for instance, J.M. Beattie, *Crime and the Courts in England, 1660-1800* (Oxford: Clarendon Press, 1986), 113-24; and Jackson, "Suspicious Infant Deaths."

11. It was aimed partly at amending the Coventry Act, "under which no man who wounded, maimed, or defaced another, could be convicted, unless the lying-in-wait, with a view to commit the offence was proved" (Cobbett, *The Parliamentary History of England, 1801-03*, 36:1245), and at incorporating it with the Irish Chalking Bill. On this see William Woodfall, *Parliamentary Register* (London, 1803), 2:390.

12. See *Journals of the House of Commons* 58 (1802-03): 425.

13. The discussion in Parliament endorsed English prejudices about the primitiveness and savagery of the Irish. Lord Carleton raised the point that only the Irish knew the meaning of the word *chalker*: "a person who maliciously cut or maimed another." Ellenborough presents the Chalking Bill as though it were an Irish joke. He claims, "It stated in one part, that 'whosoever shall cut, wound, etc, in the face, head, limbs, or any other part of the body' etc. Now . . . where could any person be cut or wounded, except in his body?" See Woodfall, *Parliamentary Register*, 2:355.

14. The bill followed other repressive legislation, for instance, the Habeas Corpus Suspension Bill (1801). Ellenborough supported this as well as the continuation of martial law in Ireland in 1801. He strongly opposed the admission of Catholics to political rights, claiming that "the palladium of our protestant, and, indeed of our political security, consists principally in the oath of supremacy." Cited in *Dictionary of National Biography*, s.v. "Edward Law, 1st Baron Ellenborough."

15. On Emmet's rebellion, see Marianne Elliott, *Partners in Revolution: The United Irishmen and France* (New Haven: Yale University Press, 1982), 282-322.

16. On legal reform and Ellenborough's resistance to it, see Leon Radzinowicz, *A History of English Criminal Law and Its Administration from 1770*, vol. 1, *The Movement for Reform, 1750-1830* (New York: Macmillan, 1948), esp. 506 n. 39.

17. "At present the judges were obliged to strain the law for the sake of lenity, and to admit the slightest suggestions that the child was still born, as evidence of the

fact": Cobbett, *The Parliamentary History*, 36:1246. Burke et al. had made a similar point in 1772.

18. Jean Donnison, *Midwives and Medical Men: A History of Inter-Professional Rivalries and Women's Rights* (London: Heinemann, 1977).

19. On Ellenborough's role in the Warren Hastings trial, see John Campbell, *Lives of the Lord Chief Justices of England* (New York: Cockcroft, 1878), vol. 4.

20. See Debate in the Commons, 19 April 1772, Cobbett, *The Parliamentary History of England, 1771-74*, 17:451; Hoffer and Hull, *Murdering Mothers*, 85.

21. Cobbett, *The Parliamentary History*, 17:451.

22. Adam Smith, *Theory of Moral Sentiments* (Oxford: Clarendon Press, 1976), 209-10. This argument comes in the context of a discussion about the impact of custom on moral behavior. The examples are raised in an effort to deflect the accusation against Smith of moral relativism.

23. *The Journals of Captain Cook*, vol. 2, *The Voyage of the Resolution and the Adventure, 1772-1775* (Cambridge: Cambridge University Press, 1961). Cited in Roy Porter, "The Exotic as Erotic: Captain Cook in Tahiti," in *Exoticism in the Enlightenment*, ed. G.S. Rousseau and Roy Porter (Manchester: Manchester University Press, 1989), 128. Not all commentators were as disapproving as Cook; some found the sexual habits of the Tahitians attractive. See, for instance, Diderot's *Supplément à la voyage de Bougainville*.

24. *Asiatic Researches* 4 (1799): 340-42. Cited by Malthus in *Essay on the Principle of Population*, ed. Patricia James (Cambridge: Cambridge University Press, 1989), I: 118, II: 258.

25. On the campaign, see Kanti B. Pakrasi, *Female Infanticide in India* (Calcutta: Editions Indian, 1970). On sati, see Lata Mani, "Contentious Traditions: The Debate on Sati in Colonial India," in *Recasting Women*, ed. Kumkum Sangari and Sudesh Vaid (New Delhi: Kali, 1989), 88-126; for a summary of recent debates concerning sati, see Ania Loomba, "Dead Women Tell No Tales: Issues of Female Subjectivity, Subaltern Agency, and Tradition in Colonial and Postcolonial Writings on Widow Immolation in India," *History Workshop* 6 (1993): 209-27. Like female infanticide, sati is a site in which arguments about modernization and tradition are played out. The parallels between infanticide and sati have yet to be fully explored.

26. David Hume, "On the Populousness of Ancient Nations," in *Philosophical Essays in Morals, Literature, and Politics* (Georgetown, 1817), 2:393-94. See Ernest Campbell Mossner, "Hume and the Ancient-Modern Controversy, 1725-1752," *University of Texas Studies in English* 28 (1949): 139-53.

27. England lagged behind continental Europe in the establishment of foundling hospitals. Captain Thomas Coram created the London Foundling Hospital in 1739; the impetus behind its establishment was a desire to prevent the deaths of illegitimate children. See Ruth K. McClure, *Coram's Children: The London Foundling Hospital in the Eighteenth Century* (New Haven: Yale University Press, 1981). The hospital was able to accommodate only a fraction of the children in need. See Wilson, "Illegitimacy in Mid-Eighteenth-Century London."

28. William Alexander, *The History of Women from the Earliest Centuries to the Present, Giving Some Account of Almost Every Interesting Particular Concerning the*

Sex, Among All Nations, Ancient and Modern, 2 vols. (London, 1789), 1:174-75. On Alexander, see Sylvana Tomaselli, "The Enlightenment Debate on Women," *History Workshop* 20 (1985): 101-24.

29. For an account of the positions, see J.R. Poynter, *Society and Pauperism: English Ideas on Poor Relief, 1795-1834* (London: Routledge, 1969), 165-85, 225-71; and Kenneth Smith, *The Malthusian Controversy* (London: Routledge, 1951).

30. The best example of this is Malthus's exposition of the problem of population through the use of statistics, which provoked Hazlitt to complain that "the principle of population is a mechanical thing." See William Hazlitt, *A Reply to the Essay on Population, by the Rev. T.R. Malthus. In a Series of Letters. To which are added, Extracts from the "Essay," with Notes* (1807), in *Complete Works*, centenary ed., ed. P.P. Howe (London: Dent, 1930), 1:247. On Malthus and mathematics, see Frances Ferguson, "Malthus, Godwin, Wordsworth, and the Spirit of Solitude," in *Solitude and the Sublime: Romanticism and the Aesthetics of Individuation* (London: Routledge, 1992), 114-28.

31. Cf. Catherine Gallagher, "The Body versus the Social Body in the Works of Thomas Malthus and Henry Mayhew," in *The Making of the Modern Body: Sexuality and Society in the Nineteenth Century*, ed. Catherine Gallagher and Thomas Laqueur (Berkeley: University of California Press, 1987), 83-106. Gallagher argues that the significance of Malthus is that he reconceptualizes the relationship between the body and the social body, whereby the vigorous body is no longer a sign of a healthy society but a sign of society's imminent decay. See also Mary Jacobus, "Malthus, Matricide, and the Marquis de Sade," in *First Things: The Maternal Imaginary in Literature, Art, and Psychoanalysis* (London: Routledge, 1995), 83-104. Jacobus points out that it is specifically the female reproductive body that poses the threat of overproduction.

32. William Godwin, *Thoughts Occasioned by the Perusal of Dr. Parr's Spital Sermon* (1801), in *Political and Philosophical Writings* (London: Pickering, 1993), 2:199. On Malthus and Godwin, see Donald Winch, *Riches and Poverty: An Intellectual History of Political Economy in Britain, 1750-1834* (Cambridge: Cambridge University Press, 1996), 223-48.

33. Charles Hall, *The Effects of Civilization on the People of the European State* (1805; London, 1850), 9n. On Hall, see J.R. Dinwiddy, "Charles Hall, Early English Socialist," *International Review of Social History* 21 (1976): 256-76.

34. William Godwin, *Enquiry concerning Population* (London, 1820), 320.

35. *Works of Anna Letitia Barbauld* (London, 1825), 1:348. On Barbauld's critique of Malthus, see Isobel Armstrong, "The Gush of the Feminine: How Can We Read Women's Poetry of the Romantic Period?" in *Romantic Women Writers: Voices and Countervoices*, ed. Paula R. Feldman and Theresa M. Kelley (Hanover, N.H.: University Press of New England, 1995), 13-32.

36. William Hazlitt, *Reply to the Essay on Population*, in *Complete Works*, 1:236. In a review of this work published in the *Edinburgh Review* in August 1810, the reviewer accuses Hazlitt of failing to read Malthus. The reviewer also points out that savages are known to be unproductive, which was a key factor in contemporary debates about the relative sizes of colonial populations. It is suspected that this reviewer was Malthus.

37. See Higginbottom, "'Sin of the Age.'"

38. On the bastardy provisions, see Lisa Cody, "The Politics of Bastardy in an Age of Reform," in her *Politics of Body Contact: Disciplines of Reproduction in Britain, 1688-1834*, Ph.D. diss., University of California at Berkeley, 1993.

39. "Marcus," *An Essay on Populousness* (London: privately printed, 1838), 22. See George K. Behlmer, "Deadly Motherhood: Infanticide and Medical Opinion in Mid-Victorian England," *Journal of the History of Medicine* 34 (1979): 415. Another essay by "Marcus," published in the same year, "On the Possibility of Limiting Populousness," was generally available and later reissued as the *Book of Murder* (London, 1839).

40. On Malthus's role in the formation of the Poor Law, see Poynter, *Society and Pauperism*; and Anne Digby, "Malthus and the Reform of the English Poor Law," in *Malthus and His Time*, ed. Michael Turner (London: Macmillan, 1986), 157-69.

41. The ideology of separate spheres and domesticity has been well documented since Leonore Davidoff and Catherine Hall's *Family Fortunes: Men and Women of the English Middle Class, 1780-1840* (London: Hutchinson, 1987). See also Elizabeth K. Helsinger, Robin L. Sheets, and William Veeder, *The Woman Question: Society and Literature in Britain and America, 1837-1883* (Manchester: Manchester University Press, 1983), esp. vol. 1. See also Sally Shuttleworth, "Demonic Mothers: Ideologies of Bourgeois Motherhood in the Mid-Victorian Period," in *Rewriting the Victorians: Theory, History, and the Politics of Gender*, ed. Linda M. Shires (London: Routledge, 1992), 31-51. Shuttleworth points out that "motherhood and all processes leading up to it were firmly associated in Victorian eyes with murderous lust" (34), and she links this with the dangerous ideological importance that had been ascribed to mothers.

42. See, for example, Lynda Nead, *Myths of Sexuality* (Oxford: Basil Blackwell, 1988); Nina Auerbach, *Woman and the Demon: The Life of a Victorian Myth* (Cambridge: Harvard University Press, 1982); and Helsinger et al., *The Woman Question*, vol. 3.

43. Mary Wollstonecraft, *A Vindication of the Rights of Woman* (London: Dent, 1982), 209. In her treatment of mothers, Martineau borrows much from Wollstonecraft.

44. Harriet Martineau, "Weal and Woe in Garveloch," in *Illustrations of Political Economy*, 2d ed. (London: William Fox, 1832), 2:100.

45. "Song"—"They sold the chairs, they took the bed, and went." In Ebenezer Elliott, *Poetical Works* (London, 1876), 1:26, lines 6-10. See also Elliott's poem "Withered Wild Flowers." My thanks to Karen S. Wolven for these references.

46. See Williams, *Culture and Society, 1780-1950* (London: Chatto and Windus, 1958); and Terry Eagleton, *Literature and Ideology* (London: Verso, 1977).

47. Hetty's punishment is transportation, and she dies just as she is about to be rehabilitated. On the significant spatial transformations in *Adam Bede*, see my *George Eliot* (Plymouth: Northcote House Press, 1997), chap. 1. For an excellent discussion of maternity and infanticide in *Adam Bede*, see Jill L. Matus, *Unstable Bodies* (Manchester: Manchester University Press, 1996), 167-79.

48. Joan Manheimer, "Murderous Mothers: The Problems of Parenting in the Victorian Novel," in *Feminist Studies* 5 (fall 1979): 530-46, 543. Although this is sug-

gestive, we should also bear in mind that Dinah's Methodism would align her with industrial cities and certain forms of modernization.

49. See Rita Felski, "The Gender of Modernity," in *Political Gender: Texts and Contexts*, ed. Sally Ledger, Josephine McDonagh, and Jane Spencer (Hemel Hempstead: Harvester, 1994), 144-55; Sally Ledger, "The New Woman and the Crisis of Victorianism," in *Cultural Politics at the Fin de Siècle*, ed. Sally Ledger and Scott McCracken (Cambridge: Cambridge University Press, 1995), 22-44; and Ledger, *The New Woman* (Manchester: Manchester University Press, 1997).

50. The debate provoked by the case of Caroline Beale, the British woman arrested at JFK Airport in New York in 1994 with the corpse of her recently deceased infant strapped to her body, demonstrates the persistence of these terms in modern accounts of the nation. See my "Infanticide and the Nation: The Case of Caroline Beale," *New Formations* 32 (autumn/winter 1997): 13-23. In Ireland, the furor in the 1980s over another infanticide, the Kerry Baby case, provides a further example. In the intense debate, questions of national identity, modernization, and reproduction became inextricably entangled. See Nell McCafferty, *A Woman to Blame* (Dublin: Attic Press, 1987).

51. Matthew Arnold, "The Function of Criticism at the Present Time," in *Complete Works*, ed. R.H. Super (Ann Arbor: University of Michigan Press, 1962), 3:258-85.

"Happy Shall He Be, That Taketh and Dasheth Thy Little Ones against the Stones"

Infanticide in Cooper's
The Last of the Mohicans

"I am . . . a white man without a cross."

Cotton Mather's 1702 narration of the massacre of Hannah Dustan's family provides one of the earliest accounts of infanticide in the New World: "On March 15, 1697, the Salvages made a Descent upon the Skirts of Haverhill. . . . The Nurse trying to Escape, with the New-born Infant, fell into the Hands of the Formidable Salvages; and those furious Tawnies coming into the house, bid poor Dustan rise . . . ; but e'er they had gone many Steps, they dash'd out the Brains of the Infant, against a Tree."[1]

Similar reports of white children massacred by Native Americans recur in both autobiographical captivity narratives and their fictional descendants. In Ann Eliza Bleecker's novel *The History of Maria Kittle*, for example, two mothers lose their infants to "Salvages" while their husbands are away from the settlement: "An Indian, hideously painted, strove up to Comelia . . . and cleft her white forehead deeply with his tomahawk. . . . [H]e deformed her lovely body with deep gashes; and tearing her unborn babe away, dashed it to pieces against the stone wall." This account of violence to mother and fetus is followed by a baby-killing only a few pages later when another mother "re-signed [her infant] to the merciless hands of the savage, who instantly dashed his little forehead against the stones."[2] The scenario recurs in Catherine Maria Sedgwick's nineteenth-century novel *Hope Leslie*: "The Indian . . . now sprang forward and tore the infant from its mother's breast . . . tossed him wildly around his head, and dashed him on the doorstone."[3] And in Cooper's *The Last of the Mohicans*, an angry Huron warrior at Fort William Henry "dash[es] the head of [a white] infant against a rock, and cast[s] its quivering remains to [its mother's] very feet."[4]

Forty years ago, R.W.B. Lewis described the hero of American fiction as "happily bereft of ancestry," noting that America's political parentlessness is often figured in post-Revolution literature as biological parentlessness; however, given the range of possible fates for young white children available to such fiction writers as Bleecker, Sedgwick, and Cooper, the recurrence of depictions of offspring killed by Native Americans suggests that this literature might also express America's anxiety over the possibility of being bereft of descendants. Like the "redundancy of [the] phrase and figure" of the headlong Indian, which Lora Romero examines in her insightful essay, "Gender, Empire, and New Historicism," the repeated figure of a nursing babe murdered by savages while a hysterical mother looks on and a father is absent, as well as the repetition of the verb *dash* in all of these representations, suggest that infanticide functions more as a sensationalist figure manifesting anxiety about the security of the nation's future than as an empirical fact of colonial warfare.[5]

Most recent historians of Native America agree that no ethnographic evidence exists of consistent war practices of infanticide among northeastern Native American tribes during this period. Historian James Axtell and others have argued that rather than killing them, East Coast tribes customarily took English women and children as prisoners, either selling them to the French or adopting them: "The pattern of taking women and children for adoption was consistent throughout the colonial period. . . . [Native Americans] captured English settlers largely to replace members of their own families who had died, often from English musketballs or imported diseases. Consequently, women and children—the 'weak and defenceless'—were the prime targets of Indian raids." Daniel K. Richter claims that restoring populations decimated by disease or battle was the major goal of most raids launched by the Iroquois during the eighteenth century: "The essential measure of a war party's success was its ability to seize prisoners and bring them home alive." John E. Ferling acknowledges that "troublesome small children" were sometimes killed, but these murders were committed en route to the raiding parties' camps if the children irritated their captors rather than during a raid.[6] Although some of the more sensational captivity narratives describe the massacres of infants, many others testify that children as young as fourteen days old were made captives or adopted and that white mothers were often assisted in caring for their infants by their Native American captors.[7]

The reiteration of the verb *dash*, like the recurrence of the trope of infanticide itself, in fictional and nonfictional accounts of colonial American history suggests discursive rather than strictly documentary significance. The source for this usage seems to be the Old Testament, a text familiar to many American colonists and settlers, which features numerous descriptions of infants "dashed to pieces" within the context of the Jews' struggle to preserve their minority culture within communities of "heathens."[8] In Psalm 137, for example, the singer cries, "O daughter of Babylon . . . / Happy shall he be, that taketh and dasheth thy little ones against the stones."[9] The author of the Book of Nahum recounts the destruction of the immoral city of Nineveh in a similar manner: "Woe to the bloody city! It is full of lies and robbery. . . . Her young children also were dashed in pieces at the top of all the streets" (Nahum 3:1-10). In these and other biblical examples, infants' heads are dashed when immoral (i.e., non-Jewish) societies are purged of their wickedness by a wrathful Yahweh. Elsewhere in the Old Testament, however, God's chosen people, the children of Israel, are also "dashed to pieces" by their enemies. In the apocryphal Book of Judith, for example, Hebrew children are threatened by the Assyrian armies of Holofernes. And in 2 Kings, Elisha weeps because he knows "what thou wilt do unto the children of Israel: their strong holds wilt thou set on fire, and their young men wilt thou slay with the sword, and wilt dash their children, and rip up their women with child" (2 Kings 8:12).

Thematically, all of these biblical examples of infanticide foreground the Jews' concerns over the survival of their culture threatened with ethnic and moral contamination. Infants are the battleground on which these cultures fight for future dominance. Most significant about these biblical references, however, is the doubled hermeneutic: When the immoral societies of Babylon, Nineveh, and Samaria are destroyed at the hands of the purifying Yahweh, it can be read as part of a "just" war, yet when the chosen people are its victims, infanticide can be read as immoral barbarism.

Given the lack of historical evidence of infanticidal practices among the northeastern Native American nations and the variety of references to infanticidal violence in Old Testament texts, what accounts for the recurrence of this theme in early American literature? What might the repetition of both figure and phrase signal? What are the ideological contradictions surrounding representations of America simultaneously as a new and fertile landscape and as a society in which all possibilities of a future for the colonizers are brutally extinguished when their offspring are systematically exterminated?

In an attempt to answer these questions, I would like to examine James Fenimore Cooper's novel *The Last of the Mohicans* (1826), a text ostensibly propelled by the quest to reunite broken families—Munro with his daughters, the Mohicans with their Delaware relatives—but punctuated by the brutal sacrifices of offspring. Although the literal massacre of a white infant and its mother is pinned on a Native American enemy, more metaphorical infant-killings such as the slaughter of an innocent colt and the acts of disowning one's children are perpetrated by Natty and Munro, suggesting that the colonizers are also implicated as agents of the destruction of America's future.

Earlier critics like Leslie Fiedler have discussed this novel in terms of "homosocial bonding," the "perpetual blood brother theme," and the "almost inarticulate, but unquestioned love" that binds Chingachgook to Natty Bumppo. While relationships between men are crucial in this novel, more recent critics have focused on the interactions of other groups. Jane Tompkins, for example, has read the novel as "an attempt to calculate exactly how much violation or mixing of its fundamental categories [ethnicity, nationality, and class] a society can bear." I would argue that a powerful gender subtext lies beneath the novel's more overtly manifest concerns about these other fundamental categories; this subtext is everywhere, from the oft-repeated slur that "the Delaware are women" to Natty Bumppo's repeated anxiety that being tied to their mothers' apronstrings has ruined white men's ability to survive on the frontier. I would suggest, then, that the recurring examples of violence toward offspring in this text signal resistance to a much more complicated sort of mixing than Tompkins imagines: a crossing that is at once sexual (through biological reproduction) and racial (through miscegenation). Like the Old Testament examples, the violence directed at offspring in Cooper's text seems to highlight conflict between opposing communities. But if the violence marks attempts to purify the frontier of alterity, Cooper's novel defines alterity not exclusively in terms of race but also in terms of gender. Taunts linking women and Native Americans recur, such as Magua's repeated accusation that "the Delaware are women!" implying, as Shirley Samuels has suggested, that when Native American men are killed in *Mohicans*, it is because they resemble women. Like Native Americans who, through their understanding of sustainable agricultural and hunting practices, perpetuate the fertility of the wilderness, and therefore intrude on the novel's fantasy of white male sufficiency, women threaten white male fantasies of self-making because they are biologically necessary for the white population's future on the American frontier. Women represent two undesirable qualities in Cooper's text: the transmission and preservation of a conservative feminized and feminizing culture, which Natty links with the impracticality of book-learning, and sexual corruption, which is traditionally viewed in terms of original sin but here is viewed as well in terms of miscegenation. For these reasons, both women and Native Americans are defined in the novel as the unwanted Other.[10]

The instances in which offspring are killed conflate the text's anxieties over these two controversial issues of race and gender, suggesting to me that white America may be "bereft of descendants," not because of the mythical barbarism of Native Americans, but because of its own interconnected anxieties about racial and sexual purity and about the female-centered processes of biological reproduction by which families and cultures regenerate themselves. Whereas historical romances typically depict racial or ethnic conflicts resolved through a marriage between representatives of the feuding peoples, their miscegenated offspring serving to cement the alliance, in *Mohicans* the possibility of interracial union is eliminated when Cora and Uncas are killed; mothers are excluded; and offspring, both animal and human, are brutally killed.[11] Violence toward offspring seems to stand in for unrepresented fantasies of mother-killing.

What emerges as an alternative to female-dependent reproduction is a fantasy of male parthenogenesis which assumes men can be free from dependence on women in order to re-create themselves, a fantasy which continues in contemporary American science's attempts to bypass biological generation. Inspired by this fantasy, Natty's boast that he is a "man without a cross" can be read as meaning not only that he is not the result of miscegenation but also that he is self-reproducing rather than reliant on women-centered reproduction. This fantasy of retaining the American frontier as a private domain exclusively for the white male, however, has as its logical consequences sterility and extinction. The recurring trope of infanticide then can be read as exposing a relationship between white America's fantasies of racial and sexual dominance and its fears of racial domination and annihilation. While simultaneously using depictions of "savages" attacking white families to justify white genocidal treatment of Native Americans, these fantasies implicate white Americans as agents of their own destruction.

Infanticide in The Last of the Mohicans

The most literal example of infanticide in Cooper's *Mohicans* is the massacre of a white baby by an angry Huron warrior in chapter 17. Although not perfectly homologous, two other moments in the novel when the colonizers themselves sacrifice or disown offspring for the greater good of the patriarchal "nation" complicate the reading of this climactic moment in Cooper's text. In all of these examples, the deaths of offspring are blamed on external enemies— Native American brutality, warfare, miscegenation—but closer readings reveal a countermyth: white Americans as agents of their own elimination.

In the earliest example of offspring-killing, Natty kills a colt whose rustling in the bushes threatens to expose the Munro party to their "Mingo" pursuers. Here, the captivity narrative convention of beastly savages brutally murdering the children of morally superior colonists is reversed. Instead, the rational Natty Bumppo justifies the slaughter of an innocent colt by explaining it in terms of the conflict between a person's individual survival and the survival of his dependents: "When men struggle for the single life God has given them," Natty argues, "even their own kind seem no more than the beasts of the wood" (*LM* 47). Like a child who threatens a parent's survival, the colt must be sacrificed.[12] The psalmodist David Gamut, however, resists this rationalization and urges Natty to "spare the foal of Miriam! It is the comely offspring of a faithful dam" (LM 47). Gamut insists on seeing Natty's violence as directed not only at the offspring but also at its mother when he demonstrates pity for the butchered colt as well as for the "motherly animal" (LM, 39), "Poor Miriam!" (LM, 51).

The mare's name and the song Gamut sings after the colt has been killed— "First born of Egypt, smite did he, / Of mankind, and of beast also" (LM, 51)—recall two biblical accounts of infanticide that illuminate the novel's concerns for racial purity: the pharaoh's plot to keep Jews from outnumbering their Egyptian oppressors and Yahweh's plague on the Egyptian first-born (Exodus 1 and 12). Miriam is the name of Moses' sister, who helps him escape the pharaoh's policy of Hebrew infanticide and go on to lead the chosen people to the promised land. Gamut's song refers specifically to Yahweh's tenth plague, which killed all Egyptian first-born but passed over Hebrew homes marked with lamb's blood. Both of these Old Testament stories foreground fears of racial contamination between the enslaved Hebrews and their Egyptian oppressors. The marking of Hebrew homes at Passover demonstrates a desire for visible differences between two feuding peoples, differences which miscegenation through intermarriage might obliterate.

The Mosaic myth was familiar to many of Cooper's readers, including descendants of New England Puritans who had described their own exodus from the tyranny of England in the typological terms of the Jews' escape from Egypt.[13] Using this typological framework, Cooper contextualizes the novel's quest for the reunification of the Munro family in terms of deliverance from the threats of racial contamination. Natty's rescue of Cora and Alice from Magua not only reunites the family but frees Cora from the miscegenation that Magua threatens.[14] Like Moses, who is born a Hebrew but raised by the pharaoh's daughter, Natty is biologically of one race and culturally incorporated into another, and he can therefore represent a living compromise between two conflicting races while he denies any potential for permanent reconciliation through interracial marriage. Natty's sacrifice of a colt linked with Moses, then, seems an act as shocking as suicide. It presages his own expendability—his inability to regenerate his temporary compromise between the two races—and underlines the inherent imbrication of white fantasies of racial dominance and fears of racial domination.

More metaphorical killings of offspring in the novel are occasioned by fathers' refusals to acknowledge their children. Both Colonel Munro and the Delaware sachem Tamenund resist their biological paternity, preferring to use the family metaphorically to connote their political patriarchies rather than literally to signify "their own kind." Munro, for example, ignores his daughter Alice's call in order to play the part of colonel to his larger "family," the inhabitants of the fort. As he explains to Heyward, "All that you see here claim alike to be my children" (*LM*, 171). Similarly, when Cora attempts to remind Tamenund of a recent event involving his child, the Delaware patriarch interrupts to put her familial account into context within the long political history of Delaware contact with whites. When she asks, "Is Tamenund a father?" he puts her off by replying, "Of a nation" (*LM*, 305). Here the politics of warfare, which breaks up the family, also usurps its vocabulary; political alliances structured by the "fathers" of nations replace biological alliances dependent on the participation of mothers.[15]

The humiliated father of a Huron youth named Reed-that-bends makes a similar denial of paternity when his son is denounced for cowardice: "I had no son! He who was called by that name is forgotten; his blood was pale, and it came not from the veins of a Huron; the wicked Chippewas cheated [me of] my squaw!" (*LM*, 247). Like the sacrifice of the colt, this denial of paternity can be read as an act of covert violence against the mother. By blaming intertribal mixing and infidelity for his son's weakness, the father of Reed-that-bends isolates Woman as the site of racial and moral contamination.

The most literal instance of infanticide is the Huron killing of a white baby during the Fort William Henry massacre. Like the previous examples, the incident foregrounds anxiety about both racial and sexual mixing. The incident begins with a description of a truant provincial "being plundered of those very effects, which had caused him to desert his place in the ranks" (*LM*, 174-75). This emphasis on the redistribution of trade goods is followed by a second scene of bartering, in which a Huron warrior is attracted by a white woman's shawl:

> As the female crowd approached them, the gaudy colours of a shawl
> attracted the eyes of a wild and untutored Huron. He advanced to seize it,
> without the least hesitation. The woman, more in terror, than through
> love of the ornament, wrapped her child in the coveted article, and
> folded both more closely to her bosom. . . . [Suddenly] the savage
> relinquished his hold of the shawl, and tore the screaming infant from her
> arms. Abandoning every thing to the greedy grasp of those around her, the
> mother darted, with distraction in her mien, to reclaim her child. The
> Indian . . . extended one hand, in sign of a willingness to exchange,
> while, with the other, he flourished the babe above his head, holding it by
> the feet, as if to enhance the value of the ransom. (*LM*, 175)

Most literally, the passage seems to be about a kind of protoconsumer desire run amuck—a cross-cultural economic perversion—among the Native Americans, but I think the deviant economics also maps on to a deviant erotics.[16] Indeed, the passage conflates the languages of economic exchange and eroticism. When the Huron adopts a position of barter, assuming that the child he holds is now rightly his to trade for whatever the mother can offer, the mother cries out her terms of barter: "'Here—here—there—all—any—every thing!'. . . tearing the lighter articles of dress from her person. 'Take all, but give me my babe!'" (*LM*, 175). Her desperate efforts to retrieve her infant resemble a striptease, but her stuttering bid, the only direct speech by a white mother in the entire novel, is insufficient to appease the angry warrior: "The savage spurned the worthless rags, and perceiving that the shawl had already become a prize to another, his bantering but sullen smile, changing to a gleam of ferocity, he dashed the head of the infant against a rock, and cast its quivering remains to her very feet" (*LM*, 175). That the mother almost disrobes in the process of trying to retrieve her child conveys in microcosm the dilemma of the novel itself: Cooper's text offers the titillation of interracial union, such as Uncas's union with Cora, but prohibits its consummation at the very last moment, replacing it with violence against children. The mother's subsequent death by a "tomahawk [driven] into her own brain" (*LM*, 175) seems the text's cruel punishment for her willingness to engage in an economic exchange that might also signal an erotic exchange with the racial Other.

This final instance of infanticide simultaneously confirms and challenges the white fantasy of a racially pure continent. If the baby's death personalizes the massacre of American colonists, casting them as morally superior victims of a barbarous attack, then it can justify their subsequent genocidal treatment of their Native American aggressors. But if the Huron can be read as adopting the child as his own, thereby exhibiting a willingness to engage in cultural and sexual exchange, then the child is killed by white culture's anxious rejection of miscegenation as a possible solution to racial conflict. The bartering represents a moment of potential equality between the two races and the possibility of economic, cultural, and sexual exchange, but its dysfunctioning reveals the price of the text's prohibition of interracial union. As the only white infant in the novel, the baby's fate foretells a limited future for Anglo-Americans on the continent. Its elimination implies that the last of the Mohicans forecasts the last of the Munros as well.

All these examples of infanticide conflate anxieties about race and gender by locating contamination, both moral and racial, in women's bodies: The colt's death recalls Egyptian and Hebrew fears of racial intermingling and Moses' ambiguous significance as culturally mixed yet racially pure; the denial of paternity by Reed-that-bends's father similarly rests on claims that his cowardice stems from his mother's miscegenation; and finally, the massacre of the white child and mother at the fort forbids the possibility of interracial exchange. Each of these instances of infanticide suggests that the displays of white Americans' roles as victims of Native American violence conceal less flattering readings of white Americans as their own aggressors.

"Partial Relatives"

Structured as a historical romance, *Mohicans* has as its ostensible quest the reunification of families: while Cora and Alice travel to meet their father, Uncas and Chingachgook attempt to locate their Delaware relatives. But a closer examination of the novel reveals that all families in *Mohicans* are, in their unified states, characterized by incompleteness—by half sisters, displaced or adopted children, and single parents. The Munro family itself comprises a father and two grown daughters born of different mothers, as well as a potential son-in-law who has "no father to expect [him]" (*LM*, 102). The family of Uncas and Chingachgook is limited to a father-and-son team, supplemented by the kinless Natty Bumppo's role as "Uncas' father's brother" (*LM*, 273) and Uncas's adoptive father (*LM*, 263). The quest for a reunited family, then, signifies a return to the patriarch rather than to a family that includes both mother and father.

Mothers, in fact, are systematically excluded from the text. Other than the mother at the fort, who loses her life and the life of her child, there are no white mothers represented in the novel. Only Cora appears as a doubled figure of maternity and childhood, since she represents "my more than sister, my mother" (*LM*, 115) to Alice and "my babe" to Munro. A source of affection and comfort to the younger sister, Cora is described as looking at the innocent Alice with "maternal fondness" (*LM*, 156). In contrast to Alice's virginal simplicity, Cora describes herself as a woman of "experience," implying a degree of sexual knowledge: "That I cannot see the sunny side of the picture of life, like this artless but ardent enthusiast, . . . is the penalty of experience" (*LM*, 150). For the same fantasies of racial and sexual purity that motivate the other instances of infanticide in the novel, Cora must also be sacrificed.

It is worth noting that, although the rescues of women and reunions of the family propel the plot, these reunions are only temporarily achieved. In a description of a brief moment of domestic comfort at Munro's tent, Cooper's prose betrays the impermanence of the colonial family structure: "Not only the dangers through which they had passed, but those which still impended above them, appeared to be *momentarily* forgotten, in the *soothing indulgence* of such a family meeting. It seemed as if they had profited by the *short truce*, to devote an *instant* to the purest and best affections: the daughters forgetting their fears, and the veteran his cares, in the security of the *moment*" (*LM*, 156, my emphasis).

Even though Natty Bumppo and the Mohican scouts deliver Alice and Cora to their father at the fort, they are soon separated again during the Huron massacre, and when the Munro/Bumppo party arrives to rescue Cora from her imprisonment by Magua, the Munro reunion is immediately interrupted by her death. At the level of narrative, these reunions are temporary because external threats separate or kill family members, but on a symbolic level, one can interpret the transience of these reunions as evidence that the family without a mother has no means of perpetuating itself into futurity.[17]

Cora's death marks the end of the "short truce" of the Munro family reunion and the destruction of the potential for family and future that Cora's sensuality promises. Her death is the moment at which all the potential significations of infanticide and mother-killing converge. The resistance to the maternal, shown here as a resistance to Cora, is also inevitably a resistance to miscegenation. The conflation of sexual experience and mixed ancestry in the character of Cora reveals that the "cross" Natty insists he is without refers to both race and sexuality. This is shown most evocatively when Munro's explanation of the absent mothers in the text also explains Cora's mixed ancestry. Cora's origins are described by her father as a "curse entailed on Scotland, by her unnatural union with a foreign and trading people" (*LM*, 159). Munro's "shedding blood in different lands," "form[ing] a connexion" with a nameless woman of mixed race, from a "foreign and trading people"—all these details represent Munro's marriage to his first wife, Cora's mother, in the conventions of a fling by a soldier in a strange land so that, like the explanation of the cowardice of Reed-that-bends, Cora is explained by her mother's contamination.

In the final chapters, the novel shifts its focus irrevocably from the dark and sensual Cora as romantic heroine to her fair and virginal opposite, Alice. In moving from the potential union of Uncas and Cora to the actual union of Heyward and Alice, the novel traces a narrative trajectory from sensuality to virginity and from potential miscegenation to racial purity. Rather than unite feuding peoples, as marriages in historical romances often do, the marriage implied at the end of the novel ensures the colonists' safety from the threats of miscegenation: "The 'open hand' had conveyed [Munro's] surviving daughter far into the settlements of the 'pale-faces,' where her tears had, at last, ceased to flow, and had been succeeded by the bright smiles which were better suited to her joyous nature" (*LM*, 348). The asexual union of Heyward and the childlike Alice suggests that the price of the desire for racial purity may be extinction.

Regeneration through Self-Making

The instances of violence toward offspring depicted in *Mohicans* suggest that sensational descriptions of Native American attacks on the chosen people of colonial America may mask white Americans' own anxiety about their genocidal treatment of Indians in North America and their ability to reproduce their own culture biologically and culturally after they have exterminated the racial Other. The trope of infanticide provides a lens through which the self-annihilation of white American culture can be viewed, since these acts of violence directed against children and their mothers are also directed at American culture itself.

Cora's death and the instances of infanticide preceding it imply that reproduction with motherhood at its center cannot function on the frontier represented in *Mohicans*. Although Richard Slotkin has suggested that American fiction offers a model of regeneration through violence rather than biological reproduction, Cooper offers another alternative to biological reproduction in *The Last of the Mohicans*—a fantasy of male parthenogenesis on a frontier that only men inhabit. It is the American myth of the self-made man, a myth that has captivated American writers from Benjamin Franklin to F. Scott Fitzgerald. For female reproduction, Cooper substitutes the image of the self-reliant hero who, without engaging in sexual relations, reproduces himself through near escapes from death and the adoption of new names or multiple identities. Natty is the primary example of this self-made man. Described by Balzac as "a magnificent moral hermaphrodite born between the savage and the civilized worlds," he resists marriage throughout the Leatherstocking Tales and ultimately leaves no offspring.[18] Instead, he changes his own identity throughout: "Leatherstocking," "Pathfinder," "Trapper," "Hawkeye," "Deerslayer," and "la Longue Carabine" are only a few of the many names he achieves through the performance of new feats and the acquisition of new skills.

In the character of Natty, Cooper presents a counter to the biological model of reproduction and a safeguard to the miscegenating risks of this model. As an absolute opposite to Cora, Natty claims to be both racially and sexually pure. Natty's resistance to miscegenation becomes resistance to all breeding, not simply culturally sanctioned unions. Natty succeeds in effecting the compromise between the two races, not through intermarriage but through the self-making that allows him to learn the skills of his Mohican friends. But Natty's compromise can only be short-term. Like the cross-bred mule in Cooper's *The Prairie*, he is sterile; he can provide only a temporary, and therefore unsatisfactory, resolution to the racial and sexual contradictions of America.

For this reason, Cooper's *Mohicans* is a problematic work for contemporary readers. No utopian moment of relations between the sexes or the races emerges from the historical romance Cooper sets up. At the same time that his text forbids miscegenation, it recognizes it retrospectively as the only possible solution to racial conflict in America. The supposed ideal of reproduction through self-making has its obvious limits. The doubled readings of the killing of innocent offspring examined here suggest that the infanticide theme simultaneously attempts to justify white genocide of Native Americans and implicates white males in their culture's own sterility. Violence toward the mother and women in general is camouflaged by violence toward children, assumed to be caused by external racial conflict but in actuality demonstrating an internal conflict. The double place that white women inhabit as both white (and therefore same) and female (and therefore different) means that the distinction between agent and victim is never stable. As white, they can be aggressors driven by desires for racial domination; as women, they are victims of the white male desire for racial and sexual purity. This relation between figures of infanticide and the consequent sterility of the culture is significant, not only because Cooper establishes it in *The Last of the Mohicans* but because this novel is only one of several written during the early nineteenth century in America that feature this convergence of sexual and racial politics. The fantasy of the self-made man, as an alternative to female-centered reproduction, is at once a practical myth of economic opportunity in the New World and a naive denial of the place of the Other in American society.

Notes

I wish to thank Shirley Samuels, Charlotte Sussman, Heather Zwicker, and D. Mark Simpson, each of whom offered extensive advice on earlier drafts of this essay.

1. Cotton Mather, "Magnalia Christi Americana" (1702), in *Narratives of the Indian Wars*, ed. Charles Lincoln (New York: Scribner, 1913), 264.

2. Ann Eliza Bleecker, *The History of Maria Kittle* (Hartford, Conn., 1797), 19-20, 21.

3. Catherine Maria Sedgwick, *Hope Leslie* (New Brunswick, N.J.: Rutgers University Press, 1987), 65. In "Distresses of a Frontier Man," in *Letters from an American Farmer* (1782; New York: E.P. Dutton, 1951), Hector St. John de Crèvecoeur invokes what must by then have been a familiar refrain to acknowledge the threat of violence that war with England represented to the new Americans: "Must I then, in order to be called a faithful subject, cooly and philosophically say it is necessary for the good of Britain that my children's brains should be dashed against the walls of the house in which they were reared; that my wife should be stabbed and scalped before my face?"

(206-7). What is significant about this passage is that Crèvecoeur invokes the familiar images of a Native American raid—scalping, children's brains dashed against walls, etc.—but assigns agency to Britain rather than to "savages."

4. James Fenimore Cooper, *The Last of the Mohicans* (1826; New York: Penguin Books, 1986), 175; hereafter cited in the text and abbreviated *LM*.

5. R.W.B. Lewis, *The American Adam: Innocence, Tragedy, and Tradition in the Nineteenth Century* (Chicago: University of Chicago Press, 1958), 5; Lora Romero, "Gender, Empire, and New Historicism," *American Literature* 63 (1991): 385-404. Romero argues that "the redundancy of both phrase and figure in Cooper's novel signals that text's participation in and instantiation of a larger antebellum cultural discourse in which the ethnographic and pedagogic overlap" (387).

6. James Axtell, *The Invasion Within* (New York: Oxford University Press, 1985), 304; Daniel K. Richter, "War and Culture: The Iroquois Experience," in *The American Indian: Past and Present*, ed. Roger L. Nichols (New York: Alfred A. Knopf, 1986), 109; John E. Ferling, *A Wilderness of Miseries: War and Warriors in Early America* (Westport, Conn.: Greenwood Press, 1980), 51.

7. Elizabeth Hanson's account of her captivity (1728) includes this anecdote: "The captain, though he had as great a load as he could well carry, and was helped up with it, did, for all that, carry my babe for me in his arms, which I took to be a favor from him." See Joseph Norman Heard's *White into Red: A Study of the Assimilation of White Persons Captured by Indians* (Metuchen, N.J.: Scarecrow Press, 1973), 54. In addition to Hanson's account, Heard provides other examples of infants made captive by northeastern tribes (125, 131).

8. The *Oxford English Dictionary* definition of *dash* cites ships, cities, oystershells, teeth, and roses but does not mention infants' heads as possible objects of the verb.

9. Psalm 137:8-9. See also Isaiah 14:16 and Hosea 13:16.

10. Fiedler quoted in Wayne Fields, ed., *James Fenimore Cooper: Twentieth-Century Views* (Englewood Cliffs, N.J.: Prentice Hall, 1979), 53; Jane Tompkins, *Sensational Designs: The Cultural Work of American Fiction, 1790-1860* (New York: Oxford University Press, 1985), 106; Shirley Samuels, "Generation through Violence: Cooper and the Making of Americans," in *New Essays on "The Last of the Mohicans,"* ed. Daniel H. Peck (Cambridge: Cambridge University Press, 1992), 87-114.

11. See Richard Slotkin, *Regeneration through Violence: The Mythology of the American Frontier, 1600-1860* (Middletown, Conn.: Wesleyan University Press, 1973).

12. Samuels claims Cooper confounds distinctions between animals and humans throughout *Mohicans*, but particularly in this scene where Gamut gives the colt human status by describing it as the "comely offspring of a faithful dam" (*LM* 47), thereby inviting readers to make the equation between the colt and human offspring. See Samuels, "Generation through Violence," 87.

13. See John McAleer, "Biblical Analogy in the Leatherstocking Tales," *Nineteenth-Century Fiction* 17 (1962): 217-35.

14. Cora is, of course, already a product of miscegenation as the daughter of a white man and Creole woman, but only Munro and Heyward know this.

15. Like *Mohicans*, *The Pathfinder* is structured by the return of an adolescent daughter to a widowed army man and explores the family/nation homology. But un-

like the heroines of the earlier novel, *The Pathfinder*'s heroine, Mabel Dunham, rejects her father's military metaphors for family relations as well as the corresponding authority he attempts to impose on her in terms of her marriage partner.

16. Miscegenation and commerce are also linked when Munro blames Cora's mixed race on a "foreign and trading people," suggesting colonial trade and miscegenation are homologous.

17. Although the plot seems initially directed by the male restoration of a family torn apart by threats to female chastity, ironically all the dangers that Cora and Alice encounter are caused by their political and familial leader. Like Serjeant Dunham in *The Pathfinder*, Colonel Munro in *Mohicans* actually endangers the family when he attempts to transfer his daughters from their home to the realm of war.

18. Quoted in Richard Chase, *The American Novel and Its Tradition* (Garden City, N.Y.: Doubleday, 1957), 63.

Reforming the Body

"Experience" and the Architecture of Imagination in Harriet Jacobs's *Incidents in the Life of a Slave Girl*

The sentimentalist paradigm for Harriet Jacobs's 1861 slave narrative, *Incidents in the Life of a Slave Girl*, is the story of a chaste young woman heroically fending off—or tragically falling victim to—a villainous man's sexual advances. Jacobs's rhetorical problem with this paradigm, however, is that the domestic ideology behind literary sentimentalism equates a woman's sexual morality (chastity for unmarried women, maternity for those who are married) with her credibility. Jacobs has failed to adhere to these standards, and this is precisely her point: slavery should be condemned because it makes conventional morality impossible, as she herself exemplifies. Yet because she is writing her own story, her physically and therefore morally damaged body may deflect her audience's sympathy from the story itself, even though she needs to rely on the text of that body to gain sympathy.[1] Jacobs must negotiate between the reality of her experience and the sensibility of her white northern audience. While her narrative dramatizes the gap between their experiences, it also represents the opportunity to bridge this gap by revealing the common desires shared by black and white women. Hazel Carby, Jean Fagan Yellin, and others have established that Jacobs overtly espouses domestic values to persuade her audience of her credibility, but she also sees those values as inadequate and even harmful for slave women. As Carby puts it, Jacobs subverts domestic rhetoric through "an exposition of her womanhood and motherhood contradicting and transforming an ideology that could not take account of her experience."[2]

"Experience," Space, and Motherhood under Slavery

Although Carby does not specifically develop a theory of "experience" in her reading, her association of womanhood and motherhood with experience reflects the central referentiality among these concepts in *Incidents*.[3] In what follows, I will demonstrate that Jacobs's pregnant body and the interiors of buildings with which her body has come into contact are portrayed in the narrative as contiguous spaces that represent each other metonymically. Jacobs's spatialized representations of unspeakable experiences of domestic space not only reveal her imaginative uses of pregnancy to free herself from various forms of confinement but also create a politicized spatial language for enslaved mothers.

As used in antebellum reformist texts such as *Incidents*, the word *experience* announces the speaker's moral authority, as developed through a direct physical engagement with the material world. Although the process is not solely physical, it is thought that the body—especially the state of one's physical health—will make one's experience visibly evident. According to the Emersonian model,

> When [a man] comes to give all the goods he has year after year collected, in an estate to his son . . . and cannot give him the skill and experience which made or collected these, and the method and place they have in his own life, . . . what a change! Instead of the masterly good humor and sense of power and fertility of resource in himself; instead of those strong and learned hands, those piercing and learned eyes, that supple body, and that mighty and prevailing heart which the father had, whom nature loved and feared . . . we now have a puny, protected person, guarded by walls and curtains, stoves and down beds.[4]

The man without experience, whose body and spirit are not strengthened through the physical creation of space, becomes emasculated and imprisoned in space. However, although confinement to interior space reveals a lack of experience here, having experience, as Emerson argues elsewhere, allows the man to enter a sanctified interior space from which he can speak with authority: "One class [of teachers] speaks from within, or from experience, as parties and possessors of the fact; and the other class from without, as spectators merely. . . . It is of no use to preach to me from without. . . . [I]f a man do not speak from within the veil, where the word is one with that it tells of, let him lowly confess it."[5]

The veil, while in part alluding to ancient religious rituals in this passage, refers almost ubiquitously in antebellum literature to the concealment of the female body, a tradition evident in *Incidents*. In Jacobs's text, the lifting of the veil reveals the experienced female body; Linda Brent's body, reshaped by pregnancy, becomes the text of her experience.[6] Those who see the body with the "veil withdrawn," in this case Jacobs's readers, obtain knowledge of the sexual history of her body.[7]

Lydia Maria Child's preface to *Incidents* uses the veil image to show, as both a warning and an enticement, that readers of this narrative will experience a sexually damaged female body and learn of that body's experience:

"The experiences of this intelligent and much-injured woman belong to a class which some call delicate subjects, and others indelicate. This peculiar phase of Slavery has generally been kept veiled; but the public ought to be made acquainted with its monstrous features, and I willingly take the responsibility of presenting them with the veil withdrawn."[8] So, while experience confers authority to speak, and in Child's interpretation even makes speech essential, representations of experience as a concept tend toward images of "veiled" interiors rather than verbal articulation.[9] The problem stems partly from the fact that the word *experience* is a linguistic signifier of antilanguage: it is a generalization of particular events that are supposed to critique such generalities. The word signifies physical and psychological events that seem private and unrepresentable, like the celebrated mysteries of the female body to which experience is linked; but speech, according to its basic function, generalizes these events for public comprehension. To counteract its externalization in speech, images of experience strive to maintain its interiority. The theoretical difficulties of translating private phenomena into public discourse are greatly enhanced in *Incidents* by the rigid conventionality of sentimentalism and by Jacobs's use of her individual experience to call for collective political action.

More important, in Jacobs's narrative, the representation of experience *as* interior space also results from the impossibility of narrating her particular experience *of* interior space. For reasons of decorum and because of the pain it causes her personally, Jacobs avoids articulating her own rape by her master, even though rape constitutes her claim to the authority of experience.[10] However, as I will show, she reveals her rape by imagistically substituting her pregnant body for the literal enclosed spaces where sexual violence takes place in her narrative. For Jacobs, the interiority of experience (her rape and subsequent confinement in the garret) is fact, not theory. The practice of showing spaces rather than speaking of events becomes an opportunity for Jacobs to tell her story while undermining the domestic ideology of the home as sanctified space. Indeed, she uses these revisions of space to dismantle the notion of material space, thus effecting both her ultimate escape and, as a result, her lasting political power. A brief discussion of antebellum architectural ideology, to which I will now turn, reveals the particular spatial terms for Jacobs's experience; I will then show how Jacobs reconceptualizes those terms through images of damaged, inverted, even impossible domestic spaces.

The Flowery Home Ravaged

When Jacobs imagistically undermines homes, she questions the material foundations of the cult of domesticity. The domestic architecture reform movement, led by Andrew Jackson Downing in the 1840s and 1850s, mass-produced inexpensive pattern books to show individuals how to build domestic ideology into the very walls of their homes: the house would shape and paradoxically also reveal the moral character of the family within.[11] In many ways Downing's is a more ideologically programmatic version of the dynamics between body and space in the Emersonian images of experience. Downing shows how vines, or architectural imitations of them (such as twisted columns), can literally enclose the house in the virtues of domesticity and its close relative, pastoralism: vines "embower" houses, "partly concealing and partly adorning their walls" and giving them "that expressive beauty of rural and home feeling which makes them so captivating to every passer-by." As Downing makes clear, vines are a metonymy for the idealized white women who live inside: such vines are planted "generally by the mother or daughter, whose very planting of vines is a labor of love offered up on the domestic altar, it follows, by the most direct and natural associations, that vines on a rural cottage always express domesticity and the presence of heart." Women and vines are engaged in a mutual process of ideological construction, through which they come to represent each other.[12]

The coyness displayed by vines ("partly concealing and partly adorning") recalls the iconographic white woman who discreetly invited male attention by adorning herself (and being an adornment), but conceals any improper intimations with a modesty that makes her all the more captivating. Thus the ability of pastoral scenery simultaneously to hide and invite attention to the house and the women who live there is one of the ways in which it effaces the border between interior and exterior, enabling a symbolic ambiguity that is central to American pastoralism.[13] Women train vines to make the house and the household appear to be "embowered," lovingly sanctioned by the natural world. According to Jacobs, slave owners use the same landscaping tricks to demonstrate that slavery is a "natural" and therefore moral system: a hypothetical visitor from the North "walks around the premises, and sees the beautiful groves and flowering vines, and the comfortable huts of favored household slaves. He asks them if they want to be free, and they say, 'O, no, massa.' This is sufficient to satisfy him" (74). Along with the slaves' self-protective dishonesty, the "comfortable" slave huts and the "beautiful groves and flowering vines" conceal cultural violence with images of nature and culture in harmony.

Jacobs's critique of pastoralism as it specifically relates to domesticity exploits the symbolic interior/exterior ambiguity of the vine-covered house. She makes the ambiguity explicit in an image of a "flowery home" where a young bride from the North, her mind filled with conventional pastoral fantasies, encounters their southern revision. Jacobs exposes the slave owners' concealment of the abuses of slavery by appropriating and then dismantling the "flowery home" image in a rhetorical inversion intended particularly to distress northern mothers:

> Reader, I draw no imaginary pictures of southern homes. I am telling you
> the plain truth. Yet when victims make their escape from this wild beast of
> Slavery, northerners consent to act the part of bloodhounds, and hunt the
> poor fugitive back into his den, "full of dead men's bones, and all
> uncleanness." Nay, more, they are not only willing, but proud, to give
> their daughters in marriage to slaveholders. The poor girls have romantic
> notions of a sunny clime, and of the flowering vines that all the year
> round shade a happy home. To what disappointments are they destined!
> The young wife soon learns that the husband in whose hands she has
> placed her happiness pays no regard to his marriage vows. Children of
> every shade of complexion play with her own fair babies, and too well she
> knows that they are born unto him of his own household. Jealousy and
> hatred enter the flowery home, and it is ravaged of its loveliness. (35-36)

Jacobs redirects the process of silent witnessing that is motherhood under slavery, forcing northern white mothers to watch their own daughters in the way that slave mothers watch theirs.[14] Like their own mothers, young brides from the North—now mothers themselves—watch helplessly while their husbands humiliate them and commit crimes against women whom they should consider their sisters. By depicting the entrance of jealousy and hatred into the flowery home, Jacobs exposes the vines as mere ornament, unable to conceal the interior reality, in much the same way that she will expose the reality of Flint's secluded cottage. The violent hatred that enters the house, an image (like children's complexions) that shows rather than speaks the rape of slave women, tears the vines from the walls, deracinating the architectural expression of pastoral ideology from its false organic connection to nature. By portraying the southern home as a scene of invasion, Jacobs rhetorically positions the white woman as a fellow victim who, unlike the slave, is not raped but ravaged of her beliefs. The veil has been violently withdrawn, and the bride—representing the reader or her daughter—is now experienced through her knowledge of the sexual history of the female slave body. And this will happen again: for every fugitive slave the northerners send back to the South according to the Fugitive Slave Law, one young white woman will go, too, and become trapped in the hell of southern motherhood. Jacobs's strategy, as we will see again, is to use the language of rape to explode the pastoral language that enables the concealment of violence by those who commit or condone it.

The rhetorical ravaging of northern concepts of domestic space at an early point in the narrative suggests that the reader might interpret other domestic spaces as similarly inverted. Such a reading not only reveals the unwritten dimensions of Jacobs's personal experiences of houses—specifically, the fact of her rape—but also shows how these experiences inspired her strategy of spatial inversion.[15] In the turning point of the narrative, Flint attempts to use a pastoral space to consolidate his power: he constructs a secluded cottage where he can keep Brent as his mistress. Flint cleverly manipulates what he believes to be Brent's devotion to domestic ideals by telling her that the cottage will be "a home of [her] own" that will "make a lady" of her (53). But Brent knows what this language means for slave women; she may be mistress of the house, but only in the sense of a sexual captive; and Flint would forcibly remake her body, like the cottage, into a container for his children. This episode in Jacobs's narrative represents yet another revision of pastoralism. In Downing's discussion of vine-covered cottages, he describes them as "bewitching" and possessed of "charms."[16] In this period, identical language was used to signify the uncontrollable occult dimension of black women's nature with which they were accused of seducing white men.[17] Yet Jacobs inverts this cultural stereotype by positioning a white man as the bewitching seducer of a black woman, who is wise enough to see through his adornment of both the cottage and language.

Unable to prevent rape itself—as her complicated structural references will reveal—Brent blocks Flint's ability to increase his supply of slave children (through his own efforts) by voluntarily becoming pregnant with a white neighbor just before the rape becomes inevitable:

> At last, [Flint] came and told me the cottage was completed, and ordered me to go to it. I told him I would never enter it. He said, "I have heard enough of such talk as that. You shall go, if you are carried by force; and you shall remain there."
> I replied, "I will never go there. In a few months I shall be a mother."
> He stood and looked at me in dumb amazement, and left the house without a word. (56)

Turned inside out, like the "flowery home," this scene translates Brent's refusal to enter the cottage into her refusal to let Flint enter her. Jacobs renegotiates the instability of pastoral boundaries between inside and outside by changing Brent's body from an immobile container (like the cottage) for Flint's future slaves into an agent who determines whether or not she will cross the threshold or, more precisely, let her threshold be crossed. At the end of the scene, in another inversion, Flint becomes the silent witness to one maternity that he cannot control.

As several critics have pointed out, the narrative itself never explains how the affair with Sands could possibly have defeated Flint if his desire were solely to rape her.[18] The plan makes sense only if we read the cottage as a version of Brent's pregnant body. Brent cannot be made to enter the cottage, because her own body has already become exterior space, enclosing another being—and by becoming the "house" of a child other than Flint's, she can take on the active role of deciding not to enter his "household" (36). The presence of Brent's child expels Flint from the house/body, denying him the role of "father" in this twisted domestic scenario. At the same time, Jacobs strongly suggests that she herself was raped by Flint both by offering an inadequate explanation for avoiding his advances and by complicating the distinction between interior and exterior space. When Brent announces her second pregnancy to Flint, he is "exasperated beyond measure" and again rushes from the house. This time, however, he brings back scissors with which he cuts off all her hair. He also swears and strikes her (77). The physical violence seems to signify another rape; the hair-cutting (reminiscent of the deracination of the vines) specifically suggests that Brent has been "ravaged."

That Brent is able to determine her child's paternity despite this abuse becomes not only a matter of personal dignity for her and her children but a confrontation with the southern law stating (in Jacobs's words) that "'the child shall follow the condition of the mother,' not of the father; thus taking care that licentiousness shall not interfere with avarice" (76). Although this meant that Brent's children would still be Flint's slaves, they would not be direct results of his attack: she rendered him impotent to produce fruit from his own labor. Moreover, the white neighbor has the means to buy and free their children. Brent's rejection of chastity can now be reread by her potentially offended audience as a complex strategy to protect her children from the pain of being products of rape and to arrange for their freedom even before they are born. Under the distortion of values that slavery produces, voluntary premarital sex is the best way of becoming the self-sacrificing mother of sentimentalism.[19]

In the physical and rhetorical inversions that enable Brent to escape Flint's cottage, that is, to escape being the mother of his children, Jacobs also suggests that a slave woman's ability first to choose her own lover and then to become pregnant makes her body a truly pastoral place that further exposes the false uses of pastoralism. Although she attacks slavery's distortion of pastoralism, Jacobs strongly supports the pastoral as an ideal that can and must be recovered through political action.[20] Her recovery of her body as a pastoral place becomes apparent in the chapter entitled "The Lover" (concerning Brent's first and only true love, a freed black man whom Flint forbids her to marry), which begins by continuing her reconceptualization of vine imagery:

> Why does the slave ever love? Why allow the tendrils of the heart to twine
> around objects which may at any moment be wrenched away by the hand
> of violence? When separations come by the hand of death, the pious soul

can bow in resignation, and say, "not my will, but thine be done, O Lord!" But when the ruthless hand of man strikes the blow, regardless of the misery he causes, it is hard to be submissive. (37)

Such tendrils appear all over nineteenth-century American literature.[21] In close juxtaposition to the "flowery home" image that concludes the preceding chapter, however, they continue that passage's revision of pastoralism. The "flowery home" is a containment device for the bodies of black and white women, whereas these "tendrils of the heart" grow out from inside a black woman's body, a spontaneous expression of love and desire—a pastoral ideal. The violent wrenching further highlights the physicality of this otherwise conventional trope, as does the real "stunning blow" that Flint gives Brent, a few pages later, when she tells him of her plans to marry (39). The tearing of the tendrils by the "ruthless hand of man" (which looks very much like Flint's hand) recalls the "ravaging" of the "flowery home," another use of pastoral imagery in the depiction of sexual violence.

Vine imagery used in conjunction with Brent's maternal body after she gives birth reveals her love for her children and confirms it as a truly natural kind of love. Because she has chosen their father and loves her children, Brent's body is sanctioned by nature: this maternal body quietly contrasts itself to the force with which Flint manufactures houses and babies. Brent calls her son "the little vine [that] was taking deep root in my existence" (62), and says later that she will miss her grandmother's house, "where my children came to twine themselves so closely round my desolate heart" (155). This later instance, in which the "natural" maternal body is located in the grandmother's house, doubly exemplifies ideal pastoralism. Jacobs has presented Brent's grandmother as both the exemplar of true womanhood and the yeoman farmer of Jeffersonian fame. A former slave, Aunt Martha cultivates a small garden and makes preserves and other culinary specialties much sought after by the whole community.

Aunt Martha plays the role of mother for Brent, since her real mother died when Brent was a child. *Incidents* is in many ways a story of mother-substitutes: Brent's several mother figures (including her grandmother, a kind childhood mistress, relatives, and friends both black and white) reflect slavery's disruptions and distortions of families—and the slaves' equally powerful impulse to recuperate those families in whatever form possible. I suggest that the interplay of body and house in the narrative reflects, among the other strategies I have already described, Brent's attempts to recuperate her dead mother by incorporating her. Brent's figurative reunion with her mother's body takes place during her seven-year confinement in her grandmother's attic. But this "reunion," as we will see, really means that Brent makes herself into her own mother; that is, she becomes a mother on her own spatial and verbal terms.[22]

The Maternal Body and the Hiding (of) Place

Gaston Bachelard implies a connection between a pregnant body and a house in daydreams about a shell:

> We shall never collect enough daydreams, if we want to understand phenomenologically how a snail makes its house; how this flabbiest of creatures constitutes such a hard shell; how, in this creature that is entirely shut in, the great cosmic rhythm of winter and spring vibrates nonetheless. [This problem] arises automatically, in fact as soon . . . as we start to dream of a house that grows in proportion to the growth of the body that inhabits it. How can the little snail grow in its stone prison?[23]

Bachelard never explicitly connects the shell to pregnancy, but it seems a powerful presence here, on the order of Jacobs's motherhood. My apparently insulting association of Brent with what Bachelard calls "this flabbiest of crea- tures" reflects my interest in the possibility of a being, apparently totally vul- nerable, who is still able to create an enclosure that is as nurturing on the inside as it is hard on the outside. As opposed to Downing's idea of "natural" proportion—that people should build their homes to reflect their unchange- able social status—Bachelard suggests that the body inside the house could be the standard for the house's measurement, a relationship in harmony with "the great cosmic rhythm." What is exterior to the house does not determine the house's dimensions. Brent's pregnancy by Sands makes her "impregnable" like the shell, if not to Flint's sexual aggression, then at least to impregnation with his baby. The attic is an architectural version of the idea of the pregnant body as a protective shell, whose walls, as we will see, are reconstructed both literally and rhetorically by Brent's body.

The escape plan that drives Brent into the attic is conceived as follows: convinced that Brent has fled to the North, Flint will sell her children— whom he can no longer use to threaten her into staying—to their father, Sands, who has promised to free them. Brent's voluntary concealment in the body- sized attic above Aunt Martha's house is also, of course, an imprisonment: her physical and psychological sufferings receive the most vivid, detailed de- scriptions that the usually reserved Jacobs presents.[24] By confining herself to a tiny interior, Brent represents the imprisoned status of even the best-treated slaves; however, this act also inverts the master-slave power structure, sending Flint on the run while Brent stays put: she "contains" him through a series of fruitless, Ahab-like searches for her in the North. Brent inspires these searches by sending letters to Flint, through a friend, with northern postmarks, exem- plifying a strategy that we will see repeated: Jacobs undermines the concept of real physical location by textualizing and then disseminating representations of her body.[25] Indeed, fictionalizing herself as Linda Brent and then publishing the narrative reenacts the trick that Brent plays on Flint. Moreover, when Brent conceals herself in the crawl space, she chooses and enters her own "secluded cottage," so that in still another way she has created her own imagistic language by inverting Flint's imposed terms.

In translating her body's spatial experiences into textual reimaginings of space, Jacobs reveals motherhood itself as an act of spatial and ultimately literary imagination.[26] Indeed, it is through the scenes in the attic that Brent becomes her own mother, giving birth to herself as she reconstructs the ideological norms imposed upon her body. By entering the attic, Brent creates a maternal body around herself, like the mollusk that exudes its own shell in Bachelard's image. A very uncomfortable and unnourishing womb, the attic is at once "natural" like the shell, since the positive associations of Aunt Martha's house with pastoralism now hold Brent's body, and also "unnatural," since hiding in the attic represents the extremes—including having to be one's own mother—to which slave mothers are driven. That Brent cannot walk but only crawl around in the attic further suggests that she is in a state of infancy from which she will be reborn in some other form. The attic is the place where Jacobs will invert, fully and finally, the terms of the southern law that the child follows the mother's condition. Here, Brent reconstructs herself as her own mother, giving new meaning to the law's suggestion that the mother and child are somehow the same. In another inversion of the law, Brent hides in the attic to secure her children's emancipation before her own; now she follows *their* condition, letting these supposed products of slavery lead her into freedom: even though her grandmother tries to discourage her from finally leaving, telling her, "You'll break my heart," Brent says, "My children were continually beckoning me to the north" (149).

As we have already seen, Jacobs inverts the domestic space of the slave owner (the "flowery home" and the "secluded cottage") by exposing its concealed brutality. Through the use of her imagination, she also inverts her own "domestic" space (the garret) by transforming it into a site of refuge. Elaine Scarry tells us that seeing and hearing are the senses most frequently invoked by poets as the sensory analogues for the imagination. Through them, one seems to become disembodied, either because one seems to have been transported hundreds of feet beyond the edges of the body into the external world or because the images of objects from the external world have themselves been carried into the interior of the body as perceptual content and seem to reside there, displacing the dense matter of the body itself.[27]

Brent sees the attic as a place of freedom: "It seemed horrible to sit or lie in a cramped position day after day, without one gleam of light. Yet I would have chosen this, rather than my lot as a slave, though white people considered it an easy one" (114). When she bores a hole in the attic wall, through which she can watch her children, her vision (imagination) allows her to forget momentarily her bodily pain. Once again, we see motherhood as silent witnessing, but here it is as much a sign of the happiness of motherhood as of its fears and sorrows: "Presently two sweet little faces were looking up at me, as though they knew I was there, and were conscious of the joy they imparted" (115). Vision and imagination cannot fully substitute for communication. Brent adds, "How I *longed* to tell them I was there!" Still, with this seemingly small gesture of boring a hole, Brent makes her mark on the surroundings that have marked her for so long. In terms of the Emersonian model, Brent's body and spirit are strengthened through the physical creation (or alteration) of space.[28] As I have already suggested, this translation of a site of bodily experience into a site of spatial refiguration reveals Jacobs's strategy of simultaneously affirming her body's presence in her narrative and disembodying herself.

Experience, as we have seen, leads to linguistic as well as individual reconstruction: the marks of experience at once testify to the truth of the narrative's events and highlight the impossibility of locating the bodily site of those events. Brent tells us that her scars are the tangible proof (or text) of the seemingly fantastic occurrences in the attic: "I hardly expect that the reader will credit me when I affirm that I lived in that dismal hole, almost deprived of light and air, and with no space to move my limbs, for nearly seven years. But it is a fact; and to me a sad one, even now; for my body still suffers from the effects of that long imprisonment, to say nothing of my soul. Members of my family, now living in New York and Boston, can testify to the truth of what I say" (148). Brent suggests that the reader look up her family members for verification, which would make no sense if one looked for the Brent family: fiction and testimony collide. Even more strikingly, she hints that the skeptical readers should look at her body—which exists only as the verbally constructed image of Linda Brent—if they really want proof. The implied reader of these lines, who suspects the author's credibility but not her existence, would be sent on a Flint-like search for a fictional body: that desire for proof, it seems, can lead to violations on the order of Flint's that must be diverted. Through her experience in the attic, then, Jacobs has remade herself in two ways: her own body is claimed as a tangible and therefore politically inspiring critique of conventional pastoral space, but the body as the site of proof slips away into fictionalized prose.

Accordingly, Jacobs concludes her narrative with a lament of placelessness: "Reader, my story ends with freedom; not in the usual way, with marriage. . . . The dream of my life is not yet realized. I do not sit with my children in a home of my own" (201). Racism and poverty are to blame on the historical level; on the rhetorical level placelessness results from the narrative's repeated conversions of tangible places (bodies and houses) into written images—new spaces which are often inside out or otherwise impossible in the physical world. The vividly portrayed, physically confining attic paradoxically confirms the final unlocatability of the human body in written text. Within the narrative, the attic is a place where Jacobs's readers can pinpoint Brent's location when the other characters think she is anywhere but there (they are, in fact, unaware of the attic). But at the time Jacobs wrote *Incidents*, Brent's counterpart in the real world was long gone from the attic, and it was not until 1987 that Jean Fagan Yellin definitively established that Jacobs was the book's author. The narrative, then, is Jacobs's most revolutionary act, inasmuch as it is also her most effective act of self-concealment. Because it fundamentally deconstructs and diffuses temporal and spatial locations, the text is the hardest shell of all. Refusing to be fixed in space and time, Jacobs instead uses the central location of her experience—her body—to translate real architectural spaces into less tangible but more earthshaking sites of writing.[29]

Notes

Special thanks to Patricia Manganello for her help in revising and editing this article.

1. Jacobs's authorial position is complicated by the fact that although her story does not fit into the framework of conventional morality, her body, as the site of oppression, attains the status of a text, and thus to separate the body and the story is problematic. The fact that Jacobs/Brent was a mulatto signifies that, even before she was raped, her body symbolized the sexual abuse of slave women by their masters. For more on the idea of the body as text, see Karen Sanchez-Eppler, "Bodily Bonds: The Intersecting Rhetorics of Feminism and Abolition," *Representations* 24 (fall 1988): 28-59.

2. Hazel Carby, *Reconstructing Womanhood: The Emergence of the Afro-American Woman Novelist* (New York: Oxford University Press, 1987), 49.

3. I will not, however, draw explicit distinctions between womanhood and motherhood, because the two are already largely elided in sentimentalism and in the language of slavery.

4. See Ralph Waldo Emerson, "Man the Reformer," in *Selected Essays* (New York: Penguin Books, 1982), 136-37. Other references will be to this edition.

5. Emerson, "The Oversoul," in ibid., 218.

6. For purposes of clarification, I will use Jacobs when I am referring to the author and Brent when referring to the fictionalized character. At times, however, this distinction is arbitrary.

7. See David S. Reynolds, *Beneath the American Renaissance* (Cambridge: Harvard University Press, 1988), 211-24.

8. *Incidents in the Life of a Slave Girl*, ed. Jean Fagan Yellin (Cambridge: Harvard University Press, 1987), 3-4. All references to *Incidents* will be cited in the text by page number.

9. Charles Altieri criticizes contemporary feminist formulations of experience particularly for the ways in which they spatialize the term: "Unless one can theoretically indicate how we distinguish and link experiences, especially in terms of development and change (and perhaps in terms of internal and external relations), using the concept does little more than provide another transcendental substitute for Kant's noumena on the other side of representation." See Altieri, "Temporality and the Necessity for Dialectic," *New Literary History* 23 (winter 1992): 139. For another important critique, see Joan Scott's "Experience," in *Feminists Theorize the Political*, ed. Judith Butler and Joan W. Scott (New York: Routledge, 1992), 22-40.

10. Franny Nudelman has shown this irony in Jacobs's position as a writer of her own story: "While unreserved communication with an audience of white women is the premise for Jacobs's narrative, her authorship resulted from an instance in which complete revelation proved unacceptable." Nudelman, "Harriet Jacobs and the Sentimental Politics of Female Suffering," *ELH* 59 (winter 1992): 956.

11. For an overview of the domestic architecture reform movement and its relationship to the cult of domesticity, see Clifford Clark Jr., "Domestic Architecture as an Index to Social History: The Romantic Revival and the Cult of Domesticity in America, 1840-1870," *Journal of Interdisciplinary History* 7 (summer 1976): 33-56. See also Richard and Jean Carwil Mastellar, "Rural Architecture in Andrew Jackson Downing and Henry David Thoreau: Pattern Book Parody in *Walden*," *New England Quarterly* 57 (December 1984), 483-510; this article also discusses the confusion between instruments and symbols of morality as it surfaces in Downing's writings (evidently unnoticed by him).

12. Andrew Jackson Downing, *The Architecture of Country Houses* (New York, 1852), 207.

13. See Leo Marx, "Pastoralism in America," in *Ideology and Classic American Literature*, ed. Sacvan Bercovitch and Myra Jehlen (New York: Cambridge University Press, 1986), 36-69, for a discussion of the role of this ambiguity in Manifest Destiny and related expansionist projects.

14. When a slave woman's maternity was the result of a rape by her master she had to remain silent about it to avoid further punishment and to spare her family (especially her mother) from pain. Jacobs describes Linda Brent's watchfulness over her daughter, Ellen, whose master was harassing her: "She never made any complaint about her own inconveniences and troubles; but a mother's watchful eye easily perceived that she was not happy" (178). Earlier in the story, Brent's grandmother observes Brent with the same all-perceiving eye: "I think she knew something unusual was the matter with me. The mother of slaves is very watchful" (56). Throughout the narrative, Jacobs comments on the attention paid by slaves and masters to the facial features of slave children: a light-skinned child with his or her master's features indicates the rape that cannot be discussed.

15. I agree with P. Gabrielle Foreman and Elizabeth Fox-Genovese, who believe neither that the sexual threats to Jacobs by her master in reality remained on the level of language nor that Jacobs could ultimately have resisted his assaults, although *Incidents* claims both to be true for these individuals' fictionalized counterparts. Foreman writes that in Brent's condemnations of her owner, Dr. Flint, "the passion in her

language does not seem to have a correct correlation with what she claims Flint 'says.' Jacobs transfers Linda's (unacknowledged) violated body to the body of the word. By serving for and providing the theme for physical abuse, words act both to describe her violation and to absorb it." See Foreman, "The Spoken and the Silenced in *Incidents in the Life of a Slave Girl* and *Our Nig*," *Callaloo* 13 (spring 1990): esp. 317-18; and Fox-Genovese, *Within the Plantation Household: Black and White Women of the Old South* (Chapel Hill: University of North Carolina Press, 1988), 392.

16. Downing, *Architecture of Country Houses*, 207.

17. Carby, *Reconstructing Womanhood*, 27.

18. For example, see Foreman, "The Spoken and the Silenced," 322.

19. In "The Spoken and the Silenced," Foreman cites Carby's response to Blassingame in order to add this important qualification of Brent's "choice" of Sands: "Responding to historian John Blassingame's assertion that 'slave women were literally forced to offer themselves willingly,' Carby reveals the tension between 'forced' and 'willingly' and upbraids him for his ambivalence in recognizing that what this juxtaposition articulates is the dynamics of rape (Carby, *Reconstructing Womanhood*, 22-23). Although, in this exchange, they speak to the relations between slave and master, I would suggest that this language, and these dynamics, fit Linda's situation precisely—she is forced by Dr. Flint's behavior to submit herself willingly to Mr. Sands" (322).

20. This corresponds with the genre of pastoral critique in antebellum (and later) American works such as *Moby Dick* and *The Scarlet Letter*. See Marx, "Pastoralism in America," 59-60.

21. Illustrating the use of the word *tendril* in the context of attachment (excessive, dangerous, or otherwise) to an object, the *Oxford English Dictionary* points to examples from "Man the Reformer" and *Uncle Tom's Cabin*: "Inextricable seem to be the twinings and tendrils of this evil" (Emerson); "Her own earnest nature threw out its tendrils, and wound itself around the majestic book" (Stowe).

22. For another interpretation see Jennifer Fleischner, who argues that we cannot fully understand Jacobs if we think back only through her mothers. Her escape to freedom evolves primarily out of her identification and association with men in her family and not the women who, though they support her, cannot show her the way. When Linda visits her parents' graves, it is her father's voice she hears encouraging her to fight for her freedom. While she is in the garret, her brother and uncle care for her. Fleischner suggests that Brent recovers her family by incorporating her father's spirit of rebellion and her mother's capacity for self-sacrifice. Jennifer Fleischner, *Mastering Slavery: Memory, Family, and Identity in Women's Slave Narratives* (New York: New York University Press, 1996).

23. Gaston Bachelard, *The Poetics of Space*, trans. Maria Jolas (Boston: Beacon Press, 1969), 118.

24. Nudelman identifies the detail in this section as the clearest example of what she calls Jacobs's "rhetoric of contrast," through which "she demand[s] sympathy and attention on the basis of exceptionality rather than universality": "While Jacobs never discloses the details of her sexual experience, she offers painstaking accounts of the discomforts of her seven-year captivity. . . . The experience that most completely

figures the difference between white and black women, which is least available as a basis for identification, is the experience that Jacobs is able to communicate most accurately" (959-60).

25. Carolyn Sorisio suggests a connection between literacy and the notion of space in *Incidents*. "The spoken and written word are represented as noncorporeal. . . . Jacobs's emphasis on literacy can be interpreted as creating a space in which she is not viewed solely in terms of her body": Sorisio, "'There Is Might in Each': Conceptions of Self in Harriet Jacobs's *Incidents in the Life of a Slave Girl, Written by Herself*," *Legacy* 13, no. 1 (1996): 15.

26. Foreman, in arguing that Jacobs's imagery is of rape rather than of mere verbal harassment, says that Jacobs translates the events of her life to the level of discourse: "The Spoken and the Silenced," 317. My argument is that Jacobs's disembodiment, which corresponds to an equally strong insistence on bodily presence, has particular implications for the politics of space as enacted by the narrative itself.

27. Elaine Scarry, *The Body in Pain* (New York: Oxford University Press, 1985), 165.

28. In "'There Is Might in Each,'" Sorisio suggests that Jacobs revises Emerson's and Thoreau's transcendental individualism: "Her challenge as an author was to write the knowledge that came through her embodied experience without reifying scientific essentialism. She does so by writing about her life while asserting an amorphous and transcendent will that exists outside her slave's body" (3).

29. See Houston A. Baker Jr., *Blues, Ideology, and Afro-American Literature* (Chicago: University of Chicago Press, 1984). By including a reading of Jacobs in his book, Baker indirectly compares her to a blues singer, whose signature is one of placelessness: "The blues singer's signatory coda is always atopic, placeless: 'If anybody ask you who sang this song / Tell 'em X done been here and gone.' Nevertheless, the 'you' (audience) addressed is always free to invoke the X(ed) spot in the body's absence" (5).

Contributors

Carol Barash is the author of *English Women's Poetry, 1649-1714* (Oxford, 1996) and has edited the works of Aphra Behn, Anne Finch, and Olive Schreiner. She received her Ph.D. from Princeton University in 1989.

Toni Bowers, the author of numerous articles for such journals as *Eighteenth-Century Fiction, English Literary History*, and *Studies in American Fiction*, wrote *The Politics of Motherhood: British Writing and Culture, 1680-1760* (Cambridge, 1996). She teaches English and women's studies at the University of Pennsylvania and is writing a book on eighteenth-century British seduction stories.

Mary Chapman is an associate professor of English at the University of Alberta. She is coeditor, with Glenn Hendler, of *Sentimental Men: Masculinity and the Politics of Affect in Nineteenth-Century America* (University of California Press, 1999) and the author of several articles on issues of maternity in works by Louisa May Alcott, Louise Erdrich, and Leslie Marmon Silko.

Julie Costello is an assistant professor of English at Hope College and an assistant editor of *Bullán: An Irish Studies Journal*. She is currently completing her book, *Romanticism, Nationalism, and Maternity: Mothers on Trial in the Late Eighteenth and Early Nineteenth Centuries*.

Julia Epstein, a former professor of comparative literature at Haverford College, is the author of *The Iron Pen: Frances Burney and the Politics of Women's Writing* (Wisconsin, 1989) and *Altered Conditions: Disease, Medicine, and Storytelling* (Routledge, 1995). She coedited *Body Guards: Sexual Ambiguity and the Politics of Culture* (Routledge, 1991) and *Shaping Losses: Cultural Memory and the Holocaust* (Illinois, forthcoming in 1999).

Ann Gelder is a multimedia developer and writer. She received her Ph.D. in comparative literature from the University of California, Berkeley, in 1995.

Susan C. Greenfield, an associate professor of English at Fordham University, is the author of several articles on women novelists. Her work has appeared in *Eighteenth-Century Fiction, The Eighteenth Century: Theory and Interpretation, English Literary History, PMLA*, and other journals. She is currently completing a book entitled *Mothering Daughters: Politics, Desire, and Kinship from Burney to Austin.*

Claudia L. Johnson, a professor of English at Princeton University, is the author of *Jane Austen: Women, Politics, and the Novel* (Chicago, 1988) and *Equivocal Beings: Politics, Gender, and Sentimentality in the 1790s* (Chicago, 1995). She is editing *The Cambridge Companion to Mary Wollstonecraft* and finishing a book on the development of novel studies.

Eve Keller is an associate professor of English at Fordham University. She has published essays on a variety of seventeenth-century figures, such as Milton, Hobbes, and Cavendish, and on topics related to early modern theories of generation. Her work has appeared in *Women's Studies* and *English Literary History*, and an article is forthcoming in *Eighteenth-Century Studies*. Keller is currently working on a book about the rhetorics of reproduction in early modern England.

Kimberly Latta is an assistant professor of English at Saint Louis University in Saint Louis, Missouri. She received a master's degree in comparative literature from the University of California, Berkeley, and a doctorate in English from Rutgers University in New Brunswick. Her current research concerns the figuring of gender and economics in English literature from 1640 to 1720.

Anita Levy is an assistant professor of English at the University of Rochester. The author of *Other Women: The Writing of Class, Race, and Gender, 1832-1898* (Princeton 1991) and numerous essays on nineteenth-century British culture, she has just completed a book entitled *Reproductive Urges: Popular Novel-Reading, Sexuality, and the English Nation* (Pennsylvania, forthcoming).

Josephine McDonagh, a lecturer in humanities in the English department at Birkbeck College, University of London, is the author of *De Quincey's Disciplines* (Clarendon Press, 1994) and *George Eliot* (Northcote House, 1997). She is working on a book about the rhetorical uses of child murder in eighteenth- and nineteenth-century British culture.

Index

DATE DUE